This book focuses on KAM implementation as well as strategy, making it a great addition to the guides for key account managers, especially the chapter on the use of information technology and artificial intelligence.
George S Yip, Emeritus Professor of Marketing and Strategy, Imperial College London and author of *Total Global Strategy and Managing Global Customers*

The UK is the global leader in KAM research and practice, due, in no small measure, to the years of best practice experience gathered and codified at Cranfield. *The High Performing Key Account Manager* collects together some of the best Cranfield thinking and will be an invaluable source of advice and leadership for both academics and practitioners.
Neil Rackham, speaker, writer and author of *SPIN Selling*

The High-Performing Key Account Manager is a critical resource for anyone serious about driving significant revenue and building lasting partnerships with strategic clients. This isn't just a theoretical text; it delivers practical, immediately actionable guidance that you can apply to your key accounts right away. Whether you're a veteran key account manager looking to sharpen your edge or a rising star aiming for rapid impact, this book provides the essential knowledge and practical tools to not just manage key accounts, but to truly excel.
Steven Elsham. Head of Marketing, Commerce, Service & Revenue Clouds EMEA Commerce Champion, Saleforce Nederland

An essential resource for anyone interested in strategic sales. The team have brought together a great mix of KAM theory with practice-relevant insights sourced from some of the brightest and best KAM thinkers from around the world. Grounded in an extensive body of research, this book is destined to being one of the great KAM resources of our time!
Daniel Prior, Associate Professor of Buyer-Supplier Engagement, Cranfield University

This is a highly relevant and engaging book on key account management. The authors have not only provided a strategic take on this topic, but also provide a practical, hands-on approach for managing high-value clients, covering essential topics like relationship building, value co-creation, and long-term customer retention. In particular, their use of testimonials from key account managers in combination with evidence from academic research, makes this a must read for executives, business school faculty, and for university students.

Deva Rangarajan, Professor of Marketing and Sales at IESEG School of Management, France

Every good seller should always be thinking about Key Account Management. A toolkit such as this book is great to refer to and remind yourself of some key points to help keep you on track with your customers. If KAMs were to adopt even a few strategies from this book you will be more successful than your peers. If you work for a company who supports KAM you won't go far wrong.

Kate Rotheram, BMS Specialist, Intelligent Buildings

This book brings together perspectives from leading academics and practitioners in the field. A welcome message that emerges from their work is that culture, customer understanding and flexibility are as important as structure and processes in making companies customer-focused and generating high performance. Of course, key account managers need to do their analytical homework and manage a data-rich environment, but the role of trust and the importance of collaboration and of mutual understanding in successful key account relationships is set out here.

Prof Lynette Ryals OBE, Deputy Vice-Chancellor, Faculty of Business and Management, Cranfield University

This book is an essential guide for account managers dedicated to driving value creation. With practical advice and real-world examples from different industries, this book provides hands-on tools to demonstrate measurable value, foster growth, and navigate complex business environments. A mustread for those looking to elevate their impact and drive long-term success.

Prof Christoph Senn, CEO Valuecreator, AG, and Adjunct Professor, INSEAD

Comprehensive, up to date, extremely well-referenced, this book is a brilliant insight into the world of contemporary key account management with a great blend of academic research and practitioner insight. This must read for anyone in key account management, we shall certainly be including the book on our reading lists.

Philip Squire, CEO, Consalia Sales Business School

The High-Performing Key Account Manager

*Creating sustained value
with strategic customers*

Javier Marcos, Rodrigo Guesalaga,
Andrew Hough and Richard Vincent

KoganPage

First published in Great Britain in 2025 by Kogan Page Limited

Kogan Page

Kogan Page Ltd, 2nd Floor, 45 Gee Street, London EC1V 3RS, United Kingdom
Kogan Page Inc, 8 W 38th Street, Suite 90, New York, NY 10018, USA
www.koganpage.com

EU Representative (GPSR)

Authorised Rep Compliance Ltd, Ground Floor, 71 Baggot Street Lower, Dublin D02 P593, Ireland
www.arccompliance.com

Kogan Page books are printed on paper from sustainable forests.

ISBNs

Hardback	978 1 3986 2041 4
Paperback	978 1 3986 2030 8
Ebook	978 1 3986 2040 7

British Library Cataloguing-in-Publication Data

A CIP record for this book is available from the British Library.

Library of Congress Control Number

2025934393

Typeset by Integra Software Services, Pondicherry
Print production managed by Jellyfish
Printed and bound by CPI Group (UK) Ltd, Croydon, CR0 4YY

CONTENTS

FOREWORD

As the President and CEO of SAMA – the Strategic Account Management Association – I have the privilege of engaging with some of the most innovative and foremost thinkers in the field of strategic and key account management. SAMA membership comprises a worldwide nexus of practitioners, experts and thought leaders whose collective wisdom fuels our ecosystem of shared best practices for today's strategic account managers (SAMs) and key account managers (KAMgrs).

Few people embody this spirit of shared knowledge better than Professor Javier Marcos Cuevas, whose articles and contributions to SAMA's *Velocity* magazine have long captured not only the attention of our global community, but the heart and soul of what I like to call SAMA's 'human network'. His widely acclaimed series on 'The High-Performing SAM' always delivered deep insights and actionable takeaways that truly resonated with readers, wherever they may be on the path of key account management. However, his series really took flight because it spoke to those looking to access a higher level in their pursuit of strategic-account excellence – people who didn't want to settle for good, but instead wanted to strive for greatness.

Now, with this book – Javier and his co-authors elevate the conversation to new heights. Built on the foundation of academic research and expertise from the renowned Cranfield School of Management, plus a combined business acumen that boasts decades of extensive management and consulting experience, this book provides a comprehensive guide on *how* to excel at the highest levels in the dynamic and complex world of key account management.

I emphasize the word *how* for good reason. Countless resources in the milieu of strategic account management focus too heavily on the what and the *why*, but Javier, Rodrigo, Andy and Richard masterfully address the *how*. Through a unique combination of cutting-edge research, real-world examples and practical frameworks, this book equips readers with the tools necessary to bridge theory and practice.

In fact, SAMA's own mission is imbued with this very concept – the union of the theory and practice. Consequently, this book embodies the values and principles that define SAMA's community. In fact, I welcome this book as another essential resource that will empower and enrich our ecosystem even further. As you embark on this journey, I speak to all readers when I say: don't just read this book – *apply* it. Think of it as a roadmap that not only reveals direct, beneficial routes, but unfolds the science and art of key account management and the nuances therewithin.

At its core, *The High-Performing Key Account Manager* celebrates the human element of strategic account management, based on real-life scenarios with leading companies such as Siemens, Caterpillar, Honeywell Group and CISCO Systems. Practical use cases like these are more than just demonstrations of success. To me, they're concrete, proof-of-concept end results that highlight what happens when you prioritize collaboration in customer relationships full of trust: the harmony of co-value creation.

This outside-in mindset challenges us to think beyond our traditional approaches and, instead, embrace a more agile, customer-centric strategy – one that integrates (and interprets) the grand desires of our customers with the operational realities they face every day. For SAMs and KAMs of all stripes, it's about honing your skills to such a fine point that you can anticipate and communicate your customers' needs before they do – and this book will lead you there.

At SAMA, we pride ourselves on holding a mirror up to 'what good looks like' and reflecting that image back to our community so they can visualize what's possible and emulate the excellence they see. In much the same way, I see *The High-Performing Key Account Manager* as another reflection in our mirror and I welcome you to have a look for yourself.

Whether you're a seasoned practitioner or a rising star, this book offers essential guidance on how to unlock your full potential – as an individual or team member. In the business world, strategic and key account management is a higher calling that asks SAMs and KAMs to elevate their proficiency and create long-lasting, ongoing value for their customers. Question is: can you rise to the challenge?

As you navigate this book, if you look deep enough, you'll discover the reflection of your own potential upon these pages. Once you see it, you'll find yourself empowered not only with solutions, but with a framework to reimagine your role as a key account manager and launch a whole new chapter of exponential growth for you and your organization.

Gordon Galzerano
SAMA President and CEO

PREFACE

Managing key account relationships has never been a more challenging, yet exciting job. Strategic customer relationships lie at the heart of business strategy, driving growth and innovation. Global trade and its associated economic development rely on the ability of key account managers to establish and develop relationships between corporations.

Why read or listen to a book about key account management when you can find content on this topic freely available? Web-based and AI queries may enable you to identify the factors influencing excellence in key account management (KAM). You may be able to find some critical factors involved in a key account manager role. Further exploration through online content may give you an insight into *why* these are critical factors. However, no amount of searches through free content will provide you with insight into *how* to achieve excellence in the science and art of KAM by blending academic research, with decades of managerial and consulting experience. This book brings together a unique combination of perspectives to give you well-grounded and actionable insights to succeed in your key account manager role.

In this book, we will (constructively) challenge your thinking with concepts and questions about KAM excellence, its underpinning drivers and manifestations. This book focuses on *how* key accounts managers, regardless of revenue and company size, achieve excellence in practice. The book will give insights into the execution of the KAM theory, and the embedding of best practices, reinforced by perspectives from the world's leading academics and practitioners in the field of KAM. As you progress through the book together, we will help you answer questions such as:

- What makes your customers key accounts and what are the implications for the way you do business with them?
- Why is a key account to your company, and what experience do they have with your company that is different from the experience other customers get?
- Will those accounts always be key or strategic to you and your company? If not, why not?

- Whose strategy is at the centre of your planning and operational activities?
- How do you use outside-in strategies to identify potential future key or strategic accounts by avoiding the inside-out view of the world?
- What does it take to manage key accounts and navigate through processes of value creation, value capture and multifaceted relationships?

And overall, the question this book addresses is how can you identify and develop the capabilities to become a high performing key account manager?

We hope this book will help you answer this question, and in so doing help you in both addressing the challenges and enjoying the excitement of being a key account manager!

ACKNOWLEDGEMENTS

The process of writing and completing a book like this is often the result of inspiration and collaboration with colleagues and clients. We are regularly engaged in programmes and interventions that require us to think beyond, question established practices and develop new ways of working for key account managers and KAM organizations. All this work underpins the content of the book. Here, we sincerely express our gratitude to all our partners. This book would not have happened without them.

First, we are indebted to those who contributed to the book by offering their perspectives in interviews: Andrea Clatworthy, Beth Rogers, Dominique Côté, John Downer, Prof Malcolm McDonald, Mark Bailey, Nicolaas Smit, Stuart Blakeley, Stuart Roberts, Dr Sue Holt and Tim Chapman. They are all experts in KAM and their insights and experience greatly enriched the content of the chapters.

Our colleagues at the Cranfield Centre for Strategic Marketing and Sales, Vasilis Theoharakis, Annmarie Hanlon, Tamira King, Sharifah Alwi, Dennis Esch and Marwa Tourky, inspired us with their research and scholarship.

Associates at the Key Account Management Forum at Cranfield School of Management shared with us invaluable lessons. Thank you, Richard Brooks, Mark Davies, John MacDonald-Gaunt, Peter Kerr, Daniel Prior, John Viner-Smith and Matt Wilkinson. Many thanks to Liang Sun for sharing his doctoral research on top management sponsorship.

The Institute of Professional Sales provided a fertile context to engage with practice and disseminate our initial ideas. Thank you, Guy Lloyd, Patrick Joiner and Gordon Galzerano.

We are also grateful to our Global Sales Science Institute (GSSI) colleagues for their camaraderie and stimuli to our research and thought leadership.

We have special appreciation to our colleagues at the Strategic Account Management Association (SAMA), Gordon Galzerano, Nic Halverson, Libby Souder and Joel Schaafsma, for their collaboration and encouragement with this project.

Thank you to Bobbi-Lee Wright, Donna Goddard, Jeylan Ramis and the team at Kogan Page, for their commitment and for helping us turn a loosely defined idea into a book reality.

Lastly, we would like to thank our students and the delegates to our programmes. They may not be aware, but they also greatly motivated us to write this book. We hope you will use it and that it will help you in your practice and/or studies.

INTERVIEWEES

We interviewed 11 experts about KAM. Their insights appear interleaved between the chapters. We also quote from them in the text.

MARK BAILEY

Board Director, non-exec and former Group Director of Customers and Services at Rolls-Royce. Visiting Fellow Cranfield University (page 186)

STUART BLAKELEY

Global Key Account Consultant, Grundfos (page 126)

TIM CHAPMAN

Sales Leader and Consultant Vice President of Sales at Elliptic, and Managing Partner at Sales EQ (page 306)

ANDREA CLATWORTHY

Account-based marketing expert, Director and Head of Marketing Transformation, Fujitsu (page 333)

DOMINIQUE CÔTÉ

Cosawi CEO and founder, board member, SAM/KAM AND ABM Roadmaps adviser. Visiting Fellow Cranfield University (page 216)

JOHN DOWNER

Key account leader and business growth expert. Visiting Fellow Cranfield University (page 158)

SUE HOLT PHD

Academic, educator and joint author of *Implementing Key Account Management*. Visiting Fellow Cranfield University (page 243)

PROF MALCOLM MCDONALD PHD DLITT DSC

Author, KAM expert and Emeritus Professor at Cranfield University (page 25)

STUART ROBERTS

Vice President of Client Development & Sales, Securitas Global Clients (page 96)

BETH ROGERS PHD

Academic, educator and lead author of *Selling Professionally* (page 277)

NICOLAAS SMIT

Strategic business relationships consultant and Triple Fit 360 Business Plan Coach. Visiting Fellow, Cranfield University (page 61)

PART ONE

Traversal capabilities

01

Strategizing and planning for your customers

Overview

Key account managers (KAMgrs) are expected to operate at their highest level of performance in highly volatile contexts. This results in a role that is becoming more sophisticated and multifaceted. In today's business markets, key account managers have to develop competencies to face increasingly complex and potentially transformational jobs.

In this chapter, we describe the role of the KAMgr as a 'strategist' and address how KAMgrs develop their account strategy and align it with the corporate strategy of their firms.

Why is it important to plan and strategize the relationships with your customers?

In today's competitive business landscape, fostering strong and enduring relationships with customers is paramount to long-term success. Planning and strategizing customer relationships allow businesses to move beyond transactional interactions and cultivate mutually beneficial partnerships that drive growth and profitability. By taking a deliberate and proactive approach to managing customer relationships, businesses can reap a multitude of benefits. Here are some of these benefits.[1,2,3]

- **Increased customer loyalty and retention:** When businesses invest time and effort in understanding and meeting customer needs, they create a sense of value and appreciation that fosters loyalty. Loyal customers are more likely to make repeat purchases, generate positive word-of-mouth referrals and remain committed to the business even in the face of competitive offers.

- **Enhanced profitability:** Acquiring new customers is significantly more expensive than retaining existing ones. By nurturing strong customer relationships, businesses can reduce customer churn, leading to increased customer lifetime value and improved profitability. Moreover, satisfied customers are often willing to pay a premium for products and services they perceive as valuable, further contributing to profitability.

- **Improved customer insights:** Through strategic planning and engagement, businesses can gain a deeper understanding of customer preferences, needs and pain points. These insights can inform product development, marketing strategies and customer service initiatives, enabling businesses to better tailor their offerings to meet customer expectations and anticipate future needs.

- **Competitive advantage:** In an increasingly crowded marketplace, businesses that excel at building strong customer relationships differentiate themselves from the competition. By consistently exceeding customer expectations and providing a superior customer experience, businesses can establish a distinct competitive advantage that attracts and retains customers.[4]

- **Enhanced collaboration and innovation:** Strategically managed customer relationships foster an environment of open communication and collaboration. By working closely with customers, businesses can identify opportunities for joint innovation, develop new products and services that better meet market needs and co-create solutions that drive mutual value.[5]

- **Improved risk management:** Strong customer relationships can provide a buffer against market volatility and economic downturns. When businesses have established trust and loyalty with their customers, they are more likely to weather challenging times together, minimizing the impact of external factors on business performance.

WHY STRATEGY AND PLANNING IS IMPORTANT

Strategic value creation:

- Increases customer loyalty and retention
- Enhances profitability through reduced churn
- Creates competitive differentiation
- Enables premium pricing opportunities

Customer understanding:

- Deepens insight into customer preferences
- Improves anticipation of future needs
- Facilitates better solution development
- Enables proactive problem resolution

Risk management:

- Provides a buffer against market volatility
- Reduces the impact of economic downturns
- Protects against competitive threats
- Minimizes customer churn risk

Innovation and collaboration:

- Fosters joint innovation opportunities
- Enables co-creation of solutions
- Strengthens product development
- Accelerates time to market

Cross-functional alignment:

- Improves internal resource coordination
- Enhances service delivery
- Strengthens stakeholder engagement
- Creates better customer experience

Key account management (KAM) emerges as a crucial strategy for effectively planning and managing customer relationships. KAM involves identifying, engaging and nurturing relationships with a select group of strategically important customers, often referred to as key accounts. These accounts are typically characterized by their high revenue potential, their influence within their industry and/or their potential for long-term growth and collaboration.

WHAT KEY CUSTOMERS EXPECT FROM THEIR SUPPLIERS

Anticipate customer needs:

- Competitive advantage
- Proactive solution development

Value creation:

- Higher customer retention
- Increased revenue opportunities

Strategic partnership development:

- Long-term relationship security
- Access to higher-level decision-makers
- Greater influence

Innovation opportunities:

- Competitive differentiation
- Increased customer value

Cross-functional alignment:

- Better customer experience
- New solution development

Performance measurement:

- Better ability to demonstrate and measure value creation

This book focuses on the core characteristics of high-performing key account managers. In this chapter, we describe the role of the KAMgr as a 'Strategist' and address how you, as a KAMgr, can develop your account strategy and align it with your firm's corporate strategy.

Understanding your customers' 'pragmatic' strategy

More than two decades ago, research revealed two key factors linked to the performance of the KAMgr: strategic ability and intrapreneurial ability. Strategic ability refers to the cognitive skill of analysing vital customers' business context and organization, focusing on their long-term interests, opportunities and challenges, and being able to use that analysis to create clear and practical strategies that will allow them to achieve their goals. Strategic ability often emerges from blending functional expertise, codified information and knowledge with professional judgment grounded in tacit understanding. In other words, as a good KAMgr, you need to use your accumulated knowledge and experience to interpret all the disparate and partial information you receive about the customer and use that interpretation to create a clear and effective strategy, which you can articulate to the customer in a way they understand and buy into.

One source of insight can be information found in annual reports or similar strategy documents belonging to your customer. Understanding their strategic priorities and their commitments to investors (in the case of public and listed companies) is a good starting point. However, it is unlikely to offer actionable insights you can use to advance your relationship with the account without further development.

Consider the following joint message from Jim Hagemann Snabe and Søren Skou, the Chairman and the CEO, respectively, of A.P. Moller-Maersk. Addressing their strategy in the context of their evolution from a diversified conglomerate to a focused and integrated global logistics company, they said: 'Our strategy is built on... building competitive advantage through technology. We are digitizing the interaction with our customers while offering unique digital products and leveraging Maersk.com.[6]

This statement tells you very little about the architectures, applications and areas of investment in digital technologies that are a priority for one of the world's largest supply chain operators. While this information wouldn't give you much advantage if you worked for a digital solutions company, as an indication of the company's future direction, it is invaluable.

You cannot rely solely on written information or formal company documents to decipher your accounts' strategies. Your customers' strategy will rarely emerge exclusively from formal or structured analytical tools like SWOT, PESTEL or road mapping. The strategy that your key customer implements will be the result of the interplay between the 'grand' desires (i.e. the strategy communicated to the market and investors) and the 'mid-range' wants that are materialized in operational decisions. Thus, the question becomes how to understand what your customers really want.

This very question appeared on the front page of a *Harvard Business Review* issue (September 2016), and is as relevant today as it was when it was published. A significant hurdle that must be overcome when trying to find out what your customers want so you can use that information to inform your account strategy is that they often struggle to articulate their wants and needs. Partially as a consequence of this, there may be many inconsistent and contradictory viewpoints within the company which you'll need to help resolve into a single coordinated approach to have any chance of success.

Traditional research methods, such as surveys and focus groups, offer limited insights. A technique called 'maximum difference scaling', or MaxDiff, addresses the shortcomings of conventional methods. This method requires customers to select the most and least important attributes from a subset of product or service features. Customers are invited to make a sequence of explicit trade-offs, resulting in a list of attributes ranked by their perceived importance that allows comparisons.[7]

Another technique to find valuable knowledge about your accounts' strategy is the hidden needs analysis.[8] Pioneered by Keith Goffin, a Professor of Innovation, it employs techniques from psychology and anthropology that can help understand how people think, as opposed to what they tell market researchers.

For instance, Bosch's production-line equipment division used a technique called 'repertory grid', which put them in direct communication with the production-line operators of a pharmaceutical company.[9] This allowed them to see how some design features of existing equipment could either enable or hinder them from reaching their production targets. With this unique information, they could create new product features and designs to help their customer achieve their strategy.

Whatever approach you use for needs analysis, there's much to be gained by ensuring that input is taken from multiple stakeholders with different roles within the customer's company. It is not uncommon to discover, at this point, that there is no general consensus within the organization. When this is the case, it must be (tactfully) brought to the attention of the customer and resolved. Keeping the initiative and being the catalyst for this resolution is invaluable because it allows you to focus on the options and trade-offs where you can add value, and a successful resolution can be a critical first step in building customer trust and confidence.

One of the critical aspects of KAM is the orchestration of various roles within the pharmaceutical industry, such as market access, medical liaison, and commercial teams. The Key Account Manager acts as a connector, bringing together different functions to create a cohesive strategy aligned with the customer's objectives.

Dominique Côté

When senior executives of your key account know the 'grand' strategy and other people in the account organization have access to the 'mid-range' wants and aspirations, you can create what we call a 'pragmatic' strategy. This involves using your insights to create a set of actionable, relevant and meaningful goals for your account that you can deliver against. An understanding of their needs can help you transform your key-customer business, but you must do it one opportunity at a time.

John MacDonald-Gaunt of IBM pioneered a simple but practical approach to helping customers resolve their internal priorities. When faced with a large group of stakeholders within a single customer, all of whom had conflicting priorities, he gained agreement from the customer to bring all of the stakeholders together for a day. He gave each one 10 marbles and asked them to distribute those between three containers, representing conflicting options such as product quality, delivery time and product cost. At the beginning of the session, most of the participants put all 10 of their marbles in one or other of the three containers. However, they soon realized that for everyone to be satisfied with the eventual outcome, they needed to look at getting a clearer understanding of their overall joint priorities. Each would need to compromise to achieve an internal consensus before being able to deliver a clear message to John and IBM about their needs.

Understanding your customer's pragmatic strategy is essential for building strong, long-term relationships and aligning your business for mutual success. This requires moving beyond simply knowing their immediate needs and digging deeper into their long-term objectives, challenges and the competitive landscape in which they operate. This can become a daunting task, so the following are a few key areas to focus on.

Focal areas of the customer strategy and key questions to ask

Business objectives and goals

- What are your customer's overall business objectives and goals?
- What are they striving to achieve in the short and long term?

Understanding your key customer's strategic priorities allows you to tailor your offerings and demonstrate how your products or services can contribute to their success.

Market position and competitive landscape

- What is your customer's current market position?
- Who are their main competitors?
- What are the key trends and challenges within their industry?

Understanding your key customer's competitive landscape provides context for their decisions and helps you anticipate their future needs.

Internal structure and decision-making processes

- What is the internal structure of your customer's organization?
- Who are the key decision-makers?
- What are their decision-making processes?

Understanding your key customer's internal workings allows you to navigate their organization effectively, build relationships with the right people and tailor your communication to resonate with their specific needs and expectations.

Challenges and opportunities

- What are the biggest challenges and pain points your customer is facing?
- What obstacles are preventing them from achieving their goals?

By identifying your key customer's challenges and opportunities, you can position your business as a solution provider and demonstrate how your expertise and offerings can address their specific needs.

Vision for the future

- Where does your customer see their business going in the future?
- What are their aspirations and long-term goals?

FIGURE 1.1 The role of the key account manager

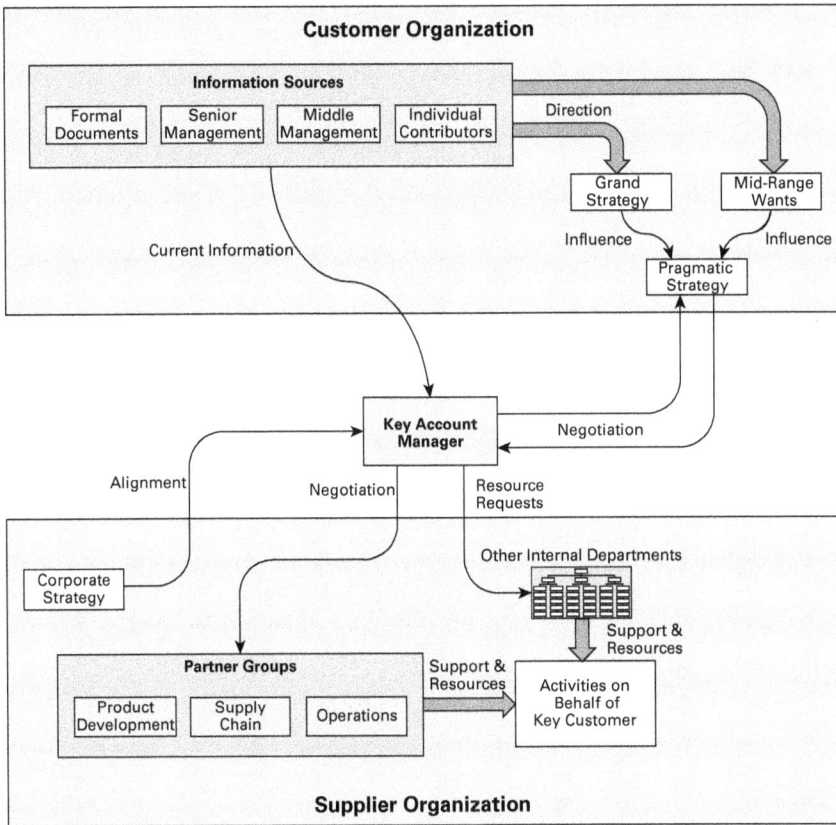

Understanding their vision for the future allows you to anticipate their evolving needs and develop solutions that support their long-term growth trajectory.

By investing time and effort in gathering information and insights into your customer's strategy, you build a foundation for a strong and enduring relationship. You position yourself as a valuable partner who understands their business, anticipates their needs and is committed to their long-term success.

Aligning your organization's strategy with that of your customer

In addition to having the competence to identify meaningful key account opportunities, as a KAMgr, you need to develop the ability to galvanize the support of executives in your own organization to create the products and services that will address the identified account's 'pragmatic' strategy. However, the challenge is that you're often measured against customer outcomes. In companies that are new or inexperienced at KAM, you might be asked to maximize the time you invest with your customers at the expense of time working inside your organization. A study[6,10] that explored the internal dimensions of 29 KAMgrs across US and UK companies, identified 112 incidents of intra-organizational and interpersonal conflict. To successfully implement key account management, your supplying company will have to be prepared to make internal changes to better align to your customer's priorities, and those changes will need to be driven by you.

In Chapters 11 and 12, we will cover the subtleties of engaging top management support and leading and influencing from different positions in greater detail, but, at this point, it is worth saying that to get the internal agreement you need – which will inevitably pull colleagues away from their previously agreed goals and objectives – it is not only imperative that you have top management support but that you have visible top management support. Having a VP or board-level sponsor who can be called on to reinforce the importance of supporting the KAM group is invaluable.

> In my experience with companies like Tetrapak and SKF, which are proficient in KAM, I've observed that key account managers spend about 60 per cent of their time internally, making things happen within their own company.
>
> Prof Malcolm McDonald

You engage with colleagues from a number of areas such as new product development, logistics, supply chain and operations to secure their support and to bring relevant innovation to their key customers. It is a prerequisite of your role that you're able to do this with a good understanding of each of these areas and the respect of the colleagues concerned. Negotiating internally differs significantly from commercial negotiations with external clients. There needs to be symmetry in the flow of information. In most cases, you must maintain harmonious relationships with your colleagues. The significance of these relationships should inform your negotiation strategy, collaborating or possibly compromising as needed. In situations where you need your organization to make a major investment in winning a substantial opportunity with a key customer, and you have a strong business case, your best approach may be a competitive one. This primarily focuses on internal interests and their alignment with those of the key account.

You must identify who will implement collaboration and how to do so as part of your 'strategist' role. Interestingly, despite the established assumption that effective collaboration with the customer drives your performance, a study found that it is the combined effect of internal and external collaboration that has a significant impact on your performance as an account manager.[11] That's why we refer to alignment across boundaries: internally and externally.

Consider the example of Repsol, the energy and chemical company headquartered in Spain. They developed a more sustainable polymer called Reciclex. Through chemical recycling, Reciclex is produced using plastic that cannot be recycled in any other way and that would otherwise become landfill waste. To sell this product, key account managers in the chemical division of the company had to 'negotiate' the design and implementation of new processes and practices upstream and downstream to ensure the successful launch of Reciclex and the realization of its benefits by some of their key customers, such as food and beverage manufacturers.

To reduce the conflict and complexity of managing internally, you need to ensure tight alignment between your organization's corporate strategy and the business strategy of your key accounts. That often calls for negotiating trade-offs between short- and long-term goals. For instance, postponing some revenues to introduce an improved product versus achieving next-quarter returns with an existing, less optimal product. As the adage goes, 'In business, you don't get what you deserve; you get what you negotiate' (see Chapter 8).

Once you have a thorough understanding of your customer's strategy, the next crucial step is to align your organization's strategy to ensure a mutually beneficial partnership. We cover this in detail in the rest of the section.

Skills that support alignment

Collaborative planning

Engaging in joint planning sessions with your customer to develop a shared vision for the future of the relationship. Establish clear goals, define roles and responsibilities, and outline a roadmap for achieving mutual success.

Open communication

Fostering a culture of open and transparent communication between your organization and your customer. Establish clear channels for sharing information, feedback and updates to ensure alignment and address any potential issues promptly

Flexibility and adaptability

Being willing to adapt your approach as your customer's needs evolve. The business landscape is constantly changing, and a successful partnership requires flexibility and a willingness to adjust to new challenges and opportunities.

> For key accounts (high potential from the supplier perspective, high strength of the supplier from the customer perspective), I'm convinced that a business manager with MBA-level skills is necessary. These individuals should have strategic business planning functions, help customers anticipate and define needs, maintain multi-function contact between organizations, develop joint solutions and innovations, lead internal account teams, promote cross-boundary relationships, orchestrate activities, and act as high-level arbiters, negotiators and ambassadors for the customer.
>
> Prof Malcolm McDonald

Aligning your organization's strategy with your customer's strategy is crucial for building strong and mutually beneficial long-term relationships. **This means understanding your customer's goals, challenges and overall business direction, and then adapting your offerings, communication and internal processes to support their success.** It's about moving beyond transactional interactions and becoming a true partner who actively contributes to their growth and development.

> Understanding our customers deeply is crucial – not just their immediate
> needs, but their overall business structure, challenges, and goals.
>
> Stuart Blakeley

1. Identifying areas of synergy

Begin by carefully examining your customer's strategy and identifying areas where your organization's strengths and capabilities can directly support their needs and objectives. For instance, if a customer is focused on expanding into new markets, and your organization possesses strong international logistics capabilities, there's an obvious synergy that you can leverage. Similarly, if a customer is prioritizing innovation, your company's research and development expertise could be a valuable asset.

> Example: A software company (the supplier) discovers that a major retail
> customer is focused on enhancing their online shopping experience. The
> supplier can align their strategy by offering personalized product
> recommendations, integrating loyalty programmes into the customer's
> platform, and providing ongoing support for their e-commerce platform.

2. Adapting your offerings

Once you've identified areas of synergy, it's essential to adapt your products, services and solutions to meet the specific requirements of your customer. This might involve:

- **Customization:** Tailoring existing products or services to align with the customer's unique needs.
- **Bundling:** Combining multiple offerings into a comprehensive package that provides a complete solution.
- **Developing new offerings:** Investing in research and development to create entirely new products or services that directly address the customer's specific challenges and contribute to their strategic goals. [conversation history]

- **Example:** A logistics company (the supplier) learns that a key manufacturing customer is struggling with supply chain disruptions. The supplier can align by offering tailored solutions such as expedited shipping, real-time tracking and inventory management services to mitigate the customer's challenges. [conversation history]

3. Embracing collaborative planning

Building a true strategic partnership requires moving beyond one-sided presentations and engaging in joint planning sessions with your customer. This fosters a sense of shared ownership and ensures both parties are working towards a common vision. Collaborative planning can involve:

- **Developing a shared vision:** Articulating a clear and concise vision for the future of the relationship, outlining the desired outcomes for both parties.
- **Establishing clear goals:** Setting specific, measurable, achievable, relevant and time-bound (SMART) goals that guide the partnership and provide benchmarks for measuring progress.
- **Defining roles and responsibilities:** Clearly outlining who is responsible for what, ensuring accountability and efficient execution of the agreed-upon plan.
- **Creating a roadmap for success:** Developing a detailed timeline that outlines key milestones, activities and deliverables, providing a clear path forward for achieving the shared vision and goals.
- **Example:** A marketing agency (the supplier) partners with a client in the hospitality industry to develop a comprehensive marketing strategy. They hold joint planning sessions to define target audiences, establish key performance indicators (KPIs) and outline a content calendar for social media campaigns, website updates and email marketing initiatives.

4. Fostering open communication

Open and transparent communication is the lifeblood of any successful partnership. Establish clear channels for communication and ensure information flows freely between your organization and your customer. This can involve:

- **Regular meetings:** Scheduling regular meetings, both formal and informal, to discuss progress, address challenges and exchange ideas.

- **Dedicated communication channels:** Utilizing tools like email, instant messaging and project management software to facilitate efficient and timely communication.

- **Transparency and feedback:** Creating a culture where both parties feel comfortable sharing feedback, both positive and negative, to ensure continuous improvement and address any concerns promptly.

- **Example:** A financial services firm (the supplier) provides regular portfolio updates and market analysis to their key clients. They also host webinars and online forums to share insights and address client questions. This open communication helps build trust and transparency in the relationship.

5. Cultivating flexibility and adaptability

The business landscape is constantly evolving, and so too must your approach to strategic customer relationships. Flexibility and adaptability are essential for navigating change and ensuring the partnership remains relevant and mutually beneficial. This involves:

- **Monitoring the market:** Keeping abreast of industry trends, competitive shifts and emerging technologies that could impact your customer's business and your partnership.

- **Being open to change:** Being willing to adjust your strategy, offerings and approach as needed to address new challenges, capitalize on new opportunities and ensure your solutions remain aligned with your customer's evolving needs.

- **Embracing a growth mindset:** Viewing challenges as opportunities for learning and improvement, fostering a culture of innovation and a willingness to experiment and adapt. [conversation history]

- **Example:** A technology company (the supplier) initially partnered with a customer to implement a cloud-based storage solution. As the customer's needs evolved, the supplier adapted their offering to include data analytics and cybersecurity services, ensuring the partnership remained valuable and aligned with the customer's changing priorities. [conversation history]

6. Establishing practices for enhanced understanding and coherence

The alignment between your organization's strategy and that of your key customer needs to be supported by certain processes and systems.

For instance, **customer immersion** practices, such as the 'voice of the customer', encourage key members of your business to spend time 'in the customer's shoes', understanding their day-to-day operations, challenges and culture. This can involve shadowing employees, participating in customer events or engaging in joint workshops and brainstorming sessions.

Some functions within your organization may not be in close contact with the customer. Thus, in order to achieve **cross-functional alignment** you may need to create dedicated customer teams or establish clear communication channels and processes for sharing information and coordinating efforts. Once these are established, **shared metrics and reporting** will help track progress towards achieving the shared goals of the supplier-key customer partnership.

> I also advocate for a multidimensional model of measurement at the individual level, similar to a spider diagram. This model would include factors such as understanding the customer's business and the type of relationship desired, in addition to traditional metrics like sales volume and profit.
>
> Prof Malcolm McDonald

These practices, many of which are rather prescribed, need to be coupled with informal processes that favour **relationship development**. Go beyond formal business interactions and invest in relationship-building activities that foster trust and rapport. This can involve social events, team-building exercises or simply taking the time to connect on a personal level.

By embracing these deeper alignment tactics, you can transform your customer relationships from transactional exchanges to true strategic partnerships that drive mutual growth, innovation and success.

By fostering internal alignment, you ensure everyone in your organization is working together to deliver a seamless and exceptional customer experience, strengthening the partnership and driving long-term value creation.

Balancing planned and emerging strategy

It would be unrealistic to think that your key customers will have an unambiguous, widely supported and agreed-upon strategy and that they will turn to you with the question: How can you help us achieve goals X, Y and Z of our strategy?

Deliberate strategies are approaches that arise from mindful, considerate and structured decision-making by the organization and its executives. They typically emerge from the rigorous scrutiny of information, market analysis and resource-evaluation techniques. But organizations often pursue unplanned, unintentional or 'emergent' strategies, as Henry Mintzberg, Cleghorn Professor of Management Studies, calls them. An emergent strategy results from spontaneous actions and decisions that are not pre-planned and organized.[12] Emergent strategies occur when new opportunities for business growth are realized, but executives had not previously planned to focus on them. Emergent strategies will be even more common post-Covid due to the greater rate of business change.[13]

Your key customers will likely focus on a strategy that is a blend of planned and emerging strategies. For instance, Cargill, a key supplier to Unilever, defined specific, planned approaches to help Unilever in its new product development cycle. This was a 'planned strategy'. As Unilever further pursued its mission of 'Making sustainable living commonplace' and increased its commitment to sustainability, Cargill's emergent strategy gradually shifted towards sustainability, in line with some of its key accounts' priorities.

One implication for you in embracing both planned and emergent strategies is that you need to sense signals and detect relevant information not just from your key customers' senior managers and middle managers, but also from people at all levels of the company, including operators and others, to achieve a more comprehensive picture of customers' strategic priorities. Also, you need to be comfortable incorporating both focused initiatives that address the account's planned and emergent strategies into your own account plans.

In the best-case scenarios, over time, customers will come to embrace the advantages of working with you as a supplier and partner. In the 2010s, Fujitsu was one of the customers that realized the benefits of this approach and institutionalized Joint Planning and Joint Development process with a few key partners such as Hewlett Packard Storage. This involved regular meetings both for executives and individual contributors where detailed, long-term strategic plans and shorter-term product and range plans were shared. The benefits to both sides were enormous, ensuring that new product development could be started in some cases many years ahead of the product need. As a supplier, HP knew there would be guaranteed demand for the products being developed and so could invest in them with a strong guarantee of return. As a customer, Fujitsu had assurance that their future performance needs would be met. However, the trust and confidence in the relationship that both parties must have to be able to share at this level is immense. In this case that was particularly so given that in other areas these two companies were direct competitors and rivals. This means that relationships of this strength can only be built up slowly, over many years of close cooperation, so patience may sometimes be required.

Overall, the essential dimension of your performance is strategic ability. Unlike other functions where the strategy is fundamentally inward-looking, you need to conceive rounded strategies that connect your firm's corporate strategy with that of your key accounts in mutually reinforcing ways. Being prepared to change or adjust your strategies to meet the needs of key customers is a fundamental requirement of key account management. However, in doing that it is imperative that you do not lose sight of your overall strategic direction and get sidetracked into areas or programmes where you cannot add value. The relationship must remain one of trusted equals where the final directions are agreed on by all and if this cannot be achieved it is better to acknowledge the situation and part ways.

> Being a key account manager primarily involves orchestrating the entire account team and shifting the mindset from an inside-out to an outside-in perspective. The key account manager's role is to move beyond the traditional sales approach of being a mere marketing billboard to becoming a customer-centric partner who understands and addresses the needs of the entire customer ecosystem: a strategist and mini key account CEO.
>
> Nicolaas Smit

Summary and application

An integral part of implementing effective key account management is anticipating customers' needs faster than they can do it themselves. If you are new to the world of KAM, you may think this sounds impossibly difficult and doubt that it can be achieved. However, research shows that it is not only possible but essential.[14] Becoming a better strategist in managing customer relationships requires a proactive and deliberate approach. Table 1.1 shows 10 tactics you can use to enhance your ability to strategize.

Figure 1.2 shows key drivers, tools, behaviours and success factors when strategizing and planning for your key customers.

TABLE 1.1 Ten tactics to enhance your ability to strategize

	Action	Description
1.	Develop analytical skills	You need strong cognitive skills to analyse customers' business contexts, focusing on long-term interests and challenges.
2.	Understand the 'pragmatic' strategy of your key accounts	You must go beyond formal company documents to decipher your accounts' true strategies, which often result from a mix of 'grand' desires and 'mid-range' operational wants.
3.	Use innovative needs analysis	Techniques like MaxDiff and hidden needs analysis can reveal genuine customer needs that may not be articulated through traditional research methods.
4.	Foster internal alignment	You must negotiate within your own organization to secure support for creating products and services that address the account's strategy.
5.	Balance internal and external collaboration	The combined effect of collaborating both internally and externally significantly impacts your performance.
6.	Navigate planned and emergent strategies	Customers often blend deliberate and emergent strategies. You need to be adaptable and sense signals from various levels within customer organizations.
7.	Boost continuous innovation	It is crucial for you to constantly innovate and reinvent value propositions, creating novel solutions that anticipate and exceed customer needs.
8.	Develop cross-functional understanding	You need a good understanding of various business areas (product development, logistics, supply chain, operations) to effectively negotiate internally.
9.	Promote strategic alignment	You must align your organization's priorities with those of key accounts, carefully choosing which internal 'battles' to fight.
10.	Seek comprehensive information relentlessly	To get a full picture of customer priorities, you should gather information from all levels of the customer's organization, not just senior management.

FIGURE 1.2 Key drivers, tools, behaviours and success factors

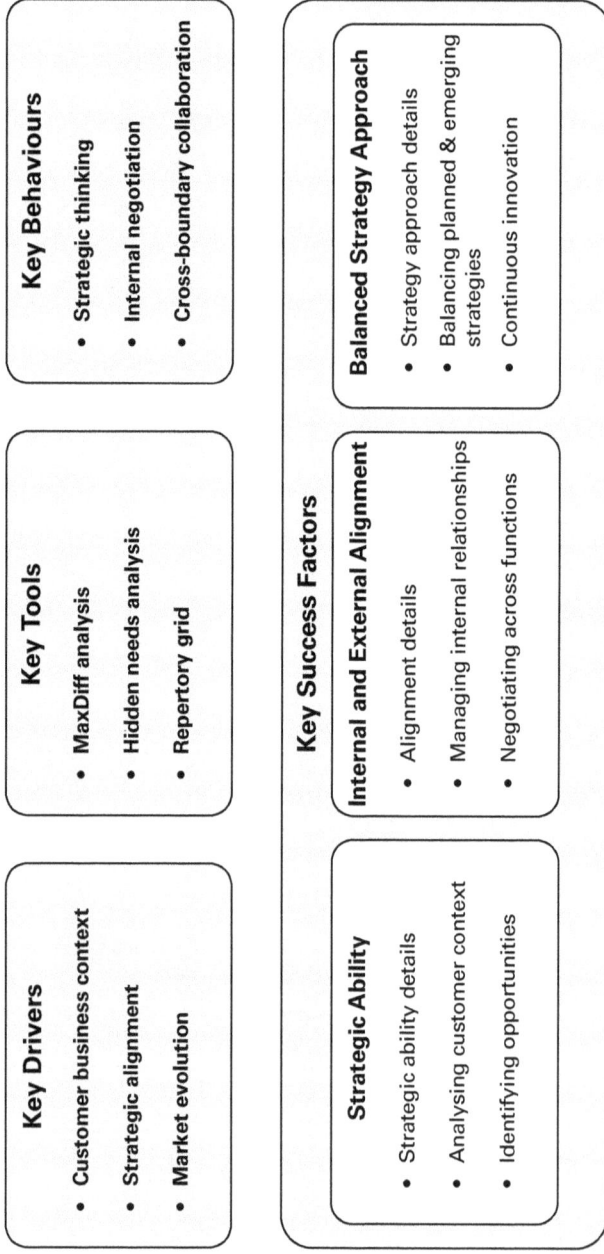

Key Drivers

- **Customer business context**
- **Strategic alignment**
- **Market evolution**

Key Tools

- **MaxDiff analysis**
- **Hidden needs analysis**
- **Repertory grid**

Key Behaviours

- **Strategic thinking**
- **Internal negotiation**
- **Cross-boundary collaboration**

Key Success Factors

Strategic Ability

- Strategic ability details
- Analysing customer context
- Identifying opportunities

Internal and External Alignment

- Alignment details
- Managing internal relationships
- Negotiating across functions

Balanced Strategy Approach

- Strategy approach details
- Balancing planned & emerging strategies
- Continuous innovation

Notes

1 I A Davies and L J Ryal. The effectiveness of key account management practices, *Industrial Marketing Management*, 2014, 43 (7), 1182–94, www.sciencedirect.com/science/article/pii/S0019850114001059 (archived at https://perma.cc/Y97Y-DWA2)

2 S Gounaris and N Tzempelikos. Relational key account management: Building key account management effectiveness through structural reformations and relationship management skills, *Industrial Marketing Management*, 2014, 43 (7), 1110–23

3 R Guesalaga, M Gabrielsson, B Rogers, L Ryals and J Marcos Cuevas. Which resources and capabilities underpin strategic key account management? *Industrial Marketing Management*, 2018, 75, 160–72, https://doi.org/10.1016/j.indmarman.2018.05.006 (archived at https://perma.cc/BP2K-T698)

4 J Feste, B S Ivens and C Pard. Key account selection as a political process: Conceptual foundation and exploratory investigation, *Industrial Marketing Management*, 2020, 90, 417–34, https://doi.org/10.1016/j.indmarman.2020.07.024 (archived at https://perma.cc/5L9T-K8E5)

5 T Hakanen. Co-creating integrated solutions within business networks: The KAM team as knowledge integrator, *Industrial Marketing Management*, 2014, 43 (7), 1195–203, www.sciencedirect.com/science/article/abs/pii/S0019850114001394 (archived at https://perma.cc/T2DY-DPN9)

6 J Hagemann Snabe and S Skou. Message from the Chairman and the CEO. A.P. Møller – Mærsk A/S, 10 February 2021, www.maersk.com/news/articles/2021/02/10/message-from-the-chairman-and-ceo (archived at https://perma.cc/F6LZ-75CM)

7 A A Marley and J J Louviere. Some probabilistic models of best, worst, and best-worst choices, *Journal of Mathematical Psychology*, 2005, 49 (6), 464–80

8 D I Baxter, K Goffin and M Szwejczewski. The repertory grid technique as a customer insight method, *Research-Technology Management*, 2014, 57 (4), 35–42, www.tandfonline.com/doi/abs/10.5437/08956308X5704229 (archived at https://perma.cc/TC6F-AHQF)

9 I. Speakman and L. Ryals,. Key account management: the inside selling job, *Journal of Business & Industrial Marketing*, 2012, 27 (5), 360–69, https://doi.org/10.1108/08858621211236034 (archived at https://perma.cc/637G-CA3T)

10 T Stobiersk. Emergent vs. deliberate strategy, *Harvard Business Review*, 19 November 2020, https://online.hbs.edu/blog/post/emergent-vs-deliberate-strategy (archived at https://perma.cc/F7PZ-FDYD)

11 S Y Tarba, J G Frynas, Y Liu, G Wood, R M Sarala and S Fainshmidt. Strategic agility in international business, *Journal of World Business*, 2023, 58 (2), 101411

12 T Stobiersk. Emergent vs. deliberate strategy

13 C Bratianu and R Bejinaru. COVID-19 induced emergent knowledge strategies, *Knowledge and Process Management*, 2021, 28 (1), 11–17

14 S Holt (2003). The role of the global account manager: a boundary role theory perspective, PhD Thesis, Cranfield University

Malcolm McDonald

In my 68 years of work experience, including 25 years in my current company, I've worked with hundreds of companies on key account management over at least a quarter-century. From this extensive experience, I can confidently say that understanding the types of key account is crucial when defining the roles and responsibilities of key account managers.

In my view, key accounts should be classified according to their potential for growth in profits and the supplier's strength with that account. This classification results in four types of key accounts: strategic, status, star and streamline. Each type, I believe, requires a different approach and skillset from a key account manager.

For strategic accounts (high potential, high strength), I'm convinced that a business manager with MBA-level skills is necessary. These individuals should have strategic business planning functions, help customers anticipate and define needs, maintain multi-function contact between organizations, develop joint solutions and innovations, lead internal account teams, promote cross-boundary relationships, orchestrate activities and act as high-level arbiters, negotiators and ambassadors for the customer.

Star accounts require a higher level of entrepreneurial skills, whilst status accounts require a more project management approach in order to maintain profitable cash flows. Streamline accounts (accounts that do not hold much potential for future growth and where the supplier does not enjoy an excellent relationship with the customer) needs a manager who can control costs to serve and who can maximize cash flows.

In my experience with companies like Tetrapak and SKF, which are proficient in KAM, I've observed that key account managers spend about 60 per cent of their time internally, making things happen within their own company. This aligns with what I've seen in other successful KAM implementations.

When it comes to defining key accounts, in my opinion, it's not just about size but strategic importance. I'd say it's the supplying company who thinks of them as a strategic customer, somebody who's like a market in their own right. This could include smaller customers who are opinion leaders in their industry.

In terms of organizational structure, I typically see key account managers reporting to a sales and marketing director. However, I've noticed that in some organizations, particularly in fast-moving consumer goods companies, key account managers might have their own dedicated teams with dotted-line relationships to various departments like accounting, production and distribution.

Regarding the academic background of key account managers, I'm a strong advocate for MBA graduates due to the multidisciplinary nature of the role. In my view, finance is the most crucial discipline to master, as that's all companies are really interested in. I've found that individuals with a finance background often make the best key account managers.

On the topic of performance measurement, I strongly believe in using shareholder value added or profit as the primary metric at an organizational level. In my experience, if you're creating shareholder value for the company and you can prove it, then the board will support you. If you can't prove it, you don't know what you're doing.

However, I also advocate for a multidimensional model of measurement at the individual level, similar to a spider diagram. This model would include factors such as understanding the customer's business and the type of relationship desired, in addition to traditional metrics like sales volume and profit.

When it comes to key capabilities for key account managers, I'd prioritize four main areas:

1 Researching and seeking value creation opportunities (50 per cent)
2 Managing information and conducting financial analysis (20 per cent)
3 Strategizing and planning (20 per cent)
4 Achieving top management involvement and support (10 per cent)

In my opinion, researching and seeking value creation opportunities is the most critical capability. If you're trying to create value, you've got to understand the client's processes, their business model, their market, their customers, their strengths and weaknesses. Otherwise, you've got no chance of creating value.

Regarding the development of these capabilities, I believe in ongoing training, especially in emerging areas like digital technologies. In my view, key account directors play a crucial role in assessing their team's skills and addressing any gaps through appropriate training.

I must say, I'm critical of the current state of KAM education. It's an absolute disgrace that it's not taught in business schools. It's not taught on university courses. It's not on the curriculum in most places. I praise institutions like Cranfield and Portsmouth for their focus on KAM, but I believe more needs to be done to develop these crucial skills in future business leaders.

In conclusion, based on my decades of experience, I can say that key account management is complex and multifaceted. It requires strategic thinking, multidisciplinary skills, and a deep understanding of both the client's business and one's own organization. I firmly believe in tailored approaches to different types of key accounts and the critical role of ongoing education and training in developing effective key account managers.

Malcolm H B McDonald is a British educator and the first marketing professor to have created an app and recorded his full lectures. He founded the Key Account Management Forum at Cranfield School of Management and recently celebrated its 25th anniversary.

Malcolm was, until recently, Professor of Marketing and Deputy Director at Cranfield University School of Management and is now an Emeritus Professor at the university and an Honorary Professor at Warwick Business School. He has consulted for many major companies in the United Kingdom, Europe, the USA, the Far East, Southeast Asia, Australasia and Africa in strategic marketing and marketing planning, market segmentation, key account management, international marketing and marketing accountability.

Malcolm is also chairman of six companies and works with the operating boards of some multinational corporations, and his opinions and advice carry great weight across the globe, from classroom to boardroom.

He has written over 40 books, including Marketing Plans: How to prepare and use them *(translated into French among many languages)*, Marketing Value Metrics, Creating Powerful Brands; *and* Marketing and Finance: Creating shareholder value. *With Tony Millman and Dr Beth Rogers, Professor McDonald was involved in Cranfield's first research projects on key account management.*

www.linkedin.com/in/professormalcolmmcdonald

02

Researching and seeking value-creation opportunities

Developing an inquiring mindset and analytical skills to explore business opportunities with key accounts

Overview

In the intricate tapestry of modern business, key accounts represent the crown jewels of any company's client portfolio. These accounts, often the largest and most strategically significant, warrant a unique management, development and growth approach. Key accounts are more than high-revenue clients; they represent pivotal strategic partnerships critical to long-term success. Their significance lies in the opportunity for sustained growth, innovation and competitive differentiation. By focusing on these relationships, companies can create mutually beneficial opportunities that extend beyond traditional buyer-supplier dynamics.

Effective key account management begins with thorough research. Understanding a key account's industry landscape, internal operations and strategic goals allows account managers to align solutions closely with client needs. The ability to analyse trends, anticipate challenges and co-create solutions elevates the partnership, transforming vendors into trusted advisors. The ultimate goal of researching and seeking value-creation opportunities is to foster a collaborative environment where both parties thrive. Tailored solutions, strategic alignment and proactive engagement build trust and loyalty. These efforts ensure that key accounts not only remain profitable but also become advocates and innovators within their respective industries.

This chapter delves into the critical practice of researching and seeking value-creation opportunities within key accounts. It emphasizes the necessity of understanding the underlying reasons for these activities and underscores the imperative role of key account knowledge as the foundation for robust, bi-directional business relationships. We present a framework centred on three pillars: the external environment, the customer's business and the supplier organization. By examining each, key account managers (KAMgrs) can identify opportunities for growth and collaboration. Tools such as PESTEL analysis and the GRASP framework provide practical methodologies for gathering actionable insights.

Why is research on your key accounts so important?

The importance of meticulously researching and seeking value-creation opportunities for these accounts cannot be overstated. As a key account manager, these efforts are essential for several reasons, which we now present.

Strategic intelligence

Strategic intelligence is paramount for effective KAM. By actively researching market trends and customer needs, KAMgrs can provide early warnings of market shifts and threats. This capability allows organizations to anticipate changes and prepare adequately, avoiding disruptions that could harm relationships with key clients. Additionally, identifying emerging customer needs ensures that offerings remain aligned with client expectations, making the organization indispensable to its strategic accounts.

Proactive relationship management is another critical aspect of strategic intelligence. Rather than reacting to client requests, key account managers who leverage strategic intelligence can anticipate client needs, positioning themselves as forward-thinking partners. The value of a key supplier is helping your customers avoid unforeseen problems; see the quote from Dr Beth Rogers in the following box. This proactive stance is crucial in maintaining the key account's confidence and satisfaction, preventing potential problems from escalating and demonstrating the supplier's commitment to the client's success. It also enhances the ability to better anticipate disruptions, ensuring that both the organization and the client can navigate unforeseen challenges more effectively.

> The value of a key supplier is helping your customers avoid unforeseen problems more than it is solving known problems.
>
> Dr Beth Rogers

Knowledge-driven value creation

The ability to create value through knowledge is a hallmark of successful KAM strategies. Developing tailored solutions involves deeply understanding a client's unique challenges and crafting specific responses that address those needs. These personalized offerings enhance the perceived value of the relationship and strengthen the client's trust in the organization.

Facilitating innovation opportunities is another key dimension of knowledge-driven value creation. Key accounts are often at the forefront of their industries, driving trends and setting standards; by working closely with clients, KAMgrs can uncover unique insights to co-develop new products, services or processes that drive mutual growth. This collaboration fosters a sense of shared ownership and commitment to the partnership. Supporting co-creation initiatives further reinforces this collaborative bond, enabling both organizations to leverage their strengths and achieve greater success together. Moreover, this collaborative approach not only benefits the key account but also allows the supplier to develop cutting-edge solutions that can be scaled across the broader market.

Finally, enhanced competitive differentiation is achieved through knowledge-driven strategies. In highly competitive markets, the ability to understand and anticipate the needs of key accounts better than competitors can serve as a significant differentiator. By proactively seeking value-creation opportunities, supplier companies can deliver unique and customized offerings, distinguishing themselves from competitors and solidifying their position as the partner of choice for strategic clients.

Customer understanding

A deep understanding of the client's business is central to building and sustaining strategic relationships. Key account managers achieve this by gaining deep insights into customer challenges. This involves thorough research and active engagement with clients to uncover the underlying issues they face. Armed with this knowledge, KAMgrs can offer more relevant and impactful solutions.

Better alignment with customer goals is another crucial outcome of enhanced customer understanding. By ensuring that the partnership's objectives align with the client's broader business goals, key account managers can demonstrate their commitment to the client's success. Additionally, improved ability to anticipate needs allows KAMgrs to provide solutions before challenges escalate, further cementing their value to the client.

Enhanced relationship development is the natural result of these efforts. Demonstrating an intimate knowledge of a key account's business builds trust and credibility. Clients are more likely to view the supplier as a trusted advisor rather than just a vendor. This shift in perception can lead to more significant collaborative opportunities and a greater willingness to invest in joint ventures. By building trust and demonstrating a deep commitment to understanding and addressing client needs, key account managers foster stronger, long-term relationships that are resilient to competitive pressures.

Strategic alignment

A deep understanding of a key account's strategic objectives allows the supplier to align its offerings and initiatives with the client's long-term goals, which creates a synergistic relationship where both parties work towards mutual success, reinforcing the partnership's importance and longevity. Strategic alignment ensures that resources and capabilities are deployed efficiently to meet the needs of key accounts. Making better resource allocation decisions involves prioritizing investments in areas that deliver the most value to strategic clients. This careful allocation ensures that both the organization and the client benefit from optimal use of time, talent and financial resources.

Improved capability matching aligns the organization's strengths with the client's specific requirements. This tailored approach not only enhances the effectiveness of solutions but also demonstrates a deep understanding of the client's business. Setting clearer partnership objectives further strengthens this alignment by providing a shared vision and roadmap for achieving success. More effective solution development is another key outcome of strategic alignment. By leveraging synergies between the two organizations, KAMgrs can design and implement solutions that are both innovative and practical, ensuring mutual value creation.

Sustained growth and risk management

Finally, growth and effective risk management are essential for sustaining long-term partnerships. Key accounts often provide a steady stream of revenue, crucial for the financial health of a supplier's business. Identifying new avenues for value creation ensures that these accounts remain profitable and can even expand their business with the supplier, thereby contributing to the company's long-term growth and stability. This involves identifying and addressing potential vulnerabilities that could disrupt the client relationship.

Early threat identification allows key account managers to recognize and mitigate risks before they escalate. This includes monitoring market dynamics, competitive actions and internal challenges that could impact the partnership. Growth opportunity recognition is another critical aspect of risk management, enabling KAMgrs to identify and pursue new avenues for collaboration and mutual benefit.

Additionally, more accurate strategic planning minimizes uncertainty and enhances decision-making. By combining insights from risk management with broader strategic intelligence, KAMgrs can create robust plans that support both the client's and the organization's long-term success.

The following box provides a summary of the main points that justify researching and seeking value-creation opportunities in KAM.

WHY RESEARCHING AND SEEKING VALUE-CREATION OPPORTUNITIES IS IMPORTANT

Strategic intelligence

- Early warning of market shifts and threat
- Identification of emerging customer need
- Proactive relationship management
- Better disruption anticipation

Knowledge-driven value creation

- Development of tailored solutions
- Facilitation of innovation opportunities
- Support for co-creation initiatives
- Enhanced competitive differentiation

Customer understanding

- Deep insight into customer challenge
- Better alignment with customer goal
- Improved ability to anticipate needs
- Enhanced relationship development

Strategic alignment

- Better resource allocation decisions
- Improved capability matching
- Clearer partnership objective
- More effective solution development

Sustained growth and risk management

- Sustained revenue stream protection
- Early threat identification
- Growth opportunity recognition
- More accurate strategic planning

Fundamental components of researching and seeking value-creation opportunities

Key account managers must excel in researching and seeking value-creation opportunities to ensure the growth and sustainability of their relationships with key clients. They need to be proactive in gathering first-hand information about evolving trends, as well as customer needs and priorities. Furthermore, KAMgrs must also gather insights internally, from the KAM team, executives from other functional areas and senior management, as this will help align internal resources, capabilities and strategies to create value for key customers.

First, key account managers must have a deep grasp of industry and market underlying forces, such as economic shifts, technology advances, political events, legal restrictions and social or cultural trends. Second, they need to fully understand their key account's needs and preferences, pains, business model and strategy. Third, KAMgrs should also be conscious of their own (supplier) company's resources and capabilities that are in place to support their job; therefore, they need to gather insights from the KAM team, executives from other functional areas and senior management. These tools help in aligning internal resources, capabilities and strategies to create value for key customers.

The benefits of actively obtaining and analysing such information can be substantial. For instance, KAMgrs would be well-equipped to be responsive and even anticipate customer needs, drive co-creation with key accounts, provide valuable inputs for innovation and tailored solutions, and build a competitive advantage through a researching competency. The consequence will be the identification of novel and promising business opportunities with key accounts.[1]

The three components of researching and seeking value-creation opportunities are: external environment, customer's business and (own) supplier company. We now develop these components further and provide some advice on the types of secondary and primary sources of data that could be used to obtain valuable qualitative and quantitative insights. Figure 2.1 presents a summary of these components, and the data sources key account managers could consider in their research.

FIGURE 2.1 Components of researching and seeking value-creation opportunities

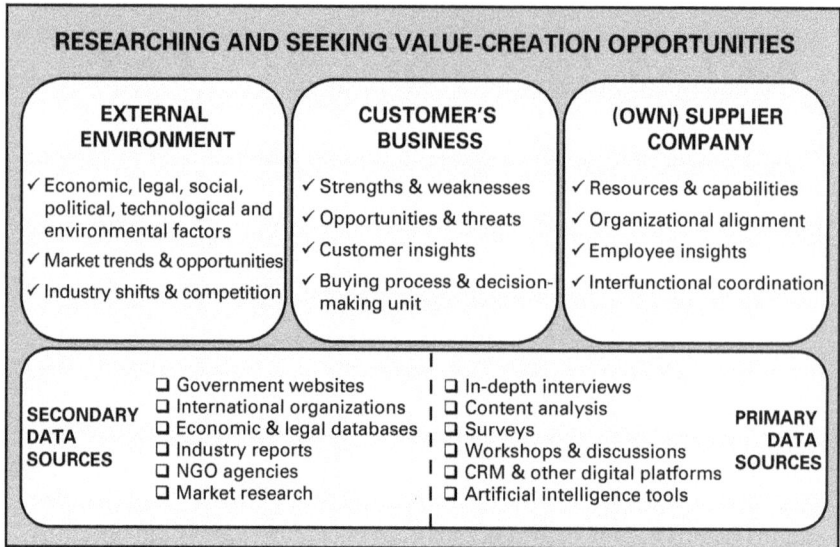

RESEARCHING AND SEEKING VALUE-CREATION OPPORTUNITIES

EXTERNAL ENVIRONMENT	CUSTOMER'S BUSINESS	(OWN) SUPPLIER COMPANY
✓ Economic, legal, social, political, technological and environmental factors	✓ Strengths & weaknesses	✓ Resources & capabilities
✓ Market trends & opportunities	✓ Opportunities & threats	✓ Organizational alignment
✓ Industry shifts & competition	✓ Customer insights	✓ Employee insights
	✓ Buying process & decision-making unit	✓ Interfunctional coordination

SECONDARY DATA SOURCES
- ❑ Government websites
- ❑ International organizations
- ❑ Economic & legal databases
- ❑ Industry reports
- ❑ NGO agencies
- ❑ Market research

PRIMARY DATA SOURCES
- ❑ In-depth interviews
- ❑ Content analysis
- ❑ Surveys
- ❑ Workshops & discussions
- ❑ CRM & other digital platforms
- ❑ Artificial intelligence tools

External environment

In the world of KAM, the landscape is rarely still. Shifts in customer needs, competitor strategies and industry trends can rapidly reshape the business environment.

To navigate this ever-evolving terrain, key account managers need to gather and interpret data on the variety of environmental factors that affect their company's business, their key accounts and the quality of buyer-supplier relationships. These factors are economic, legal, social, political, technological and environmental.

In addition, KAMgrs should keep track of the main market trends and the potential opportunities that may arise for their company and with key accounts. Likewise, they must deeply understand the industry shifts and dynamics, and the power balance and types of relationships among buyers and sellers. Additionally, they ought to analyse the competitive situation among industry players, and identify organizations that lead innovations and, thus, represent role models for other firms.

Customer's business

Understanding what key customers truly value is like having a backstage pass to the show: you get an inside view of what's working, what's missing and where future hits might lie.

Customer business analysis involves a deep dive into the client's internal operations, financial health, strategic objectives and pain points. Key account managers must understand their customer's business model, types of revenue streams and operational challenges to identify areas where they can add value. Incorporating the viewpoints and feedback from key accounts contributes to a more customer-centric approach to strategic decision-making, which leads to greater customer satisfaction, loyalty and long-term collaborative partnerships.[2]

Key account managers are encouraged to conduct external and internal audits for customers to identify their opportunities and threats, their strengths and weaknesses, and the resulting strategies they could follow. Regular business reviews, close communication with various stakeholders within the customer's organization and a trusting relationship are essential for effective client business analysis.

A major responsibility of KAMgrs is to analyse their key customer's buying process, understanding the critical stages, touchpoints, success factors and relevant metrics. Moreover, they should have a sound grasp of the members, interests and relative power within the customer decision-making unit.

(Own) Supplier company

Key account managers also need support from their (own) supplier organization to perform well. First, they need to rely on the company's most strategic resources and capabilities to be able to differentiate the value propositions to key accounts. Second, the organization needs to be aligned to better serve and manage key account relationships, with a special emphasis on top management involvement. Third, key account managers should bring in insight from their company's employees to obtain a more objective perspective on the initiatives that can be taken successfully for or with strategic customers. Fourth, there needs to be good coordination among functional departments to effectively and efficiently develop long-term relationships with key accounts.

> One of the unique aspects of our approach is the high level of empowerment we give our CEs [Client Executives]. They have a lot of authority to make decisions and drive initiatives forward.
>
> Andrea Clatworthy

Sources of data

The usefulness of the KAMgrs researching efforts depend on the quality of the data obtained. Ideally, a combination of secondary and primary sources of data will provide the information that is needed to effectively manage key accounts.

Secondary data sources: These refer to data that has been gathered before for various purposes, which is available to the KAMgrs. The following sources have proven to be useful to researching and seeking value-creation opportunities:

- Government websites
- International organizations (e.g. World Bank, International Monetary Fund, Organization for Economic Co-operation and Development)
- Economic databases (e.g. Eurostat, United Nations Data, World Trade Organization Data)
- Legal databases (e.g. Westlaw International, LexisNexis, WorldLII, Global Regulation)
- Industry reports (e.g. Statista, Euromonitor)
- Technology reports (e.g. Gartner, Forrester)
- NGO agencies (e.g. World Resources Institute, Environmental Protection Agency)
- Market research (e.g. Nielsen, Ipsos, GfK)

Primary data sources: These constitute data that is gathered specifically to understand a managerial problem or proactively learn about key customers, the external environment and the (own) supplier company. The following sources are typically used:

- In-depth interviews with key informants (e.g. purchasing managers, senior managers, experts in the industry)
- Content analysis of relevant text (e.g. customer reviews, discussion forums)
- Surveys (e.g. with customers and end users)
- Workshops and structured group discussions (e.g. internal meetings with people in different functional units)
- CRM and other digital platforms
- Artificial intelligence tools (e.g. account insights, data enrichment, deal intelligence, conversation analytics, account engagement)

FIGURE 2.2 Tools for researching and seeking value-creation opportunities

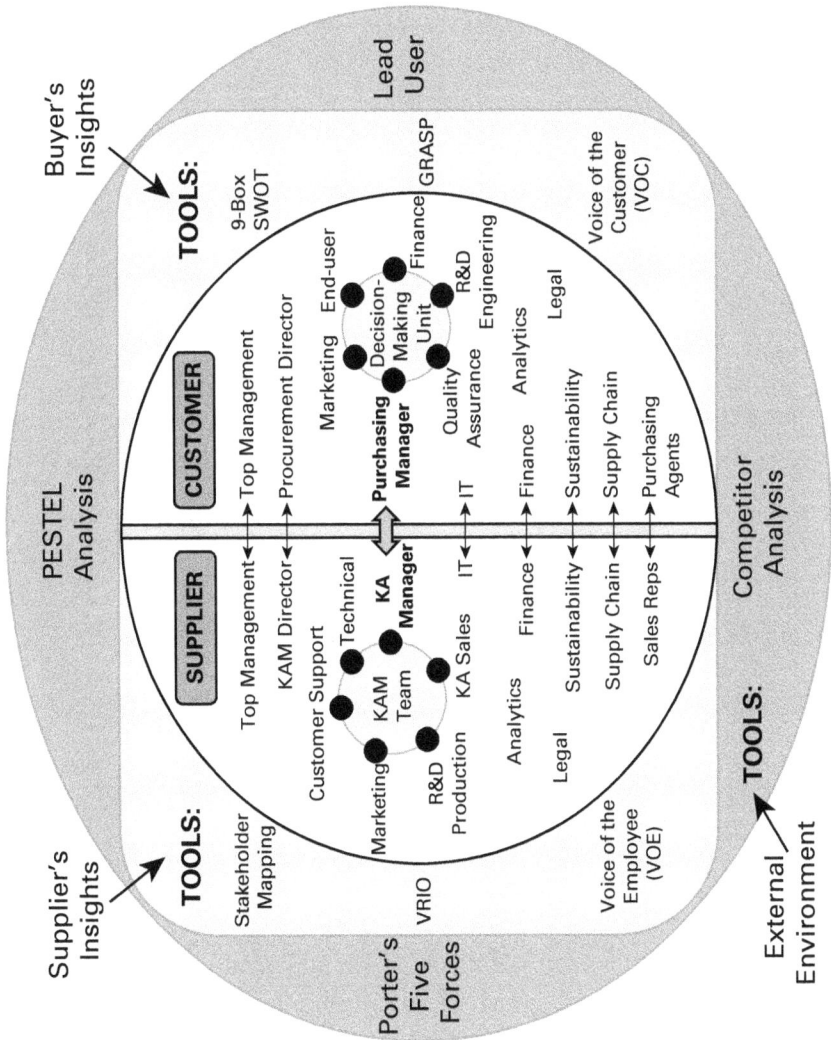

Tools for researching and seeking value-creation opportunities

Figure 2.2 presents a framework of tools for researching and seeking value-creation opportunities. The outside oval shows the tools that key account managers can use for researching the external environment, whereas the inside diagram presents tools to be used to investigate the customer business and the (own) supplier company.

Researching the external environment

PESTEL ANALYSIS

A PESTEL analysis is used to understand the macro-environmental factors that could impact industries and markets, as well as the overall business environment for a company.[3] The acronym stands for: Political, Economic, Social, Technological, Environmental and Legal. Table 2.1 presents a general definition of each PESTEL factor and some suggestions of specific elements that could be particularly relevant in the context of key account management and B2B relationships.

TABLE 2.1 PESTEL factors in key account management

PESTEL factor and definition	Relevant factors for KAM
Political factors refer to the influence of government policies, regulations and political stability on business operations.	**Regulatory changes:** Understanding how changes in regulations, such as trade policies, taxation and labour laws, might affect the customer's business operations. **Government stability:** Monitoring the political environment and potential risks in key markets that could affect the customer's supply chain or market access. **Industry-specific legislation:** Staying informed about industry-specific legislation that could impact the customer's industry.
Economic factors encompass the broader economy's conditions, such as inflation, interest rates and economic growth, which can influence business performance.	**Economic growth trends:** Keeping track of economic growth in key markets to anticipate demand for the customer's products or services. **Exchange rates:** Monitoring exchange rates that could affect pricing strategies and profitability for customers operating internationally. **Inflation and interest rates:** Understanding how inflation and interest rates might impact the customer's cost structure, pricing and purchasing power.

(continued)

TABLE 2.1 (Continued)

PESTEL factor and definition	Relevant factors for KAM
Social factors include demographic trends, cultural attitudes and consumer behaviours that can affect market demand and business practices.	**Demographic changes:** Analysing shifts in demographics, such as aging populations or urbanization, that could influence the customer's target market and product offerings. **Cultural trends:** Being aware of cultural trends and values that could affect consumer preferences and, subsequently, the customer's product positioning. **Workforce trends:** Monitoring changes in workforce dynamics, such as remote work, gender diversity or talent shortages, that could impact the customer's operations and strategic priorities.
Technological factors refer to innovations and technological advancements that could influence the way businesses operate and compete.	**Emerging technologies:** Identifying emerging technologies that could disrupt the customer's industry or create new opportunities for innovation. **Digital transformation:** Understanding the customer's digital transformation initiatives and how they align with industry trends and technological advancements. **Cybersecurity:** Staying informed about cybersecurity risks and trends, especially where sensitive data is involved.
Environmental factors include ecological and environmental aspects, such as climate change, sustainability and environmental regulations.	**Sustainability initiatives:** Understanding the customer's sustainability goals and how environmental regulations might impact their operations. **Climate change impacts:** Analysing how climate change could affect the customer's supply chain, particularly in industries reliant on natural resources. **Environmental regulations:** Monitoring changes in environmental regulations that could impose new requirements on the customer's operations or products.
Legal factors encompass laws and regulations that govern business practices, including employment laws, competition laws and intellectual property rights.	**Compliance requirements:** Ensuring that the customer is aware of and compliant with relevant legal requirements, especially in highly regulated industries. **Contract law:** Understanding changes in contract law that might affect B2B agreements, including terms and conditions, dispute resolution and liability. **Intellectual property:** Keeping track of intellectual property laws that could impact the customer's ability to protect and leverage their innovations.

PORTER'S FIVE FORCES

Porter's Five Forces[4] is one of the most renowned frameworks for analysing the competitive environment. It helps assess the intensity of competition and the profitability of an industry by examining the following five forces.

Competitive rivalry: Who's in the arena?

Competitive rivalry is the intensity of competition among existing players in an industry. Think of it as the level of 'noise' in the market – the higher it is, the tougher it is to stand out. In high-competition markets, firms often vie for similar customers, pushing down margins and making it harder for any one company to dominate.

For key account managers, understanding the level of competition that your company and account face is crucial. If you're working with key accounts in a crowded industry, your customers are likely bombarded with offers from rivals, each promising a better deal or innovation. This scenario might mean focusing on unique value propositions and differentiators – what makes your offer uniquely better?

Key questions for KAMgrs:

- What strategies are competitors using to appeal to our key accounts?
- How loyal are our key accounts, and what risks exist of them switching to competitors?
- Are there unique value-added services that could keep us top of mind?

Threat of new entrants: The gate crashers

Every industry has an entry barrier, and some are higher than others. Low barriers mean new players can jump in quickly, potentially disrupting established relationships and pricing norms. If it's easy for new entrants to enter the market, companies need to stay alert to protect their share and key accounts.

New entrants are always on the lookout for ways to win over customers – including your key accounts. If you're aware of new players who might enter the market, you can proactively communicate the security, reliability and history your company provides, which can be hard for newcomers to replicate.

Key questions for KAMgrs:

- What might motivate new companies to enter our market?
- How easy would it be for them to lure away our key accounts?
- Could we consider stronger, long-term contracts to fortify our customer relationships?

Bargaining power of buyers: Who holds the cards?

The bargaining power of buyers indicates how much influence customers (or, in the KAM world, key accounts) have in dictating terms. The stronger their bargaining power, the greater their ability to push for lower prices, better quality or additional services.

When buyers wield high bargaining power, they can turn to competitors or demand concessions that cut into profit margins. Key account managers with high-power customers need to develop strategies to build loyalty that transcends mere pricing – customer experience, service responsiveness and innovation are critical.

Key questions for KAMgrs:

- How likely are our key accounts to switch suppliers?
- Do our key accounts have more or less power over us, and how can we manage this balance?
- What aspects of our relationship could make it costly or undesirable for accounts to leave?

Bargaining power of suppliers: The puppet master

Just as buyers can hold power, so too can suppliers. Supplier bargaining power affects the cost structure of your product or service. If suppliers can easily increase prices or limit supply, they can squeeze profit margins, making it more challenging to meet account demands at competitive prices.

While key account managers don't typically manage supplier relations directly, understanding supplier power helps them anticipate cost fluctuations or constraints that may affect product availability or pricing for key accounts. When supplier power is high, KAMgrs should communicate transparently with accounts and work with internal teams to manage expectations.

Key questions for KAMgrs:

- Are we reliant on a few key suppliers, and how does this impact our offerings?
- How do fluctuations in supplier pricing affect price stability for key accounts?
- Are there ways to work with suppliers to gain more control over pricing and supply?

Threat of substitutes: The new kid on the block

Substitutes aren't direct competitors but rather alternative products or services that could fulfil the same needs as yours. A substitute is like a wild card that appears out of left field, giving customers an entirely different way to achieve their goals, often at a lower cost or with a unique feature.

Key account managers should keep an eye on the broader market for substitutes, as they can entice key accounts to shift resources or change priorities. For example, a new technology offering similar functionality to that of the supplier but at a lower price is a red flag.

Key questions for KAMgrs:

- Are there emerging products that could replace or mimic our offerings?
- How likely are key accounts to view these substitutes as viable alternatives?
- How can we innovate or adapt our offerings to differentiate them?

Pulling it all together: Strategic moves for key account managers

Using Porter's Five Forces is about vigilance and adaptation. By understanding the five forces shaping the environment, key account managers can prepare strategies that not only address immediate challenges but also foster long-term account loyalty and growth. Here's how to turn insights into action:

- **Map out the market**: Create a visual map showing competitors, suppliers, substitutes and customer power dynamics for each key account. This exercise helps identify where your influence lies and where it's threatened.
- **Build relationships across forces**: Look beyond the account itself. A KAMgr who has good relationships with suppliers, competitors (within legal limits) and alternative technology providers can offer well-rounded insights that few other team members can.
- **Anticipate shifts**: Use trend analysis to track changes in each of the five forces. Anticipate new entrants, substitutes and any shifts in buyer or supplier power before they happen, enabling proactive strategies.

COMPETITOR ANALYSIS

Competitor analysis involves assessing the strengths and weaknesses of current and potential competitors.[5] A KAMgr can use competitor analysis to identify areas where competitors are strong or weak and develop strategies to differentiate their company's offerings. Understanding competitors' value propositions helps the KAMgr position their own products or services more effectively.

In a competitor analysis, KAMgrs monitor the actions and strategies of both their (own) supplier company competitors, as well as the key account's competitors. Understanding competitors' strengths, weaknesses and market positioning helps in identifying potential threats and opportunities for supplier-customer relationships.

The effectiveness of competitor analysis can be measured by the comprehensiveness of the competitive intelligence gathered, the strategic recommendations made based on this intelligence and the impact of these recommendations on the client's competitive positioning.

The **Competitor Profile Matrix (CPM)** is a strategic tool used to evaluate and compare the strengths and weaknesses of key competitors within an industry. It provides a structured approach to understanding the competitive landscape, allowing firms to identify areas where they can achieve a competitive advantage.

The CPM has four main components:

Critical success factors (CSFs): These are the essential areas of activity that must be performed well for a company to achieve its mission and objectives. CSFs vary by industry but typically include factors such as product quality, customer service, innovation, pricing, market share and brand reputation.

Weighting: Each CSF is assigned a weight based on its relative importance to the industry's success. The weights usually sum up to 1.0 or 100 per cent. This reflects the significance of each factor in determining the overall competitive advantage.

Rating: Each competitor is rated on each CSF on a scale, commonly from 1 to 4:

4 = Major strength

3 = Minor strength

2 = Minor weakness

1 = Major weakness

Score: The score for each competitor on each CSF is calculated by multiplying the weight by the rating. These scores are then summed up to provide an overall score for each competitor.

Table 2.2 shows a template for a CFM, illustrating the analysis for an industrial supplier of mining services. These companies provide critical solutions to mining operations, such as equipment, maintenance, safety solutions and optimization services. Mining companies seek partners who excel in product reliability, cost-efficiency, innovation and technology, customer support and service, sustainability practices and local market expertise.

TABLE 2.2 CPM template illustrating industrial providers of mining services

		Your Company		Competitor 1		Competitor 2	
Critical Success Factor	Weight (%)	Rating	Score	Rating	Score	Rating	Score
Product reliability	25	3	75.00	4	100.00	3	75.00
Cost efficiency	20	2	50.00	2	50.00	4	100.00
Innovation and technology	20	4	100.00	3	75.00	2	50.00
Customer support and service	15	2	50.00	2	50.00	3	75.00
Sustainability practices	10	3	75.00	2	50.00	1	25.00
Local market expertise	10	2	50.00	3	75.00	4	100.00
Total Score	100		400.00		400.00		425.00

Competitive Profile Matrix (CPM) Template

LEAD USER METHODOLOGY

Lead User methodology[6] is an innovation approach that involves identifying and collaborating with lead users – those at the forefront of market and industry trends and who have needs that will become common in the market but are not yet widely recognized. These users often develop their own solutions to address unmet needs, making them valuable sources of innovative ideas. The concept was pioneered by Eric von Hippel, who emphasized that lead users can provide insights into future market demands and innovations.

Lead users normally anticipate obtaining high benefits from a solution to their needs so they are willing to invest and innovate;[7] they are at the edge of critical trends in a market or an industry, and they typically experience needs and challenges that other users will face in the future.[8] By engaging with them, key account managers can gain early insights into emerging trends that can be capitalized later with key accounts.

Lead users often have practical experience in solving problems that others in the market will eventually face. Their insights can help KAMgrs co-create innovative solutions and exploit value-creation opportunities that are more likely to succeed. Also, by leveraging the expertise and knowledge of lead users, the supplier company can reduce the uncertainty, risks and time involved in developing solutions for their key accounts. The process can be split into three stages.

1. Identify lead users

- *Industry*: Conduct thorough research within the industry. Lead users are often the first to experience new challenges and are actively seeking or developing solutions. They may not always be the largest or most well-known companies but are typically those pushing the boundaries in their field.
- *Networking and referrals*: Use industry networks, trade associations and referrals from existing customers or partners to identify companies or individuals that exhibit lead user characteristics.
- *Innovators*: Look for companies that are early adopters of new technologies, have a history of innovation or have made efforts to address emerging challenges.

2. Engage lead users

- *Meetings*: Organize interviews, site visits or collaborative innovation workshops with identified lead users to understand their specific needs, challenges and the solutions they have developed or are seeking.
- *Build relationships*: Develop long-term relationships with lead users by involving them in ongoing innovation processes. This can include co-development projects, pilot testing of new solutions or participation in advisory boards.

3. Analyse insights

- *Commonalities*: Analyse the information gathered from lead users to identify common needs and challenges that may soon affect the broader market.
- *Emerging trends*: Look for patterns or trends that indicate potential market shifts or opportunities for innovation.

Researching the customer business

9-BOX SWOT TOOL

The 9-Box SWOT tool is an extension of the traditional SWOT analysis, which provides a more structured and strategic approach to evaluating strengths, weaknesses, opportunities and threats from a specific business situation. The 9-Box SWOT grid (see Figure 2.3) combines these elements into a matrix that helps visualize and prioritize strategies based on the interplay between internal and external factors, and key organizational objectives.

FIGURE 2.3 9-Box SWOT tool

Objectives	Strengths	Weaknesses
1.	1.	1.
2.	2.	2.

Opportunities		
1.	ATTACK (A)	CONVERT (C)
2.		

Threats		
1.	BLOCK (B)	DEFEND (D)
2.		

The steps to apply the 9-Box SWOT tool for customer analysis are:

Step 1: Determine the key strategic objectives of the customer.

Objectives: Key strategic objectives of the customer.

Step 2: Conduct a traditional SWOT analysis.

Strengths: Internal attributes that give the customer an advantage.

Weaknesses: Internal attributes that put the customer at a disadvantage.

Opportunities: External factors that the customer can exploit to its advantage.

Threats: External factors that could cause trouble for the customer.

Step 3: Define the strategies of the 9-Box SWOT tool.

ATTACK (SO): matching strengths and opportunities. How can the customer use their strengths to benefit from an opportunity?

BLOCK (WT): matching weaknesses and threats. How can the customer manage their weaknesses to avoid the potential damage of a threat?

CONVERT (WO): matching weaknesses and opportunities. How can the customer reduce their weaknesses to benefit from an opportunity?

DEFEND (ST): matching strengths and threats. How can the customer use their strengths to face a threat?

FIGURE 2.4 Example of a 9-Box SWOT tool application in a B2B context

Objectives	Strengths	Weaknesses
Increase annual revenues by 20% in a period of 3 years.	Strong in-house engineering teams.	Slow decision-making processes.
Increase the annual net profit margin from 12% to 16% in 3 years.	Significant budget for technology investments.	Legacy systems that are difficult to integrate with new technologies.
	Long-standing industry reputation and relationships.	Limited experience with digital transformation initiatives.
Opportunities	**ATTACK (A)**	**CONVERT (C)**
Growing demand for Industry 4.0 solutions.	Leverage the client's engineering teams and budget to implement Industry 4.0 solutions, capitalizing on government incentives.	Introduce modular and scalable technology solutions that can integrate with existing infrastructure.
Government incentives for technology upgrades in manufacturing.	Use the client's reputation to seek partnerships with technology providers to enhance the digital transformation process.	Provide training to enhance the client's experience with digital transformation, ensuring smoother implementation.
Potential to streamline operations and reduce costs with automation.		
Threats	**BLOCK (B)**	**DEFEND (D)**
Rising competition from agile startups offering cutting-edge technology.	Mitigate the risk of competition by focusing on unique, customized solutions that competitors cannot easily replicate.	Use the client's reputation to invest in cybersecurity measures that mitigate digital transformation risks.
Economic downturn impacting investment decisions.	Minimize the impact of economic downturns by offering flexible pricing or phased implementation plans.	Speed up decision-making by aligning new technology projects to reduce the impact of slow internal processes.
Cybersecurity risks associated with digital transformation.		

Step 4: Prioritize and execute.

The strategies will then be prioritized based on the customer's specific needs and available resources.

Example of a 9-Box SWOT tool application in a B2B context: Let's consider a key account manager at a software solutions provider who is analysing a strategic business customer – a large manufacturing company. The unit of analysis here is the customer (the manufacturing company). Figure 2.4 illustrates the application of a 9-Box SWOT tool in this example.

GRASP FRAMEWORK

The effective development of key account relationships requires a good assessment of the decision-making unit (DMU) within the customer. The DMU – also called the 'buying centre' – is represented by all the individuals, groups, business units, functional areas and other entities that participate in the organizational buying process. By mapping out the decision-makers and influencers within a key customer organization, a KAMgr can develop strategies to engage the right stakeholders, build stronger relationships and uncover value-creation opportunities.

There are several roles within the DMU, which on occasions are concentrated in a few people or units, and in other situations are spread among several or many people or units. The following roles have been identified:[9]

Initiator: Recognizes the need, opportunity or problem that leads to considering the purchase of a product, service or solution.

User: Uses or works with the product, service or solution, and normally has a say on determining the specifications that the offering must have.

Influencer: Influences the decision by providing inputs on the requirements and/or alternatives available. This role is usually related to technical expertise.

Gatekeeper: Controls the flow of information among the members of the DMU, and often influences the extent and means of communication between the supplier and the customer.

Decider: Makes the final decision on the purchase, by having formal authority or other sources of power.

Controller: Determines the budget for the purchase and other restrictions (usually of a financial nature).

TABLE 2.3 Example of the GRASP framework applied to a customer

	Purchasing Manager	Chief Engineer	Finance Director	Technical Team	Chief Executive Officer (CEO)	CEO Personal Assistant
Goal	Position ourselves as a reliable and flexible supplier	Demonstrate quality of our product and explore the customer's need for post-sale services	Translate the quality of our machine into financial savings for the customer	Recover a positive brand image from a previous incident and prove our reliability	Obtain a top-to-top meeting with our CEO to discuss opportunities for co-creation	Keep a friendly interaction and gather information about the buying process
Role	Buyer Influencer	Initiator User Decider	Controller Decider	Influencer	Decider	Gatekeeper
Appeal	Efficiency in the buying process Flexibility in delivery	Performance Quality of images	Price of purchase Obsolescence Profitability	Product specifications Safety	Return on investment Functionality	Internal recognition Socialization
State	We have a close and good relationship with her	We do not have previous interaction with him	He is a close friend of one of our team members	They had a bad experience with our brand in the past	There is no previous interaction, and she knows very little about our company	She gets along with our key account manager
Power	She shortlists suppliers and establishes payment conditions	He has high decision-making power and is well respected among his peers	He recently joined the company and does not have the power to influence a decision	They have a high influence on the Chief Engineer, based on their knowledge	She holds high hierarchical power in the organization	She manages the agenda of the CEO, who trusts her very much

Buyer: Makes the purchase and leads the ordering process; people in this role usually have some power in selecting suppliers and determining some conditions for the deal, such as the payment terms or timings for the delivery of products and services.

In KAM, it is extremely important to have a good knowledge of the customer's decision-making unit and the goals that the supplier company needs to accomplish with each of its members. To analyse the DMU, we propose the **GRASP** approach, which stands for:

Goal: What are our goals and action plans with respect to this DMU member?

Role: What are the roles that this member plays in the buying process?

Appeal: What appeals to this DMU member about the offering and buying process?

State: What is the state of our relationship with this member of the DMU?

Power: What level and source of power does this DMU member have?

Table 2.3 provides an example of how the GRASP framework is applied to a customer, an industrial manufacturer of machinery.

> Understanding our customers deeply is crucial – not just their immediate needs, but their overall business structure, challenges, and goals.
>
> Stuart Blakeley

VOICE OF THE CUSTOMER (VOC)

Voice of the Customer (VOC) programmes gather and analyse customer feedback to understand their needs, preferences and perceptions. A KAMgr can use VOC insights to refine value propositions, improve service delivery and identify areas where the company can add value. Regularly engaging with customers through surveys, interviews or feedback loops can reveal opportunities for innovation or process improvement.

For key account managers and their line managers, a VOC programme isn't just a nice-to-have; it's a powerful tool for proactively managing accounts, building loyalty and identifying opportunities that can elevate both the customer's business and yours.

Simply put, a VOC programme is a systematic approach to gathering feedback from customers and using it to inform decisions. But it goes far beyond annual surveys or quarterly check-ins. A robust VOC programme involves multiple touchpoints, continuous feedback loops and advanced data analysis to capture the nuances of what customers are saying – or, sometimes, not saying – outright. In the context of KAM, a VOC programme is often customized to gather insights specifically from strategic customers, meaning those key accounts that represent significant revenue, influence or growth potential for the company.

Here's why VOC programmes are essential for KAM:

- **Pre-empting customer churn:** By continuously listening to strategic customers, key account managers can detect early warning signs of dissatisfaction and address issues before they become deal-breakers.

- **Spotting growth opportunities:** Strategic customers are often willing to share insights on what products, services or innovations would add value to their operations. VOC programmes create a formal mechanism for these ideas to flow to key account managers.

- **Building trust and loyalty:** Actively listening to and acting on feedback demonstrates to key accounts that their voices are heard and valued, reinforcing their commitment to the relationship.

Designing a VOC programme for key accounts   Building a VOC programme specifically for KAM is like tailoring a suit – it needs to fit the unique contours of each key account while also being adaptable enough to evolve. Here are the main steps to designing a VOC programme that drives meaningful insights:

1 **Define objectives and scope:** What do you want to achieve with the VOC programme? Are you looking to improve customer satisfaction, identify unmet needs or gather insights on emerging trends? Clearly defining your objectives will help shape the programme's design and the questions you ask.

2 **Choose the right feedback channels:** One size doesn't fit all when it comes to feedback channels. For KAM, the best VOC programmes blend multiple formats to capture a fuller picture.

   o **Structured interviews:** In-depth, one-on-one discussions with account stakeholders to explore their challenges and needs.

   o **Surveys:** Targeted surveys designed to measure satisfaction across specific touchpoints (e.g. service, product quality, support).

   o **On-site observations or customer advisory boards:** Involving key account representatives in hands-on settings can reveal much about how your offerings integrate into their daily operations.

3 **Develop a feedback loop:** To avoid a 'set it and forget it' approach, create a feedback loop that brings insights back to the KAM team and other relevant departments. This loop should include clear channels for reporting insights, an action plan for implementing changes and a follow-up process to close the loop with customers.

4 **Ensure confidentiality and transparency:** VOC programmes often touch on sensitive topics, particularly when gathering feedback from high-stakes accounts. Be transparent about how feedback will be used and ensure that responses are handled with discretion.

Analysing and acting on VOC insights   A well-designed VOC programme doesn't stop at gathering feedback; the real value comes from analysis and action. Here's how key account managers can turn VOC insights into impactful outcomes:

- **Segment and prioritize feedback:** Not all feedback is equally actionable. Segment responses by urgency, impact and feasibility to identify quick wins, long-term improvements and potential innovations.

- **Identify patterns and themes:** Often, VOC insights will reveal patterns across multiple accounts. By identifying recurring themes, KA managers can address systemic issues and propose improvements that resonate with multiple customers.

- **Involve cross-functional teams:** VOC insights can touch on various parts of the business, from product development to customer support. Regularly share feedback with cross-functional teams to ensure that actions align with customer needs and that internal teams have a chance to address underlying issues.

- **Communicate actions back to the customer:** Closing the loop is vital. Let customers know when their feedback has led to changes, enhancements or new initiatives. This not only validates their contributions but also builds goodwill and encourages ongoing engagement.

Researching the (own) supplier company

STAKEHOLDER MAPPING

Stakeholder mapping is a strategic tool that helps key account managers identify and understand the various internal stakeholders involved in delivering value to key customers.[10] This process focuses on mapping relationships in terms of their level of interest and power, plus any other desirable metric or characteristic.

- *Primary internal stakeholders* are the members of the KAM team, which typically includes marketing, R&D and production, customer support, technical support and key account sales. They are directly involved in the day-to-day management of key accounts and collaborate closely to identify customer needs, provide tailored solutions and make sure customer expectations are met. For researching in KAM, these stakeholders should contribute with up-to-date information about customer perceptions, activities, pain points, and ideas for innovation and supplier engagement.

- *Secondary internal stakeholders* usually include top management, the KAM director, information technology, analytics, finance, legal, sustainability, supply chain and sales representatives. They play a more indirect but equally important role, providing essential support such as data analysis, risk management, financial guidance and compliance oversight, which is crucial for creating sustained value. Importantly, mapping these stakeholders allows KAM teams to identify opportunities for executive sponsorship and cross-functional collaboration with respect to key accounts, ensuring that the right resources are mobilized to address customer needs effectively and uncover value-creation opportunities.

MENDELOW'S MATRIX

Mendelow's Matrix is a model for mapping stakeholders based on their levels of power and interest.[11] In the context of KAM, power is stakeholders' ability to influence other members of the KAM team, other internal stakeholders outside of the KAM team and external stakeholders (e.g. customers, industry players, policymakers, etc.). In turn, interest refers to stakeholders' motivation and involvement with the pursuit of succeeding in KAM.

Stakeholder mapping helps identify and analyse key internal stakeholders who can contribute to value creation for key accounts. A KAMgr can map out the relevant internal stakeholders, such as executives from sales, marketing, R&D, finance and operations, to understand their roles, interests and influence. Engaging these stakeholders in discussions can provide valuable insights into how their areas can contribute to meeting the needs of key customers.

Figure 2.5 represents Mendelow's Matrix.

FIGURE 2.5 Mendelow's Matrix

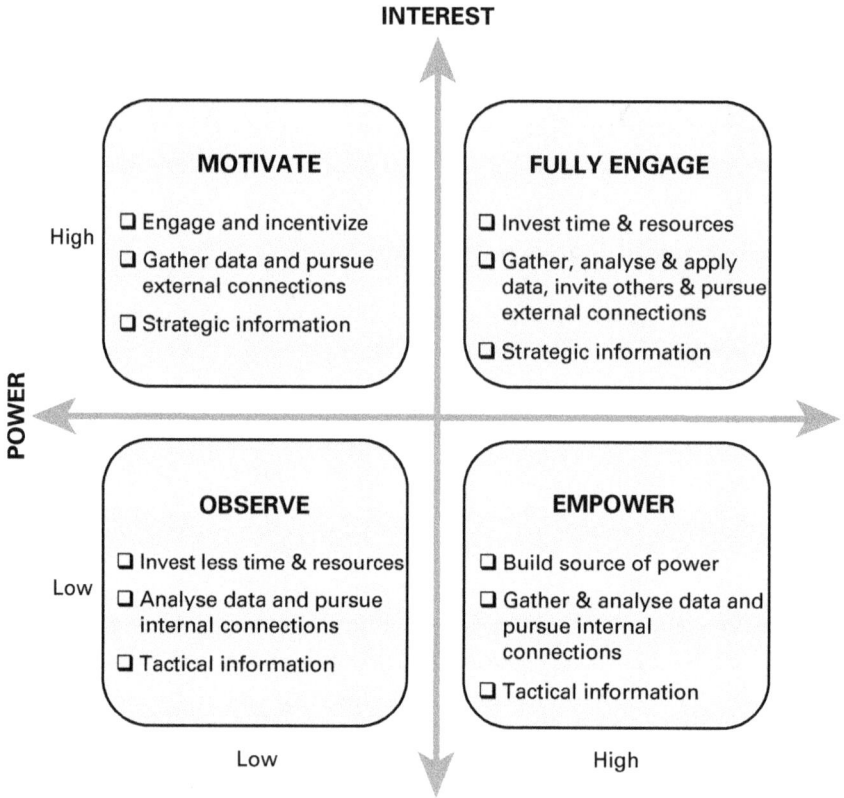

VRIO FRAMEWORK

The VRIO framework[12] is a strategic analysis tool used to evaluate a firm's resources and capabilities to determine whether they can provide a sustained competitive advantage.[13] The acronym VRIO stands for Value, Rarity, Imitability and Organization:

- **Value:** Does the resource or capability allow the firm to exploit opportunities or defend against threats? A resource is valuable if it helps the firm create strategies that improve efficiency or effectiveness.

- **Rarity:** Is the resource or capability controlled by a small number of firms? A resource must be rare enough that it provides some competitive advantage.

- **Imitability:** Is it costly for other firms to imitate the resource or capability? If a resource is valuable and rare but can be easily imitated, it will not provide a sustained competitive advantage.

TABLE 2.4 Example of a VRIO framework for an IT consulting services firm

Value	The firm has developed proprietary AI-driven software that significantly reduces the time and cost of managing IT infrastructure for its clients. This resource is valuable because it addresses a critical pain point for business customers, offering them significant cost savings and efficiency improvements.
Rarity	The firm's AI-driven software is based on a unique algorithm developed by a specialized team of data scientists. Only a few competitors in the market offer anything similar, making the software a rare resource.
Imitability	The software is protected by patents, and the firm's data scientists have specific expertise that is not easily replicated by competitors. This makes the resource difficult and costly to imitate.
Organization	The firm has a well-established sales and support team that is highly trained in explaining the benefits of the software to clients and providing ongoing support. The firm's organizational structure is designed to fully exploit the AI software's advantages, from development through to client delivery.

- **Organization:** Is the firm organized to exploit the resource or capability? Even if a resource is valuable, rare and costly to imitate, the firm must be organized to capture the value from it.

To illustrate, let's consider a firm that sells IT consulting services and software solutions to business customers. Table 2.4 shows how the VRIO framework could be applied.

Based on this VRIO analysis, the AI-driven software is likely to provide a sustained competitive advantage for the firm, as it is valuable, rare, difficult to imitate and the firm is well-organized to capture its value.

VOICE OF THE EMPLOYEE (VOE)

Voice of the Employee (VOE) programmes[14] play a pivotal role in fostering cross-functional collaboration, uncovering latent challenges and identifying opportunities to enhance the value delivered to key customers.

Key account managers often serve as the bridge between customers and internal teams. They are uniquely positioned to recognize the importance of engaging with employees from various functions – such as marketing, operations, product development and customer support – whose contributions

FIGURE 2.6 Implementing a Voice of the Employee (VOE) programme

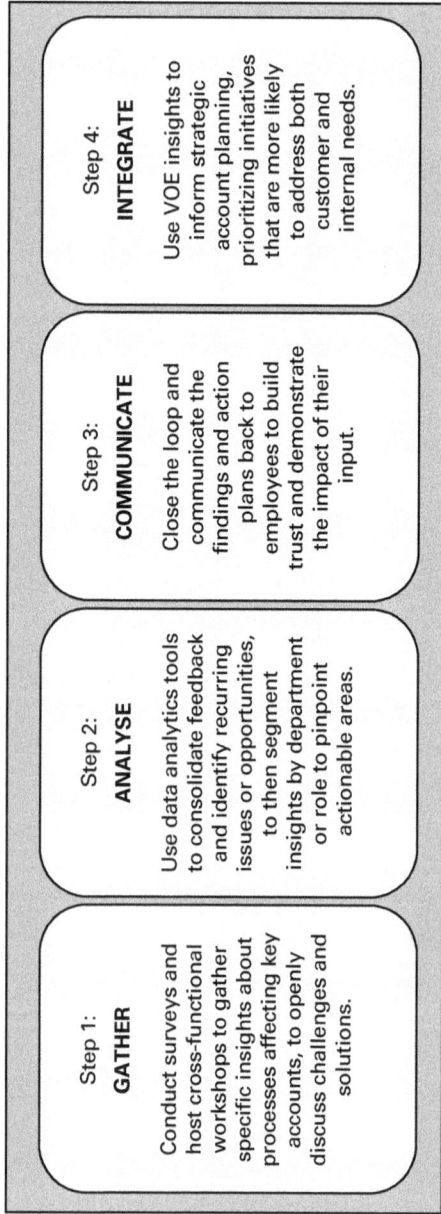

Step 1:
GATHER

Conduct surveys and host cross-functional workshops to gather specific insights about processes affecting key accounts, to openly discuss challenges and solutions.

Step 2:
ANALYSE

Use data analytics tools to consolidate feedback and identify recurring issues or opportunities, to then segment insights by department or role to pinpoint actionable areas.

Step 3:
COMMUNICATE

Close the loop and communicate the findings and action plans back to employees to build trust and demonstrate the impact of their input.

Step 4:
INTEGRATE

Use VOE insights to inform strategic account planning, prioritizing initiatives that are more likely to address both customer and internal needs.

directly or indirectly affect customer experience. By using VOE programmes, key account managers can:

- **Identify bottlenecks:** Gather feedback on internal processes that may hinder timely delivery or service quality.

- **Discover innovation opportunities:** Tap into the frontline knowledge of employees who interact with customers or products daily.

- **Enhance engagement:** Involve employees in the customer success journey, fostering a shared sense of purpose.

- **Bridge silos:** Highlight interdepartmental dependencies and promote a culture of collaboration.

Implementing VOE in KAM   Figure 2.6 demonstrates the four-step implementation framework for the Voice of the Customer in key account management.

Summary and application

If you don't have the mindset to adopt an 'outside-in' view of your company from your customer's perspective, you are going to fail. More importantly, what does an outside-in view illustrate to you in terms of addressable opportunity? What could you develop together as mutual revenue opportunities compared to what you achieve today? The essence of creating value for key accounts lies in the depth and breadth of knowledge a company possesses about these clients for mutual value creation, not for the exploitation of revenue opportunities. The need for sustained growth, competitive differentiation and innovation drives the imperative to research and seek value-creation opportunities in key accounts. At the heart of these efforts lies key account knowledge, forming the foundation of effective and enduring business relationships.

The identification of value-creation opportunities involves synthesizing insights from the external environment, the customer's business and the (own) supplier company. As a result of this process, not only will new opportunities arise, but also the likelihood of developing innovative solutions that drive mutual growth will increase, which will help develop customer trust and loyalty. This could include, for example, new product or service offerings, process improvements, cost-saving initiatives or strategic partnerships.

TABLE 2.5 Recommended actions for key account managers

	Action	Description
1.	Adopt an 'outside-in' perspective	Understand your client's perspective by considering how they view your company, and co-create solutions that align with their strategic priorities, such as a more sustainable business.
2.	Map the decision-making unit (DMU)	Use the GRASP framework to identify key stakeholders and their roles within your client's organization and engage gatekeepers and influencers early in the sales process to smooth negotiations.
3.	Conduct regular business reviews	Schedule in-depth reviews with key accounts to assess performance and explore opportunities. For example, host quarterly workshops to align on KPIs and discuss potential innovations.
4.	Monitor industry trends	Apply the PESTEL framework to stay ahead of shifts that might affect your accounts. For example, if new environmental regulations arise, proactively offer solutions that align with these changes.
5.	Build cross-functional teams	Collaborate across departments to ensure comprehensive support for key accounts. For instance, integrate insights from R&D and marketing to tailor a new product for a client's needs.
6.	Invest in Voice of the Customer (VOC) programmes	Collect and act on client feedback to refine offerings. For example, use surveys and interviews to discover pain points and prioritize fixes that drive customer satisfaction.
7.	Strengthen internal alignment with Voice of the Employee (VOE) programmes	Utilize employee feedback to address internal barriers affecting client relationships and streamline workflows based on suggestions from frontline staff.
8.	Embrace innovation through lead users	Collaborate with innovative clients to develop forward-thinking solutions. For example, partner with a tech-savvy client to pilot a new AI-driven service model.
9.	Utilize competitive intelligence	Continuously analyse competitors' strategies and positioning and use the CPM matrix to highlight areas where your offerings outperform competitors in cost or innovation.
10.	Enhance digital competencies	Leverage CRM systems and AI tools to gain actionable insights. For example, use conversation analytics to identify patterns in client interactions that can inform tailored engagement strategies.

In summary, researching and seeking value-creation opportunities is a multi-faceted capability requiring key account managers to be adept at analysing the industry and the market, monitoring competitors, understanding the customer's business and leveraging relevant internal information, all of which would result in pursuing strategic initiatives. The effectiveness of these efforts can be assessed through various metrics that highlight the impact of their insights and actions on the customer's success and the overall business relationship.

Table 2.5 suggests recommended actions for key account managers to foster research and seek value-creation opportunities.

Notes

1   L George and A Eggert. Key account managers' role within the value creation process of collaborative relationships, *Journal of Business-to-Business Marketing*, 2003, 10 (4), 1–22

2   P O Brehmer and J Rehme. Proactive and reactive: Drivers for key account management programmes, *European Journal of Marketing*, 2009, 43 (7/8), 961–84

3   G Johnson, K Scholes and R Whittington (2008) *Exploring Corporate Strategy*, 8th edn, Pearson Education

4   M E Porter. How competitive forces shape strategy, *Harvard Business Review*, March/April 1979, 137–45

5   R Groves, K Lueck and S Redaelli. Commercial Excellence: Your path to growth, McKinsey & Company, 24 October 2018, www.mckinsey.com/capabilities/growth-marketing-and-sales/our-insights/commercial-excellence-your-path-to-growth (archived at https://perma.cc/6374-5KVQ)

6   E von Hippel. Lead users: A source of novel product concepts, *Management Science*, 1986, 32 (7), 791–805

7   E L Olson and G Bakke. Creating breakthrough innovations by implementing the Lead User methodology, *Telektronikk*, 2004, 100, 126–32

8   N Franke, E Von Hippel and M Schreie. Finding commercially attractive user innovations: A test of lead-user theory, *Journal of Product Innovation Management*, 2006, 23 (4), 301–15

9   M Johnston and G Marshall (2016) *Sales Force Management: Leadership, innovation, technology*, Routledge

10 B Schaninger and T Lauricella. A data-backed approach to stakeholder engagement, McKinsey Organization Blog, 28 May 2020, www.mckinsey.com/capabilities/people-and-organizational-performance/our-insights/the-organization-blog/a-data-backed-approach-to-stakeholder-engagement (archived at https://perma.cc/K8WU-Z28E)

11 A L Mendelow (1981) Environmental scanning – the impact of the stakeholder concept, Proceedings of the International Conference on Information Systems

12 J B Barney. Firm resources and sustained competitive advantage, *Journal of Management*, 1991, 17 (1), 99–120

13 C Bradley, A Dawson and A Montard. Mastering the building blocks of strategy, *McKinsey Quarterly*, 2013, 4, 36–47

14 T J Turner (2023) Employees seek personal value and purpose at work. Be prepared to deliver, Gartner, www.gartner.com/en/articles/employees-seek-personal-value-and-purpose-at-work-be-prepared-to-deliver (archived at https://perma.cc/V6F6-MHZG)

Nicolaas Smit

I've built extensive experience in key account management, beginning with my role in consulting at Cisco Systems and subsequently in the Cisco Global Accounts Programme and after Cisco in my private practice working with many different companies and organizations. My primary focus was, and still is, on our most strategic customers, aiming to transform their perception of our company and create value in innovative ways. In my view, this experience laid the foundation for my understanding of the complexities involved in managing key accounts.

The role of a key account manager, particularly in global accounts, is multifaceted and complex. It extends beyond mere sales to encompass value creation for the customer and orchestration of global resources. Our objectives included shifting perceptions, driving innovation and developing transferable solutions across different customers. In my opinion, this breadth of responsibility is what makes the role both challenging and rewarding.

Performance measurement in key account management is nuanced. While revenue remains a critical metric, we also considered factors such as project types, relationship levels and solution complexity. Our focus was on delivering comprehensive solutions that enhanced our customers' business capabilities, rather than simply selling individual products. I believe this holistic approach to performance measurement is crucial for long-term success in key account management.

Key account managers require a diverse skill set. Among the most crucial are strategizing and planning, developing lasting relationships and promoting customer centricity. Additionally, creating opportunities, building teams and leading without formal authority are essential competencies. In my experience, these skills are not innate but can be developed over time with conscious effort and practice.

Listening skills are paramount in this role. It's crucial to prioritize understanding the customer's challenges over pushing for sales. This involves not just hearing words but comprehending their deeper meaning and asking insightful questions. From my perspective, effective listening is the foundation upon which all other aspects of key account management are built.

Empathy plays a complex role in key account management. While understanding the customer is vital, excessive empathy can hinder effective negotiation. However, empathy becomes increasingly important when leading internal teams. In my view, striking the right balance is key – being empathetic enough to build strong relationships, but not so much that it compromises your ability to make tough decisions.

In my opinion, adaptability is what separates great key account managers from good ones. The role demands juggling multiple priorities and being able to pivot strategies quickly. I've found that focusing on outcomes rather than specific methodologies and trusting team members to find optimal solutions is key. Broad business experience significantly enhances one's adaptability in this role. In my opinion, adaptability is what separates good key account managers from great ones.

Psychological safety, in my experience, is fundamentally about trust. Building trust requires demonstrating a genuine understanding of the customer's business and challenges, consistently delivering on promises and ensuring that actions align with stated intentions. At the same time, trust is crucial in internal cross-functional team collaboration. People need to feel psychological safe to perform at their best. I believe that creating an environment of psychological safety is essential for fostering open communication and innovation in key account relationships.

The essence of successful key account management lies in approaching the role as a business manager rather than solely as a sales manager. It involves managing the success of both the customer and your own company within the relationship. This requires a comprehensive understanding of both businesses and a diverse skill set. In my view, this broader perspective is what enables key account managers to create truly strategic partnerships.

A crucial piece of advice for key account managers is to recognize when to involve other team members. Rather than attempting to handle everything personally, it's important to bring in the right expertise at appropriate times to showcase the company's capabilities and add credibility to your propositions. I've found that this approach not only enhances the customer's experience but also builds stronger internal relationships.

In conclusion, effective key account management centres on creating value, building trust and driving growth for both the customer and your own organization. While challenging, the role can be immensely rewarding when executed successfully. From my perspective, the key to success lies in continuous learning, adaptability and a genuine commitment to creating mutual value.

In reflecting on my career, I've come to believe that key account management is as much an art as it is a science. It requires a blend of strategic thinking, interpersonal skills and business acumen. The most successful key account managers, in my opinion, are those who can seamlessly integrate these various elements.

One aspect that I think is often overlooked is the importance of cultural awareness, particularly in global account management. Understanding and navigating different cultural contexts can be crucial in building and maintaining relationships with key accounts across different regions.

Lastly, I believe that the future of key account management will be increasingly influenced by technological advancements. Embracing digital tools and data analytics can provide key account managers with valuable insights and help them make more informed decisions. However, in my view, these tools should complement, not replace, the human elements of relationship building and strategic thinking that are at the core of effective key account management.

Nicolaas Smit is a seasoned business strategist with over 25 years of experience, including 17 years at Cisco Systems, where he held several senior positions, including Managing Director of Global Industry Marketing and Business Development. His expertise spans strategic sales leadership, global account management and customer partnerships, with a particular focus on the oil and gas and utility sectors, where he managed portfolios exceeding $1 billion. At Cisco, he played key roles in transforming business relationships from transactional to high-value partnerships and led global initiatives in industry marketing, sales enablement and business development.

Currently, Nicolaas serves as a Strategic Business Relationships Consultant and Triple Fit 360 Business Plan Coach, while holding academic positions as a Visiting Fellow at Cranfield School of Management and Visiting Faculty at Rotterdam School of Management. He specializes in developing one-page customer partnership plans to create 10 times the value and boost growth, focusing on transforming traditional buyer-seller relationships into strategic partnerships. His approach combines practical experience from organizations of various sizes with proven methodologies to improve revenue, margins and customer loyalty. Additionally, he serves on the Supervisory Board of Waterbedrijf Groningen, focusing on digital strategy and operational technology.

www.linkedin.com/in/nicolaas-smit (archived at https://perma.cc/RG4R-WTAH)

03

Managing information and financial analysis overview

Overview

Key account managers (KAMgrs) are the central processors and analysers of complex information flow between supplier and customer organizations. These information flows are multifaceted, spanning financial, operational and strategic domains, requiring sophisticated analysis and interpretation to create value for strategic accounts.

The success of KAM programmes increasingly depends on the ability to effectively gather, analyse and leverage information to drive strategic decision-making. The growing complexity of business environments and the exponential increase in available data demand that KAMgrs develop strong information management and financial analysis capabilities.

This chapter explores key dimensions in managing information and conducting financial analysis to deliver value to your most important customers. We'll examine how to identify and leverage various information sources, establish effective analysis frameworks and create data-driven value propositions that resonate with key accounts.

We address the challenges of information management in an era of technological advancement and data explosion, distilling practical strategies for navigating the complexity while focusing on customer-centric goals. This chapter also tackles common challenges when dealing with financial analysis and information interpretation. We blend research insights with practical applications to offer actionable guidance on how KAMgrs can enhance their effectiveness through superior information management and financial acumen.

The following box highlights why managing information and financial analysis is important for KAM.

WHY MANAGING INFORMATION AND FINANCIAL
ANALYSIS IS IMPORTANT

Complexity management:

- Handles increasing volume of business data
- Enables systematic analysis approaches
- Supports multifaceted customer relationship
- Improves resource allocation decision

Credibility enhancement:

- Establishes authority with C-suite stakeholder
- Demonstrates deep business understanding
- Strengthens internal organizational support
- Facilitates strategic-level discussion

Financial performance analysis:

- Identifies growth patterns and trends
- Evaluates operational efficiency
- Assesses working capital optimization
- Monitors profitability metrics

Value demonstration:

- Quantifies impact in financial terms
- Validates investment decisions
- Measures performance improvement
- Tracks value creation over time

Why information management and financial analysis matter in KAM

Traditionally, key account management has emphasized relationship-building and sales skills. We argue that the ability to effectively manage information and conduct sophisticated financial analysis increasingly determines success in multifaceted customer relationships. These capabilities are crucial for at least three reasons: complexity, credibility and value demonstration.

Consider the experience of a Global Account Director at Salesforce, who notes: 'In today's data-driven environment, key account managers need to be as comfortable with financial statements and data analytics as they are with customer relationships. The ability to translate complex data into actionable insights separates strategic partners from mere suppliers.'

Complexity

It is widely accepted that the volume and complexity of information in business markets have grown exponentially and that buying organizations expect more sophisticated analysis and insights from their suppliers. No single individual can process and analyse all relevant information manually. Thus, systematic approaches to information management and analysis must be developed to address the complexity of modern business relationships.

A study of Fortune 500 companies revealed that organizations with structured approaches to information management and analysis in their KAM programmes achieved 23 per cent higher customer satisfaction scores and 18 per cent better retention rates than those without such systems. Moreover, this work showed that effective information management can enhance decision-making quality and enable better resource allocation.[1]

Take, for example, the case of a global technology company's key account team working with a major retail client. The team implemented a structured approach to analysing the client's revenue trends using index numbers, allowing them to identify growth patterns across different business segments. By setting their base year revenue as an index of 100, they could track how different product categories performed over time. This analysis revealed that while the client's overall revenue grew by 35 per cent over three years, their digital services segment grew by 128 per cent, highlighting a strategic opportunity for technology solutions.[2]

> Another critical capability, in my view, is the ability to manage information effectively. I've observed that many key account managers could improve in utilizing information from various sources within their organization. High-performing managers stand out by taking a holistic view and actively gathering insights from all customer touchpoints.
>
> Dr Sue Holt

Credibility

The second crucial reason for developing strong information management and financial analysis capabilities is establishing and maintaining credibility both internally with the finance department and senior management and externally with senior stakeholders in customer organizations. This is particularly important as KAM relationships increasingly involve interaction at the C-suite level. It is important that credibility is viewed through external and internal perspectives, as credibility built on financial acumen evaluates your client's view of you as a KAMgr. Likewise, demonstrating the impacts of proposals on your organization as a key supplier increases your credibility internally and makes sign-offs and internal support easier.

Consider the view of one of the authors of this book who was always taught by his mentors: 'Remember you get relegated to who you sound like!' A KAMgr must demonstrate a deep understanding of business metrics and financial implications to be a C-suite advisor. It's not just about having the data – it's about turning that data into strategic insights.

Consider the example of a senior account director at SAP who was tasked with expanding their relationship with a significant manufacturing client. She recognized that more than traditional relationship-building was required. By developing a comprehensive analysis of the client's operational efficiency metrics, benchmarking against industry standards and creating a detailed financial model showing potential value-creation opportunities, she secured regular access to the client's C-suite. She significantly expanded SAP's footprint within the account as a result of higher access levels.

Understanding financial performance indicators

Key account managers must develop proficiency in analysing and interpreting various financial performance indicators. One fundamental approach is understanding how to analyse revenue trends and patterns effectively. For instance, when examining a key account's financial statements, KAMgrs should look beyond simple year-over-year growth figures to understand the underlying dynamics.

Consider a scenario where a key account reports annual revenue of $500 million. While this top-line number is essential, what's more crucial is understanding how this revenue is generated and whether it represents healthy growth. Using index numbers provides a straightforward way to track growth trajectories. If we set a base year index of 100, we can more easily visualize growth patterns across different business segments or geographical regions.

For example, one global manufacturer presented revenue growth across five business segments over five years. While their total revenue showed steady growth with an index increasing from 100 to 122, individual segment performance varied dramatically. Their emerging technologies segment grew to an index of 208, while their legacy products segment declined to 82. This type of analysis helps KAMgrs identify growth opportunities and potential areas of concern within their accounts.

Value demonstration

The third critical dimension quantifies and demonstrates value creation in concrete financial terms. In an era of increased scrutiny on business investments, articulating value propositions in clear financial terms has become paramount.

Research indicates that KAMgrs who consistently quantify the financial impact of their solutions are significantly more likely to achieve their account growth targets than those who rely on qualitative value propositions.[3]

Understanding working capital management provides another crucial avenue for value demonstration. Key account managers who can help their clients optimize their cash-to-cash cycle often engage in strategic conversations with senior leadership. This cycle, which combines inventory, accounts receivable and accounts payable days, provides a comprehensive view of working capital efficiency.

For instance, when analysing a retail client's working capital metrics, a KAMgr might discover that their inventory days are significantly higher than industry standards. This insight could lead to discussions about supply chain optimization solutions that could free up working capital. Consider a case where a retailer has:

- Inventory days: 45
- Accounts receivable days: 30
- Accounts payable days: 60
- Resulting in a cash-to-cash cycle of 15 days

By implementing improved inventory management solutions, the KAMgr might help reduce inventory days to 35, improving the cash-to-cash cycle to just five days and freeing up substantial working capital.

The nature of information management in KAM

Jon Katzenbach's[4,5] framework for high-performing teams can be adapted to understand effective information management in KAM. Just as teams need clear goals and complementary skills, information management requires clear objectives, structured processes and integrated capabilities.

Figure 3.1 shows an overview of information and financial analysis in KAM.

FIGURE 3.1 An overview of information and financial analysis in KAM

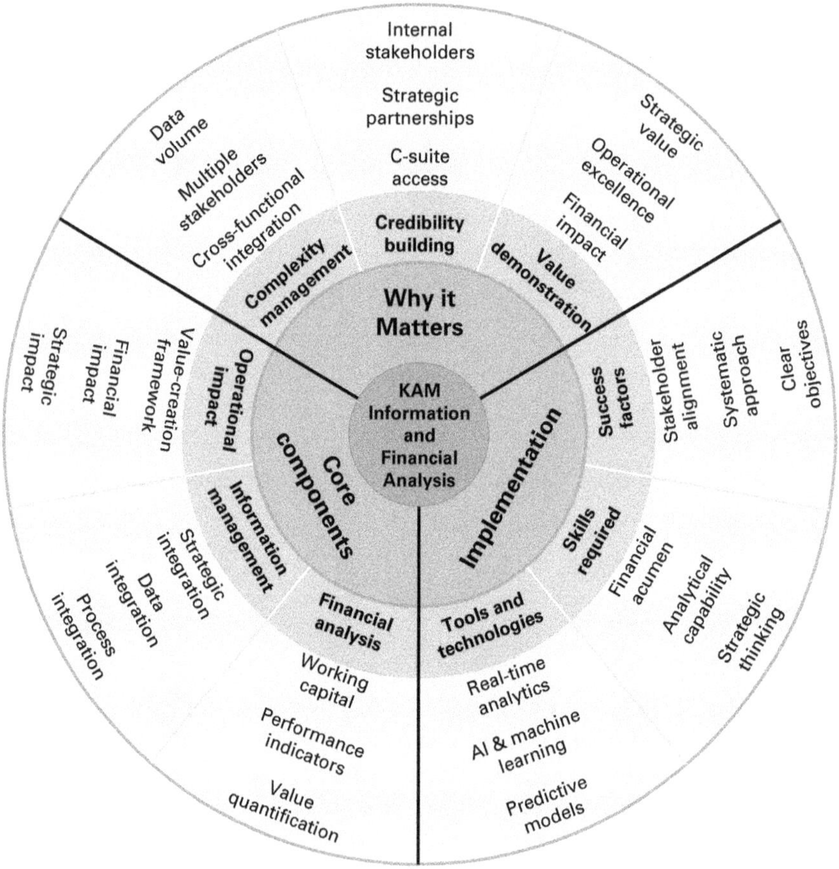

Financial analysis framework

A robust financial analysis framework helps KAMgrs identify opportunities for value creation. This includes understanding key profitability metrics such as:

Operating profit margin = (Operating income / Revenue) × 100 Return on capital employed = (Operating Income / (Total assets – Current liabilities)) × 100

These metrics provide insights into both operational efficiency and capital utilization. For example, one technology company's KAM team identified that their client's ROCE (return on capital employed) had declined from 15 per cent to 12 per cent over three years, primarily due to increasing capital intensity. This led to discussions about asset-light solutions that could improve returns while maintaining operational capability.[6]

Looking toward the future, I believe the role of key account manager will become even more strategic. While artificial intelligence and automation will handle many transactional aspects, I'm convinced there will always be a place for human relationships in strategic business partnerships.

Dr Sue Holt

Creating effective information management systems

Is it enough to understand the nature of information management to deliver high-performing customer relationships? Not really. KAMgrs must understand the dynamic processes underpinning effective information management and some of the silent killers of analytical effectiveness.

Consider how, as a KAMgr, you manage information in your strategic account. As a team, you must coordinate inputs from product managers, technical specialists, financial analysts and industry experts to create comprehensive insights that drive customer value. But how can a KAMgr effectively orchestrate these diverse information streams? Take a moment to consider how you would do this in your account.

Establishing systematic financial analysis processes

A systematic financial analysis approach begins with understanding your key account's complete financial picture. This means going beyond surface-level metrics to understand the story behind the numbers. For instance, when analysing profitability, KAMgrs should examine multiple layers.

Research by Gregory Huszczo[7] suggests that excellence in information management emerges from deliberately cultivating seven critical elements: clear objectives, robust processes, quality controls, analysis frameworks, sharing protocols, leadership engagement and technological support. This research is set in a team context based on clarity of purpose, coordination, complementary skills, commitment, conflict management and cultural alignment.

Consider the Strategic Account Director at a large IT company working with a significant manufacturing client. By implementing a systematic approach to financial analysis, he was able to demonstrate that their proposed digital transformation solution would deliver:

- 15 per cent reduction in operational costs

- 23 per cent improvement in production efficiency
- 8 per cent market share gain potential
- 30 per cent faster time-to-market for new products

This systematic approach involved analysing multiple years of financial data, including:

1 Income statement analysis: Understanding revenue trends, cost structures and profit margins over time. For example, tracking gross margin trends revealed that while revenue had grown 15 per cent over three years, margins had compressed by 200 basis points, highlighting the need for operational efficiency improvements.[8]

2 Balance sheet analysis: Examining asset utilization, working capital management and capital structure. Analysis showed that the client's return on capital employed had declined despite revenue growth, primarily due to increasing working capital requirements.

3 Cash flow analysis: Understanding the client's cash generation capacity and working capital efficiency. This revealed that despite strong EBITDA growth, free cash flow was constrained by working capital inefficiencies.

Leveraging financial insights for strategic value

The ability to translate financial analysis into strategic insights sets apart exceptional KAMgrs.

Consider a key account's working capital management. Understanding the components of the cash conversion cycle can reveal significant opportunities:

Inventory Days + Receivable Days − Payable Days = Cash Conversion Cycle

A manufacturing client might show: Base Year:

- Inventory days: 65
- Receivable days: 45
- Payable days: 30
- Cash conversion cycle: 80 days

After implementing strategic improvements:

- Inventory days: 45
- Receivable days: 35

- Payable days: 40
- Cash conversion cycle: 40 days

This 40-day improvement in the cash conversion cycle translates to substantial working capital release, creating strategic value for the client.

> Process integration moves beyond data sharing to create synchronized decision-making frameworks... Financial planning and budgeting processes were synchronized, allowing better resource allocation and investment timing.
>
> Mark Bailey

Technology and data management in modern KAM

The technological landscape of KAM has transformed dramatically, creating both opportunities and challenges for KAMgrs. Understanding how to leverage technology while avoiding its pitfalls is crucial for success.

DIGITAL TRANSFORMATION OF FINANCIAL ANALYSIS

The integration of digital technologies in financial analysis has evolved through three distinct phases.

First, the digitization phase involved converting analogue financial data into digital formats. This meant moving from paper-based account plans to digital formats and creating electronic repositories of customer information. While this represented progress, it merely digitized existing processes rather than transforming them.

Second, the digitalization phase transformed processes by implementing integrated CRM systems, developing automated reporting and analytics, and creating digital collaboration platforms. For example, one global technology company implemented a system automatically tracking key financial metrics across their strategic accounts, providing real-time alerts when specific thresholds are crossed.

Third, we've entered the digital transformation phase, characterized by strategically reimagining how we analyse and utilize financial data. This includes leveraging AI and machine learning for insight generation, creating predictive analytics capabilities and developing digital value propositions.

Research by the Customer Service Institute shows that organizations in the third phase achieve 45 per cent higher customer satisfaction scores and 62 per cent better retention rates than those still in the first phase. This dramatic improvement stems from their ability to identify and act on opportunities more quickly and effectively.[9]

Managing the data explosion

Modern KAMgrs face an unprecedented volume of financial data from multiple sources. Success requires developing systematic approaches to data management and analysis. In 2024 we were in the era where relationships alone cannot sustain key accounts. Today's key accounts expect us to demonstrate value in concrete, financial terms. The most successful KAMgrs can translate complex solutions into clear financial benefits.

The challenge lies in managing what we call the three Vs of data (as shown in Figure 3.2):

Volume: The sheer quantity of financial data available can be overwhelming. Successful KAMgrs implement scalable storage solutions and develop efficient data processing capabilities. For example, one team created a hierarchical data structure that organized financial metrics by importance and relevance, making it easier to focus on the most critical indicators.

Velocity: The speed at which financial data changes and updates requires real-time monitoring systems and agile analysis capabilities. Modern KAMgrs utilize automated alerts and dashboards to stay current with key metrics and trends.

Variety: Financial data comes in multiple formats from diverse sources. To create comprehensive insights, KAMgrs must integrate structured data (like financial statements) with unstructured data (such as market reports and customer feedback).

Value quantification and financial impact

In today's data-driven business environment, the ability to quantify and communicate value has become a critical differentiator for key account managers. Executive decision-makers are no longer satisfied with vague promises of value or general assertions about business impact. They demand

FIGURE 3.2 The three Vs of data

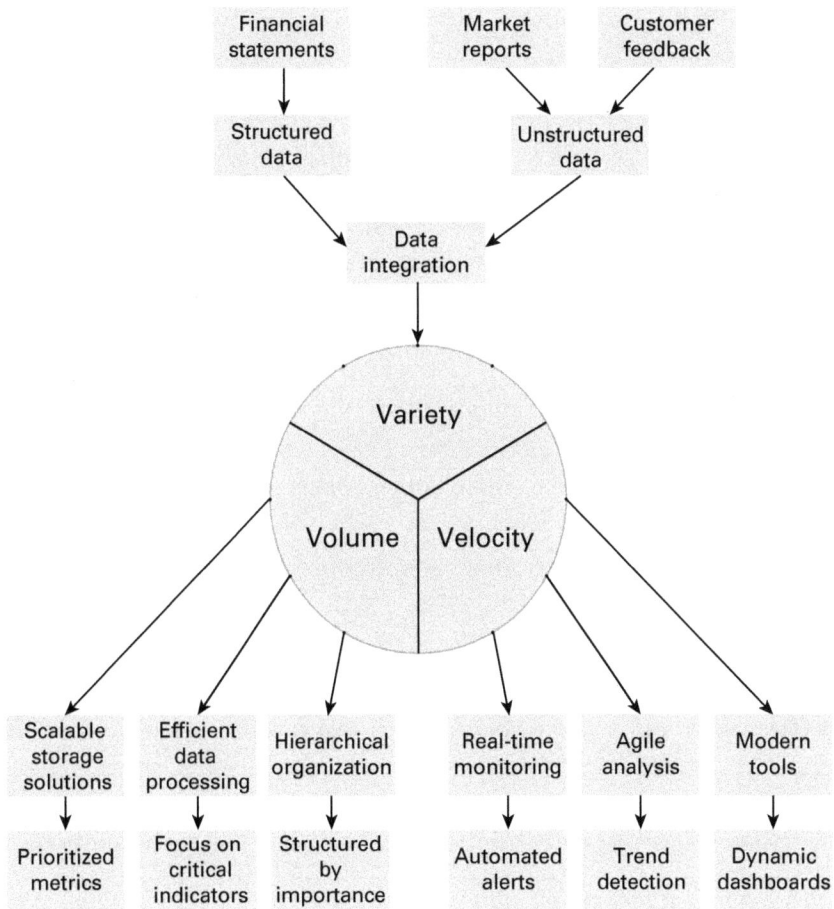

rigorous analysis and concrete evidence of return on investment, which is validated by their internal financial teams and often independent consultants.

The challenge for KAMgrs lies in creating value and measuring and communicating it in terms that resonate with senior stakeholders. This requires a sophisticated understanding of both financial metrics and value-creation mechanisms. For instance, imagine you are a senior KAMgr working at Siemens with a major automotive manufacturer; you have discovered that traditional ROI calculations significantly understated the actual value of their proposed automation solution. By expanding their analysis to include secondary benefits such as improved quality metrics, reduced warranty claims and enhanced production flexibility, you could demonstrate that the total value creation was more than double the initial estimates.

THE VALUE QUANTIFICATION FRAMEWORK

Research conducted by Stanford has revolutionized our understanding of value quantification in B2B relationships. Their comprehensive study of over 200 strategic partnerships revealed that effective value quantification must address four key dimensions: financial impact, operational excellence, strategic advancement and relationship value. Each dimension requires its analytical approach and metrics, yet all must be integrated into a coherent value story. This work was further explored by Andreas Hinterhuber (2017)[10] in his article 'Value quantification capabilities in industrial markets', in which he concluded that firms with high-value quantification skills had higher overall performance.

FINANCIAL IMPACT

The foundation of value quantification begins with direct financial impact. This encompasses both cost reduction and value creation initiatives across multiple financial dimensions. Consider how you can conduct a financial impact analysis for a global manufacturing client as a KAMgr. Consider the approach of the senior account director at SAP mentioned earlier. Rather than focusing solely on direct cost savings, she developed a comprehensive framework that examined:

1 Cost optimization: Beyond simple cost reduction, this included analysis of cost structure transformation. For instance, a supply chain solution reduced inventory holding costs by 15 per cent and improved the inventory mix, leading to better gross margins. The team constructed detailed financial models potentially showing improved forecast accuracy (22 per cent improvement) cascaded through the organization, reducing safety stock requirements, warehouse costs and obsolescence risk.

2 Revenue enhancement: The analysis demonstrated how operational improvements translated into revenue opportunities. Better forecast accuracy and reduced stockouts led to an increase in perfect order fulfilment, which should directly correlate with customer retention and share of wallet.

3 Working capital optimization: The team developed a sophisticated working capital model that showed how their solution would impact each component of the cash conversion cycle. By reducing inventory days by 12, improving receivables collection by eight days and optimizing payment terms, they demonstrated how working capital could be released for strategic investments.

4 Asset utilization improvement: Detailed analysis showed how improved planning and scheduling could increase asset utilization rates creating additional capacity for capital investment. This analysis proved particularly compelling to the CFO, who had been considering facility expansion.

The power of this approach lies in its comprehensiveness. Rather than presenting isolated metrics, the team showed how improvements in one area created ripple effects across the organization. For example, they demonstrated how improved forecast accuracy not only reduced inventory costs but also:

- Lowered transportation costs by reducing expedited shipments
- Improved production efficiency by enabling better scheduling
- Enhanced supplier relationships by providing more accurate demand signals
- Reduced working capital requirements through better inventory management

This comprehensive approach to financial impact analysis helped transform a discussion about a supply chain solution into a strategic partnership focused on enterprise value creation. The KAM team established quarterly value-tracking sessions with the client's executive team, where they monitored progress against these metrics and identified new value-creation opportunities.

> I'm a strong advocate for MBA graduates due to the multidisciplinary nature of the role. In my view, finance is the most crucial discipline to master, as that's all companies are really interested in.
>
> Prof Malcolm McDonald

Operational impact analysis

When analysing operational impact, successful KAMgrs focus on multiple dimensions, of which the most critical to clients are:

Process efficiency: Consider how one KAM team worked with a manufacturing client to analyse their production efficiency. By examining detailed cost accounting data, they identified that setup times consumed 18 per cent of available production capacity. They reduced this to 12 per cent through process improvements, translating to $3.2 million in annual savings.

Quality improvements: Financial analysis of quality metrics often reveals hidden costs. One team discovered that their client's warranty claims, while only 2 per cent of revenue, generated additional customer service costs equal to 5 per cent. By implementing quality improvement initiatives, they reduced total quality-related costs from 7 per cent to 4 per cent of revenue.

Cycle time reduction: Time is money, and sophisticated financial analysis can reveal the true cost of delays. Analysis of one retailer's supply chain showed that reducing the order-to-delivery time by two days would release $12 million in working capital through reduced safety stock requirements.

Strategic impact measurement

The future of KAM will be defined by the ability to harness emerging technologies while maintaining the human element that drives strategic relationships. This balance is particularly crucial when measuring strategic impact.

Competitive advantage creation: Financial analysis must demonstrate how strategic initiatives create sustainable competitive advantages. For example, one KAM team analysed their client's market position using financial metrics across five years, showing how technology investments had improved their cost position relative to competitors by 12 per cent.

Market position enhancement: Understanding market share dynamics through a financial lens provides crucial insights. Analysis of one consumer goods company's financial statements revealed that while their revenue was growing at 8 per cent annually, their market share was eroding due to a faster-growing market. This insight led to strategic discussions about accelerating growth through innovation.

Innovation acceleration: Quantifying the financial impact of innovation requires sophisticated analysis. One team developed a model showing how their client's R&D spending, while higher than competitors at 4.5 per cent of revenue, was generating returns 60 per cent above the industry average through better project selection and execution.

Strategic impact assessment

The third dimension focuses on long-term strategic value creation. This proves particularly challenging to quantify, yet often delivers the greatest long-term impact. Strategic value quantification requires analysis across multiple timeframes and business dimensions.

Market position enhancement: A systematic approach to quantifying strategic value examines several key areas:

Speed-to-market impact: Digital transformation initiatives typically increase speed-to-market for new products by 35–45 per cent. Historical data shows this improvement can raise new product success rates from 20–25 per cent to 30–40 per cent. This has compound effects on revenue growth and market share gains.

Pricing optimization: Real-time pricing capabilities enabled by advanced analytics typically drive margin improvements of 2–3 per cent through better market responsiveness and reduced margin leakage. For large organizations, this can translate to $10–15 million in additional annual profit.

Competitive differentiation: Strategic partnerships often create significant barriers to entry through:

- Integrated supplier networks that reduce total cost-to-serve by 8–12 per cent
- Proprietary market insights generated through advanced analytics
- First-mover advantages in emerging market segments
- Enhanced customer loyalty through improved service levels

Innovation capabilities: Quantification of innovation value requires analysis of multiple factors:

- Development efficiency: Virtual prototyping and simulation capabilities typically reduce development costs by 25–30 per cent while accelerating time-to-market by 40–50 per cent.
- Success rate improvement: Better market testing and customer insight capabilities increase new product success rates by 40–50 per cent, significantly improving return on R&D investment.
- Commercialization speed: Automated compliance and verification processes reduce time-to-market by 30–35 per cent for new products, creating substantial first-mover advantages.

Risk mitigation value: Often undervalued in traditional ROI calculations, risk mitigation creates substantial value through:

- **Supply chain resilience:** Predictive analytics reduce supply disruption impacts by 30–40 per cent through early warning and automated response capabilities.

- **Cybersecurity enhancement:** Advanced security frameworks typically provide $20–30 million protection annually based on risk-adjusted impact analysis.

- **Compliance automation:** Automated compliance systems reduce regulatory risk exposure by 40–50 per cent while decreasing compliance costs by 25–30 per cent.

Relationship value quantification

The fourth dimension examines value created through enhanced relationship capabilities. This often-overlooked aspect of value creation can deliver substantial long-term benefits.

Knowledge transfer systems: Systematic knowledge sharing creates quantifiable value through:

- Operational efficiency: Shared learning systems reduce training costs by 20–25 per cent while improving problem resolution speed by 30–40 per cent.

- Innovation acceleration: Cross-functional collaboration platforms increase innovation success rates by 25–30 per cent and reduce development cycles by 20–25 per cent.

- Decision quality: Integrated insight sharing improves accuracy by 15–20 per cent and reduces decision cycle times by 30–35 per cent.

Future opportunity value: Long-term partnership benefits include:

- Technology access: Priority access to new technologies typically accelerates adoption by 6–12 months, creating competitive advantages worth 2–3 per cent of affected revenue streams.

- Market responsiveness: Reduced time-to-market for joint initiatives improves capture rates on new opportunities by 15–20 per cent.

- Supply chain priority: Preferential treatment during supply constraints reduces lost sales opportunities by 25–30 per cent during disruption periods.

Cross-enterprise optimization: Integration benefits include:

- Planning efficiency: Aligned strategic planning processes reduce planning cycle times by 40–50 per cent while improving forecast accuracy by 15–20 per cent.

- Resource optimization: Integrated performance metrics enable a 15–20 per cent improvement in resource utilization across shared processes.

- Risk management: Joint risk management approaches reduce total risk exposure by 25–30 per cent through better coordination and shared mitigation strategies.

Implementation and measurement

Successful implementation of this framework requires systematic measurement and tracking processes:

Baseline establishment: Comprehensive documentation of current performance across all value dimensions, using both quantitative metrics and qualitative assessments.

Tracking systems: Automated data collection and analysis systems are implemented to monitor progress against value creation targets.

Regular reviews: Quarterly value-tracking sessions with executive stakeholders to review progress and identify new opportunities.

Value capture: Systematic processes to ensure realized benefits are correctly attributed and recorded, creating a compelling track record for future initiatives.

This comprehensive approach to value quantification transforms traditional vendor relationships into strategic partnerships by:

- Providing clear evidence of value creation across multiple dimensions
- Enabling more informed investment decisions
- Creating a shared understanding of partnership benefits
- Building credibility for future initiatives

The framework's success depends on rigorous analysis, clear communication and consistent measurement of outcomes. When properly implemented, it provides a robust foundation for long-term strategic partnerships that deliver substantial value to both organizations.

Integration with customer systems and processes

Success in modern KAM requires deep integration with customer systems and processes, enabling more effective information flow and value creation. The Digital Integration Consortium identifies three levels of integration that progressive KAM programmes should strive to achieve.

DATA INTEGRATION

The foundation of practical financial analysis lies in data integration. As an example, a global IT software company with a strategic partnership with a US retailer demonstrates this power, which has come from the author's own work. The KAM team:

- Established shared data platforms for retail analytics, allowing real-time analysis of key performance indicators. This enabled them to identify that shelf availability issues were costing 3 per cent in lost sales, leading to the implementation of automated replenishment systems.
- Created integrated process workflows for digital transformation, reducing manual data entry by 75 per cent and improving data accuracy by 45 per cent. This improved decision-making speed and quality across the organization, which contributed to a competitive advantage.
- Developed joint innovation initiatives in retail technology, leading to a 28 per cent improvement in supply chain efficiency and 45 per cent faster deployment of new technologies.

PROCESS INTEGRATION

Process integration moves beyond data sharing to create synchronized decision-making frameworks. Consider the situation where a Global Account Manager at a global engineering company, developed a structured framework for analysing customer operational data across multiple sites. This integration enabled:

Aligned planning cycles: Financial planning and budgeting processes were synchronized, allowing better resource allocation and investment timing.

Coordinated execution: Shared performance metrics and real-time monitoring systems enabled quick identification and resolution of issues.

Joint performance monitoring: Integrated dashboards provided visibility into key financial and operational metrics, enabling proactive management of potential issues.

STRATEGIC INTEGRATION

The highest level of integration occurs at the strategic level, where financial analysis drives joint value creation. One technology company achieved this by:

- Creating shared objective-setting processes that aligned financial targets and strategic goals

- Developing joint innovation initiatives that leveraged both companies' capabilities

- Building integrated value creation frameworks that ensured fair value distribution

Current trends and implications

As we reflect on both the current and future of information management and financial analysis in KAM, several key trends emerge that will shape the landscape.

Artificial intelligence and machine learning in financial analysis

Integrating artificial intelligence and machine learning into financial analysis has fundamentally transformed how key account managers create and demonstrate value. These technologies enable KAMgrs to move from reactive analysis to proactive value creation, identifying opportunities and risks that would be impossible to detect through traditional analytical methods.

In predictive analytics, advanced algorithms process vast amounts of historical financial and operational data to forecast customer needs accurately. For instance, one global manufacturing company's KAM team implemented an AI-driven analysis system that examines multiple data streams simultaneously: purchasing patterns, production schedules, inventory levels, market demand signals and macroeconomic indicators. This system predicts essential reorder points and identifies subtle patterns that indicate emerging opportunities or challenges.

The system recently detected that one of their key accounts was experiencing gradual increases in inventory holding costs across multiple categories, a trend that wasn't obvious in traditional financial reports. By analysing historical patterns, the AI system predicted this would lead to working capital constraints within six months. The KAM team used this insight to develop a proactive proposal for a vendor-managed inventory programme that would reduce their client's working capital requirements by 25 per cent while maintaining service levels.

Machine learning algorithms are particularly effective in at-risk identification and mitigation. These systems continuously monitor hundreds of risk indicators across financial statements, operational metrics and external market data. For example, one KAM team's ML system flagged an unusual pattern in their customer's accounts payable aging that suggested potential supply chain disruptions. This early warning enabled the team to develop contingency plans three months before the issues became apparent through conventional analysis.

In pricing optimization, AI systems now analyse massive datasets to identify opportunities for value-based pricing. These systems consider multiple factors simultaneously: customer profitability analysis, competitive positioning, market dynamics and production costs.

Perhaps most significantly, modern AI systems can generate automated insights from unstructured data sources that traditionally require extensive manual analysis. These systems can process annual reports; earnings call transcripts, industry news and social media sentiment to provide KAMgrs with comprehensive views of their accounts' strategic positions. For instance, an AI system recently identified a correlation between a customer's R&D spending patterns and their subsequent market share gains, enabling the KAM team to develop targeted innovation support programmes.

The impact of these technologies extends beyond individual account analysis to portfolio-level insights. AI systems can now identify patterns across multiple accounts that suggest broader market trends or opportunities. One team's system recognized that customers who adopted certain digital technologies showed similar patterns of working capital improvement 6–12 months later, information that proved valuable in developing value propositions for other accounts.

However, the successful implementation of AI and ML in financial analysis requires more than technology deployment. Key account managers must develop new skills to interpret and act on machine-generated insights effectively. They need to understand both the capabilities and limitations of these systems, knowing when to rely on automated analysis and when human judgment is required.

The future of AI in KAM lies not in replacing human analysis but in augmenting it. The most successful KAM teams use AI systems to handle routine analysis and pattern recognition, freeing human analysts to focus on strategic interpretation and relationship building. This combination of artificial and human intelligence creates a powerful platform for identifying and capturing value-creation opportunities.

Real-time analytics in key account management

Analysing real-time data has become a crucial differentiator in modern KAM. While historical analysis remains essential, business change demands immediate insights and rapid response capabilities. Real-time analytics transforms how KAMgrs monitor, analyse and respond to their accounts' evolving needs and challenges.

Modern KAM systems now integrate data from multiple sources simultaneously. For instance, a typical KAM dashboard might combine financial transaction data, inventory levels, production metrics, logistics information and market indicators. This integration enables account managers to see the complete picture of their account's performance as it unfolds. When a significant electronics manufacturer implemented such a system, they discovered that supply chain delays were causing inventory build-ups that wouldn't have been visible in traditional monthly reports. This real-time visibility enabled them to adjust production schedules dynamically, saving their client over $2 million in excess inventory costs annually.

Dynamic decision support systems have evolved to provide contextual recommendations based on current conditions. These systems continuously analyse incoming data against historical patterns and predetermined thresholds. For example, one KAM team's system monitors their client's production efficiency metrics in real-time. When efficiency drops below expected levels, the system automatically analyses potential causes – from material quality issues to maintenance needs – and suggests corrective actions based on successful historical interventions. This capability has reduced response time to production issues from hours to minutes.

Continuous performance monitoring across key metrics has become increasingly sophisticated. Modern systems track hundreds of performance indicators simultaneously, understanding individual metrics and the relationships between them. A global logistics provider's KAM team implemented a system that monitors real-time delivery performance, cost per shipment, fuel efficiency and customer satisfaction scores. When the system detected that faster delivery times weren't translating into improved satisfaction scores for specific routes, it revealed an opportunity to optimize delivery schedules based on customer preferences rather than assumed priorities.

Automated alerts have evolved beyond simple threshold notifications into intelligent early warning systems. These systems use pattern recognition and trend analysis to identify potential issues before they become problems. For instance, one KAM team's system monitors their customer's working capital metrics in real-time. It recently identified that while individual components of the cash conversion cycle were within normal ranges, their combined trend suggested emerging liquidity pressure. This early warning enabled the team to proactively develop a supplier financing solution three months before the issue would have impacted operations.

The power of real-time analytics lies in faster data processing and the ability to combine multiple data streams to create actionable insights. For example, when a major retailer's system detected an unusual pattern in point-of-sale data, it simultaneously analysed weather forecasts, social media sentiment and local event calendars to determine whether the pattern represented a temporary anomaly or a significant trend requiring intervention.

Implementation of real-time analytics requires careful consideration of both technical and organizational factors. Key account teams must determine which metrics require real-time monitoring versus those that can be analysed less frequently. They must also establish clear protocols for acting on real-time insights, ensuring that rapid response capabilities don't lead to reactive decision-making.

The future of real-time analytics in KAM points toward even greater integration and automation. Systems are beginning to incorporate external data sources such as social media sentiment, competitor actions and macroeconomic indicators to provide comprehensive real-time insights. However, successful KAMgrs recognize that real-time analytics complement rather than replace strategic thinking and relationship building. The goal is to use real-time capabilities to enhance rather than dictate decision-making.

The impact of real-time analytics extends beyond operational efficiency to strategic relationship development. When key account managers can demonstrate a deep, real-time understanding of their customers' businesses, they strengthen their position as strategic partners rather than mere suppliers. This enhanced relationship creates opportunities for deeper collaboration and value creation that benefit both organizations.

REAL-WORLD EXAMPLE: TURNING DATA INTO VALUE: A KEY ACCOUNT MANAGEMENT SUCCESS STORY
A fictional example

Sandra Martinez stood at her office window at Advanced Enterprise Solutions (AES), staring at the downtown Chicago skyline while contemplating her biggest challenge. As key account manager for Midwest Manufacturing Corporation (MMC), one of AES's largest enterprise software clients, she faced a critical turning point in the relationship. Despite a decade-long history of providing IT services to MMC, their partnership had stagnated. Recent conversations with MMC's procurement team made it clear that they viewed AES as just another vendor, and there were whispers about putting their entire IT services contract out for a competitive bid.

Sandra knew she needed to transform the relationship fundamentally, but more than the traditional approach of relationship building and service reliability would be needed. MMC's new executive team was focused intensely on financial performance and measurable value creation. As she reviewed MMC's latest annual report spread across her desk, she realized that the key to elevating their partnership lay in developing a deeper understanding of MMC's financial challenges and opportunities.

Over the next several weeks, Sandra immersed herself in MMC's financial statements, analysing five years of data to understand the company's trajectory and challenges. The story that emerged was concerning. While MMC had grown revenue from $2.8 billion to $3.4 billion over five years, its operating margin had steadily declined from 15 per cent to 12 per cent. Most concerning was their deteriorating working capital position – their cash conversion cycle had ballooned from 50 to 85 days, tying up an additional $180 million that could have been invested in growth initiatives.

Digging deeper into the numbers, Sandra identified that MMC's declining profitability was primarily due to something other than price pressure, as many assumed. Instead, the root cause appeared to be operational inefficiency. Their inventory days had increased significantly, suggesting problems with production planning and forecasting. Their aging manufacturing execution system, now 12 years old, needed help to cope with increasing product complexity and shorter production runs.

The financial analysis also revealed concerning trends in asset utilization. Return on capital employed had declined from 18 per cent to 13 per cent, driven by margin decline and less efficient capital utilization. Equipment downtime increased due to reactive maintenance practices, and the need for real-time visibility across their production network meant they couldn't optimize capacity utilization across facilities.

Armed with these insights, Sandra began developing a comprehensive transformation proposal. Rather than leading with technology solutions, she structured her analysis around MMC's key financial metrics. She demonstrated how implementing a modern production planning system with AI capabilities could reduce inventory days from 65 to 45, releasing $85 million in working capital. The improved production scheduling would also boost gross margins by optimizing resource utilization and reducing expedited shipping costs.

Sandra's analysis showed that modernizing MMC's supply chain management capabilities could reduce accounts receivable days from 55 to 40 by automating manual processes and providing real-time visibility. Combined with improved forecast accuracy, this would free up another $65 million in working capital. Implementing predictive maintenance capabilities across MMC's production facilities could reduce unplanned downtime by 35 per cent and improve asset utilization by 12 per cent, delivering $45 million in annual benefit through improved productivity and reduced maintenance costs.

When Sandra presented her analysis to MMC's executive team, the conversation differed from previous quarterly business reviews. Instead of focusing on service levels and project updates, they discussed transforming MMC's operations and financial performance strategically. Sandra's ability to connect technological capabilities to concrete financial outcomes resonated strongly with the executive team, particularly the CFO.

The comprehensive analysis and clear value proposition transformed the relationship. Rather than proceeding with a competitive bid, MMC signed a five-year strategic partnership agreement with AES worth $450 million – triple their previous contract value. More importantly, the nature of the relationship fundamentally changed. AES was now viewed as a strategic partner rather than a vendor, evidenced by their invitation to participate in MMC's annual strategic planning process.

Two years into the transformation programme, the results validated Sandra's analysis. MMC had reduced inventory by 22 days, releasing $92 million in working capital. Operating margins had improved to 13.8 per cent, and the return on capital employed had climbed to 16 per cent. The success of the initial programmes led to three additional strategic initiatives worth $180 million.

Sandra's experience demonstrates how sophisticated financial analysis capabilities can transform traditional vendor relationships into strategic partnerships. By developing a deep understanding of her client's economic challenges and opportunities, she identified and quantified value-creation opportunities that resonated with executive stakeholders. Her success highlighted that modern key account managers must be as comfortable with financial statements and value quantification as they are with relationship building and service delivery.

The case of Sandra Martinez and MMC illustrates a broader trend in KAM: the growing importance of financial acumen in developing and maintaining strategic partnerships. As organizations face increasing pressure to demonstrate return on investment for all major initiatives, KAMgrs who can connect their solutions to measurable financial outcomes will be best positioned to create and capture value for their organizations and clients.

Future trends and transformative technologies

The landscape of financial analysis in key account management continues to evolve rapidly.

Advanced analytics and artificial intelligence

Integrating artificial intelligence in financial analysis transforms how KAMgrs create and demonstrate value. Consider the experience of Global Technologies, where their KAM team implemented an AI-driven analysis system that processes customer financial data to identify value-creation opportunities. The system analyses patterns in working capital utilization, operational efficiency and cost structures to highlight areas where intervention could create measurable value.

In one instance, the system identified that a key account's seasonal inventory build-up created high carrying costs three months earlier than necessary. Adjusting production schedules and implementing automated replenishment systems reduced peak inventory levels by 28 per cent while maintaining service levels. This insight, which might have been missed in traditional analysis, generated $12 million in annual savings.

Predictive analytics and scenario planning

The ability to model different financial scenarios has become increasingly sophisticated. Modern KAMgrs are using predictive analytics to forecast the impact of various initiatives on their customers' economic performance. For instance, when evaluating a significant supply chain transformation project, one KAM team created a dynamic model that showed how different implementation approaches would affect their client's working capital requirements and return on invested capital over three years.

Their analysis revealed that while a rapid implementation would deliver benefits sooner, a working capital investment would be required to reduce ROCE below acceptable levels in the short term. By modelling alternative approaches, they developed a phased implementation plan that maintained ROCE above threshold levels throughout the transformation while delivering 85 per cent of the benefits within the original timeframe.

Recommendations for developing financial analysis capabilities

BUILDING ORGANIZATIONAL COMPETENCY

Successful KAM programmes require a systematic approach to developing financial analysis capabilities across the team. The Strategic Account Finance Institute's research identifies five core competencies that distinguish high-performing KAMgrs:

Financial statement analysis: KAMgrs must develop proficiency in analysing balance sheets, income statements and cash flow statements to identify opportunities and risks. This includes understanding key ratios and their implications for business performance.

Value creation metrics: Teams need the ability to quantify the impact of their initiatives across multiple dimensions, including cost reduction, revenue enhancement and working capital optimization.

Cost structure analysis: Understanding how costs behave and identifying opportunities for optimization is crucial. This includes differentiating between fixed and variable costs, analysing contribution margins and assessing operational leverage.

Working capital management: KAMgrs must understand the components of working capital and how their solutions can improve their customers' cash conversion cycle.

Risk assessment: The ability to evaluate and quantify various risk factors, including operational, financial and market risks, is increasingly important in strategic account relationships.

CREATING VALUE THROUGH FINANCIAL INSIGHTS

The actual test of financial analysis capabilities is translating insights into value creation. Consider an example of a global account director at a global SAAS provider who transformed her relationship with a major retail client.

Through detailed analysis of their financial statements, she identified that while the client's revenue was growing at 12 per cent annually, their operating margin had declined by 300 basis points over three years due to increasing complexity in their operations.

By analysing their cost structure and operational metrics, the account director developed a comprehensive proposal that showed how implementing integrated business systems could:

- Reduce administrative costs by 18 per cent through automation
- Improve inventory turnover by 25 per cent through better demand forecasting
- Increase labour productivity by 15 per cent through improved workforce management
- Generate $45 million in annual benefits against a $30 million investment

The key to success was her ability to connect operational improvements to financial outcomes that mattered to executive stakeholders.

Summary

The future of financial analysis in KAM

The evolution of KAM continues to emphasize the critical importance of sophisticated financial analysis capabilities. As we've seen through numerous examples, success in strategic account management increasingly depends on the ability to:

- Understand and interpret complex financial information to identify value-creation opportunities
- Develop and quantify value propositions that resonate with senior stakeholders
- Create actionable insights from large volumes of financial and operational data to demonstrate the tangible economic impact of strategic initiatives

The future of key account management lies in integrating advanced analytical capabilities with traditional relationship management skills. Those who master this combination will be best positioned to create and capture value in their strategic relationships. The future's most successful key account managers will be those who can seamlessly blend financial acumen with strategic insight and relationship skills. They will be as comfortable discussing return on invested capital with a CFO as they explore innovation opportunities with a CTO.

The KAMgrs who thrive in this environment will embrace these changes and continuously develop their financial analysis capabilities. They will use these skills to analyse past performance and shape future opportunities, creating value for both their organizations and their strategic accounts.

> We used a variety of tools to measure performance, with Salesforce being central to our operations. We tracked metrics like gross margin, customer satisfaction, safety leadership and the strength of client relationships. We also used AI-driven pricing algorithms to optimize our bids.
>
> John Downer

Table 3.1 outlines key actions for enhancing information management and financial analysis performance.

Figure 3.3 shows key drivers, tools, behaviours and success factors for managing information and financial analysis.

TABLE 3.1 Key actions for enhancing information management and financial analysis

	Action	Description
1.	Develop financial statement analysis expertise	Build proficiency in analysing balance sheets, income statements and cash flow statements to identify opportunities and risks, focusing particularly on understanding key ratios and their implications for business performance.
2.	Establish value quantification systems	Create comprehensive frameworks to measure and track value creation across four key dimensions: financial impact, operational excellence, strategic advancement and relationship value.

(continued)

TABLE 3.1 (Continued)

	Action	Description
3.	Implement working capital analysis	Master the analysis of cash conversion cycle components (inventory days, accounts receivable, accounts payable) to identify opportunities for working capital optimization and demonstrate value to C-suite stakeholders.
4.	Create systematic data integration	Develop structured approaches to collecting and analysing data from multiple sources, including financial metrics, operational indicators and market trends, establishing automated systems for real-time monitoring where possible.
5.	Build cost structure analysis capabilities	Develop expertise in analysing cost behaviours, differentiating between fixed and variable costs, understanding contribution margins and identifying operational leverage opportunities.
6.	Establish value-tracking processes	Implement quarterly value-tracking sessions with customer executives to monitor progress, validate impact and identify new opportunities, supported by systematic measurement and documentation processes.
7.	Develop predictive analytics capabilities	Learn to use advanced analytics and AI tools to forecast trends, identify risks and create predictive models that demonstrate potential value creation opportunities to key accounts.
8.	Create strategic impact measurement systems	Develop frameworks for measuring and communicating strategic value creation, including competitive advantage analysis, market position enhancement and innovation acceleration metrics.
9.	Implement risk assessment protocols	Establish systematic approaches to evaluating and quantifying various risk factors, including operational, financial and market risks, in strategic account relationships.
10.	Build integration frameworks	Develop structured approaches to integrating with customer systems and processes across three levels: data integration, process integration and strategic integration, enabling more effective information flow and value creation.

FIGURE 3.3 Key drivers, tools, behaviours and success factors

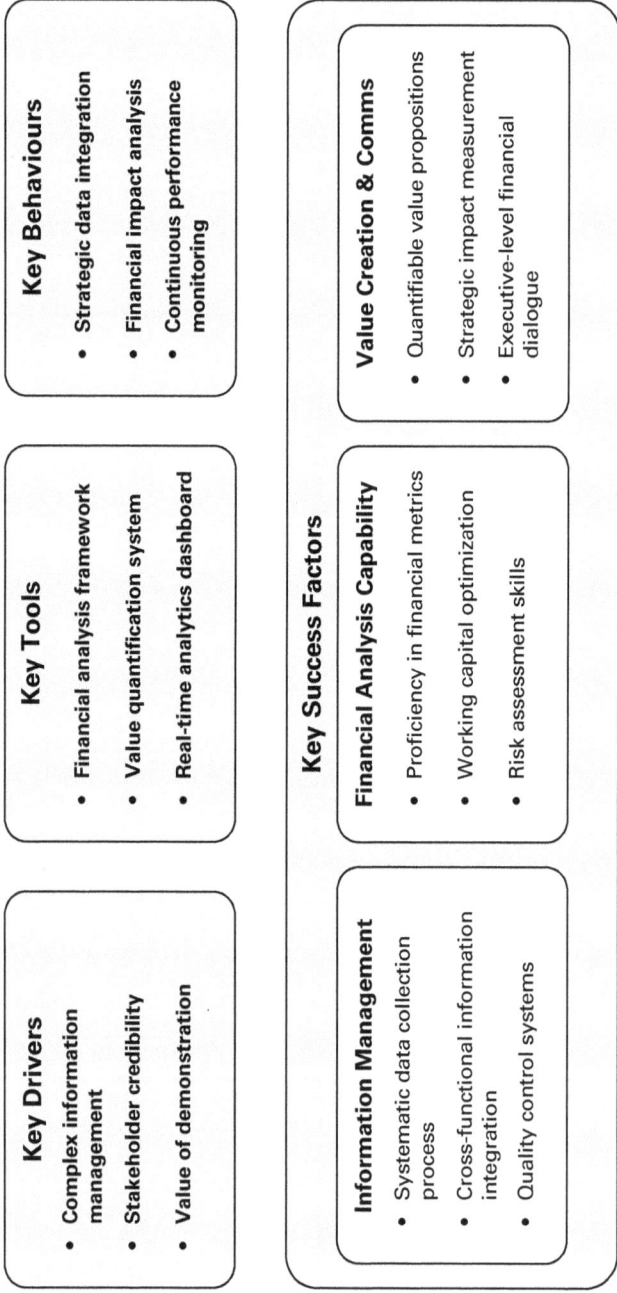

Key Drivers

- **Complex information management**
- **Stakeholder credibility**
- **Value of demonstration**

Key Tools

- **Financial analysis framework**
- **Value quantification system**
- **Real-time analytics dashboard**

Key Behaviours

- **Strategic data integration**
- **Financial impact analysis**
- **Continuous performance monitoring**

Key Success Factors

Information Management

- Systematic data collection process
- Cross-functional information integration
- Quality control systems

Financial Analysis Capability

- Proficiency in financial metrics
- Working capital optimization
- Risk assessment skills

Value Creation & Comms

- Quantifiable value propositions
- Strategic impact measurement
- Executive-level financial dialogue

Further reading

N Tzempelikos and S Gounaris. Industrial marketing management: Linking key account management, *Industrial Marketing Management*, 2015, 45, 22–34

Notes

1 S Wengler, M Ehret and S Saab. Implementation of key account management: Who, why, and how? *Industrial Marketing Management*, 2006, 35 (1), 103–12, https://doi.org/10.1016/j.indmarman.2005.08.011 (archived at https://perma.cc/5RZZ-JNAU)

2 Ibid.

3 L Georges and A Eggert. Key account managers' role within the value creation process of collaborative relationships, *Journal of Business-to-Business Marketing*, 2003, 10 (4), 1–22, https://doi.org/10.1300/j033v10n04_01 (archived at https://perma.cc/4LT2-HZ4S)

4 J R Katzenbach and D K Smith (1993) *The Wisdom of Teams: Creating the high-performance organization*, Harvard Business School Press

5 J R Katzenbach. Pride: A strategic asset, *Strategy & Leadership*, 2003, 31 (5), 34–38

6 S Wengler, M Ehret and S Saab. Implementation of key account management: Who, why, and how? *Industrial Marketing Management*, 2006, 35 (1), 103–12, https://doi.org/10.1016/j.indmarman.2005.08.011 (archived at https://perma.cc/JXF9-3MRZ)

7 G E Huszczo (1996) *Tools for Team Excellence: Getting your team into high gear and keeping it there*, Davies-Black Publishing

8 L Georges and A Eggert. Key account managers' role within the value creation process of collaborative relationships, *Journal of Business-to-Business Marketing*, 2003, 10 (4), 1–22, https://doi.org/10.1300/j033v10n04_01 (archived at https://perma.cc/4LT2-HZ4S)

9 Institute of Customer Service (2024) UKCSI – the state of customer satisfaction in the UK – July 2020, www.instituteofcustomerservice.com/product/ukcsi-jul-24/ (archived at https://perma.cc/6MRJ-CEX8)

10 A Hinterhuber. Value quantification capabilities in industrial markets, *Journal of Business Research*, 2017, 76, 163–78

Stuart Roberts

Based on my extensive experience in key account management spanning over two decades, I believe the capabilities required for success in this role represent a sophisticated blend of *relationship management*, *commercial acumen* and *strategic thinking*. Let me share my perspective on these critical capabilities drawing from my journey and my role in growing a single account from £11 million to £50 million in annual revenue over 15 years.

In my professional assessment, stakeholder relationship management forms the cornerstone of effective key account management. Early in my career, I discovered that I was more suited to being a 'farmer' than a 'hunter' – finding greater success in nurturing and growing existing relationships rather than cold calling. Through my experience, I've found that successful stakeholder management requires penetration at multiple organizational levels. A key account manager must establish authentic relationships across various functions – from finance to procurement, operations to HR. I've consistently observed that this multidimensional relationship architecture provides the foundation for sustainable account growth.

The second critical capability domain, in my experience, centres on commercial and business acumen. As I often tell my teams, 'anybody can sell a tenner for a fiver'. The real challenge lies in maintaining profitability while building strong stakeholder relationships. Throughout my career, I've encountered situations where key account managers, in their eagerness to please clients, compromised profitability by making unnecessary concessions. Understanding value creation, not just price, has been fundamental to my success. I often use the water bottle analogy to illustrate this point – the same bottle of water holds drastically different value depending on whether you're in a supermarket or stranded in a desert. This understanding of value enabled me to maintain pricing integrity through five major renegotiations while still ensuring client satisfaction.

Strategic planning capability represents another crucial dimension. When I transitioned to my last role, I was surprised to find key account managers operating without structured account plans. We addressed this by implementing comprehensive planning frameworks, including value creation spreadsheets that helped account managers articulate and track value delivery. In my view, effective account planning must look beyond immediate service delivery to envision the account's evolution over a five-year horizon.

Cross-cultural competence and the ability to lead without formal authority have proven increasingly critical in my experience managing global accounts. When I led a pharmaceutical account spanning 42 countries and 200 sites, I encountered diverse cultural dynamics that required sophisticated navigation. The challenges I faced in South America particularly illustrated this – managing relationships between Brazil, Colombia and Mexico demanded deep cultural understanding and diplomatic skills. Success in such environments requires what I term 'matrix leadership' – the ability to influence and achieve objectives without direct authority.

Technology and digital competence represent non-negotiable capabilities in modern key account management. Throughout my career, I've seen how digital tools enable effective reporting, cross-border communication and performance tracking. Without embracing technology, key account managers simply cannot function effectively in today's global business environment.

Regarding performance measurement, I've found that organizational and individual metrics must align while serving distinct purposes. At the organizational level, I focus on contract profitability, growth and retention. However, at the individual level, I prioritize customer satisfaction, followed by profitability and growth. This dual perspective enables more effective performance management while maintaining focus on both relationship and commercial outcomes.

For aspiring key account managers, I often describe the role as 'herding cats' – it requires patience, resilience and sophisticated stakeholder management skills. However, I've found it to be an immensely rewarding career path. Every day brings different challenges, requiring continuous adaptation and learning. The key to success, in my experience, lies in developing a balanced capability set spanning relationship management, commercial acumen, strategic thinking and leadership skills.

In conclusion, my career trajectory demonstrates that mastery of these capabilities can lead to significant value creation for both service providers and clients. The role demands a remarkable synthesis of soft and hard skills, and while challenging, offers extraordinary opportunities for professional growth and impact. As the business environment becomes increasingly complex, I believe these capability requirements will only grow in sophistication, making systematic capability development ever more critical for success in key account management roles.

Stuart Roberts is a distinguished Business Development Leader with over 20 years of experience in the international security and investigations industry. Currently serving as Vice President of Client Development & Sales for Securitas Global Clients Europe, he has established himself as a strategic leader with comprehensive expertise in global security operations, risk management and business development. His career trajectory includes influential roles at G4S plc, where he spent nearly 11 years as Global Account Director, and earlier positions at Chubb Security Personnel.

Throughout his career, Stuart has demonstrated an exceptional ability in developing and implementing complex security solutions for multinational clients, while maintaining a strong focus on operational efficiency and stakeholder relationship management. His expertise spans international business development, strategic planning, bid proposal management and matrix leadership, complemented by a postgraduate diploma in Applied Management from the University of Reading. Stuart's consultative approach and proven track record in fostering inclusivity and driving business growth have made him a respected figure in the security industry, known for delivering innovative solutions and maintaining strong client partnerships across Europe.

www.linkedin.com/in/stuart-roberts-73468b17 (archived at https://perma.cc/5DSK-FXLX)

04

Embracing technology and digitalization

Overview

In the ever-evolving business landscape, KAM has undergone a seismic shift, propelled by rapid advances in digital technologies in general, and generative technologies in particular.[1] The Covid-19 pandemic served as an unexpected catalyst, accelerating digital transformation across industries and fundamentally altering the way key account managers (KAMgrs) interact with their clients.

Following the pandemic's shadow and the increasing adoption of AI, the marketing functions of companies have started a journey of automation and personalization[2] that is increasingly impacting sales and KAM practices. This chapter explores the critical importance of embracing technology and digitalization in KAM, examining the rapid changes and the emerging opportunities presented by artificial intelligence.

Artificial intelligence (AI) is everywhere now and arguably the next major transformation force in business and organizations. It is very likely that in your business, there are ongoing discussions as to whether you should adopt AI, and, second, how to do it. AI tools can help across many areas of the sales and account management function, including data collection and insights, prospecting, customer engagement, intent signals, proposals, coaching and customer service. Presently, over 200 tools are already available,[3] though in this chapter we only focus on a few of them, the most relevant ones for KAMgrs.

At the Global Sales Science Institute (GSSI) annual conference in Toronto in 2023, there was a healthy debate about the topic of AI in customer management operations.[4] Kevin Peesker, President of Worldwide Small, Medium, Corporate & Digital of Microsoft, stated in his keynote speech how the leading technology firm is deploying 50,000 engineers to AI overall, a subset of which would be focused on generative AI. Why? Because generative AI will transform jobs within organizations and will often boost performance.

McKinsey & Company estimates, in their report 'The economic potential of Generative AI', that generative AI could contribute the equivalent of $2.6–4.4 trillion annually, especially in areas such as customer operations, marketing and sales, software engineering, and research and development.[5]

We invite you and your organization to explore the applications of digital tools and AI to your KAM operations carefully, as the expected enhancement in the performance of key account managers as a result of adopting digital tools are not always realized.[6]

Why do key account managers need to embrace digital and generative technologies?

The pandemic forced businesses worldwide to adapt swiftly to remote work environments, virtual meetings and digital collaboration tools. For key account managers, this shift presented both challenges and opportunities. The traditional face-to-face interactions that were once the cornerstone of relationship-building in KAM were suddenly replaced by video conferences, digital presentations and virtual networking events. This sudden transition demanded not only technical proficiency but also a reimagining of how to foster and maintain strong client relationships in a digital-first world.

> While we used various tools for project management, bid optimization, and collaboration... we always emphasized that these tools were enablers, not replacements for the human aspects of relationship building and strategic thinking.
>
> John Downer

The following table explains the importance of adopting digital and generative technologies.

WHY EMBRACING DIGITAL AND GENERATIVE TECHNOLOGIES IS IMPORTANT

Digital transformation:

- Enables virtual relationship management
- Supports remote customer engagement

- Enhances multi-stakeholder collaboration
- Facilitates global account coordination

Data-driven insights:

- Improves customer understanding
- Enables predictive analytics
- Strengthens decision-making
- Identifies new opportunities

Process optimization:

- Automates routine tasks
- Streamlines workflows
- Improves efficiency
- Enables focus on strategic activities

Customer experience:

- Enables personalized engagement
- Supports proactive service
- Enhances communication
- Improves response times

AI-powered capabilities:

- Enhance account planning
- Support performance analytics
- Enable intelligent coaching
- Optimize resource allocation

Platforms such as Zoom, Microsoft Teams, Google Meet and the like were adopted quickly, enabling key account managers to connect with buying groups and other stakeholders across the globe more readily than ever before. These tools offered numerous advantages:

1 Increased frequency of touchpoints: KAMgrs could schedule more frequent, shorter meetings with clients, maintaining consistent engagement without the need for time-consuming travel.

2 Broader stakeholder inclusion: Virtual meetings made it easier to involve a wider range of stakeholders from both the client and vendor sides, fostering more comprehensive discussions and faster decision-making.

3 Recorded sessions for reference: The ability to record meetings allowed for better information retention and sharing with team members who couldn't attend.

4 Screen sharing and collaborative features: These tools enhanced the ability to present complex information and collaborate on documents and proposals in real time.

However, the shift to virtual communication tools also brought challenges. First, 'video call fatigue', and potential mental exhaustion for both KAMgrs and clients as a result of increased reliance on video calls. Also, the difficulty in reading non-verbal cues, as virtual interactions made it harder to pick up on subtle body language and facial expressions, which are crucial in relationship-building and negotiation. Some customer communications could suffer and important meetings be disrupted due to connectivity problems and varying levels of technological proficiency among participants. Finally, reduced informal interactions led to the loss of casual conversations that often occur before or after in-person meetings, which meant fewer opportunities for relationship-building outside of formal discussions.

KAMgrs have become technology advocates, guiding their clients through the intricacies of new digital platforms and helping them navigate the challenges of remote and hybrid business operations. The rapid level of digitization of the business landscape has highlighted the need for adaptability and technological fluency in KAM. The lessons learned during the pandemic have laid the groundwork for a new era in key account management – one where digital proficiency is not just an asset but a necessity. As we progress, the integration of advanced technologies, particularly AI, is poised to change KAM practices further. AI-powered tools offer unprecedented potential to generate insights into customer behaviour, predictive analytics for sales forecasting and automated processes that streamline administrative tasks, allowing key account managers to focus more on strategy and relationship-building with their most important customers.

These AI-driven efficiencies free up valuable time for KAMgrs to focus on more human-centric tasks crucial for relationship-building. With AI handling data analysis and routine administrative tasks, KAMgrs can dedicate more time to strategic planning and account development, personal outreach and relationship nurturing, creative problem-solving and innovation for addressing client challenges, and coaching and mentoring junior team members.

As we delve deeper into this chapter, we will explore specific strategies for integrating digital technologies and AI into KAM practices. We'll examine examples of organizations that have successfully navigated digital transformation, look at emerging trends in AI and their potential applications in KAM, and discuss the skills and mindsets that KAMgrs need to cultivate to thrive in this new digital landscape. We'll also address the ethical considerations surrounding using AI in business relationships, exploring ways to ensure transparency, maintain trust and use technology responsibly in managing key accounts. Additionally, we'll look at the future of KAM, considering how emerging technologies like blockchain, the Internet of Things (IoT) and augmented reality might further reshape the field.

The digital revolution in KAM is not just about adopting new tools or platforms but fundamentally rethinking how we create value for our most important clients in an increasingly connected and digitized world. It requires a shift in mindset, a willingness to embrace change, and a commitment to continuous learning and adaptation. As we explore technology and digitalization in KAM, remember that the goal is not to replace human interaction with digital alternatives but to enhance and augment our capabilities as KAMgrs. By embracing these technological advancements, you can become more efficient, insightful and, ultimately, a more valuable partner to your key accounts. We offer you some insights and reflections on three interrelated digital technology topics:

- Scoping and enhancing the benefits of using CRM systems
- Incorporating social selling into KAM processes
- Strengthening your practices with the use of AI and generative technologies

We now turn to each of these.

Harnessing the potential of CRM systems

In today's digital age, customer relationship management (CRM) systems have become indispensable tools in sales and for KAMgrs. These platforms serve as the technological backbone for managing complex, high-value client relationships, enabling KAMgrs to enhance customer communications by collecting, structuring and organizing relevant customer data, and in so doing, drive strategic decision-making. At its core, a CRM system acts as a centralized repository for all client-related data. For key account managers, this means having instant access to rich information about their most important customers. This can range from basic information such as contact details, interaction history, purchase records, service issues, to more nuanced insights such as preferences, strategic priorities and future requirements.[7] Such has been the explosion of CRM digital technologies that companies such as Vendor Neutral[8] help enterprises to identify, select, implement and integrate the most appropriate customer management technologies.

> Modern CRM systems with relationship-mapping capabilities can help track and analyse the strength and frequency of customer connections across different organizational levels. This systematic approach to relationship management, which I call 'multi-threading', has become crucial for success.
>
> Dr Beth Rogers

How CRM systems and processes can help KAM

ENHANCING COMMUNICATION AND COLLABORATION

Information systems are another pillar of successful KAM programmes because they facilitate intra- and inter-organizational knowledge management.[9] CRM systems facilitate communication, both with clients and within the organization. Many modern CRM platforms integrate various communication channels, including email, phone and even social media interactions. This integration allows KAMgrs to maintain a complete record of all client communications, ensuring that no important details are lost.[10] Furthermore, CRM systems enable better internal collaboration particularly in large organizations where multiple teams often interact with key accounts. CRM platforms allow seamless information sharing between sales, customer service, marketing and other departments. This collaborative approach ensures that all team members are aligned in their understanding of the client's needs and expectations.

KEY ACCOUNT PLANNING AND OPPORTUNITY MANAGEMENT

One of the most valuable aspects of CRM for key account managers is its support for strategic account planning. Advanced CRM systems often include features specifically designed for complex B2B relationships, allowing KAMgrs to map out account structures, identify key decision-makers and track long-term account development plans.

These systems also aid in opportunity management. KAMgrs can use CRM to track potential deals through various stages of the sales pipeline, forecast revenues and identify cross-selling or upselling opportunities. By providing a clear overview of all ongoing and potential deals within an account, CRM systems help KAMgrs prioritize their efforts and allocate resources more effectively.

DATA-DRIVEN DECISION-MAKING

In the era of big data, CRM systems have evolved to become powerful analytical tools (see the section on AI later in this chapter). They can aggregate and analyse vast amounts of customer data to uncover trends, predict future behaviour and identify potential risks or opportunities. For key account managers, this analytical capability is invaluable. It allows them to make data-driven decisions about account strategy, backed by concrete insights rather than gut feelings. For instance, a CRM system might reveal that a key account's purchasing patterns are changing, alerting the KAMgr to a potential shift in the client's business strategy or needs.

Challenges and best practice in embedding

While CRM systems offer numerous benefits, their implementation and effective use can present challenges. One common issue is user adoption.[11] KAMgrs and other team members may resist using the system if they perceive it as complicated or time-consuming. To address this, organizations need to invest in user-friendly CRM solutions and provide adequate training and support.

Data quality is another critical concern. The effectiveness of a CRM system is only as good as the data it contains. Key account managers must be diligent in keeping client information up-to-date and ensuring that all relevant interactions are logged in the system.

The building blocks of effective CRM in KAM are:

1 Regularly update and maintain client data (Update)

2 Utilize the system's analytical capabilities to inform account strategies (Analyse)

3 Leverage CRM insights to personalize client interactions (Personalize)

4 Use the system to facilitate internal collaboration and knowledge sharing (Collaborate)

5 Continuously learn about new CRM features and best practices (Refresh and Learn)

FIGURE 4.1 Building blocks of effective CRM in KAM

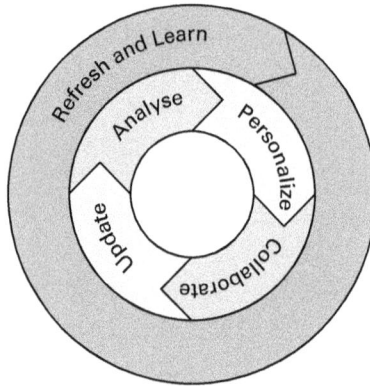

For key account managers, these advancements promise to further enhance their ability to manage complex client relationships. AI-powered CRMs might, for example, automatically suggest the next best action for an account based on historical data and current market trends.

However, while embracing these technological advancements, it's crucial for KAMgrs to remember that CRM systems are tools to augment, not replace, human relationship management skills. The most successful key account managers will be those who can effectively blend the analytical power of CRM with their own expertise, intuition and relationship-building abilities.

AI is enhancing the functionality of traditional CRM systems. As we will discuss in more detail later in this chapter, using AI, key account managers can now analyse vast amounts of data to identify patterns and trends, providing them with actionable insights about their clients' needs and preferences. This level of data-driven decision-making was once the realm of large corporations with substantial resources; now, it's becoming accessible to businesses of all sizes, levelling the playing field and raising the bar for the quality of customer engagement in key accounts from suppliers of all sizes.

In conclusion, CRM systems have become essential tools for key account managers, offering a wealth of benefits from centralized data management to strategic planning and analytics. As these systems continue to evolve, they will play an increasingly crucial role in helping KAMgrs navigate the complexities of managing high-value client relationships in the digital age.

Accelerating key account processes with social selling

Social selling is ubiquitous in B2C and in most transactional, high-volume sales operations, so you may be asking: is social selling also relevant if you are in a KAM role, involved in customer relationships with a discreet number of accounts often overseeing a small number of highly-complex, long sales cycle transactions? The answer is yes.

First, the decision to engage with a vendor is influenced by social media. Over the last decade 84 per cent of CEOs and VPs have been using social media to make purchasing decisions.[12] Secondly, according to a CMO Council study,[13] 9 out of 10 B2B buyers say online content has a moderate to major effect on purchasing decisions. Thus, in today's digital age, KAMgrs must consider the power of social media and online platforms as part of their customer engagement strategies. We argue that social selling has emerged as a critical skill for KAMgrs looking to build and maintain relationships with their most valuable clients. This section explores the concept of social selling, its importance for key account management, and strategies for effective use of social selling.

By *social selling* we refer to the use of social media platforms and digital tools to research, connect with, understand and engage potential and existing customers.[14] For key account managers, social selling is not about making direct sales pitches but rather about building and nurturing relationships, providing value and establishing thought leadership in their industry. A quick look at LinkedIn at the time of writing shows the degree of use of such professional social platforms by key account managers and strategic account managers alike.

In fact, according to LinkedIn,[15] 62 per cent of B2B buyers respond to salespeople who connect by sharing insights and over 90 per cent of them are willing to engage with sales professionals who have positioned them-

TABLE 4.1 Number of KAMgrs and SAMs active on LinkedIn

Geography	Key Account Manager	Strategic Account Manager
US & Canada	173,000	329,000
UK	83,000	33,000
Worldwide	1,600,000	366,000

selves as industry thought leaders.[16] Similarly, 87 per cent of sellers confirm that social selling has been effective for their business, according to HubSpot.[17]

> While some may question the relevance of key account managers in an increasingly digital world, I believe their role will become even more crucial. As we embrace digital tools and AI, the need for human judgment, insight and relationship-building skills will only increase.
>
> Dominique Côté

Social selling offers numerous benefits. However, KAMgrs must be aware of potential challenges such as the time investment required to ensure consistency and effectiveness. We have heard many KAMgrs highlighting the challenge of balancing online activities with other responsibilities. At the end of the day, you will want to maintain a high level of competence and represent your company and personal brand professionally in any online interaction. Also be mindful of privacy concerns and the need to respect clients' privacy and confidentiality, particularly when sharing sensitive information online.

Key platforms for social selling

We agree that social selling has its place in KAM but the question is which social media platforms to use? While numerous social media platforms exist, key account managers should focus their efforts on those most relevant to their industry and clients:

1   LinkedIn: As the world's largest professional network, LinkedIn is crucial for KAMgrs. It allows for professional networking, content sharing and direct engagement with decision-makers. This platform also offers in-depth profiles, group discussions and company pages. LinkedIn is well suited for building relationships, sharing industry insights, finding decision-makers and nurturing leads.

2   X (formerly Twitter): This platform enables real-time engagement and is adequate for sharing industry news, insights and participating in relevant industry conversations. It is well placed for quick interactions, monitoring trends, engaging with potential customers and building thought leadership.

FIGURE 4.2 Benefits and drawbacks of social media platforms

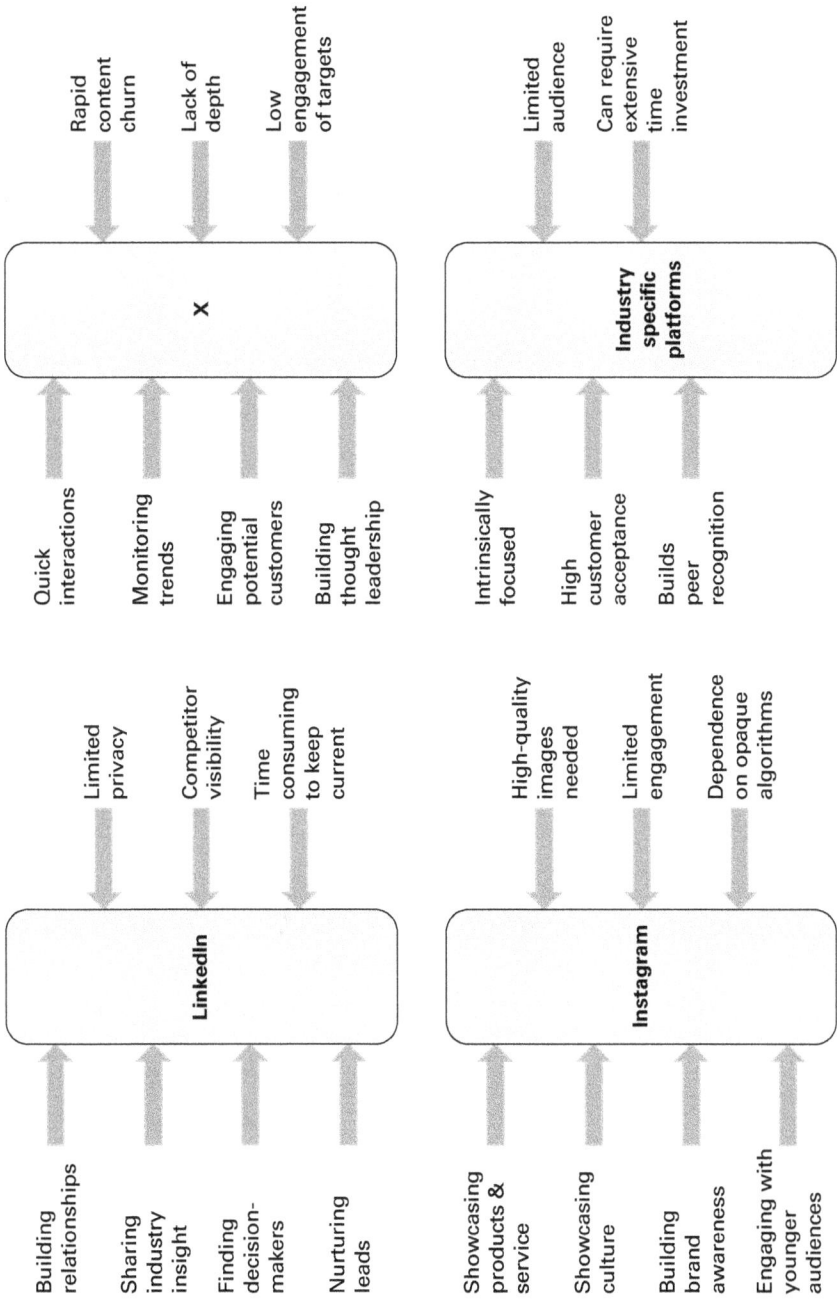

LinkedIn

Benefits:
- Building relationships
- Sharing industry insight
- Finding decision-makers
- Nurturing leads

Drawbacks:
- Limited privacy
- Competitor visibility
- Time consuming to keep current

X

Benefits:
- Quick interactions
- Monitoring trends
- Engaging potential customers
- Building thought leadership

Drawbacks:
- Rapid content churn
- Lack of depth
- Low engagement of targets

Instagram

Benefits:
- Showcasing products & service
- Showcasing culture
- Building brand awareness
- Engaging with younger audiences

Drawbacks:
- High-quality images needed
- Limited engagement
- Dependence on opaque algorithms

Industry specific platforms

Benefits:
- Intrinsically focused
- High customer acceptance
- Builds peer recognition

Drawbacks:
- Limited audience
- Can require extensive time investment

3   Instagram is great for showcasing products, services and company culture visually. It is well placed for building brand awareness, engaging with a younger audience and sharing behind-the-scenes content. It is recommended that high-quality images and videos are used.

4   Industry-specific platforms: Depending on the sector you are working in, platforms such as ResearchGate (for scientific and academic communities) or GitHub (for software development) can be valuable for specialized engagement. KAMgrs could also consider platforms such as Reddit and Quora for niche targeting.

ADOPTING SOCIAL SELLING

Embedding social media in the day-to-day tasks of a KAMgr can be an overwhelming task. Here, we offer you four tips for managing social selling effectively in your role:

1   *Optimize your professional profile*: A strong, complete profile is the foundation of social selling. On LinkedIn, for example, profiles with professional photos receive 14 times more views than those without, according to the platform itself. Thus, ensure your profile highlights your expertise, experience and the value you bring to clients. Personalize your approach when connecting with a potential customer, reviewing their profile and recent activity. Make reference to specific points and areas of interest in your outreach to demonstrate genuine interest, detailed preparation and professionalism.

2   *Listen and research*: You can use social media to establish and develop relationships but you should also use 'social listening' tools to monitor conversations about your industry, clients and competitors. This information can provide valuable insights for tailoring your approach to each key account.[18] For instance, your company can implement tools such as Hootsuite or Sprout Social to monitor mentions of your business, competitors and key industry terms. This will help the sales and marketing functions stay informed and engage in relevant conversations.

3   *Share valuable content*: The explosion of content in social media has meant that business customers and consumers alike have become more discerning about what they pay attention to. To establish yourself as a thought leader you should regularly share relevant, high-quality content. But how do you define high-quality content? This is typically industry news, insights and original content that addresses your customer's challenges, opportunities and priorities. Thus, an in-depth understanding

of your customer's priorities is needed to generate relevant, well-targeted content.

4 *Leverage the power of your organization's staff*: Encourage your colleagues to share and engage with your company content. Employee-shared content can receive eight times more engagement than content shared through brand channels.[19] Thus, you may need to lobby internally so your business supports social selling activities, encouraging you and your fellow KAMgrs to participate in content sharing, in customer engagement and in prospecting. In this respect, collaboration with marketing can hold the key to generating well-integrated, consistent, quality content. Working closely with your marketing colleagues to align your social selling efforts with broader company initiatives may have long-term payoffs.

REAL-WORLD EXAMPLE
IBM's social selling programme

IBM has been recognized as a leader in social selling, particularly in its approach to B2B and enterprise sales.[20,21] Some of the specific practices the company has implemented include:

1 Social selling programme: IBM launched a comprehensive social selling programme called 'Social Selling @ IBM'. This programme was designed to train and equip their sales force with the skills needed to leverage social media in their sales processes.

2 Training and certification: IBM developed a social selling curriculum and certification programme. Sales professionals go through training modules and must pass an exam to become certified in social selling. This ensures a consistent approach across the organization.

3 Content sharing: IBM encourages its sales professionals to share relevant content with their networks. They use a tool called Social Content Sharing, which allows employees to easily find and share pre-approved company content on their personal social media accounts.

4 LinkedIn Sales Navigator: IBM has widely adopted LinkedIn Sales Navigator for its sales force. This tool helps KAMgrs identify key decision-makers within target accounts and provides insights that can be used to personalize outreach.

5 Measuring Impact: IBM uses the Social Selling Index (SSI) on LinkedIn to measure the effectiveness of their social selling efforts.

6 Executive engagement: IBM encourages its executives to be active on social media, particularly when engaging with key accounts. This approach helps in building relationships at the highest levels of client organizations.

7 Integration with CRM: IBM integrates social selling tools with its CRM system, allowing sales professionals to track social interactions and insights alongside other customer data.

In conclusion, social selling has become an indispensable tool for key account managers in the digital age. By effectively leveraging social platforms, KAMgrs can build stronger relationships with clients, gain valuable insights and position themselves as trusted advisors. As with any strategy, success in social selling requires ongoing learning, adaptation and a commitment to providing value to your key accounts. By implementing the strategies and best practices outlined in this section, KAMgrs can enhance their digital presence, foster meaningful connections and drive significant business outcomes in an increasingly digital sales landscape.

Businesses can help KAMgrs to succeed in social selling by:

· Providing comprehensive training and support

· Encouraging the sharing of valuable, industry-specific content

· Focusing on building long-term relationships rather than immediate sales transactions

· Empowering KAMgrs to build personal brands aligned with company values

· Implementing social listening tools to identify key trends and engage with key decision-makers

· Measuring and optimizing their social selling efforts over time

Augmenting KAM with the use of AI and generative technologies

Artificial intelligence is revolutionizing sales and marketing across various industries, with recent studies showing that embracing AI can significantly boost a company's performance. Given that KAMgrs focus on building deep, strategic customer relationships, the integration of AI into KAM, in addition to other digital tools as we explored earlier, is not only appropriate but also highly beneficial.

AI's ability to analyse large datasets and predict customer behaviours can enhance the personalization and effectiveness of KAM strategies. In this section, we look at how AI could affect KAM, describing some applications as well as the associated benefits and risks. We focus on addressing the question of how AI can provide valuable insights, driving more informed decision-making and fostering stronger customer relationships.

> Lastly, I believe that the future of key account management will be increasingly influenced by technological advancements. Embracing digital tools and data analytics can provide key account managers with valuable insights and help them make more informed decisions. However, in my view, these tools should complement, not replace, the human elements of relationship building and strategic thinking that are at the core of effective key account management.
>
> Nicolaas Smit

Understanding what AI is, and what it's not

AI encompasses a broad range of computer capabilities that mimic human-like tasks. While ChatGPT's release brought AI into the spotlight, the technology has a long history and diverse applications. At its core, AI builds upon machine learning principles, where algorithms analyse data patterns to learn and adapt. Recent advancements in computing power have enabled more sophisticated 'deep learning' techniques, which use neural networks to process complex information and generate insights.

In the business world, AI's significance stems from its ability to provide comprehensive insights into customers, markets, operations and products/services. This empowers KAM teams with cutting-edge information to enhance their performance. For KAMgrs, AI offers numerous benefits, such as performance optimization. AI can streamline sales processes, predict customer behaviour, identify opportunities and improve forecasting accuracy. AI can reduce workload by automating repetitive tasks like meeting notes, emails and administrative duties, allowing KAMgrs to focus on high-value activities. As AI continues to evolve, its integration into KAM practices presents opportunities for increased efficiency, data-driven decision-making and improved work-life balance.

So, the most prominent question on your mind is likely to be, where do I start? Below, we will help you understand where, when and how you can implement AI into your role as a key account manager, as well as some of the risks you need to be cautious of.

Applications of AI in strategic account management

There are a number of tasks that you undertake in order to engage with your accounts and be successful. Some of these tasks are presented in Table 4.3 with some associated advantages and challenges.

First, AI can significantly enhance customer profiling processes. These profiles encompass a range of data, from demographics to behavioural insights. AI-driven profiling enables account managers to improve stakeholder segmentation and evaluate future business opportunities more effectively. For instance, Humantic AI profiles customers based on their digital footprint. As a KAMgr, you can use the resulting insights to judge those who may be early adopters of your solutions or become internal champions of your offerings. Additionally, AI-company AI Bees expands on the buyer profiles identified in the book *The Challenger Customer*,[22] giving the KAMgr critical insight into key stakeholder behaviours, i.e. blockers vs gatekeepers vs economic buyers.

TABLE 4.2 Summary of applications of AI in account management

Application	Advantages	Challenges
Profiling	Can accelerate the customer journey and enhance individual experiences.	Potential privacy concerns may lead some customers to avoid companies using AI-driven profiling.
Personalized account engagement	Tailored content can foster trust, boost interaction, and improve user experiences.	AI may sometimes misinterpret user preferences, resulting in poorly targeted or irrelevant personalized content.
Forecasting and predictive analytics	Helps project future customer revenues and identify non-converting deals.	AI models may struggle with unprecedented events or factors not present in training data, such as global crises.
Process optimization	Can automate mundane tasks like data input, email follow-ups and scheduling.	Implementing AI systems into existing account management workflows can be intricate and time-intensive.

(continued)

TABLE 4.2 (Continued)

Application	Advantages	Challenges
Performance analytics	AI-driven analytics enable real-time tracking of account management metrics, allowing quick responses to market or customer behaviour shifts.	Over-reliance on AI for performance analysis may diminish human oversight and critical thinking.
Account manager coaching	AI can evaluate individual performance data and offer customized feedback tailored to strengths and areas for improvement.	AI might misunderstand subtle aspects of client-supplier interactions, potentially offering inaccurate coaching advice.
Pricing optimization	Utilizes sophisticated techniques to determine optimal pricing strategies, considering various interacting factors.	Widespread adoption of AI in pricing could intensify competition, potentially leading to price wars and reduced profit margins.
Servicing the account	Capable of handling multiple customer queries simultaneously, delivering consistent service quality unaffected by human factors.	AI lacks emotional intelligence, which can be problematic for managing sensitive customer interactions or complex inquiries.
Negotiation	Advantages include enhanced data processing capabilities to analyse past negotiation patterns, real-time access to market intelligence to support decision-making, and consistent execution of negotiation strategies across multiple deals.	The inability of AI to fully comprehend complex human dynamics and relationship nuances critical in B2B negotiations, potential overreliance on historical data that may not reflect current market conditions, and difficulties in handling unexpected situations that require creative problem-solving

In account management, AI offers promising applications for personalized engagement. Accurate stakeholder profiling is crucial for tailoring content to build trust, enhance engagement and improve individual experiences. AI tools like Pathfactory can engage each buyer type and stakeholder with content that enhances their experience and propels the buyer journey forward.

Forecasting and predictive analytics represent another established AI application. KAMgrs often struggle to estimate the proportion of pipeline deals that will not convert, especially in complex scenarios involving global accounts, multiple products or highly dynamic environments. AI can significantly improve the accuracy of these predictions.

Research conducted by Matt Dixon and Ted McKenna for their book *The JOLT Effect* revealed that 40–60 per cent of deals today end in 'No decision', highlighting the importance of accurate forecasting.[23]

One of the primary advantages of AI in revenue forecasting is its ability to improve prediction accuracy by leveraging more data sources, employing sophisticated models and providing dynamic updates. AI can integrate data from various sources, including CRM systems, enterprise resource planning (ERP) software, social media, web analytics and external market data. This integration creates a comprehensive view of the sales situation, as demonstrated by platforms such as Salesforce's Einstein AI.

A related area – process optimization – is being redefined by the application of AI in large-volume sales operations. The ability to craft and direct content to your key customers is now enabled by AI. For instance, the company Lavender AI has developed an innovative email coach. This service assists account managers in real time to write better emails faster, thus helping them get more positive responses. In B2B sales, companies such as Qvidian, Proposify and Better Proposals provide solutions to optimize proposal creation. By using prebuilt templates and machine learning algorithms, they automate the process of creating personalized proposals, saving account managers valuable time.

The world of performance analytics, however, is in a state of flux. Peter Kerr, a leading sales management academic in Canada, showed how organizations need to combine both subjective and objective performance measures to better capture salesperson performance.[24] AI-powered tools such as Chorus can help account teams capture and analyse calls, meetings and emails to create more visibility, enhance account management processes and enable behavioural change. This technology helps better combine leading and lagging indicators of performance, which has fundamental implications for resource allocation, quota setting and compensation.

With better insights into how and why account managers perform differently against different indications (or otherwise), coaching can be provided to better suit the needs of specific account managers. Again, AI has a role in this. For instance, Spiky AI can be used to gain insights, identify areas of improvement and enhance the effectiveness of customer meetings. Indeed, Dixon and McKenna used such technology to analyse 8,300 sales engagements, build a model and test it against 2.3 million recorded calls.[25] This would not have been possible without AI tools to analyse the effectiveness of the engagements. Likewise, the in-depth AI sales coaching tool Dialpad can unleash a personal coach sidekick for every seller, instantly providing real-time sales recommendations and built-in speech coaching. These functions ensure that reps are armed with an answer at all times and that the conversational cadence has a natural flow.

We all know the substantial, direct impact of price on a company's profitability. Often, the question for account managers is: how to optimize and ensure that the maximum price increases can be implemented without risking losing customer business? Companies like Bubo AI offer pricing optimization tools, so suppliers can fine-tune their pricing strategies and maximize profit margins by applying targeted pricing tactics.

> Warren Buffett said that a company's ability to increase prices without driving customers to competitors is the most crucial factor in determining its business strength. When a business can raise prices while maintaining its customer base, it demonstrates exceptional market position.[26]

Key account managers invest a significant amount of time in meetings to service their accounts, and in so doing, they coordinate, align and orchestrate relationships. Most of these are, in theory, linked to the implementation of strategic account plans. We know how challenging seamless implementation of these plans is. Tools like MeetGeek automatically record video meetings, transcribe, summarize and share key insights from these meetings. This enables more accurate and speedier follow-up of actions facilitating the execution of strategic account plans. Also, large-volume customer operations can be challenging. AI can facilitate providing cost-effective, 24/7 service, ensuring consistency and speedy responses.

Lastly, AI has been used in supplier-customer negotiations in several ways. In preparation and analysis, using AI systems to analyse historical negotiation data and market conditions helps negotiators better prepare their negotiation positions. This includes identifying optimal starting points and predicting likely counteroffers.

AI has also been introduced as a decision support system to provide real-time recommendations during negotiations by processing large amounts of data about similar past deals, market conditions and available alternatives.

Some large retailers such as Walmart[27] have started to automate negotiations, for simple, standardized transactions with some suppliers. Also, AI systems have been used to conduct basic negotiations in e-commerce and digital procurement platforms. These typically involve straightforward price negotiations within predefined parameters.

However, there are important limitations to note when using AI in supplier-customer negotiations. A key one is the fact that complex negotiations still heavily rely on human judgment and relationship management and, therefore, there are concerns about transparency and accountability when AI systems are involved in negotiations.

Benefits and risks of AI in sales

Looking at the wide-ranging applications of AI outlined above, one could be tempted to focus on its benefits. These are being increasingly realized by companies, but there are also risks we would like to highlight.

The gradual implementation of AI technologies will change some of the dimensions of the roles of strategic account managers. The implementation of AI will enable these roles to improve upon the areas outlined above. However, there are several risks to AI implementation:

Overreliance on AI itself: These technologies are very limited when human judgment and intuition are required to perform a task and obtain an outcome. AI should be seen as a tool to assist sales professionals rather than a complete replacement for human decision-making.

Data bias: AI algorithms are only as good as the data they are trained on. If the training data contains biases or inaccuracies, is limited in scope or highly context-specific, the AI system may produce biased recommendations or predictions. This can have unintended consequences for people and organizations. For instance, incorrect use of performance data may result in unfair treatment of customers or staff, suboptimal allocation of resources, and flawed decisions.[28]

AI systems can also have dysfunctional effects that may not be immediately apparent: For example, automated account management processes driven by AI could result in flawed interactions with customers, particularly if they do not adequately address individual customer needs or preferences. Also, we believe that when AI tools are utilized, unless highly detailed input is used, the results could lead to standardized insights and responses (i.e. everyone is bringing the same thing to the table), which can be problematic and compromise differentiation.

Lack of transparency: Some AI algorithms, such as deep learning neural networks, can be complex and difficult to interpret for non-specialists. This lack of transparency can make it challenging to understand how AI arrives at its decisions. Those leading account management functions may face difficulties in justifying or explaining the rationale behind AI-generated recommendations. Likewise, they may struggle to get buy-in from account managers if they do not trust AI tools.

AI has triggered privacy and security concerns linked to the ethical matters: AI systems in sales often rely on collecting and utilizing large amounts of customer data. The improper handling of sensitive customer information can lead to privacy breaches and security vulnerabilities. Organizations must ensure they have robust security measures in place to protect customer data.

Ethical matters that sales leaders need to consider: AI systems in sales must adhere to ethical guidelines to avoid unethical practices or manipulation. For instance, using AI to manipulate customers' emotions or preferences in a deceptive manner could harm customer trust and brand reputation. AI-enabled customer management tools very rarely consider the emotional state of the person interacting with it. Accordingly, it cannot appropriately adapt itself.

Overall, the advantages of AI technologies can be constrained by some of its limitations. In particular, the 'approaches that work' in strategic sales and account management are context-specific, and, thus, require laser focus and precision – characteristics that some AI technologies are currently lacking.

AI in strategic account management: 'for' and 'against' considerations

Professor Ethan Mollick, author of *One Useful Thing*, the useful Substack that translates his academic research on AI and business into practical learnings,[29] claims that 'general purpose technologies are these rare events like steam power, the computer, or electrification, or maybe the internet, where a new technology comes along that touches everything'.

The integration of AI into strategic account management is poised to enhance rather than replace the role of KAMgrs. While AI will influence numerous aspects of the field, it will not fundamentally alter its core principles. Instead, KAMgrs will likely specialize in areas where AI's capabilities are limited, leveraging technology to identify and nurture crucial customer relationships.

By utilizing AI-powered tools such as Crystal Knows for automated profiling, KAMgrs will gain deeper insights into their key contacts. This enhanced understanding will enable them to tailor their approaches more effectively and conduct more productive meetings and client interactions. The unique value of KAMgrs will continue to lie in their ability to act as knowledge brokers, addressing complex and unique challenges that require human intuition and creativity – areas where AI, bound by rules and patterns, may fall short.

The rapid advancement of AI, coupled with the expanding Internet of Things (IoT), is accelerating technological change at an unprecedented rate. This progression simulates human capabilities and offers alternatives to traditional human involvement in various tasks. Futurist Gerd Leonhard raises pertinent questions about our readiness for such exponential change, asserting that conventional business models are no longer viable. He argues that technological progress has levelled the playing field in terms of business excellence, leaving a singular space for innovation in strategic account management: the strategic account managers themselves.

In this evolving landscape, the strategic use of technology will free up valuable time for KAMgrs, allowing them to focus on enhancing the experience they deliver to their accounts. This human-centric approach, augmented by AI, is likely to emerge as a significant source of competitive advantage in the field of strategic account management.

> While we can automate many aspects of our work, I believe there's no substitute for the human touch, particularly when it comes to understanding and responding to customer feedback.
>
> Stuart Blakeley

Jeff Jarvis, a professor at the Craig Newmark Graduate School of Journalism in New York and author of *The Gutenberg Parenthesis*, advocates for the inevitable ascendancy of the internet and AI. The book's title references a theory proposed by Lars Ole Sauerberg and Thomas Petite from the University of Southern Denmark, suggesting that the internet is superseding the print era. This theory posits that the print era, which began in 1455 with the first printed Bible, was an interruption in the traditional methods of knowledge creation and transfer. For millennia before this, information was primarily created and shared orally. The internet, along with its technological advancements and AI, is now steering humanity back towards this more fluid form of information exchange.[30]

TABLE 4.3 Ten practical actions that you can implement to improve performance in
a KAM role

	Action	Description
1.	Embrace Digital Tools and AI	Leverage AI-powered tools for data collection, customer engagement and sales forecasting to automate routine tasks and focus on strategic planning.
2.	Increase Frequency of Client Touchpoints	Schedule more frequent, shorter virtual meetings with clients to maintain engagement without extensive travel.
3.	Broaden Stakeholder Involvement	Include a wider range of stakeholders in virtual meetings to foster comprehensive discussions and expedite decision-making.
4.	Utilize CRM Systems	Implement a robust CRM system to centralize client data, track interactions, and manage opportunities effectively.
5.	Adopt Social Selling	Use social media platforms like LinkedIn to connect with clients, share insights and establish thought leadership in your industry.
6.	Personalize Client Interactions	Tailor communications based on insights from CRM and social media to enhance client relationships and satisfaction.
7.	Enhance Internal Collaboration	Share client insights and updates across departments to ensure all team members are aligned in understanding client needs and expectations.
8.	Regularly Update Client Data	Keep client information in the CRM system current by regularly reviewing and updating contact details and interaction history.
9.	Leverage Analytical Capabilities	Use CRM's analytical tools to uncover trends and predict future behaviour, informing account strategies with data-driven insights.
10.	Optimize Professional Profiles	Ensure your LinkedIn and other professional profiles are complete and highlight your expertise, experience, and the value you bring to clients.

In practical terms, AI is accelerating the ability of machines to communicate in human-like ways and is gradually removing human intervention from various processes, including many currently performed by salespeople. This shift mirrors the profound impact that the invention of the printing press had on society, leading to widespread literacy. In a similar vein, we might speculate whether AI will usher in an era of widespread customer centricity and value creation.

FIGURE 4.3 Key drivers, tools, behaviours and success factors for embracing technology and digitalization

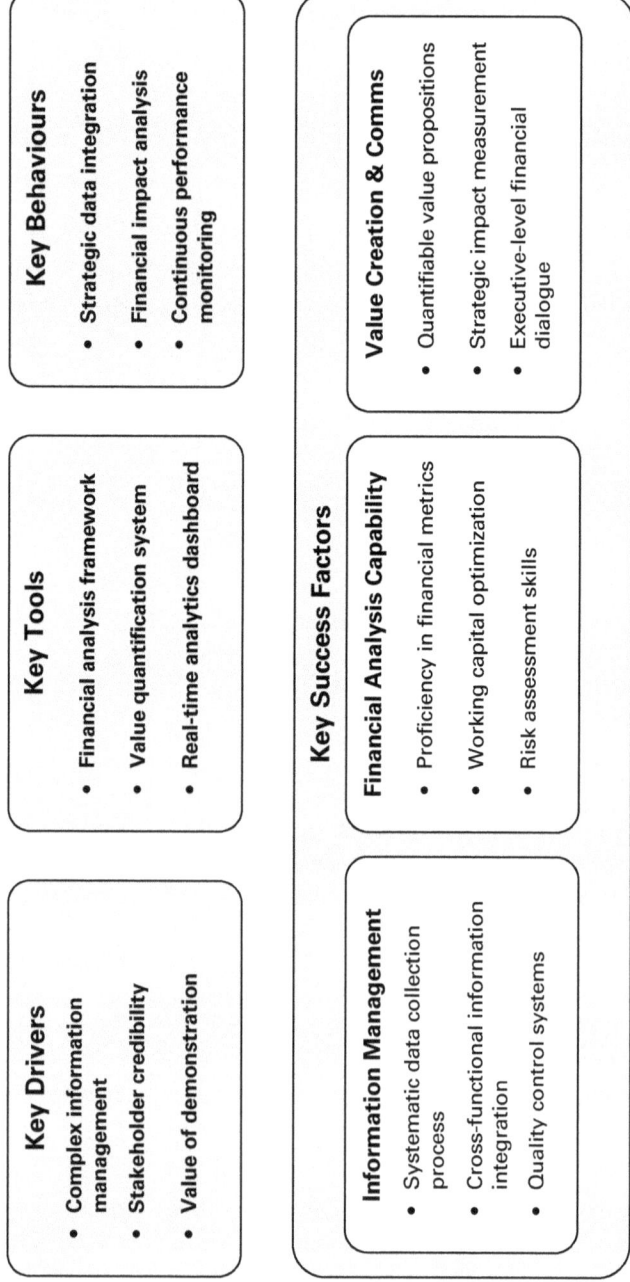

Key Drivers

- Complex information management
- Stakeholder credibility
- Value of demonstration

Key Tools

- Financial analysis framework
- Value quantification system
- Real-time analytics dashboard

Key Behaviours

- Strategic data integration
- Financial impact analysis
- Continuous performance monitoring

Key Success Factors

Information Management

- Systematic data collection process
- Cross-functional information integration
- Quality control systems

Financial Analysis Capability

- Proficiency in financial metrics
- Working capital optimization
- Risk assessment skills

Value Creation & Comms

- Quantifiable value propositions
- Strategic impact measurement
- Executive-level financial dialogue

Summary and recommendations for KAMgrs

Embracing technology and digitalization

A key point of discussion surrounding AI is its potential impact on job displacement. However, our perspective is that AI will not render the KAMgr obsolete. Instead, we anticipate a scenario where KAMgrs who possess knowledge and proficiency in AI will have a significant advantage over those who do not. This suggests that the future of strategic account management lies not in resisting AI, but in embracing and leveraging it to enhance professional capabilities and deliver superior value to clients.

Table 4.3 shows 10 practical actions that you can implement to improve performance in a KAM role.

Figure 4.3 shows the key drivers, tools, behaviours and success factors for embracing technology and digitalization.

Notes

1 M Pourmasoudi, M Ahearne, Z Hall, Z and P Krishnamurthy. The impact of the information revolution on the classical sales model, *Journal of Personal Selling and Sales Management*, 2022, 42 (2), 193–208

2 S Verma, R Sharma, S Deb and D Maitra. Artificial intelligence in marketing: Systematic review and future research direction, *International Journal of Information Management Data Insights*, 2021, 1 (1), 1–8

3 ColdIQ, The best AI sales tools, www.coldiq.com/ai-sales-tools (archived at https://perma.cc/9687-72KJ)

4 R M Peterson, D Rangarajan, H Dover and C Gordon. Artificial intelligence tsunami hits sales, GSSI, Toronto, 7–10 June 2023

5 McKinsey. The economic potential of Generative AI – The next productivity frontier, June 2023

6 B B Hengstebeck, R Kassemeier and J Wieseke. What comprises a successful key account manager? Differences in the drivers of sales performance between key account managers and regular salespeople, *Industrial Marketing Management*, 2022, 106, 392–404

7 F Buttle and S Maklan (2019) *Customer Relationship Management: Concepts and Technologies*, Routledge

8 Vendor Neutral. Precision tech integration, https://vendorneutral.com/sales-technology-consulting/sales-technology-selection-strategy/ (archived at https://perma.cc/Z8KW-VDPB)

9 D Zupancic and M Müllner. International key account management in manufacturing companies: An exploratory approach of situative differentiation, *Journal of Business-to-Business Marketing*, 2008, 15 (4), 455–75

10 A Payne and P Frow. A strategic framework for customer relationship management, *Journal of Marketing*, 2005, 69 (4), 167–76

11 F Cruz-Jesus, A Pinheiro and T Oliveira. Understanding CRM adoption stages: Empirical analysis building on the TOE framework, *Computers in Industry*, 2019, 109, 1–1

12 IDC. New IDC study reveals that the most senior and influential B2B buyers use online social networks in their purchase process, 15 September 2014, www.businesswire.com/news/home/20140915006303/en/New-IDC-Study-Reveals-That-the-Most-Senior-and-Influential-B2B-Buyers-Use-Online-Social-Networks-in-Their-Purchase-Process

13 CMO Council. BtoB content impacts customer thinking & buying decisions, www.cmocouncil.org/thought-leadership/reports/btob-content-impacts-customer-thinking--buying-decisions (archived at https://perma.cc/ZAE7-MRWJ)

14 S Belew (2014) *The Art of Social Selling: Finding and engaging customers on Twitter, Facebook, LinkedIn, and other social networks*, Amacom

15 P Simone. SALESIFICATION with LinkedIn, 4 January 2022, www.linkedin.com/pulse/top-22-reasons-social-selling-patrick-simone/ (archived at https://perma.cc/HNS6-CXXQ)

16 SlideShare. Establish your professional brand, www.slideshare.net/slideshow/establish-your-professional-brand/52913038 (archived at https://perma.cc/Q9QX-J5UC)

17 L Alfred. HubSpot, updated 18 March 2024, https://blog.hubspot.com/sales/social-selling-stats#:~:text=Of%20sales%20professionals%2C%2055%25%20harness,effective%20platform%20for%20this%20purpose (archived at https://perma.cc/3XS8-A74K)

18 O S Itani, R Agnihotri and R Dingus, R. Social media use in B2B sales and its impact on competitive intelligence collection and adaptive selling: Examining the role of learning orientation as an enabler, *Industrial Marketing Management*, 2017, 66, 64–79

19 S Sagar. Your employees are your best brand advocates, Forbes, 18 January 2022, www.forbes.com/sites/sprinklr/2022/01/18/your-employees-are-your-best-brand-advocates/ (archived at https://perma.cc/XYW9-YJH5)

20 B Umbenhauer (2017) *The Sales Revolution: How the digital revolution is changing the sales landscape*, Deloitte

21 N Schaffer (2014) *Social Selling Mastery: Scaling up your sales and marketing machine for the digital buyer*, McGraw-Hill Education

22 B Adamson, M Dixon, P Spenner and N Toman (2015) *The Challenger Customer: Selling to the hidden influencer who can multiply your results*, Portfolio

23 M Dixon and T McKenna (2022) *The JOLT Effect; How high performers overcome customer indecision*, Penguin Portfolio

24 P D Kerr and J Marcos-Cuevas. The interplay between objective and subjective measures of salesperson performance: Towards an integrated approach, *Journal of Personal Selling & Sales Management*, 2022, 42 (3), 225–42

25 Dixon and McKenna. *The JOLT Effect*

26 A Frye and D Campbell. Buffett says pricing power more important than good management, Bloomberg, 18 February 2011, www.bloomberg.com/news/articles/2011-02-18/buffett-says-pricing-power-more-important-than-good-management?embedded-checkout=true (archived at https://perma.cc/47TY-ZSR9)

27 R Van Hoek, M DeWitt, M Lacity and T Johnson. How Walmart automated supplier negotiations, HBR, 8 November 2022, https://hbr.org/2022/11/how-walmart-automated-supplier-negotiations (archived at https://perma.cc/2W24-2PRF)

28 M Franco-Santos and D Otley. Reviewing and theorizing the unintended consequences of performance management systems, *International Journal of Management Reviews*, 2018, 20 (3), 696–730

29 E Mollick. Wharton Professor Ethan Mollick on the urgency of getting in front of AI, WorkLab Podcast, 29 June 2023, www.microsoft.com/en-us/worklab/podcast/wharton-professor-ethan-mollick-on-the-urgency-of-getting-in-front-of-ai (archived at https://perma.cc/38F6-ZHS8)

30 J Jarvis (2024) *Gutenberg Parenthesis: The age of print and its lessons for the age of the internet*, Bloomsbury

Stuart Blakeley

As a global key account consultant at Grundfos, my role encompasses two main responsibilities. First, I manage a small number of globally operating key accounts, overseeing the business we have with local key account managers and sales account managers in different regions and countries. Secondly, I've been tasked with researching key account management as a discipline and setting up an internal framework to support our colleagues across different regions in upskilling their key account management practices.

In my view, one of the critical challenges in key account management at Grundfos is differentiating between sales account managers and key account managers. Many of our colleagues carry the title of key account manager but are responsible for 30–50 accounts. This raises the question of whether all these accounts are truly 'key' and whether we can provide the same level of service to such a large number.

From my perspective, the main measurements for key account performance are primarily sales-related, focusing on turnover. However, measuring end-to-end profitability can be challenging, especially when dealing with wholesalers. We also use various other metrics, such as the frequency of customer visits, quotation hit rates and online service usage.

In my opinion, there's a significant need to review how we measure key account manager performance, especially in light of advancing technologies. While we can automate many aspects of our work, I believe there's no substitute for the human touch, particularly when it comes to understanding and responding to customer feedback.

When it comes to the capabilities of key account managers, I find that developing lasting relationships and building trust are fundamental. In my experience, customers want to work with us when they trust us and feel valued. Understanding our customers deeply is crucial – not just their immediate needs, but their overall business structure, challenges and goals.

I believe that asking questions and developing empathy are critical skills for key account managers. It's not just about communicating with the customer, but also ensuring internal alignment across different functions within our organization. We use tools like Viva Engage to share updates and foster dialogue both internally and with customers.

In terms of creating psychological safety, Grundfos has a strong culture of transparency and openness. We encourage our employees to speak freely about challenges, both internally and with customers. This culture is supported by our company values and various mechanisms like employee resource groups and a works council.

Adaptability, in my view, is more crucial than ever in today's rapidly changing business environment. Our customers, particularly procurement teams, are becoming more sophisticated in their systems and expectations. To stay competitive, we need to continually innovate not just in our products, but in how we interact with and provide value to our customers.

One aspect I find particularly important is balancing experience with fresh perspectives. We have a resource group called 'Future at Grundfos' aimed at employees under 35, which helps bring new ideas into the organization and challenges the 'this is how we've always done it' mentality.

In conclusion, I believe that the key to high-performing key account management lies in providing the right tools and support for our managers, recognizing their individual strengths and areas for development. It's about elevating what we already do well to the next level, whether that's gently introducing new technologies to those who are less tech-savvy or finding ways to support our increasingly remote workforce.

The Covid-19 pandemic has changed how we interact with customers, with many now working from home or in hybrid arrangements. In response, we've developed programmes such as virtual selling and value-based selling to upskill our sales teams.

Finally, I think it's crucial to foster a sense of community among our key account managers. By building internal networks and sharing best practices, we're enabling our managers to support each other and learn from experiences across different countries and accounts.

In essence, high-performing key account management is about continuous learning, adaptability and strong relationship-building skills, all underpinned by the right organizational support and tools. It's a challenging role, but one that's critical to our success in today's complex business environment.

Stuart has almost 25 years of service at Grundfos, where he has worked in several leadership roles. He has been responsible for the strategic management of the UK Fire business. This includes developing existing companies through innovations, product solutions and services and identifying new business opportunities. He is currently at the heart of the company's key account management programme, where he coaches the key account teams to higher customer centricity and engagement.

With a BA in Business Management and a diploma in Management, Stuart has combined theory and practice to formulate views and models that impact the relationships between key suppliers and their customers. He now coaches others in best practice techniques and models that can positively impact business outcomes for both parties.

www.linkedin.com/in/stuart-blakeley

PART TWO

Inter-organizational capabilities

05

Developing lasting relationships

*Building and developing successful
long-term relationships with key accounts*

Overview

In the dynamic and competitive landscape of key account management, cultivating lasting relationships with key accounts is a cornerstone of sustainable success. This chapter explores how enduring customer relationships can elevate organizational performance through financial stability, competitive differentiation and innovative co-creation. By shifting from transactional to strategic, long-term partnerships, companies can navigate complexities, mitigate risks and achieve mutual growth.

Long-term customer relationships stabilize revenue streams and reduce costs associated with acquiring new clients. Established partnerships foster recurring purchases and create opportunities for cross-selling and upselling. Additionally, the efficiency gained in understanding client needs and optimizing service delivery enhances profitability while minimizing risks during uncertain times.

Strong, trust-based connections with key accounts serve as barriers to competition. Such relationships are not only difficult to replicate but also provide a strategic edge through privileged insights and co-created innovations. These advantages solidify customer loyalty and elevate a supplier's industry reputation. Furthermore, lasting relationships enable suppliers and customers to innovate together, addressing unique challenges with tailored solutions. These partnerships foster shared knowledge, co-development projects and mutual investments, leading to reduced time-to-market and enhanced competitiveness. As we delve deeper into this chapter, practical tools and strategies for building these relationships are outlined.

Why is developing lasting customer relationships crucial in key account management?

In the dynamic landscape of modern business, the significance of developing and nurturing lasting customer relationships cannot be overstated, particularly within the realm of KAM. As organizations navigate increasingly competitive markets and face the challenges of globalization, the ability to forge strong, enduring connections with key customers has emerged as a critical factor in achieving sustainable success. This chapter delves into the multifaceted importance of cultivating lasting customer relationships, exploring the profound impact these relationships have on organizational performance, customer loyalty and long-term business growth.

The business environment is characterized by rapid technological advancements, shifting consumer expectations and intensifying global competition. In this context, traditional transactional approaches to customer interactions have become increasingly inadequate. Key account management, with its focus on strategic, long-term relationships with a company's most valuable customers, has emerged as a crucial strategy for navigating this complex terrain.

A stated by Pamela Rucker,[1] an experienced consultant and instructor at executive programmes in Harvard University: 'It's essential for organizations to establish strategic business relationships because no company will be able to get all their customer's needs met alone in this era.'

Developing lasting customer relationships is not merely a tactical consideration but a strategic imperative, which is associated with a range of positive outcomes for organizations. These include financial performance, competitive advantage, and innovation and co-creation.

Financial performance

The financial benefits of sustaining long-term relationships with key accounts are multifaceted and strategically significant. These relationships create a robust financial ecosystem that extends well beyond traditional transactional interactions. By fostering lasting customer relationships, companies can secure a more stable revenue stream and improve their profitability and shareholder value. Some of the main mechanisms by which this happens are the following:

- **Revenue stability and predictability:** Long-term customer relationships transform revenue from volatile, unpredictable streams into more stable, forecastable income. When key accounts develop deep, trust-based partnerships with suppliers, they tend to commit to recurring purchases, engage in longer-term contracts and demonstrate higher resistance to competitive offerings. This stability is particularly crucial in turbulent economic environments, offering organizations a financial buffer against market fluctuations and economic uncertainties.

- **Cost efficiency in customer management:** In KAM, the learning that happens by building long-term relationships with customers allows supplier companies to reduce their spending pre-purchase activities, such as prospecting, promoting the brand, understanding customer needs and developing value propositions. Likewise, post-purchase activities such as service delivery, implementation monitoring, as well as training and advising, become more efficient. Additionally, strong relationships significantly mitigate customer attrition, which prevents financial burdens in researching, assessing, contacting, interacting, further engaging and so on.

- **Expanded revenue through cross-selling and upselling:** Established, trust-based relationships create fertile ground for introducing complementary products and services, expanding the scope of existing contracts, developing tailored solutions that meet evolving customer needs and co-creating business opportunities for both companies. Consequently, suppliers can increase financial performance through increased key accounts' wallet share.

- **Risk mitigation:** In times of economic uncertainty or market volatility, strong customer relationships can act as a buffer, based on trust, providing stability and resilience to organizations. Diversified, long-term relationships with key accounts reduce dependency on single revenue sources, create organizational resilience against market disruptions and enable more agile strategic responses to changing business environments.

Competitive advantage

In markets where products or services may be easily replicated, the quality and depth of customer relationships and key account managers' capabilities in pursuing this can serve as an important differentiator. Strong relationships create barriers to entry for competitors and can provide a sustainable competitive advantage.

- **Relational barriers to entry**: Deep customer relationships represent a sophisticated form of competitive protection. First, emotional and trust-based connections are not easily replicated. Second, accumulated institutional knowledge about a client's unique needs creates a complex relational ecosystem. Finally, long-term partnerships develop intricate, customized solutions that are inherently difficult for competitors to understand or reproduce.

- **Switching cost dynamics**: Strong customer relationships dramatically increase the perceived and actual costs of changing suppliers, as clients become deeply integrated with the organization's processes, systems and people. Also, transition risks and potential disruptions create a natural resistance to change, and accumulated relationship capital represents a significant psychological and operational barrier.

- **Information and insight advantage**: Sustained key account relationships provide organizations with deeper understanding of client ecosystems, privileged insights into future strategic directions, the ability to anticipate and proactively address emerging client needs and opportunities to co-create innovative solutions that pre-empt competitive threats.

- **Reputation and network effects**: Long-term relationships with strategic customers generate powerful network-driven competitive advantages. Satisfied key accounts become brand ambassadors, reference stories and testimonials carry significant credibility, and therefore industry reputation becomes a self-reinforcing competitive mechanism.

Innovation and co-creation

In the contemporary business landscape, innovation is no longer a siloed organizational function but a collaborative, interactive process that emerges from deep, meaningful customer relationships. Key account managers are pivotal in transforming traditional vendor-client interactions into dynamic innovation ecosystems. Lasting customer relationships facilitate a deeper understanding of customer needs and challenges. This intimate knowledge can drive innovation, leading to the co-creation of value and the development of tailored solutions that address specific customer pain points.

- **Collaborative knowledge generation**: Long-term relationships create unique knowledge-sharing environments that enable mutual understanding of complex business challenges, transparent exchange of strategic insights, breaking down traditional organizational boundaries and creating shared cognitive frameworks for problem-solving.

- **Structured co-creation mechanisms**: Sustained customer relationships facilitate joint innovation workshops, integrated research and development initiatives, collaborative design thinking sessions, shared technology exploration platforms and cross-organizational innovation teams.

- **Technological and operational synergies**: Deep supplier-customer relationships enable the integration of complementary technological capabilities, the alignment of operational ecosystems, the creation of interoperable solutions and the development of industry-specific innovation frameworks.

- **Successful innovations**: Innovation through customer relationships can accomplish reduced time-to-market for new solutions, lower development costs, higher probability of market acceptance, enhanced competitive positioning and improved return on innovation investments.

In conclusion, the development of lasting customer relationships stands as a cornerstone of successful KAM in the modern business landscape. The multifaceted benefits of strong, enduring customer relationships – from enhanced financial performance and increased loyalty to fostering innovation and creating competitive advantage – underscore their critical importance. By understanding why lasting customer relationships are so crucial, what constitutes their development and how to cultivate them effectively, key account managers (KAMgrs) and organizations can position themselves for sustained success in an increasingly complex and competitive global marketplace.

As we delve deeper into this chapter, we will explore the specific elements and stages involved in developing these relationships, from initial transactional to mature relational collaborative partnerships. We will then turn our attention to best practices in achieving and maintaining these valuable relationships, drawing on both theoretical frameworks and practical insights from the field.

The following box provides a summary of the main points that justify developing lasting relationships with key accounts.

WHY DEVELOPING LASTING RELATIONSHIPS WITH KEY ACCOUNTS IS IMPORTANT

Financial performance:

- Revenue stability and predictability
- Cost efficiency in customer management
- Expanded revenue through cross-selling and upselling
- Risk mitigation

Competitive advantage:

- Relational barriers to entry
- Switching cost dynamics
- Information and insight advantage
- Reputation and network effects

Innovation and co-creation:

- Collaborative knowledge generation
- Structured co-creation mechanisms
- Technological and operational synergies
- Successful innovations

Types of relationships with key accounts

For most companies, developing long-term customer relationships is critical to effective KAM. Admittedly, suppliers may have key accounts with a transactional approach to business (e.g. based on specific opportunities to win a big deal or contract). However, the greatest potential for strategic KAM lies in developing long-term relationships with customers. The continuity of a supplier-customer relationship tends to yield positive results in terms of revenue, profitability, market knowledge and new business opportunities.

In business-to-business, suppliers and customers can have different types of relationships based on two dimensions:[2]

- **Dependency/power situation:** This refers to the degree of dependency each party (supplier and customer) has in a business relationship and is primarily determined by the degree of power each party has. A typical measure of power is the degree of concentration of each party's business. For example, a retailer may be in a powerful situation if its purchases from a particular supplier represent a small portion of its total purchases, but a large portion of the supplier's sales. This would be a case of power imbalance. On the other hand, if both the customer (the retailer in this example) and the supplier have a similar degree of dependence on the other party, we consider this to be a balanced power situation. Additional elements could influence the dependency situation in supplier-customer relationships, such as access to strategic market/industry information, a leading position in the use of new technologies, access to specific customer segments, etc.

- **Transactional versus relational:** This is really a continuum, as there are many possible degrees of 'relationalism' in a supplier-customer relationship. At one extreme, the two companies may have a purely transactional relationship, where they exchange products and services and seek a payoff in each transaction. Other relationships evolve into long-term collaborative exchanges in which relational norms are established, and complex supplier-customer roles emerge. In a relational exchange, the two parties are willing to cooperate and commit to an ongoing relationship over time.

Figure 5.1 illustrates these two dimensions with the resulting types of supplier-customer relationships for different levels of dependency/power and transactional vs relational situations. The first dimension (x-axis) goes from 'supplier dependency' to 'customer dependency' and the middle section is ''mutual dependency' with a balanced power between the supplier and the customer. The second dimension (y-axis) goes from 'discrete transactions' to 'relational exchanges' with different combinations of transactional and relational components. The following types of supplier-customer relationships are identified:

- **Vulnerable supplier.** The supplier is in a high dependency position relative to the customer, and they have a transactional approach to their business relationship. The customer has the option to use this higher power to gain some benefits whilst reducing the supplier's benefits.

- **Vulnerable customer.** The customer is in a high dependency position relative to the supplier, and they have a transactional approach to their business relationship. The supplier has the option to use this higher power to gain some benefits whilst reducing those of the customer.

- **Inviting customer.** The supplier is in a high dependency position relative to the customer, and they have a relational approach to their business relationship. The customer is willing to collaborate with the supplier despite having a more powerful position.

- **Inviting supplier.** The customer is in a high dependency position relative to the supplier, and they have a relational approach to their business relationship. The supplier is willing to collaborate with the customer despite having a more powerful position.

- **Competitive interaction.** There is a mutual dependency between the supplier and the customer, and they have a transactional approach to their business relationship. They are inclined to compete for the benefits whilst reducing those of their counterpart, ending up in a win-lose situation.

- **Collaborative partnership.** There is a mutual dependency between the supplier and the customer, and they have a relational approach to their business relationship. They are inclined to collaborate for the shared benefits, looking for a win-win solution.

FIGURE 5.1 A typology of B2B supplier-customer relationships

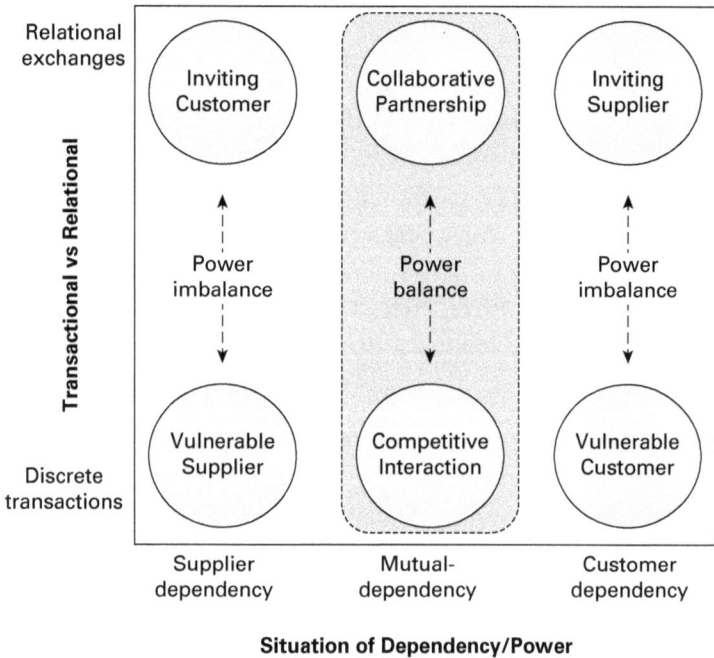

Once a supplier's key accounts are classified in the typology matrix, key account managers can use this framework to evaluate and plan for changes in these positions.

First, KAMgrs should examine the potential benefits and risks of being in a particular position and take actions that will help capitalize on the benefits and mitigate the risks. For example, if a supplier is in a 'vulnerable supplier' position, it may want to look for ways to reduce its own dependency (e.g. by broadening its customer portfolio), increase the customer's dependency (e.g. by offering customized solutions) or persuade the customer to take a more relational approach (e.g. by emphasizing the benefits of working together and/or investing in the relationship beyond specific transactions). Alternatively, a supplier may be in a comfortable 'inviting supplier' position with a large customer. The question becomes: should this supplier use its power to reap the benefits of this relationship and cause the customer to lose out, or should this supplier instead avoid using its power and favour continued collaboration with the customer, even if this pushes the relationship into one of mutual dependency?

Then, key account managers need to set a goal for where you want the relationship with the key account to be in the future, with a specific definition of the timelines and actions that need to be taken. Ideally, the supplier and customer will discuss and agree on where they want to take their relationship over time. To illustrate, a supplier and a customer may currently have a 'competitive interaction' type of relationship, based on mutual dependency but with little or no engagement in relational exchange. The supplier can invite the customer to develop their relationship into a 'collaborative partnership' that could help both companies grow their business.

A major trend in KAM is the increasing importance of collaboration between suppliers and customers, and the preference for long-term relationships with fewer customers (or suppliers) rather than short-term contracts with many accounts (or suppliers).[3] The continuity in these relationships can increase profits through reduced discretionary spending, higher customer retention and a greater likelihood of survival by being less vulnerable to the actions of competitors.[4] Moreover, recent research highlights the importance of feeding longstanding business relationships under scenarios of high turbulence and uncertainty.[5]

The process of moving from a transactional to a relational relationship is complex and takes time, as it is driven by the development of interpersonal ties. Thus, the economic exchange between a supplier and a customer is not entirely rational, as it is influenced by the existing social ties within the network of people involved in the relationship between the two companies. Clearly, the key account manager has a central role in driving long-term relationships with key customers by means of social connection and resource mobilization in both stable and unstable environments.[6]

High-quality relationships with key accounts

Relationship quality is a critical indicator of success in supplier-customer relationships. It is an assessment of the current state of the relationship between the two parties and the expectations for how the relationship will evolve. As shown in Figure 5.2, we consider the following three dimensions of relationship quality: conflict, trust and commitment.

Conflict

Conflict is a tension between a supplier and a buyer due to real or perceived differences that can often generate hostility during the interaction, create obstacles in the decision-making process and lead to distortion or withholding of information, among other behaviours.[7] A high level of conflict negatively affects the quality of the relationship between a supplier and a buyer and is therefore often referred to as dysfunctional conflict.

FIGURE 5.2 The dimensions of relationship quality in supplier-customer relationships

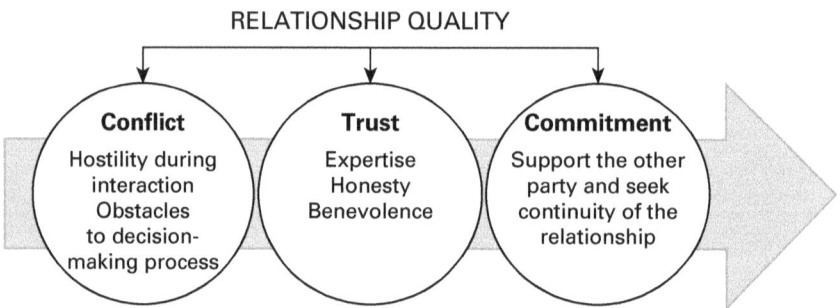

RELATIONSHIP QUALITY

Conflict
Hostility during interaction
Obstacles to decision-making process

Trust
Expertise
Honesty
Benevolence

Commitment
Support the other party and seek continuity of the relationship

However, some conflict between parties is not necessarily a bad thing, as it can stimulate productive discussion and lead to creativity, innovation and adaptation. If the disagreements are focused on how to work together and achieve common goals, conflict can be beneficial by stimulating open discussion that leads to new insights and knowledge. This is called functional conflict.

In KAM, it is expected that a certain amount of conflict will be present between the supplier and the buyer, both in day-to-day interaction and in major negotiations or joint planning. The challenge is to find the right balance, avoiding dysfunctional conflict behaviours that prevent the two organizations from trusting each other, but at the same time encouraging discussions that allow disagreements of the functional conflict type to support joint discovery of opportunities, problem solving and co-creation of value.

EXAMPLES OF DYSFUNCTIONAL CONFLICT IN KAM

- **Misaligned expectations**. The key account expects faster delivery times and more personalized service, but the supplier lacks the operational capacity to meet these demands, creating frustration on both sides.

- **Pricing disputes**. The key account demands significant discounts citing high-volume purchases, but the supplier believes these discounts would erode profitability.

- **Lack of communication or transparency**. The supplier does not inform the key account about upcoming changes to product specifications, leading to compatibility issues with the client's systems.

- **Role confusion and poor coordination**. The supplier's sales and operations teams give contradictory information to the key account about product availability, leading to missed deadlines.

- **Cultural or value misalignment**. The supplier prioritizes cost reduction, while the key account values sustainability and ethical sourcing.

- **Inequitable resource allocation**. The supplier prioritizes another key account with higher revenue potential, leaving the current key account feeling neglected.

- **Resistance to innovation or change**. The supplier proposes introducing AI-based demand forecasting, but the key account's team resists, fearing job displacement or implementation complexity.

- **Power imbalance and dominance**. The key account uses its leverage to impose unrealistic terms, such as extending payment periods, causing financial strain for the supplier.

DEALING WITH CONFLICT

The behavioural stuff you can assess and see how people develop relationships, how they deal with negotiations, how they deal with conflict. You know that sort of stuff. But there is definitely something I think you can't train and that's, you know, an attitude piece. So you'd recruit for attitude, I think as well.

Mark Bailey

Trust

In the context of KAM, building and maintaining trust is essential for navigating the complexities of long-term, strategic partnerships, especially in turbulent and uncertain environments.

Trust refers to the willingness to rely on an exchange partner in whom one has confidence.[8] It is a belief and expectation about the supplier (or buyer) based on the expertise, reliability and intentionality of the exchange partner.[9] It can reduce the perception of risk associated with engaging in a business relationship (e.g. acting opportunistically to increase one's own benefits at the expense of the other party). A trusting relationship should also increase confidence that short-term problems and grievances will be resolved over a longer period. Similarly, mutual trust between supplier and buyer can reduce transaction costs in the relationship by reducing the need to formalize each agreement between the two firms. Finally, both firms should be more willing to make idiosyncratic investments in the relationship when there is a high level of trust.

The notion of trust adopted in this book reflects two components:

1 **Trust in credibility:** The extent to which the buyer (or supplier) believes that the counterpart has the knowledge and expertise to perform effectively, and is professional, reliable and honest.

2 **Trust in benevolence:** The extent to which the buyer (or supplier) believes that the counterpart has goodwill towards the counterpart, showing intentions and motives that are beneficial to the supplier (or buyer).

To illustrate, in a highly competitive industry, you may find that several suppliers are very similar in terms of their credibility with buyers, but then there may be some important differences in terms of their goodwill toward customers. This can drive buyer preference and loyalty to only certain suppliers.

The following case is an example of a customer (key account) demonstrating trust to a supplier, showing a multiple dimension trusting relationship that goes far beyond transactional interactions into a collaborative partnership.

A large automotive manufacturer (the key account) demonstrates trust in its electronic components' supplier by:

- Sharing confidential details about its upcoming electric vehicle platform, including design specifications, production volume projections and performance requirements.

- Agreeing on a multi-year partnership agreement, including guaranteed minimum purchase volumes, joint development of next-generation components, and shared investment in research and development.

- Sharing financial risk, by offering advance payments, providing working capital support and creating joint mechanisms to manage technological development risks.

Psychological safety is a critical concept in organizational behaviour and interpersonal relationships that plays a crucial role in establishing trust, particularly in KAM relationships. In a psychologically safe environment individuals can speak up without fear of embarrassment or negative consequences, feel comfortable sharing ideas, concerns and mistakes, and are confident that they will be heard and respected.

In a supplier-key account relationship, psychological safety might look like having frank discussions about project challenges, providing candid feedback without fear of retribution, sharing each other's vulnerability and collaborating openly to resolve performance issues. For example, imagine a technology supplier working with a large telecommunications company. Psychological safety would mean the supplier can openly discuss challenges in meeting performance specifications, potential product limitations, resource constraints and unexpected technical complications. Without psychological safety, the supplier might hide these issues, potentially leading to missed deadlines, unmet performance expectations, relationship deterioration and loss of trust.

PSYCHOLOGICAL SAFETY AND TRUST

Psychological safety, in my experience, is fundamentally about trust. Building trust requires demonstrating a genuine understanding of the customer's business and challenges, consistently delivering on promises, and ensuring that actions align with stated intentions. I believe that creating an environment of psychological safety is essential for fostering open communication and innovation in key account relationships.

Nicolaas Smit

Commitment

By its very nature, key account management involves the investment of unique resources in customer relationships and the adaptation of some elements of the sales process. For example, an organizational structure with a dedicated key account manager and a KAM team, or the manufacturing of products with customized features, or an exclusive treatment in payment terms. However, it is not uncommon to find suppliers whose managers claim to have key accounts without making any specific investments; this is probably a misconception of what KAM really is.

Commitment is the desire to develop a stable buyer-supplier relationship, the willingness to make short-term sacrifices to maintain the relationship, and a sense of confidence in the stability of the relationship.[10]

A committed relationship should demonstrate not only the intentions to maintain continuity in the exchange, but also the behaviours associated with that purpose. The following example illustrates the commitment of a global manufacturer of industrial pumps (the supplier) to a multinational chemical company (the key account).

Consider a possible example of a key account that faced recurring equipment downtime due to the pumps not meeting the demands of their high-viscosity production processes. This led to delays, increased costs and reduced trust in the supplier.

The response of the supplier company was, first, to assign a cross-functional team, including a key account manager, a senior engineer and a service specialist, to work exclusively with the chemical company. Next, the supplier introduced an IoT-enabled monitoring system, allowing real-time tracking of pump performance, while offering a predictive maintenance service tailored to the account's operations. Finally, the supplier signed a multi-year service agreement, ensuring priority access to spare parts, faster repair response times and annual operational reviews to refine solutions.

These actions resulted in a reduced downtime by 25 per cent and improved production efficiency for the chemical company, plus the strengthening of the relationship between the two companies.

The extent to which a supplier's commitment to a key account adds real value depends on continuous learning and the flexibility to react to the customer's requirements, as illustrated by the following quote from Nicolaas Smit.

COMMITMENT FOR LONG-TERM KAM RELATIONSHIPS

... effective key account management centres on creating value, building trust, and driving growth for both the customer and your own organization. While challenging, the role can be immensely rewarding when executed successfully. From my perspective, the key to success lies in continuous learning, adaptability, and a genuine commitment to creating mutual value.

Nicolaas Smit

Framework on developing lasting relationships with key accounts

Figure 5.3 presents a framework on how to develop relationships with key accounts.

FIGURE 5.3 Developing lasting relationships with key accounts

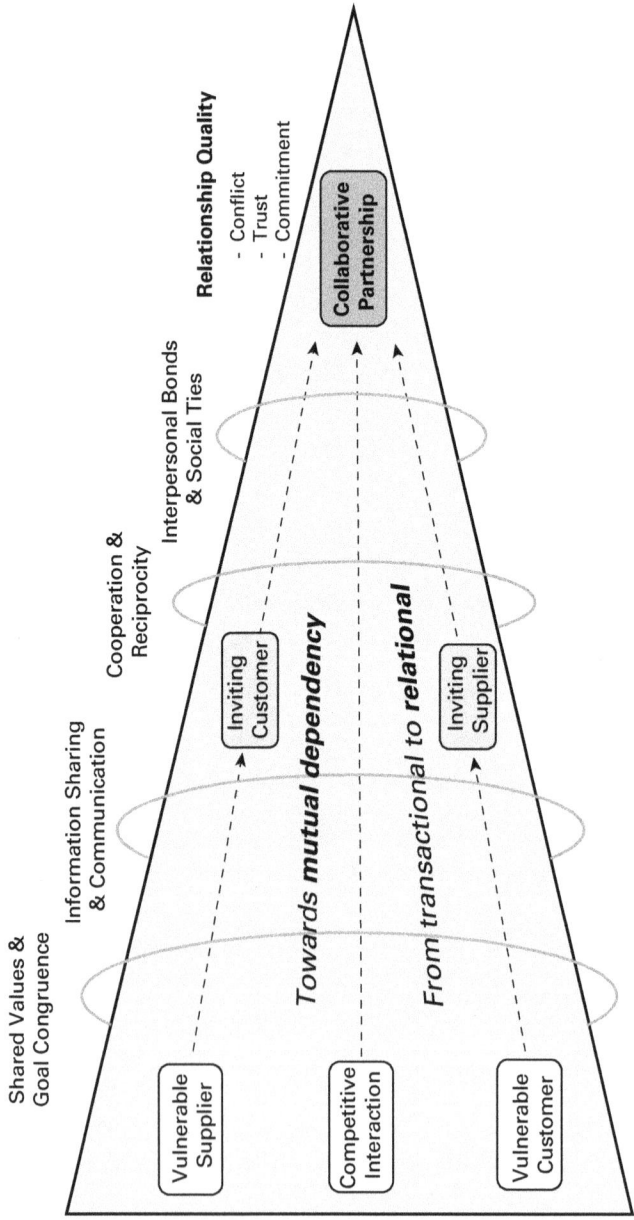

Relationship Quality
- Conflict
- Trust
- Commitment

Collaborative Partnership

Interpersonal Bonds
& Social Ties

Cooperation &
Reciprocity

Information Sharing
& Communication

Shared Values &
Goal Congruence

Inviting Customer

Inviting Supplier

Towards mutual dependency

From transactional to relational

Vulnerable Supplier

Competitive Interaction

Vulnerable Customer

First, we use a triangle to illustrate the expected evolution of customer rela-tionships from transactional to relational, together with the progression toward a situation of mutual dependency. It is expected that a 'vulnerable' type of relationship will evolve into an 'inviting' type, and then towards a 'collaborative partnership'. Likewise, in successful KAM, the 'competitive interaction' type of mutual dependency relationship should evolve into a 'collaborative partnership' type by means of moving from a transactional to a relational business approach.

Second, we establish *relationship quality* as the critical measure of success in building long-term KAM relationships, with conflict, trust and commit-ment as the main building blocks. It is expected that specific behaviours both from the supplier company and the key account manager will drive relationship quality.

Third, we use rings to represent inter-organizational drivers of relation-ship quality between the supplier and the key account: shared values and goal congruence; information sharing and communication; cooperation and reciprocity; and interpersonal bonds and social ties.

In the rest of this section, the scope is precisely on the rings of the frame-work, as they respond to *how* supplier companies can develop sustained valuable relationships with key accounts. Figure 5.4 shows the drivers of inter-organizational drivers of both a collaborative partnership and high relationship quality between the supplier and the ley account.

FIGURE 5.4 Inter-organizational drivers of relationship quality

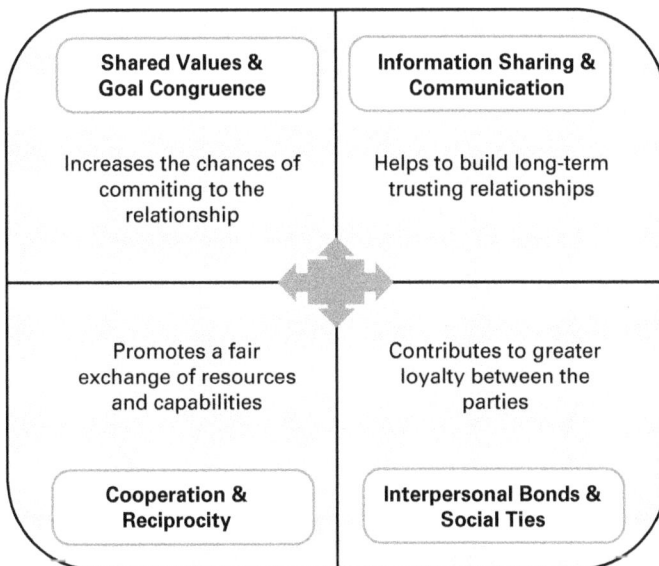

Shared Values & Goal Congruence	Information Sharing & Communication
Increases the chances of commiting to the relationship	Helps to build long-term trusting relationships
Promotes a fair exchange of resources and capabilities	Contributes to greater loyalty between the parties
Cooperation & Reciprocity	Interpersonal Bonds & Social Ties

Shared values and goal congruence

A supplier and a customer are more likely to commit to a relationship if the two companies share similar values and goals. This similarity can act as a facilitator for mutual value creation and the development of relationships that go beyond the individual to the collective.[11] Suppliers and customers may have different goals, which can lead to conflict, mistrust and sometimes opportunistic behaviour. Therefore, goal alignment and shared values facilitate the establishment of social norms of acceptable behaviour and reduce uncertainty.

The key is for the key account manager to go beyond just understanding the customer's business – they need to deeply align on mutually beneficial goals, communicate a shared vision, demonstrate reliable commitment and foster strong interpersonal connections. This creates a foundation of shared values and goal congruence that supports a thriving, long-term key account relationship.

How can a key account manager support this driver?

- Collaboratively define shared success metrics and key performance indicators that create value for both organizations.
- Ensure the goals and measures are tightly aligned to the customer's core business priorities.
- Regularly review progress against these goals and adjust as needed to maintain alignment.
- Clearly articulate how your company's mission, values and culture are compatible with and supportive of the customer's organizational identity.
- Find opportunities to reinforce these shared principles in your interactions and decision-making.
- Involve key executives from both organizations to model the collaborative mindset.
- Cultivate strong working relationships between teams at multiple levels of the organizations.
- Facilitate open and frequent communication to build personal rapport and goodwill.
- Organize social/team-building activities to strengthen the human connections.

GOAL ALIGNMENT FOR LONG-TERM STRATEGIES
WITH KEY ACCOUNTS

And so you have to strategize on what are the opportunities that we have
with this customer? What are the goals that we have as a company ourselves
and how do our goals align to the opportunities that we see at the customer
and things you never go from?

Nicolaas Smit

Information sharing and communication

The exchange of information between suppliers and buyers is essential for
building long-term relationships, as it demonstrates norms of equity and
fairness and can even prevent unethical behaviour.[12] The willingness to share
information is a signal of trust in the benevolence of the other party.
Likewise, fluent communication, either face-to-face or through technological means, is key.

The key is for the key account manager to go beyond just sharing information reactively. They need to proactively communicate, foster collaborative
exchanges, maintain transparency and personalize the experience to build
trust and strengthen the relationship over the long-term.

How can a key account manager support this driver?

- Provide regular updates on your company's strategic direction, product
  roadmaps and other information that may impact the customer.
- Quickly communicate any changes, issues or potential disruptions that
  could affect the customer's business.
- Share market insights, industry trends and benchmarking data that could
  inform the customer's decision-making.
- Invite the customer to participate in your own planning and innovation
  processes where appropriate.
- Encourage the exchange of ideas, suggestions and constructive criticism
  to continuously improve the relationship.
- Document agreements, action items and next steps from all interactions
  to ensure alignment and follow-through.

- Provide visibility into your internal processes, timelines and progress to build trust.
- Address any issues or concerns promptly and thoroughly, taking ownership and following up.
- Tailor the style, frequency and level of detail to the preferences and communication needs of each key contact.
- Actively listen to understand the customer's communication and information requirements.
- Leverage personal rapport to have more open, authentic dialogues.

THE ROLE OF KEY ACCOUNT MANAGERS IN INFORMATION-SHARING

One of the critical aspects of KAM is the orchestration of various roles within the pharmaceutical industry, such as market access, medical liaison and commercial teams. The key account manager acts as a connector, bringing together different functions to create a cohesive strategy aligned with the customer's objectives to create the strategic plan and gain mid to long-term partnership. This involves regular knowledge sharing and strategy development that considers the entire portfolio of opportunities and partnerships.

Dominique Côté

COMMUNICATION WITH THE CUSTOMER TO BUILD RELATIONSHIPS

I'm in about in the long term, you know, relationship development with customers... multifaceted relationships over the long term and very often is the person who needs to convince the organization to dedicate resources into a particular customer... And that often requires engaging communication and building trust. You know, with these customers and with the people within the customer, because sometimes the offering is complex, there will be a need for building teams and enhancing collaboration to deliver some of the things that you promised.

Tim Chapman

Cooperation and reciprocity

A supplier-customer relationship inherently exists because both firms need and depend on each other for access to resources and capabilities that are critical to their business. Thus, a bilateral relationship emerges to secure necessary resources, and cooperation is an important mechanism to achieve this.[13] Both companies need to show reciprocity and fairness in sharing the benefits and costs of the relationship, as well as in the way they act and collaborate throughout the process of value creation and relationship-building.

The key is for the key account manager to go beyond a transactional, win-lose mentality. They need to establish a collaborative, mutually beneficial relationship where both parties are invested in each other's success and willing to share risks and rewards. This fosters an environment of cooperation and reciprocity that supports a thriving, long-term key account partnership.

How can a key account manager support this driver?

- Emphasize a 'we're in this together' mentality focused on mutual success, not just individual goals.
- Actively solicit the customer's input and perspectives to demonstrate your openness to collaboration.
- Structure commercial agreements and pricing models that create shared upside when both parties thrive.
- Explore revenue-sharing, gainsharing or other innovative approaches that incentivize cooperation.
- Identify non-financial ways to recognize and celebrate joint accomplishments.
- Demonstrate your willingness to share in the financial and operational risks of the partnership.
- Jointly invest in initiatives, technologies or capabilities that benefit both organizations.
- Explore opportunities to co-develop new products, services or solutions that create interdependence.
- Develop contingency plans and commit resources to respond quickly to issues or disruptions.

Interpersonal bonds and social ties

Developing interpersonal relationships and social bonds with key contacts can bring benefits such as faster approvals, flexibility in communication, and better conflict resolution.[14] Relational and social ties between customers and suppliers contribute positively to customer loyalty and can sustain an ongoing relationship despite the occurrence of events that reduce customer satisfaction.[15]

> I'm convinced that people buy from people... The best key account managers know all the important people in their customer organizations, often on a personal level.
>
> Andrea Clatworthy

The key is for the key account manager to go beyond just a professional business relationship. They need to intentionally foster personal connections, demonstrate empathy, facilitate open communication and create shared experiences that build strong interpersonal bonds and social ties over time. This helps solidify the relationship and create a sense of mutual investment in each other's success.

How can a key account manager support this driver?

- Try to get to know key contacts on a personal level, beyond just their professional roles.
- Discover shared interests, hobbies or life experiences that can form the basis of a more meaningful connection.
- Engage in casual, social interactions that allow you to bond over common ground.
- Show a sincere interest in the customer's personal and professional well-being.
- Offer support or assistance during challenging times, even if it's not directly related to the business.
- Celebrate personal and professional milestones and accomplishments with the customer.

- Create opportunities for informal chats, virtual coffees or virtual happy hours.
- Arrange off-site events, team outings or social gatherings that bring together employees from both organizations.
- Participate in community service projects or volunteer work as a joint team.
- Encourage friendly competition through activities like sports leagues or game nights.

To assess these four drivers of relationship quality, one option is to conduct a survey, ideally with people from both the supplier and the buyer. The following box presents some statements that can be used for that purpose.

SURVEY ON DRIVERS OF RELATIONSHIP QUALITY

With respect to the relationship between your company and [name of supplier/buyer], please indicate the degree to which you agree or disagree with the following statements by circling the number that best reflects your perception, on a scale from 1 to 7, where 1 means 'Strongly disagree' and 7 means 'Strongly agree'.

Shared values and goal congruence

- Our attachment with this supplier/buyer is based primarily on the similarity of our values.
- What this supplier/buyer stands for is important to us as well.
- We and this supplier/buyer share each other's goals to a big extent.

Information sharing and communication

- We are willing to share proprietary information with this supplier/buyer.
- We frequently exchange relevant information with this supplier/buyer.
- The quality of communication between this supplier/buyer and us is very high.

Cooperation and reciprocity

- We generally cooperate with this supplier/buyer in several ways.
- We always reciprocate to this supplier/buyer when they do something valuable for us.
- The relationship with this supplier/buyer is highly collaborative.

Interpersonal bonds and social ties

- We have close personal relationships with people from this supplier/buyer.

- This supplier/buyer and our company have established strong social ties.

- We get along well with people from this supplier/buyer.

Summary and application

Relationships with strategic customers constitute a fundamental intangible asset in KAM.[16] This chapter provides an overview of how to develop lasting relationships with key accounts, underscoring the critical role of long-term relationships in KAM, highlighting how they secure financial stability, foster loyalty and provide avenues for innovation. By transitioning from transactional to relational approaches, organizations can unlock mutual benefits, ensuring sustained growth and resilience. Key account relationships thrive on trust, effective communication and aligned goals. By fostering psychological safety and shared values, companies and their clients can navigate challenges collaboratively, creating an environment conducive to innovation and long-term success.

A first step is to understand the types of supplier-customer relationships that could be established, as well as the characteristics of successful long-term relationships. In KAM, it is expected that relationships with customers will evolve into collaborative partnerships with high levels of relationship quality. Several processes support the achievement of this purpose, including goal alignment, information sharing, cooperation and interpersonal ties.

The key account managers' role in driving long-term relationships with customers is paramount,[17] especially in business environments characterized by turbulence and uncertainty. In this scenario, key actors in the customer side prioritize the establishment of social bonds with individuals in the supplier company and they would rather work with known people than with unfamiliar ones, as it reduces perceived risks and vulnerability. This is more prominent with individuals who are perceived as good communicators, flexible to adapt to the customer's needs, and able to mobilize resources and speed up the business process.

The chapter presents actionable insights into achieving relationship quality through conflict resolution, trust-building and sustained commitment. Frameworks such as shared goal alignment, reciprocity and interpersonal bonds are discussed as key drivers of partnership success. By embedding the principles of collaboration, communication and mutual investment into their strategies, key account managers can cultivate high-quality relationships that serve as the foundation for competitive advantage and innovation. These relationships not only ensure current profitability but also position organizations for future challenges and opportunities.

Table 5.1 provides recommended actions for key account managers to develop lasting relationships with strategic customers.

TABLE 5.1 Recommended actions for key account managers

Action		Description
1.	Prioritize relationship quality	Focus on building trust, managing conflicts constructively and maintaining commitment. For example, proactively resolve pricing disputes by finding mutually beneficial solutions.
2.	Embrace goal alignment	Collaborate with clients to define shared objectives and success metrics. For instance, co-create a sustainability roadmap aligning both companies' environmental goals.
3.	Foster transparent communication	Maintain open, honest and consistent dialogue with key accounts. For example, share early updates on potential delivery delays to manage expectations proactively.
4.	Develop reciprocal value propositions	Create win-win agreements where both parties share risks and rewards. An example is introducing gain-sharing contracts for co-developed innovations.
5.	Nurture interpersonal connections	Invest time in understanding personal interests and creating meaningful bonds with client stakeholders. For instance, host informal networking events to strengthen ties.
6.	Integrate cross-functional teams	Leverage internal resources to address client needs comprehensively. For example, involve R&D and marketing in brainstorming sessions for product improvements.

(continued)

TABLE 5.1 (Continued)

Action		Description
7.	Leverage data and insights	Use CRM tools to analyse customer trends and anticipate needs. For example, identify upselling opportunities through purchase pattern analysis.
8.	Adapt to changing needs	Stay agile by regularly reviewing and adapting strategies to client requirements. For instance, pivot solutions based on feedback from quarterly reviews.
9.	Facilitate co-creation	Engage clients in innovation processes, such as joint workshops to address shared challenges. An example is co-developing a digital solution for operational efficiency.
10.	Commit to long-term investments	Demonstrate dedication by allocating exclusive resources or tailored services. For example, offer a dedicated account manager and bespoke training sessions for a client's team.

Notes

1 L Parsons. How to build business relationships: Fostering business relationships can improve professional success, Harvard Division of Continuing Education Blog, 8 January 2024, https://professional.dce.harvard.edu/blog/how-to-build-business-relationships/ (archived at https://perma.cc/MZ2X-JNW7)

2 C Tangpong, M D Michalisin, R D Traub and A J Melcher. A review of buyer-supplier relationship typologies: progress, problems, and future directions, *Journal of Business & Industrial Marketing*, 2015, 30 (2), 153–70

3 S P Sandesh and J Paul. Key account management in B2B marketing: A systematic literature review and research agenda, *Journal of Business Research*, 2023, 156, 113541

4 D Bowman (2014) *Evolution of Buyer-Seller Relationships. Handbook of strategic account management: A comprehensive resource*, 277–92

5 K Zafari, S Biggemann and T Garry. Development of business-to-business relationships in turbulent environments, *Industrial Marketing Management*, 2023, 111, 1–18

6 Ibid.

7 A Menon, S G Bharadwaj and R Howell. The quality and effectiveness of marketing strategy: Effects of functional and dysfunctional conflict in intraorganizational relationships, *Journal of the Academy of Marketing Science*, 1996, 24 (4), 299–313

8   C Moorman, G Zaltman and R Deshpande. Relationships between providers and users of market research: The dynamics of trust within and between organizations, *Journal of Marketing Research*, 1992, 29 (3), 314

9   S Ganesan. Determinants of long-term orientation in buyer-seller relationships, *Journal of Marketing*, 1994, 1–19

10 E Anderson and B Weitz. The use of pledges to build and sustain commitment in distribution channels, *Journal of Marketing Research*, 1992, 18–34

11 J Marcos, S Julkunen and M Gabrielsson. Power symmetry and the development of trust in interdependent relationships: The mediating role of goal congruence, *Industrial Marketing Management*, 2015, 48, 149–59

12 S Eckerd and J A Hill. The buyer-supplier social contract: information sharing as a deterrent to unethical behaviors, *International Journal of Operations & Production Management*, 2012, 32 (2), 238–55

13 K K Kim, S H Park, S Y Ryoo and S K Park. Inter-organizational cooperation in buyer–supplier relationships: Both perspectives, *Journal of Business Research*, 2010, 63 (8), 863–69

14 Zafari, Biggemann and Garry. Development of business-to-business relationships in turbulent environments

15 D M Woisetschläger, P Lentz and H Evanschitzky. How habits, social ties, and economic switching barriers affect customer loyalty in contractual service settings, *Journal of Business Research*, 2011, 64 (8), 800–08

16 R Guesalaga, M Gabrielsson, B Rogers, L Ryals and J M Cuevas. Which resources and capabilities underpin strategic key account management? *Industrial Marketing Management*, 2018, 75, 160–72

17 M Katti (2024). A complete Key Account Management (KAM) guide for 2024, DEMANDFARM, www.demandfarm.com/key-account-management/ (archived at https://perma.cc/RFT5-SRZM)

John Downer

As the former Transportation Growth Director for Europe at Jacobs UK Limited, I've had extensive experience in key account management. In this role, I oversaw 13 client account leads and was responsible for securing the backlog of work for a significant portion of the business – about 50 per cent.

The primary focus for our key account managers, whom we called Client Account Leads (CALs), was to grow gross margin income per client. This was our key KPI, driven by the need to deliver returns to shareholders as a publicly listed company. To achieve this, we emphasized forming deep, trusted relationships with clients.

Our CALs were responsible for understanding every facet of the client's business, identifying problems or issues, and determining how Jacobs could help. We invested significantly in value creation opportunities, ranging from small interventions like providing expert consultations to large-scale projects such as developing AI solutions for industry-wide problems.

Typically, our CALs spent about 30 per cent of their time directly engaging with clients. The rest was dedicated to internal preparation, coordination, and influencing. They interacted with a wide range of stakeholders, both within Jacobs and at the client organizations, from CEOs to regional directors.

We defined key accounts based on current size, future business potential and strategic importance. Some accounts, like Transport for London, could shift in status based on changing circumstances. We were agile in our approach, willing to scale back or remove key account status when necessary.

Our CALs were typically recruited internally, often from our operations teams. We looked for individuals with a strong understanding of our business, technical expertise and the ability to influence without formal authority. Most had professional qualifications in their field and were in the 30–45 age range.

We used a variety of tools to measure performance, with Salesforce being central to our operations. We tracked metrics like gross margin, customer satisfaction, safety leadership, and the strength of client relationships.

In terms of capabilities, I believe the most crucial for a key account manager are:

1   Engaging, communicating, and building trust with key customers
2   Leading and influencing both with and without authority
3   Promoting customer centricity
4   Building teams and enhancing cross-functional collaboration

We invested heavily in developing these capabilities through various means, including formal training programs, mentoring, and on-the-job learning. We also encouraged our CALs to pursue further education, with many completing MBAs or MSc programs.

One of the key lessons I learned was the importance of investing time in individual team members. For example, I worked closely with one CAL who initially lacked confidence. Through mentoring and support, they transformed into a highly effective account manager, securing regular meetings with the client's CEO.

We fostered a collaborative environment among our CALs, encouraging them to share best practices and support each other. We treated key account management as a team sport, focusing on overall targets rather than individual performance. This approach allowed us to be flexible, shifting resources between accounts as needed.

A critical aspect of our success was having a clear, comprehensive role description for our CALs. We developed this over time, incorporating input from various stakeholders and refining it based on feedback from the team.

We also recognized the importance of being agile in our approach to key accounts. We were prepared to adjust our strategy, including scaling back or removing key account status when circumstances changed.

In terms of technology, besides Salesforce, we used various tools for project management, bid optimization, and collaboration. However, we always emphasized that these tools were enablers, not replacements for the human aspects of relationship building and strategic thinking.

Looking back, I believe our approach to key account management was highly effective. By focusing on building deep, trusted relationships, fostering a collaborative team environment, and continuously developing our people's capabilities, we were able to drive significant value for both Jacobs and our clients.

The key takeaways from my experience are:

1   Invest time in developing individual team members.

2   Foster a collaborative, team-oriented environment.

3   Be clear about roles, responsibilities and KPIs.

4   Stay agile and be prepared to adjust strategies as circumstances change.

5   Use technology as an enabler, but don't lose sight of the human element.

While there's always room for improvement, I believe our approach at Jacobs provides a strong model for effective key account management in complex B2B environments.

John has extensive strategic account management expertise, particularly in transportation and infrastructure. As Client Account Manager for Network Rail, he successfully led the winning bid for the Tier 1 Design Services Framework, achieving top-quality scores and optimal commercial rates. In his subsequent roles as Director of Sales for Rail UK & Ireland and Rail Market Director for Europe at Jacobs, he managed major client relationships. He led teams to secure over £100 million in contracts, including four successive Tier 1 contract wins. He created and implemented comprehensive client account strategies for key organizations, including Network Rail, HS2, and Transport for London.

His account management approach focused on strategic planning and transformation, influencing Jacobs's strategy for key accounts. He developed a 'Strategy 101' playbook that was adopted across the business. He pioneered new organizational structures to support client relationships, including creating specialized roles focused on Digital Rail, Intelligent Infrastructure, and Rail Decarbonization. In his most recent role as UK Growth Lead at TYLin, he is leveraging this experience to establish their infrastructure design and delivery footprint in the UK, focusing on Rail + Transit, Ports + Marine, Tunnelling, and Bridges sectors while fostering collaborations with sister companies in the Sidara Collaborative. John received the Cranfield 2023 Key Account Management Award for the best Key Account Plan.

www.linkedin.com/in/john-downer

06

Communicating and building trust with key customers

Overview

In this chapter, we explore the critical aspects of communication and trust-building in key account management. We examine how these elements form the foundation of successful supplier-customer relationships and their impact on long-term business success.

We begin by understanding that effective communication across various boundaries – internal, external and interpersonal – is essential for key account management success. Key account managers must navigate complex landscapes, coordinating between different departments within their organization while maintaining strong relationships with various stakeholders in the customer organization. This boundary-spanning role requires sophisticated communication skills and strategies to overcome potential barriers and ensure smooth information flow.

We then delve into trust, which we define as the willingness to be vulnerable to another party's actions. We explore its three key components: ability, benevolence and integrity. Trust development occurs through various approaches, including calculative assessment, prediction based on past behaviour, capability demonstration and intentionality evaluation. We examine how trust can be transferred from trusted sources and how it evolves through different stages of the relationship.

Particularly important is our discussion of the key account manager's role as a trusted advisor. We explore the trust equation, which balances credibility, reliability and intimacy against self-orientation. This framework helps us understand how key account managers (KAMgrs) can transition from being traditional salespeople to becoming indispensable strategic partners.

We also address the various barriers to trust-building, such as lack of communication, inconsistent behaviour, cultural differences and power imbalances. Understanding these challenges helps us develop more effective strategies for building and maintaining trust.

Throughout the chapter, we emphasize that building trust and maintaining effective communication are ongoing processes that require consistent effort, genuine commitment and a systematic approach to relationship management. These elements are fundamental to creating sustainable, value-generating partnerships between suppliers and their key customers.

WHY BUILDING AND LEADING TRUST DEVELOPMENT IS IMPORTANT

Personal trust development:

- Establishes professional credibility
- Creates leadership influence
- Builds stakeholder relationships
- Enables effective conflict resolution

Strategic value creation:

- Demonstrates expertise and knowledge
- Enables proactive problem-solving
- Facilitates strategic solutions
- Strengthens competitive position

Communication excellence:

- Enhances stakeholder alignment
- Improves issue resolution
- Builds transparency
- Strengthens relationship quality

Team leadership:

- Develops organizational trust
- Improves cross-functional collaboration
- Enables knowledge sharing
- Creates cultural alignment

Performance management:

- Enables systematic measurement
- Supports risk management
- Improves value tracking
- Strengthens accountability

Why communicating and building trust with key customers matters

Communicating and building trust with key customers is essential for the long-term success of any business. Trust is the foundation of any strong relationship, and this is particularly true in the context of supplier-key customer relationships. Trust can be jeopardized if a key account manager proves to be unreliable. Conversely, a highly trusted KAMgr can maintain and keep a customer's commitment to that company, even in the event of substandard service delivery.

Building trust requires an open and honest dialogue with people in the key customer organization. Suppliers need to demonstrate that they are listening to their customers' needs and challenges and that they are committed to delivering the promised solutions. Trust is a two-way street – businesses also need to be able to trust their key customers. For example, if a customer is consistently late with payments or if a customer fails to provide technical information the supplier needs, it can be challenging for a business to maintain trust in the relationship.

When trust deteriorates, it can be challenging to repair and can have a negative impact on customer loyalty and profitability. Building trust takes time, effort and consistency, but the rewards are significant. By communicating effectively and building trust, businesses can develop strong, lasting relationships with their key customers that benefit both parties.

Managing communication flows across boundaries

Effective communication is the lifeblood of successful KAM. It enables key account managers to build strong relationships, understand customer needs and align internal resources to deliver value and achieve mutual success. However, communication in KAM is rarely straightforward. Key account managers operate in a complex landscape characterized by various boundaries that can impede the flow of information and hinder collaboration. In this section, we explore the significance of managing communication flows across supplier-customer boundaries.

> When I led a pharmaceutical account spanning 42 countries and 200 sites, I encountered diverse cultural dynamics that required sophisticated navigation... Success in such environments requires what I term 'matrix leadership' – the ability to influence and achieve objectives without direct authority.
>
> Stuart Roberts

UNDERSTANDING BOUNDARIES IN KEY ACCOUNT MANAGEMENT

Boundary spanning[1,2] is a critical aspect of key account management. It involves navigating the different interfaces and interactions between individuals, departments and organizations to facilitate the flow of information, resources and decisions. KAMgrs manage across a number of boundaries:

Internal boundaries separate different departments and functions within the supplying organization. Key account managers frequently interact with various internal stakeholders, including marketing, finance, production, customer service, logistics and senior management. Research by Ian Speakman[3] identifies nine distinct departments that key account managers commonly engage with, highlighting the potential for conflict due to misaligned goals, differing priorities and varying perceptions of the sales function. For instance, conflicts can arise when sales strategies prioritize customer needs over production efficiency or when marketing campaigns do not align with the specific requirements of key accounts.

External boundaries distinguish the supplying organization from the customer organization. Managing communication across external boundaries involves effectively engaging with various buying centre members, each with their own roles, perspectives and influence on the purchasing decision. Bischoff et al[4] emphasize the importance of adapting communication strategies to the unique needs and value priorities of individual buying centre members. Key account managers need to tailor their messages to resonate with the specific concerns of technical experts, procurement officers and decision-makers within the customer organization.

Interpersonal boundaries exist between individuals within and across organizations. Communication styles, personalities, power dynamics and interpersonal relationships can significantly impact the effectiveness of communication. Speakman highlights the influence of personality clashes and personal issues on communication, suggesting that these factors can create conflicts and hinder the open exchange of information.

The permeability and complexity of these boundaries can vary depending on several factors, including on a number of factors, such as organizational structure and culture. For instance, in his relationship with Caterpillar, Dan Ahern experienced a rather rigid and silos-based setup when he was appointed Group Account Manager at ABB. These structures tend to have less permeable boundaries, hindering communication and collaboration. Organizations that foster a more open and collaborative culture tend to have more fluid boundaries, enabling easier information sharing and joint problem-solving. Sometimes, the variety of products and services developed and offered by the supplier creates greater interdependency and necessitates more frequent communication across boundaries. For example, in the ABB and Caterpillar case, Dan Ahern needed to coordinate efforts across multiple ABB divisions to present a unified solution to Caterpillar.[5]

Power imbalance and hierarchies can also create communication barriers, as individuals may be hesitant to share information or challenge decisions made by those in higher positions. In Siemens,[6] for instance, key account managers, despite having access to senior executives, preferred to start discussions at lower management levels to secure buy-in and avoid unnecessary escalation. The geographic dispersion of teams can also make communication more challenging due to time zone differences, cultural variations and the reliance on technology for interaction.

The stage of the customer relationship also affects communication patterns and the nature of interactions. These typically evolve as the customer relationship progresses. In the early stages, communication focuses on building rapport and understanding needs, while in later stages, communication may involve joint planning, problem-solving and strategic alignment.

CHALLENGES IN MANAGING COMMUNICATION FLOWS

Managing communication flows across supplier-key account boundaries presents several challenges for key account managers. Information overload, as a result of the proliferation of communication channels, coupled with the increasing volume of information exchanged in business, can lead to excessive information.[7] Key account managers must prioritize relevant information and ensure it reaches the right people in a timely manner. Information filtering can occur as information passes through different levels and departments, with key details being lost or misinterpreted.

Another challenge emerges from conflicting goals and priorities. Different departments within an organization may have differing objectives and priorities, which can lead to miscommunication and misunderstandings. Sales teams, driven by revenue targets, may prioritize closing deals, while production departments may focus on efficiency and cost optimization. Research highlights that sales strategies are often perceived as not aligned with the goals of other departments, leading to conflicts and frustration for key account managers.[8] Cultural differences, language barriers and varying communication styles can create significant challenges in understanding and interpretation. For instance, in major markets like China, cultural sensitivity in communication is crucial to operate within the Chinese business context.[9] Key account managers in China need to be mindful of cultural nuances, such as Confucianism and high-context communication styles, which emphasize indirect communication, respect for hierarchy and building relationships based on trust and harmony.

Finally, the use of technology can become a hindrance in communications. While technology can enhance communication and collaboration, it also presents new challenges. The reliance on email, instant messaging and video conferencing can lead to information overload and make it difficult to build rapport and establish personal connections. Key account managers need to strategically leverage technology to facilitate communication while maintaining a balance between face-to-face interactions and personal relationship building.

STRATEGIES FOR EFFECTIVE COMMUNICATION FLOW MANAGEMENT

Key account managers can employ several strategies to effectively manage communication flows across boundaries. First, they can establish clear communication protocols and channels: defining roles and responsibilities for communication within and across organizations, establishing preferred communication channels for different types of information, and ensuring timely and consistent communication to streamline information flow and reduce misunderstandings. Clear protocols for handling customer issues, escalating conflicts and communicating important decisions are essential for maintaining transparency and accountability.

Secondly, KAMgrs can foster a culture of open communication and transparency: organizations should encourage active listening, feedback sharing and open dialogue across departments and with customers. A collaborative approach to problem-solving and decision-making, where different perspectives are valued, can improve communication and foster a sense of shared purpose.[10] Thirdly, KAMgrs can effectively manage communication flows by developing strong relationships built on trust and mutual understanding (see the next section): building rapport and trust with key stakeholders through regular interaction, active listening and demonstrating empathy is paramount. Key account managers should act as trusted advisors who understand customer needs and advocate for their interests within the supplying organization. For example, in the ABB and Caterpillar case, Dan Ahern focused on building trust by positioning himself as 'ONE ABB' to the customer, representing all of ABB's activities and ensuring alignment across different divisions.

Fourthly, KAMgrs utilize technology to enhance communication. A growing number of communication technologies can facilitate information sharing, coordination and relationship-building. Virtual meetings, document-sharing platforms, project management tools and customer relationship management (CRM) systems can streamline communication and improve collaboration. However, it is essential to use technology strategically and avoid overwhelming stakeholders with excessive communication or replacing essential face-to-face interactions.

Fifthly, adequate communication flows require adapting communication styles and strategies to different audiences.[11] Key account managers need to tailor their communication approaches to the specific needs and preferences of different stakeholders. Cultural differences, communication styles and hierarchical levels should be considered when crafting messages and choosing communication channels. For instance, formal communication through email or written reports may be appropriate when interacting with senior management or customers in formal business settings. In contrast, informal communication through instant messaging or phone calls may be more suitable for building rapport and fostering closer relationships.

Communication flows, like many other customer-related processes, need the implementation of feedback mechanisms to evaluate communication effectiveness continuously. Regular feedback from customers and internal stakeholders can help identify areas for improvement in communication processes. Surveys, feedback forms and informal discussions can provide valuable insights into the clarity, timeliness and relevance of communication.

Overall, managing communication flows across boundaries is fundamental to successful key account management. Key account managers need to understand the complexities of different types of boundaries and the challenges they pose to effective communication. By implementing strategies that promote transparency, collaboration and trust, key account managers can overcome these challenges and foster strong relationships that benefit both the business and its key customers. Effective communication is not just about exchanging information but about building understanding, aligning goals and working together to achieve mutual success. Tightly linked to communication is the ability of KAMgrs to generate trust with key customers, a topic we now turn to.

Scoping trust in supplier-customer relationships

Trust refers to the willingness to rely on an exchange partner in whom one has confidence.[12] It is a belief and expectation about the supplier (or buyer) based on the expertise, reliability and intentionality of the exchange partner.[12] It can reduce the perception of risk associated with engaging in a business relationship (e.g. acting opportunistically to increase one's own benefits at the expense of the other party). A trusting relationship increases confidence that short-term problems will be resolved over a longer period. Similarly, mutual trust between supplier and buyer can reduce transaction costs in the relationship by reducing the need to formalize each agreement between the two firms. Finally, both firms should be more willing to make idiosyncratic investments in the relationship when there is a high level of trust.

Trust can be defined as the 'willingness of a party to be vulnerable to the actions of another party'[13] and is a critical factor in the success of any relationship, particularly in collaborative environments like supplier-key customer relationships or innovation networks.[14] When trust is present, it encourages risk-taking behaviour and a greater willingness to engage in collaborative activities despite inherent risks. The level of trust is influenced by how the trustor perceives the trustworthiness of the trustee.

Trust can be broken down into three key components: ability, benevolence and integrity.[16] Ability refers to the perceived skills, competencies and characteristics that enable a party to exert influence within a specific domain. It's about judging whether the other party is capable of fulfilling their commitments and delivering on their promises. Benevolence, on the other hand, focuses on the belief that the trustee has the trustor's best interests at heart beyond just self-serving motives. It's about believing that the other party genuinely cares about the wellbeing of the trustor and will act in a way that benefits them, even if it doesn't directly serve their own interests. In a network setting, this translates to a willingness to help and share valuable knowledge and information with other members, even when there isn't an immediate or obvious benefit for the provider. Integrity is concerned with the trustor's perception that the trustee adheres to a set of principles that the trustor finds acceptable. This encompasses several aspects:

- **Consistency between actions and words**: Does the trustee follow through on their promises and act in accordance with their stated values?

- **Strong sense of justice**: Does the trustee treat others fairly and make decisions based on ethical principles?

- **Honouring agreements**: Does the trustee abide by the rules and commitments established within the relationship or network?

For example, KAM integrity would be demonstrated by members of the supplier and the customer respecting confidentiality agreements, acting honestly in negotiations, and fairly sharing the benefits of joint projects.

Each of these dimensions plays a distinct role in shaping trust and influencing behaviour within a relationship or network. Understanding these components is crucial for building and maintaining trust, which is essential for effective collaboration, knowledge sharing and successful innovation. To illustrate, in a highly competitive industry, you may find that several suppliers are very similar in terms of their credibility with buyers, but then there may be some important differences in terms of their goodwill toward customers. This can drive buyer preference and loyalty to only certain suppliers.

The following case is an example of a customer (key account) demonstrating trust to a supplier, showing a multiple dimension trusting relationship that goes far beyond transactional interactions into a collaborative partnership.

A large automotive manufacturer (the key account) demonstrates trust in its electronic components' supplier by:

- Sharing confidential details about its upcoming electric vehicle platform, including design specifications, production volume projections and performance requirements.

- Agreeing on a multi-year partnership agreement, including guaranteed minimum purchase volumes, joint development of next-generation components and shared investment in research and development.

- Sharing financial risk, by offering advance payments, providing working capital support and creating joint mechanisms to manage technological development risks.

Psychological safety is a critical concept in organizational behaviour and interpersonal relationships that plays a crucial role in establishing trust, particularly in KAM relationships. In a psychologically safe environment, individuals can speak up without fear of embarrassment or negative consequences, feel comfortable sharing ideas, concerns and mistakes, and are confident that they will be heard and respected.

In a supplier-key account relationship, psychological safety might look like having frank discussions about project challenges, providing candid feedback without fear of retribution, sharing each other's vulnerability and collaborating openly to resolve performance issues. For example, imagine a technology supplier working with a large telecommunications company. Psychological safety would mean the supplier can openly discuss challenges in meeting performance specifications, potential product limitations, resource constraints and unexpected technical complications. Without psychological safety, the supplier might hide these issues, potentially leading to missed deadlines, unmet performance expectations, relationship deterioration and loss of trust.

PSYCHOLOGICAL SAFETY AND TRUST

Psychological safety, in my experience, is fundamentally about trust. Building trust requires demonstrating a genuine understanding of the customer's business and challenges, consistently delivering on promises and ensuring that actions align with stated intentions. I believe that creating an environment of psychological safety is essential for fostering open communication and innovation in key account relationships.

Nicolaas Smit

Trust development approaches and processes

Trust isn't built overnight. It's a gradual process that evolves over time through various interactions and shared experiences. This section explores the approaches and processes involved in trust development, highlighting key enablers and barriers that shape these dynamics.

The first approach is the *calculative*. This approach, often rooted in economic principles, involves assessing the costs and benefits of trusting another party. The trustor evaluates the potential risks and rewards of the trustee acting in an untrustworthy manner.[17] For example, a buyer might consider the financial implications of a supplier failing to deliver on time. If the costs of supplier unreliability outweigh the potential benefits of switching to a new supplier, the buyer might be more inclined to trust the existing supplier.

Investments and contracts underpin large, relationship-specific investments by the supplier, such as dedicated production lines or customized solutions. These demonstrate commitment and raise the cost of opportunistic behaviour, thus fostering trust. Similarly, well-defined contracts with clear performance metrics and penalties for non-compliance can create a framework of accountability, mitigating risks and encouraging trust.

Prediction: Repeated interactions and positive experiences help a trustor predict the trustee's future behaviour with greater accuracy.[18] This predictability reduces uncertainty and builds confidence in the relationship. For instance, consistent on-time delivery, adherence to quality standards and responsiveness to queries over time can lead a buyer to trust a supplier's reliability. Open and frequent communication is vital for enabling predictability. Sharing information about production schedules and potential delays and proactively addressing concerns demonstrates transparency, allows the buyer to anticipate and plan accordingly, and fosters a sense of trust.

> Modern CRM systems with relationship mapping capabilities can help track and analyse the strength and frequency of customer connections across different organizational levels. This systematic approach to relationship management, which I call 'multi-threading,' has become crucial for success.
>
> Dr Beth Rogers

Capability: Trust can develop through assessing the trustee's competence and ability to fulfil its promises.[19] Demonstrating expertise, technical capabilities and a track record of successful project completion enhances the trustor's confidence in the trustee's reliability. For instance, a supplier showcasing industry certifications, advanced technology or a team of experienced engineers can instil trust in their ability to deliver high-quality products or services. Sharing success stories and expertise and providing evidence of past successes, such as case studies or testimonials from satisfied customers, can showcase capability and build trust. Active participation in industry events or publishing thought leadership articles can further reinforce a supplier's expertise and trustworthiness in their domain.

Intentionality: This process focuses on interpreting the trustee's motives and intentions. If the trustor perceives the trustee's actions as genuinely motivated by a desire to benefit the relationship or the trustor's wellbeing, trust is more likely to develop. For instance, a supplier offering proactive support, going beyond contractual obligations to help the buyer solve a problem or demonstrating a commitment to mutual growth can signal benevolent intentions and foster trust. Relationship-building by investing time in understanding the buyer's business goals and challenges, offering solutions tailored to their needs and engaging in open dialogues about future collaborations demonstrates a genuine interest in the buyer's success. Such actions go beyond transactional interactions and contribute to a stronger, trust-based relationship.

Transference: Trust can be transferred from a trusted source to a new party with whom the trustor has limited direct experience. For instance, a supplier recommended by a trusted industry partner or association benefits from the existing trust associated with the referring entity. Similarly, a new salesperson representing a well-reputed supplier firm inherits the trust built by the company's brand and past performance. For instance, leveraging industry networks and endorsements and actively engaging in industry associations, seeking partnerships with reputable organizations, or obtaining endorsements from respected individuals can facilitate trust transference. These associations create a halo effect, enhancing the supplier's perceived trustworthiness based on their connection to trusted entities.

Table 6.1 shows strategies for enhancing supplier-customer trust.

TABLE 6.1 Strategies for enhancing supplier-customer trust

Trust-building Strategy	Actions
Initial trust building	Systematically mapping key decision-makers, influencers and end-users while understanding their priorities, concerns and communication preferences. Personalized engagement plans aligned with stakeholders' working styles and objectives, creating tailored interaction strategies. Regular communication with predictable touchpoints through scheduled reviews, updates and informal check-ins. Value-tracking mechanisms to document and measure the impact of initiatives on client objectives.
Ongoing trust maintenance	Relationship health checks regularly assess engagement quality, satisfaction levels and partnership strength across stakeholder groups. Proactive value demonstrations identifying and implementing new opportunities for improvement before clients request them. Knowledge sharing informing clients of industry trends, best practices and relevant innovations.
Trust recovery	Quick issue acknowledgement, taking immediate ownership when problems arise, and communicating the impact and initial response. Resolution plans outlining specific steps, timelines and responsibilities for addressing issues. Progress updates to maintain transparency throughout the resolution process. Post-resolution analysis to examine root causes and lessons learned to prevent recurrence.
Internal alignment	Executive sponsorship to provide high-level support and resources for trust-building initiatives. Incentive alignment to ensure teams are rewarded for building strong client relationships rather than just short-term wins. Success metrics to establish clear benchmarks for measuring relationship strength and value delivery.
Team development	Training programmes to equip teams with essential skills in relationship management, communication and value creation. Mentoring relationships to pair experienced staff with newer team members to transfer knowledge and best practices. Knowledge-sharing sessions to facilitate learning from successes and challenges across accounts.
Process implementation	Communication protocols to establish clear guidelines for client interaction and internal coordination. Standard operating procedures to ensure consistent service delivery and quality control. Performance tracking mechanisms to measure success against established metrics.

(continued)

TABLE 6.1 (Continued)

Trust-building Strategy	Actions
Measuring success through metrics	Quantitative metrics like satisfaction scores, relationship longevity and share of wallet provide objective measures of success. Qualitative indicators, including stakeholder feedback and collaboration levels, offer deeper insights into relationship health. Regular assessment through relationship reviews and performance evaluations ensures ongoing effectiveness.
Adaptation and evolution	Engagement strategies to meet changing client needs and market conditions. New tools and technologies are needed to keep service delivery current and efficient.

> One aspect that I believe is often overlooked is the importance of stamina and persistence. Key account managers need to be resilient, able to take knocks and keep moving forward. As I often say, we can't have 'rabbits in the headlights' when problems arise.
>
> Dr Sue Holt

Enablers for building supplier-key customer trust

In the context of supplier-key customer relationships, several factors can enable and accelerate trust development:

Shared values and vision: When both parties align on core values, ethical principles and long-term goals, it fosters a sense of shared purpose and mutual understanding. This alignment reduces the likelihood of conflicts arising from differing priorities and encourages trust-based decision-making. For instance, if both the supplier and the customer value sustainability and ethical sourcing practices, it strengthens their partnership and promotes trust.[20,21]

Open and transparent communication: Clear, consistent and timely communication builds trust by reducing uncertainty and fostering a sense of partnership. Regular updates on production progress, potential delays and proactive problem-solving demonstrate a commitment to keeping the customer informed and involved. Using multiple channels for communication, such as face-to-face meetings, video conferences and detailed reports, can cater to different preferences and ensure information clarity.[22]

Willingness to be vulnerable: Trust requires both parties to be willing to take risks and depend on each other. Sharing confidential information, involving the customer in product development processes or granting access to internal systems can demonstrate vulnerability and signal a high level of trust. These actions require careful consideration and a clear understanding of the risks involved, but they can significantly strengthen the relationship.[23]

Mutual dependence and investment: When both parties are invested in the relationship's success and have a clear understanding of their interdependence, it creates a strong incentive to act in a trustworthy manner. For instance, a supplier investing in dedicated resources or infrastructure to serve a key customer demonstrates commitment and fosters trust. Similarly, a customer providing long-term contracts or volume commitments assures the supplier of their loyalty and encourages reciprocal trust.[24]

Effective conflict resolution: Disagreements are inevitable in any relationship. However, how these conflicts are handled significantly impacts trust development. Establishing clear processes for addressing disputes, focusing on collaborative problem-solving and actively listening to each other's perspectives can prevent conflicts from escalating and damaging trust. Fair and transparent conflict resolution mechanisms, such as involving a neutral third party or mediation, can further strengthen trust by ensuring that both parties feel heard and respected.[25]

Barriers to trust building

While the aforementioned processes and enablers facilitate trust development, several barriers can hinder or even damage trust:

Lack of communication or transparency: Limited communication, withholding information or being evasive when addressing concerns creates suspicion and undermines trust. For instance, failing to inform the customer about production delays or changes in product specifications can lead to distrust and damage the relationship.

Inconsistent behaviour: Trust is built on predictability and reliability. Inconsistent behaviour, such as fluctuating product quality, missed deadlines or unmet promises, erodes trust and raises doubts about the supplier's competence and commitment. It's crucial to align internal processes with customer expectations and ensure that actions consistently reflect commitments.[26]

Cultural differences: Differences in national or organizational cultures can lead to misunderstandings, conflicting expectations and communication barriers that hinder trust development. For instance, varying approaches to negotiation, decision-making or communication styles can create friction and distrust. Investing time in understanding cultural nuances and adapting communication strategies to bridge these differences is essential.

Power imbalances: A significant power imbalance in the relationship can create a sense of vulnerability and distrust for the less powerful party. For example, a dominant customer might dictate terms or exert pressure on a smaller supplier, leading to resentment and distrust. Balancing power dynamics, fostering mutual respect and ensuring that both parties have a voice in decision-making can mitigate this barrier.

Past trust violations: Previous negative experiences, such as breaches of contract, dishonesty or opportunistic behaviour, can severely damage trust and make it challenging to rebuild. Rebuilding trust after a violation requires acknowledging the breach, taking responsibility, implementing corrective actions and consistently demonstrating trustworthiness over time.

Developing trust in supplier-key customer relationships is an ongoing process that requires commitment, effort and a genuine desire to build a mutually beneficial partnership. By understanding the key processes involved, focusing on enablers and proactively addressing barriers, organizations can cultivate strong, trust-based relationships that lead to enhanced collaboration, innovation and long-term success.

> Trust has cultural and developmental aspects – how we learn to trust or distrust is shaped by our early experiences and social context.
>
> What's your perspective on this? Do you tend to think of trust as more of a thinking process or an emotional one in your experience?

The key account manager as a trusted advisor

We argue that a key capability of a KAMgr is to generate trust and to foster trustworthy key customer relationships. KAMgrs are increasingly expected to function as trusted advisors,[27] delivering strategic guidance, insightful perspectives and effective solutions that contribute significantly to their key customers' enduring success. This transition necessitates a more profound comprehension of the nature of trust and the specific actions KAMgrs can implement to cultivate it.

A **trusted advisor** transcends the conventional role of a salesperson. They are individuals upon whom clients depend for their specialized knowledge, impartial judgment and genuine concern for the client's wellbeing. Perceived as invaluable partners, they offer guidance, unwavering support and constructive challenges that empower clients to attain their objectives. Trusted advisors possess a distinctive fusion of competence, integrity and genuine care, inspiring confidence and fostering enduring partnerships. Clients seek them out not only for their technical proficiency but also for their capacity to grasp their needs, perspectives and ambitions.

> Trust is the foundation of every successful relationship. In our industry, where contracts can span decades and involve billions of dollars, trust is the foundation of every successful relationship. Without it, even the most innovative solutions or competitive prices won't secure long-term partnerships.
>
> Mark Bailey

The **trust equation**, as elucidated in Maister and colleagues' seminal book *The Trusted Advisor*,[28] provides a valuable framework for comprehending the intricacies of trust. It proposes that trustworthiness comprises four fundamental components:

- **Credibility**: This refers to how the trustor perceives the advisor's expertise, knowledge base and experience. It is crucial for the advisor to demonstrate a deep understanding of the client's situation and business.
- **Reliability**: This element centres on the consistency and dependability of the advisor's actions and their commitment to fulfilling promises. Clients need to be able to rely on their advisors to deliver on their commitments.
- **Intimacy**: Intimacy encompasses the emotional connection and the sense of safety and vulnerability that the client experiences when sharing information and confiding in the advisor. It involves active listening, understanding the client's feelings and demonstrating empathy.
- **Self-orientation**: This aspect concerns the degree to which the advisor focuses on their own interests as opposed to the client's needs. A trusted advisor prioritizes the client's needs and demonstrates a genuine desire to help them succeed.

FIGURE 6.1 Key elements of engaging, communicating and building trust with customers

$$\text{Trustworthiness} = \frac{\text{Credibility} + \text{Reliability} + \text{Intimacy}}{\text{Self-Orientation}}$$

The trust equation indicates that trustworthiness strengthens as credibility, reliability and intimacy increase. Conversely, a high degree of self-orientation erodes trust.

The path to becoming a trusted advisor: Strategies for key account managers

Building trust is a gradual process that demands consistent effort. Key account managers can utilize the trust equation to cultivate specific behaviours and practices that nurture trust within their key accounts:

ENHANCING CREDIBILITY: LAYING THE FOUNDATION OF EXPERTISE

Enhancing credibility involves establishing a strong perception of competence and knowledge in the eyes of the client. A key question for KAMgrs becomes – how can you develop credibility? Here are some tactics:

- **Deep industry and customer knowledge:** A trusted advisor possesses an in-depth understanding of their clients' industries, the business challenges they face and the competitive landscape in which they operate. KAMgrs can enhance their credibility by continually expanding their knowledge of their key accounts' operational intricacies, strategic aspirations and the dynamics of their markets.

Imagine a KAMgr working with a major supermarket chain. To deepen their industry knowledge, they could research trends in food retail, such as the rise of online grocery shopping, the increasing demand for organic produce and the impact of changing consumer preferences. This understanding would allow the KAMgr to offer relevant advice on supply chain optimization, product assortment and marketing strategies.

- **Showcasing expertise and insights:** Sharing pertinent industry trends, best practices gleaned from experience and innovative solutions demonstrates a KAMgr's knowledge and capacity to deliver tangible value. Active engagement in industry events, contributions to thought leadership articles and presentations of compelling case studies can further solidify their expertise.

- **Building a proven track record:** The foundation of trust is often built upon a history of success. Consistently exceeding expectations, meeting deadlines and delivering on promises builds a reputation for reliability and competence. Documenting successful projects, gathering positive customer testimonials and sharing favourable outcomes progressively reinforce credibility over time.

FOSTERING RELIABILITY: THE CORNERSTONE OF DEPENDABILITY

This centres on consistently delivering on promises and demonstrating a commitment to meeting the client's expectations

- **Consistency and predictability:** Reliability stems from consistent actions and predictable outcomes. KAMgrs should strive for uniformity in their communication style, responsiveness and follow-through. Transparent communication regarding timelines, expectations and potential hurdles helps manage uncertainty and cultivates trust.

- **Honouring commitments:** Delivering on promises, regardless of magnitude, is paramount for establishing trust. KAMgrs must be realistic in the commitments they make, avoiding the pitfall of overpromising. Should unforeseen circumstances necessitate adjustments or delays, transparent and timely communication is essential.

> If a KAMgr promises to deliver a proposal by a specific date, they should strive to meet that deadline. If unforeseen circumstances cause a delay, they should communicate transparently and proactively offer an updated timeline. Failing to deliver on promises erodes trust and damages the relationship.

- **Proactive problem solving:** Anticipating potential challenges and proactively addressing them exhibits a commitment to the client's success. By assuming ownership of issues, presenting viable solutions and surpassing contractual obligations, KAMgrs fortify their reliability and cultivate trust.

A KAMgr working with a manufacturing company notices potential delays in their client's production schedule due to an upcoming supplier holiday. They proactively contact the client, inform them of the potential issue and offer solutions such as adjusting delivery schedules or identifying alternative suppliers. This proactive problem-solving showcases the KAMgr's commitment to the client's success and strengthens their reliability.

CULTIVATING INTIMACY: BUILDING GENUINE CONNECTIONS

This goes beyond simply fulfilling business transactions; it involves establishing a deeper, more personal connection with the client:

- **Building personal rapport:** Enduring relationships are founded upon personal connections and shared understanding that extend beyond mere professional interactions. KAMgrs can nurture intimacy by dedicating time to getting to know their clients on a personal level, fostering a sense of shared values and mutual respect.

- **Active listening and empathy:** Genuine interest in the client's viewpoint, actively listening to their concerns and demonstrating empathy for their emotional context build rapport and create a safe environment for candid and open communication.

When a client expresses frustration about challenges within their organization, a KAMgr should listen attentively, acknowledge their feelings and demonstrate empathy by saying things like 'I understand how frustrating that must be', or 'It sounds like you're facing a difficult situation'. This active listening and empathy demonstrate genuine concern and build rapport.

- **Appropriate vulnerability:** Trust flourishes in an environment of reciprocity. By judiciously sharing pertinent personal experiences or acknowledging past missteps, KAMgrs can demonstrate vulnerability and encourage a similar level of openness from their clients. This necessitates careful judgment and a focus on fostering a sense of shared humanity.

MINIMIZING SELF-ORIENTATION: PRIORITIZING THE CLIENT'S NEEDS

It requires consciously shifting the focus away from one's own agenda, motivations or desires and placing the client's needs at the forefront of all interactions.

- **Focusing on client needs**: Trusted advisors inherently prioritize their clients' interests above their own. KAMgrs should exhibit a genuine desire to assist their clients in achieving success, even if it entails foregoing short-term gains or recommending solutions that don't directly benefit their own company.

A KAMgr presented with the opportunity to sell a high-value product that might not fully address the client's needs could choose to recommend a more suitable, even less expensive, solution. This demonstrates a commitment to the client's best interests, even if it means a smaller immediate profit for the KAMgr's company.

- **Transparency and honesty**: Openly addressing potential conflicts of interest, being upfront about limitations and presenting a balanced perspective on all options – even suggesting a competitor's solution when appropriate – builds trust through honesty and transparency.
- **Seeking feedback and asking questions**: Regularly soliciting client input, asking clarifying questions and actively seeking feedback demonstrate a commitment to comprehending their needs and customizing solutions accordingly.

By consistently applying these principles and embodying these behaviours, KAMgrs can successfully transition from transactional salespeople to indispensable trusted advisors. In doing so, they forge deeper, more meaningful relationships and contribute significantly to the ongoing success of their key accounts. This transformation elevates the KAMgrs' role, creating a powerful synergy that benefits both the client and the advisor.

Summary and application

Success in communicating and building trust development requires a comprehensive approach combining personal actions, team leadership and systematic processes. The most effective KAMgrs balance personal relationship building with systematic approaches, creating sustainable trust-based relationships that deliver value for both organizations. Here are some actions for you to consider to become a genuine communicator and trust builder.

Table 6.2 shows actions for genuine communication and trust building. Figure 6.2 shows key drivers, tools, behaviours and success factors.

TABLE 6.2 Actions for genuine communication and trust building

Action		Description
1.	Create personalized stakeholder communication plans	Map all key decision-makers and influencers within the customer organization. Document their preferred communication channels and styles. Set up regular touchpoints tailored to each stakeholder's needs.
2.	Implement structured information sharing	Establish clear communication protocols for different types of information. Set up regular status updates and performance reviews. Create standardized reporting templates for consistency.
3.	Practice proactive problem identification	Monitor potential issues before they become problems. Alert customers to possible challenges early. Present solution options alongside problem identification.
4.	Demonstrate industry expertise strategically	Share relevant market insights and trends. Present case studies from similar situations. Offer thought leadership without being promotional.
5.	Build personal connections systematically	Schedule regular informal check-ins. Learn about stakeholders' personal motivations and challenges. Show genuine interest in their career goals and pressures.
6.	Document and track value delivery	Create value-tracking mechanisms. Regularly measure and report impact on client objectives. Maintain a record of successful initiatives.
7.	Foster transparency through open communication	Share both positive and negative information promptly. Be upfront about limitations or constraints. Acknowledge mistakes when they occur.
8.	Develop internal coordination processes	Create clear protocols for internal communication. Establish service level agreements with internal teams. Set up regular cross-functional meetings.
9.	Build psychological safety	Create environments where difficult topics can be discussed. Encourage open feedback. Respond constructively to concerns.
10.	Institute regular relationship health checks	Conduct formal relationship reviews. Gather feedback from multiple stakeholders. Use structured assessment tools to measure trust levels.

FIGURE 6.2 Key drivers, tools, behaviours and success factors

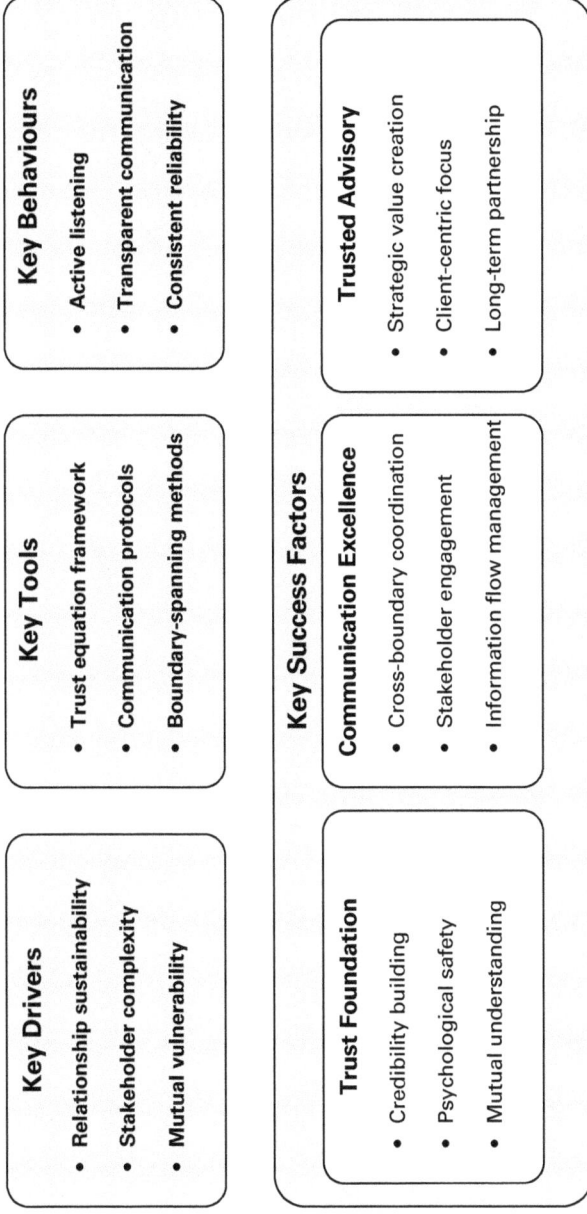

Key Drivers

- Relationship sustainability
- Stakeholder complexity
- Mutual vulnerability

Key Tools

- Trust equation framework
- Communication protocols
- Boundary-spanning methods

Key Behaviours

- Active listening
- Transparent communication
- Consistent reliability

Key Success Factors

Trust Foundation

- Credibility building
- Psychological safety
- Mutual understanding

Communication Excellence

- Cross-boundary coordination
- Stakeholder engagement
- Information flow management

Trusted Advisory

- Strategic value creation
- Client-centric focus
- Long-term partnership

Notes

1   K M Judson, G L Gordon, R E Ridnour and D A N C Weilbaker. Key account vs. other sales management systems: Is there a difference in providing customer input during the new product development process? *Marketing Management Journal*, 2009, 19 (2), 1–17

2   L Peters, B S Ivens and C Pardo. Identification as a challenge in key account management: Conceptual foundations and a qualitative study, *Industrial Marketing Management*, 2020, 90, 300–13, https://doi.org/10.1016/j. indmarman.2020.07.020 (archived at https://perma.cc/E5VQ-WPMZ)

3   J I F Speakman and L Ryals. Key account management: The inside selling job, *Journal of Business & Industrial Marketing*, 2012, 27 (5), 360–66, https://doi.org/10.1108/08858621211236034 (archived at https://perma. cc/77FY-LWUL)

4   P Bischoff, J Hogreve, L Elgeti and M KleinaltenKAMp. How salespeople adapt communication of customer value propositions in business markets, *Industrial Marketing Management*, 2023, 114, 226–42, https://doi.org/10.1016/j. indmarman.2023.08.009 (archived at https://perma.cc/K3ZK-7LXR)

5   N Winter, T E Vollman and I Francis. ABB and Caterpillar (A): Key account management, IMD, August 2007

6   T Steenburgh, M Ahearne and E Cors. Siemens: Key Account Management, Harvard Business School, June 2012, 9, Case 512-110

7   R J Schultz and K R Evans. Strategic collaborative communication by key account representatives, *Journal of Personal Selling & Sales Management*, 2002, 22 (1), 23–31

8   Speakman and Ryals. Key account management

9   J Zhang (2023) Trust-building techniques of key account managers: A Chinese perspective, MSc thesis, Cranfield School of Management

10 C Moorman, G Zaltman and R Deshpande. Relationships between providers and users of market research: The dynamics of trust within and between organizations, *Journal of Marketing Research*, 1992, 29 (3), 314–28

11 Bischoff, Hogreve, Elgeti and KleinaltenKAMp. How salespeople adapt communication of customer value propositions in business markets

12 Moorman, Zaltman and Deshpande. Relationships between providers and users of market research

13 S Ganesan and R Hess. Dimensions and levels of trust: Implications for commitment to a relationship, *Marketing Letters*, 1997, 8, 439–48

14 R C Mayer, J H Davis and F D Schoorman. An integrative model of organizational trust, *Academy of Management Review*, 1995, 20 (3), 709–73

15 H Svare, A H Gausdal and G Möllering. The function of ability, benevolence, and integrity-based trust in innovation networks, *Industry and Innovation*, 2020, 27 (6), 585–604

16 Ibid.

17 P M Doney and J P Cannon. An examination of the nature of trust in buyer-seller relationships, *Journal of Marketing*, 1997, 61 (2), 35–51, http://search.ebscohost.com/login.aspx?direct=true&db=bth&AN=970501168 5&site=ehost-live (archived at https://perma.cc/3NK9-XUFK)

18 G G Bell, R J. Oppenheimer and A Bastien. Trust deterioration in an international buyer-supplier relationship, *Journal of Business Ethics*, 2002, 36, 65–78

19 Ibid.

20 Doney and Cannon. An examination of the nature of trust in buyer-seller relationships

21 Bell, Oppenheimer and A Bastien. Trust deterioration in an international buyer-supplier relationship

22 Moorman, Zaltman and Deshpande. Relationships between providers and users of market research

23 Bell, Oppenheimer and A Bastien. Trust deterioration in an international buyer-supplier relationship

24 Ibid.

25 Moorman, Zaltman and Deshpande. Relationships between providers and users of market research

26 Ibid.

27 D H Maister, R Galford and C Green (2021) *The Trusted Advisor*, Free Press

28 Ibid.

Mark Bailey

As the former Director of Customers and Services at Rolls-Royce plc, I've accumulated 32 years of experience in the aerospace and power industry. Throughout my career, I've gained extensive insights into key account management, and I'd like to share my perspective on this crucial business function.

In my view, the role of a key account manager is multifaceted and goes far beyond traditional sales. I've always seen it as encompassing four main areas: understanding the customer and their market, providing targeted sales and support activities, managing ongoing relationships and overseeing service delivery throughout contracts. This holistic approach is essential in industries like ours, where long-term relationships and large contracts are the norm.

When it comes to defining key accounts, we never relied solely on size. While revenue is important, we also considered an account's strategic importance, influence in the market and potential for future growth. In fact, sometimes we'd consider an account 'key' even if it wasn't currently generating business. A prime example of this was our approach to Japanese customers, whom we pursued for 20 years before seeing tangible results. This long-term vision is crucial in KAM.

At Rolls-Royce, we structured our KAM function within a matrix organization. Key account managers reported to regional leaders while simultaneously working closely with product programme teams. This setup allowed for both geographical focus and product expertise. We expected our key account managers to have a deep understanding of both their customers' needs and our own capabilities. This dual knowledge was crucial for co-creating solutions that truly added value for our customers.

Performance measurement was an area we approached with great care. We implemented a balanced system that considered various factors. Of course, we looked at financial metrics like revenue and profitability, but we also paid close attention to operational performance, customer satisfaction, and behavioural aspects. I always emphasized the importance of including both objective and subjective measures. While it's easier to quantify financial results, factors like trust and relationship quality are equally crucial, even if they're harder to measure. In my experience, these softer elements often underpin long-term success in KAM.

Based on my years of experience, I've identified four key capabilities that are essential for effective key account managers:

1 Engaging, communicating, and building trust with key customers (40 per cent)

2 Building teams and enhancing cross-functional collaboration (25 per cent)

3 Fostering value-based selling and co-creating solutions (20 per cent)

4 Leading and influencing with and without authority (15 per cent)

I've assigned percentages to these capabilities to indicate their relative importance, though all are crucial. The ability to build trust is paramount. In our industry, where contracts can span decades and involve billions of dollars, trust is the foundation of every successful relationship. Without it, even the most innovative solutions or competitive prices won't secure long-term partnerships.

The second capability - building teams and enhancing cross-functional collaboration - is often overlooked but is critical to success. Key account managers rarely have direct authority over all the resources they need. They must be skilled at influencing and coordinating across different departments and levels of the organization. This requires excellent communication skills, a deep understanding of the company's operations, and the ability to align diverse stakeholders around common goals.

Fostering value-based selling and co-creating solutions is where the rubber meets the road in KAM. It's not about pushing products; it's about truly understanding the customer's business and working together to create solutions that drive their success. This often involves bringing together expertise from various parts of our organization and sometimes even from external partners.

The ability to lead and influence without formal authority ties all of these capabilities together. Key account managers need to be able to rally resources, drive decisions, and resolve conflicts, often without direct control over the people or processes involved. This requires a unique blend of leadership skills, business acumen, and interpersonal savvy.

Talent development was always a top priority in our KAM function. We took a comprehensive approach, starting with recruitment. We looked for individuals who already possessed some of these key capabilities, but we also invested heavily in ongoing training and development. We developed detailed competency frameworks, set up external accreditation programmes, and even created MSc-level training programmes in partnership with universities. This investment in our people was crucial to our success.

A crucial aspect of KAM that I consistently emphasized was its role in addressing complex issues that transcend multiple customers and geographies. In high-tech, global industries like aerospace, such challenges inevitably arise. Our key account managers often found themselves on the front lines, balancing the specific needs of their customers with the broader organizational response. This required a delicate touch, strong communication skills, and the ability to maintain trust even in challenging circumstances.

To conclude, I've always viewed key account management as going far beyond traditional sales functions. I often described the role as that of an 'orchestra leader,' where sales is a significant component but not the only one. The key account manager must harmonize various elements - customer needs, company capabilities, market trends, and internal resources - to create a symphony of mutual value creation.

The focus should always be on building long-term customer relationships that create value for both the customer and the company. This approach, in my experience, is what truly drives success in key account management. It's not always easy, and it requires a unique set of skills and a long-term perspective. But when done right, it creates partnerships that can withstand market fluctuations, technological disruptions, and competitive pressures. That's the true power of effective key account management.

Mark started his 30-year career at Rolls-Royce in 1988 as a commercial executive, before taking on several roles in programme management, aftermarket, and supply chain before eight years as Group Director of Customer and Service. He was responsible to the executive board for developing and implementing the TotalCare© customer service model, which is now a bedrock of Rolls-Royce across all divisions.

He is an executive-level coach (ILM l7), a visiting fellow, and a recognized teacher, and he teaches executive education programmes on key account management and strategic leadership. Mark spends time with executives, helping them explore the complex and intricate relationships between suppliers and key customers and how frameworks and programmes can be implemented to build successful relationships. At the time of publication, he was a Non-Executive Director on two NHS boards and a Trustee at Ashgate Hospice.

www.linkedin.com/in/mark-baileyned (archived at https://perma.cc/J5LM-CBTL)

07

Fostering value-based selling and co-creating solutions

The art of creating shared value with key accounts

Overview

Key accounts always ask for more from their suppliers, often in the form of added and distinctive value. Key account managers (KAMgrs) are crucial in building long-term relationships with key customers and in creating value for them as well as capturing that value. In this chapter, we describe approaches KAMgrs can adopt to create customer value in ways that foster loyalty, advocacy and profitability.

The approaches for value creation that we will outline in this chapter are based on several premises we want to share with you up front. First, a key assumption is that multilevel relationships are established. Key account managers are the architects of building strong relationships with various functions of their customers in a way that enables regular communication, understanding their business challenges and needs, and often personal interests and constraints. So, if your customers are willing to do business with you exclusively via requests for proposals (RFPs) or online auctions, these value creation principles do not apply.

The second premise is that you, as a key account manager, have some leeway in personalizing the solutions you sell to your strategic customers and how you sell them. Each customer has idiosyncratic needs and specifications, and the extent to which you tailor your products and services to your customer's unique requirements creates value that is more relevant and impactful. If you are in a commodity business, characterized by a single delivery channel, then little can be done to create value beyond the product or service.

The third premise is that your organization values both what and how you sell. If your sole KPI is sales revenue, and it is focused on the short term (e.g. quarterly sales quota), then establishing trust, enhancing your customers' environmental, social and governance (ESG) goals, and helping the customer get their job done will likely become secondary priorities in your agenda.

So, assuming that you interact with multiple stakeholders in your customer organization, that your product/service solution and customer engagement processes can be tailored to address meaningful customer interests, and that you and your business care about multiple dimensions of customer success, the remainder of this chapter aims to address the crucial question: *How can key account managers engage in value-selling and co-create value with their key customers?*

Its importance to key account managers

The significance of value-based selling and co-creating solutions cannot be overstated in the dynamic landscape of business-to-business sales and key account management. This approach represents a paradigm shift from traditional product-centric selling to a customer-centric model that prioritizes the delivery of tangible value and collaborative solution development. As organizations strive to differentiate themselves in increasingly competitive markets, the adoption of these strategies has become not just beneficial, but essential for sustainable growth and success.

ON FOSTERING VALUE-BASED SELLING AND CO-CREATING SOLUTIONS

Fostering value-based selling and co-creating solutions is where the rubber meets the road in KAM. It's not about pushing products; it's about truly understanding the customer's business and working together to create solutions that drive their success. This often involves bringing together expertise from various parts of our organization and sometimes even from external partners.

Mark Bailey

Value-based selling and co-creation support building stronger and more enduring customer relationships, drive innovation and maximize the lifetime value of their key accounts. Moreover, these strategies enhance sales efficiency, align with complex B2B buying processes, and contribute to organizational learning and capability development. They also provide resilience in the face of economic uncertainties and allow companies to address growing concerns around sustainability and corporate responsibility.

As the business landscape continues to evolve, those organizations that excel in value-based selling and solution co-creation will be best positioned to thrive, fostering mutually beneficial partnerships that drive sustained growth and success for both them and their key accounts. The shift towards these approaches is not just a trend, but a fundamental reimagining of the supplier-customer relationship in the B2B space, one that promises to shape the future of key account management and B2B sales more broadly.

Shifting economic environment and customer expectations

In times of economic uncertainty or downturn, the importance of value-based selling and co-creation becomes even more pronounced. When budgets are tight, the ability to clearly articulate and demonstrate value becomes crucial in justifying purchasing decisions. Co-created solutions often lead to more efficient use of resources on both the supplier and customer sides, which is particularly valuable in challenging economic conditions.

Also, today's B2B customers are more informed, discerning and value-conscious. They seek more than just products or services; they want solutions to complex problems and partnerships that contribute meaningfully to their business objectives. One-size-fits-all offerings are increasingly ineffective. Customers expect solutions tailored to their specific challenges and objectives. Value-based selling and co-creation directly address these evolving expectations by prioritizing the customer's unique needs and involving them in the solution development process.

The B2B buying process has become increasingly complex, often involving multiple stakeholders and decision-makers. Value-based selling and co-creation align well with this evolving landscape, since the collaborative nature of these approaches helps engage multiple stakeholders within the customer organization, addressing diverse concerns and priorities. By focusing on value and involving key stakeholders in solution development, suppliers can facilitate consensus-building within the customer's organization.

Importantly, the collaborative nature of value-based selling and solution co-creation fosters stronger, more enduring customer relationships. By prioritizing the customer's success and involving them in the solution development process, suppliers build trust and credibility. Moreover, the co-creation process necessitates a profound understanding of the customer's business, challenges and goals, leading to more meaningful and productive relationships. Customers who perceive high value and feel invested in co-created solutions are more likely to remain loyal and resistant to competitive offers.

Improving opportunities for differentiation, efficiency and effectiveness

In markets where products and services are becoming increasingly commoditized, the ability to articulate and deliver unique value propositions is a critical differentiator.

Value-based selling shifts the conversation away from price comparisons to focus on the overall value delivered, reducing the pressure to compete solely on cost. Likewise, by co-creating solutions, companies can develop offerings that are inherently differentiated, ensuring that the value delivered is precisely aligned with each key account's specific needs and objectives, creating a compelling reason for customers to choose and remain loyal to the supplier.

In addition, value-based selling and co-creation can lead to more efficient and effective sales processes. By focusing on value creation, sales teams can more easily identify and prioritize prospects who are likely to benefit most from their offerings and decision-making processes can be accelerated as the alignment between offering and need is more apparent.

Value-based selling and co-creation are particularly effective in maximizing the long-term value of key account relationships. A deep understanding of customer value drivers opens opportunities for cross-selling and upselling, and customers who perceive high value and are invested in co-created solutions are less likely to switch to competitors. Furthermore, satisfied customers who recognize the unique value provided are more likely to become advocates and provide referrals, further driving growth.

Enabling innovation, organizational learning and sustainability

The process of co-creating solutions with key accounts serves as a powerful driver of innovation. Close collaboration with customers provides invaluable insights into emerging market trends, challenges and opportunities. Similarly, co-creation allows for quick feedback loops and iterative improvements, accelerating the pace of innovation while ensuring that their offerings remain relevant and aligned with market needs.

The practice of value-based selling and solution co-creation also drives continuous learning and capability development within the selling organization. These approaches often require collaboration across different departments (sales, marketing, product development, etc.), fostering a more integrated and agile organization. Sales professionals and key account managers develop deeper industry knowledge, stronger consultative skills and enhanced business acumen through the practice of value-based selling and co-creation. Insights gained from co-creation processes with one key account can often be applied to benefit other accounts, enhancing the overall value proposition of the organization.

Increasingly, B2B customers are factoring sustainability and corporate responsibility into their purchasing decisions. Value-based selling allows for the incorporation of broader value elements, including environmental and social impacts, into the overall value proposition. Besides, co-creation processes can explicitly incorporate sustainability goals, leading to solutions that not only meet business objectives but also contribute to broader corporate responsibility initiatives. This strengthens the alignment of values between supplier and customer, further solidifying the relationship.

The following box provides a summary of the main points that justify developing lasting relationships with key accounts.

WHY FOSTERING VALUE-BASED SELLING AND CO-CREATING SOLUTIONS IS IMPORTANT

Shifting economic environment and customer expectations:

- Approaching the customer under economic uncertainty
- Meeting evolving customer expectations
- Addressing buying process complexity
- Building stronger relationships

Improving opportunities for differentiation, efficiency and effectiveness:

- Differentiating in commoditized markets
- Streamlining the sales process
- Maximizing key account value
- Driving advocacy and growth

Enabling innovation, organizational learning and sustainability:

- Driving innovation
- Fostering organizational learning
- Incorporating sustainability
- Strengthening relationships

Value-based selling

Solution to a problem and a strategic sales approach

Let's consider a company, TechFlow Solutions, that provides industrial software for manufacturing optimization. Their key customer, ManuCore, is a medium-sized manufacturer aiming to improve production efficiency and reduce costs. In a product-centred sales strategy, TechFlow's sales pitch would focus on features and price points. The pitch might go like this:

> Our software is cloud-based, supports up to 10,000 data points per second and integrates with most ERP systems. The annual subscription is $50,000, and you can add modules for an additional $10,000 each.

The focus is purely on the product specs and cost, leaving ManuCore to figure out how it aligns with their business goals. While this approach may resonate with some technical teams, it doesn't engage the decision-makers who care about ROI or strategic benefits. Consequently, ManuCore's purchasing manager might compare this offer directly with competitors, focusing only on price and features, which can lead to price-driven negotiations and potentially a lower-margin deal for TechFlow.

Let's think now of a different selling approach, where TechFlow shifts the conversation to outcomes and business impact, tailoring the discussion to ManuCore's specific challenges. The pitch might go like this:

> We've analysed your current production metrics and estimate our software can reduce downtime by 15 per cent and energy costs by 10 per cent, saving you around $500,000 annually. By improving production visibility, you'll also be able to shorten lead times, which could unlock new contracts with your key customers.

In this second pitch, instead of selling a product, TechFlow sells a solution to a problem. They use data, industry benchmarks and even offer a case study of another manufacturer who achieved similar results. This sales pitch centres on value, and ManuCore's executives can see the software as a strategic enabler, not just a cost item. They're less likely to push for discounts and more likely to view TechFlow as a partner and not just as a regular supplier.

This shift from product to value is not just about better sales techniques; it's about deeply understanding the customer's business and aligning your offer with their strategic goals. That's the kind of partnership that keeps customers coming back.

Value-based selling (VBS) is a strategic sales approach that focuses on creating and communicating the unique value a product or service can provide to customers, rather than emphasizing features, benefits or price. This approach aligns the seller's offerings with the customer's business objectives, challenges and value drivers, ultimately aiming to demonstrate how the proposed solution can positively impact the customer's bottom line.[1,2] VBS is customer-centric in that it prioritizes understanding the customer's business, identifying their specific needs and pain points, and then articulating how the supplier's product or service can address these issues in a way that creates measurable value for the customer.

VBS has become a critical selling approach in today's business environment.[3] It involves collaborating with customers to craft a compelling customer value proposition and quantifying the value of that proposition in monetary terms.[4] Thus, this approach requires sales executives or key account managers to act more as consultants or business advisors, helping customers understand and realize the full potential value of the proposed solution.

Dimensions of value-based selling

There are three main dimensions of value-based selling[5] that are worth examining in detail, which are explained in the next paragraphs. Building on the work by Terho and colleagues, these dimensions are expanded considering the current business landscape, which requires a more dynamic, technologically integrated, sustainable and ethically conscious approach. Figure 7.1 shows these dimensions.

FIGURE 7.1 Dimensions of value-based selling

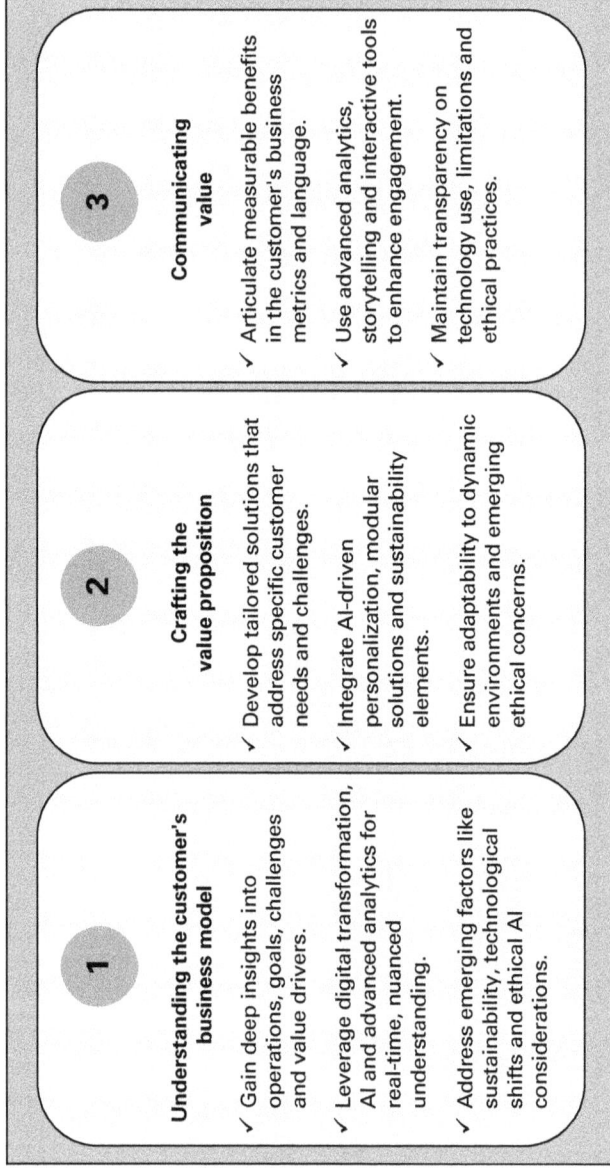

1

Understanding the customer's business model

✓ Gain deep insights into operations, goals, challenges and value drivers.

✓ Leverage digital transformation, AI and advanced analytics for real-time, nuanced understanding.

✓ Address emerging factors like sustainability, technological shifts and ethical AI considerations.

2

Crafting the value proposition

✓ Develop tailored solutions that address specific customer needs and challenges.

✓ Integrate AI-driven personalization, modular solutions and sustainability elements.

✓ Ensure adaptability to dynamic environments and emerging ethical concerns.

3

Communicating value

✓ Articulate measurable benefits in the customer's business metrics and language.

✓ Use advanced analytics, storytelling and interactive tools to enhance engagement.

✓ Maintain transparency on technology use, limitations and ethical practices.

In the contemporary business landscape, VBS has transcended traditional transactional paradigms to become a holistic strategic framework that demands profound customer understanding and collaborative value creation. The digital transformation has equipped sales professionals and KAMgrs with sophisticated analytics, artificial intelligence and customer relationship management tools that enable unprecedented granularity in identifying and articulating customer value propositions. Where historical approaches focused primarily on product features and price, modern value-based selling integrates comprehensive insights into customer business models, operational challenges and strategic objectives, allowing sales professionals to position solutions as transformative investments rather than mere commodities.

Moreover, the ethical dimension of value-based selling has gained critical prominence in an era of increasing corporate accountability and stakeholder transparency. Organizations now recognize that authentic value creation extends beyond immediate financial metrics to encompass broader societal impacts, sustainability considerations and long-term partnership potential. This evolution requires sales teams to develop a more nuanced capability of value articulation – one that demonstrates not just economic benefits, but also environmental, social and governance (ESG) contributions. By aligning sales strategies with these multidimensional value propositions, companies can differentiate themselves in competitive markets, build more resilient customer relationships, and contribute to a more sustainable and interconnected business ecosystem.

1. UNDERSTANDING THE CUSTOMER'S BUSINESS MODEL

This dimension involves gaining deep insights into the customer's operations, goals, challenges and value drivers. It is critical because it forms the foundational knowledge that enables truly value-creating solutions. By deeply understanding a customer's business model, companies can move beyond surface-level interactions to become strategic partners who can genuinely impact the customer's performance.

For example, consider a software company selling enterprise resource planning (ERP) solutions. Instead of simply pitching features, they first conduct an in-depth analysis of the potential client's supply chain, revenue streams, operational bottlenecks and strategic goals. They might discover that a manufacturing client struggles with inventory management inefficiencies that are directly impacting on their profit margins.

The digital transformation, advanced analytics and the use of artificial intelligence have dramatically enhanced how we can understand customer business models, by bringing in much deeper, real-time insights into business operations. For instance, machine learning algorithms can help predict potential challenges and opportunities within a customer's business model, while digital twins and comprehensive data integration allow for more nuanced, predictive understanding of business ecosystems.

With respect to other emerging considerations, sustainability metrics must now be integrated into business model understanding, rapid technological changes mean business models are more fluid and require more frequent reassessment, and ethical AI and data privacy considerations add complexity to deep business model analysis.

2. CRAFTING THE VALUE PROPOSITION

This dimension of VBS refers to developing a tailored value proposition that demonstrates how their offering can address specific customer needs and create value. The value proposition is the critical bridge between a company's capabilities and the customer's specific needs. It transforms a generic offering into a targeted solution that directly addresses the customer's unique challenges and opportunities.

To illustrate, a cloud computing provider doesn't just sell server space, but crafts a value proposition that shows how their specific cloud solution can for example reduce a financial services firm's IT infrastructure costs by 40 per cent, improve data security and enable faster digital transformation.

In the new landscape, the use of AI enables value propositions to become increasingly personalized and dynamic. In addition, modular and adaptable solutions are replacing one-size-fits-all approaches, while real-time data allows for continuous refinement of value propositions. These new elements must address emerging concerns like data privacy and ethical technology use.

Additionally, value propositions gradually integrate elements of sustainable development, both from an environmental and a social perspective. Finally, value propositions must also show resilience and adaptability in uncertain global environments.

3. COMMUNICATING VALUE

This VBS dimension focuses on effectively articulating and quantifying the value of the proposed solution in terms that resonate with the customer's business metrics and objectives. Effective value communication transforms potential benefits into tangible, measurable outcomes. It's about translating technical capabilities into business language that resonates with decision-makers.

For instance, instead of presenting technical specifications, a cybersecurity firm demonstrates how their solution can prevent potential data breaches that could cost the client millions in lost revenue, regulatory fines and reputational damage.

In recent years, value communication has become more sophisticated, and data driven. Advanced analytics provide more precise, real-time value measurement, while interactive dashboards and predictive modelling allow for more dynamic value communication. Likewise, storytelling and visual communication tools have become more advanced than before.

Communicating value to customers requires transparency about the use of AI and technology and their limitations, together with clear communication of ethical considerations.

REAL-WORLD EXAMPLE
Applying the dimensions of value-based selling

GreenFuture, a B2B provider of advanced energy management systems (EMS), is targeting GlobalTech, a multinational manufacturing company struggling with high energy costs, inefficient production processes and increasing pressure to meet ESG (environmental, social, governance) goals. GreenFuture's EMS leverages AI-driven analytics, IoT devices and cloud-based platforms to optimize energy use, reduce operational inefficiencies and support sustainable practices.

Dimension 1: Understanding the customer's business model

GreenFuture begins by conducting a comprehensive analysis of GlobalTech's operations, including their production lines, energy consumption patterns and ESG reporting. GreenFuture discovers that:

- GlobalTech's energy expenditure constitutes 25 per cent of its operational costs.
- Their production downtime due to inefficiencies averages 8 per cent, causing significant revenue losses.
- ESG compliance is becoming a critical priority for their stakeholders, with particular focus on reducing carbon emissions by 30 per cent within three years.

Using advanced analytics and IoT sensors, GreenFuture collects real-time data on GlobalTech's energy usage, uncovering patterns of waste during non-peak hours and opportunities for process automation. Sustainability metrics are integrated to assess the carbon footprint across their operations.

Dimension 2: Crafting the value proposition

Based on the insights gathered, GreenFuture develops a tailored value proposition for GlobalTech:

GreenFuture's AI-driven EMS will reduce GlobalTech's energy costs by up to 20 per cent, optimize production processes to decrease downtime by 50 per cent, and help achieve your ESG goals by cutting carbon emissions by 35 per cent within three years. This solution not only improves operational efficiency but also enhances GlobalTech's reputation as a leader in sustainable manufacturing.

The value proposition emphasizes:

- **Economic value**: Cost savings through energy optimization and reduced downtime.
- **Operational efficiency**: Real-time monitoring and predictive maintenance.
- **Sustainability impact**: Meeting and exceeding ESG targets.

The use of modular and adaptive EMS solutions ensures flexibility, allowing GlobalTech to scale or modify their system as their needs evolve. Ethical AI practices are highlighted, assuring transparency and compliance with data privacy regulations.

Dimension 3: Communicating value

GreenFuture employs a data-driven and customer-centric approach to communicate the proposed value:

- **Quantitative insights**: Interactive dashboards showcase potential savings, operational improvements and carbon emission reductions based on predictive modelling. For example, 'In the first six months, energy savings of $1.2 million are achievable, with a 20 per cent reduction in downtime.'
- **Storytelling**: GreenFuture shares a case study of a similar manufacturing client who achieved a 25 per cent reduction in energy costs and enhanced their ESG compliance through the EMS.
- **Visual tools**: Infographics illustrate how the EMS integrates seamlessly with GlobalTech's existing infrastructure, and 3D visualizations demonstrate real-time system monitoring.
- **Addressing concerns**: Clear communication about data privacy safeguards and the ethical use of AI builds trust.

By aligning the proposed solution with GlobalTech's strategic objectives and presenting measurable outcomes, GreenFuture ensures that decision-makers understand both the immediate and long-term value of their offering.

Outcome: After a series of value-focused discussions, GlobalTech agrees to implement GreenFuture's EMS. Within the first year, GlobalTech achieves a 22 per cent reduction in energy costs, a 40 per cent decrease in downtime and a

30 per cent cut in carbon emissions, surpassing their ESG targets. The collaboration evolves into a long-term partnership, with GreenFuture providing continuous support and system enhancements.

Value co-creation

A strategic decision based on mutual trust, shared goals and commitment

Value co-creation is a collaborative approach where suppliers and their strategic customers work together to generate mutual value. It constitutes a paradigm shift from traditional, firm-centric views of value creation to a more collaborative, customer-centric approach. In the context of key account management, it involves a joint effort between the supplier and the strategic customer to create value that neither party could achieve independently.[6]

According to Vargo and Lusch,[7] value co-creation is rooted in the service-dominant logic, which posits that value is always co-created through the interaction of various actors, rather than being embedded in products or services. In key account management, this translates to a deep, strategic

FIGURE 7.2 Indicators of readiness for value co-creation

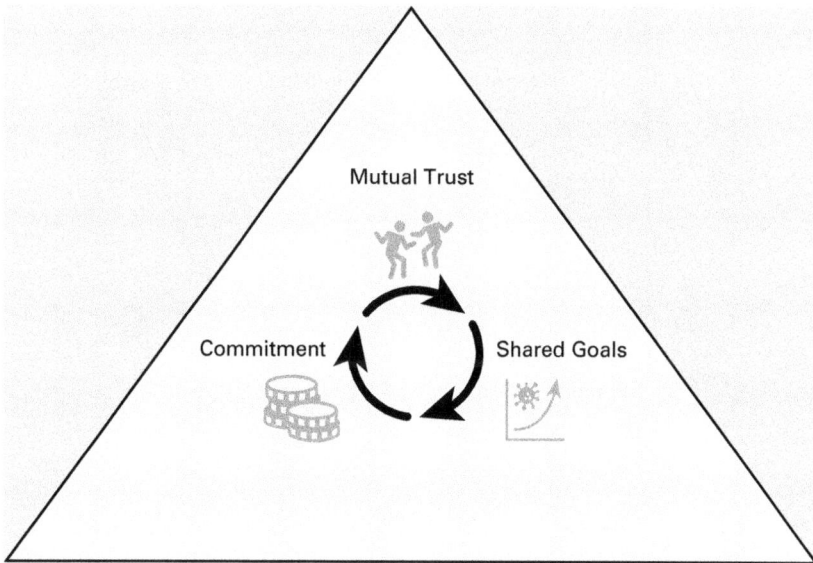

partnership where both parties contribute resources, knowledge and capabilities to achieve shared goals and create mutually beneficial outcomes.[8]

A critical question that both the supplier and the buying company should ask before fully engaging in value co-creation is: *Are we ready for it?* Readiness for value co-creation between a supplier and a key account hinges on foundational elements that enable effective collaboration. Figure 7.2 presents a summary of these readiness for value co-creation indicators.

Mutual trust is a critical indicator, as it establishes a safe environment where both parties feel confident sharing sensitive information, strategic goals and challenges. Trust allows for open communication and reduces the fear of exploitation, enabling the co-creation process to thrive. For instance, when a supplier and a key account trust each other, they are more likely to disclose insights about internal inefficiencies or market pressures, which can lead to the development of tailored, high-impact solutions.

Another vital indicator is *shared goals* between the supplier and the key account. Both parties must have a clear understanding of the desired

FIGURE 7.3 Dimensions of value co-creation in KAM

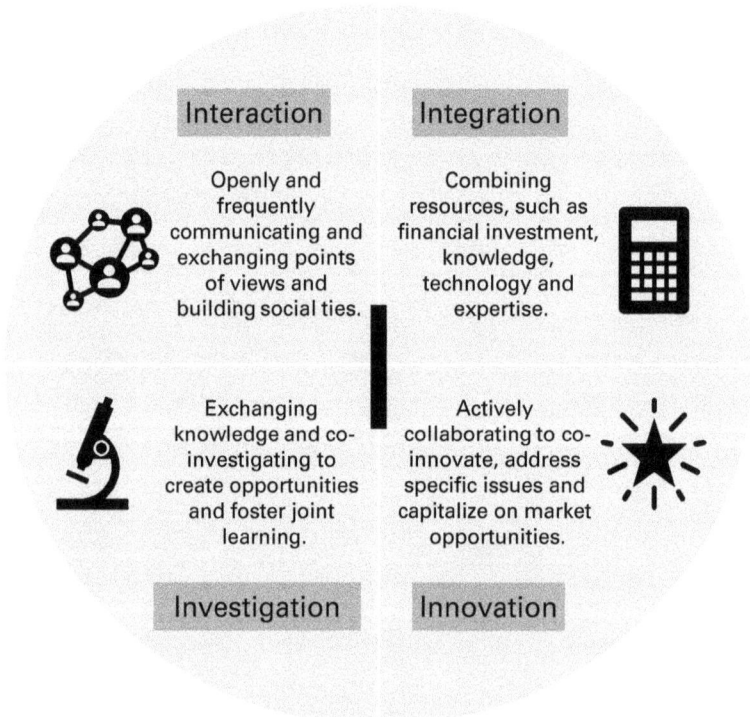

outcomes and a commitment to achieving them together. Misaligned objectives can lead to wasted resources and strained relationships, undermining the value co-creation process. Shared goals create a sense of purpose and direction, ensuring that efforts are not only collaborative but also strategically focused. For example, a shared objective of achieving carbon-neutral operations could drive joint initiatives like developing sustainable supply chain practices or green technology solutions.

In addition, *organizational commitment* to resource availability is a crucial indicator of readiness. Both the supplier and the key account must allocate dedicated teams, time and budgets to support the co-creation process. Without these resources, even the best intentions and aligned goals may falter. Furthermore, the cultural and operational adaptability of both organizations is essential for integrating new processes or co-developed innovations. For example, if a supplier is willing to adapt its manufacturing processes to meet a client's unique product specifications, it demonstrates readiness to contribute meaningfully to co-creation efforts. Collectively, these indicators ensure that both parties are not only willing but also able to co-create value effectively.

Dimensions of value co-creation

The dimensions of value co-creation refer to the ways by which a supplier company and a key account should engage in co-creation activities. We propose the *Four I* framework for value co-creation in KAM, which is depicted in Figure 7.3.

1. INTERACTION

Interaction in KAM revolves around open and frequent communication, as well as the exchange of perspectives to build strong social ties. Open dialogue ensures that both the supplier and the key account are aligned on strategic priorities and operational details, reducing misunderstandings and creating a foundation of trust. For example, a supplier might schedule regular review meetings to discuss project progress, identify challenges and propose adjustments collaboratively. Such structured interactions not only keep both parties informed but also foster a sense of partnership.

Frequent communication also strengthens the relationship by making both parties feel heard and valued. Informal interactions, such as lunch meetings or social gatherings, allow account managers and client representatives to connect on a personal level, which is crucial in building rapport. A key account manager might, for instance, arrange quarterly off-site workshops to brainstorm solutions and deepen the professional bond. These events create opportunities for open exchange and relationship building beyond day-to-day transactions.

Building social ties through interaction is particularly valuable during periods of conflict or uncertainty. When trust and communication channels are established, both sides are more willing to collaborate on finding mutually beneficial solutions. For example, a supplier facing a delay in delivery can proactively communicate with the key account, offering transparency and alternative solutions, such as expedited shipping for critical components. The established social ties ensure that such challenges are met with understanding rather than frustration, strengthening the long-term partnership.

2. INTEGRATION

Integration in KAM involves combining resources such as financial investments, knowledge, technology and expertise to create joint value. This process ensures that the strengths of both the supplier and the key account are leveraged for mutual benefit. For instance, a technology provider might co-develop a tailored software solution with a key client, sharing expertise and resources throughout the process. This collaborative effort often leads to superior outcomes that neither party could achieve independently.

Financial investments are another critical component of integration. A supplier might invest in advanced infrastructure or specialized training programmes tailored to the key account's needs, ensuring long-term compatibility and efficiency. For example, a logistics company could develop a dedicated fleet or warehouse facilities specifically for a high-value client. This demonstrates commitment to the relationship and enhances the customer's operational capabilities, deepening the partnership.

Knowledge-sharing and technology integration also drive co-creation. A key customer and supplier might establish joint task forces or innovation teams to integrate their expertise. For example, a pharmaceutical company and a healthcare provider might combine their data analytics and medical expertise to improve patient care outcomes. By aligning resources and goals, integration fosters innovation and creates tangible value for both parties.

3. INVESTIGATION

Investigation in KAM refers to the collaborative exchange of knowledge and joint exploration to uncover opportunities and foster learning. Through shared efforts, suppliers and key accounts can better understand each other's needs, market dynamics and potential areas for growth. For example, a supplier and client might co-investigate market trends to identify emerging consumer demands, leading to the development of new product lines.

This dimension emphasizes the value of shared insights and learning. By working together to analyse challenges, both parties can create solutions that are both innovative and practical. For instance, a manufacturing firm and its key supplier might conduct joint root cause analysis to address quality control issues. This approach not only resolves immediate concerns but also enhances both organizations' capabilities for future problem-solving.

Investigation also builds trust and commitment by involving both parties in the decision-making process. When clients feel they are part of the exploration and ideation phases, they are more likely to buy into proposed solutions. For example, a renewable energy provider might invite a key corporate client to collaborate on designing a customized sustainability plan. By engaging the client in the investigative process, the provider not only enhances the plan's effectiveness but also reinforces the client's sense of partnership and shared purpose.

4. INNOVATION

Innovation in KAM focuses on active collaboration to co-create solutions, address specific challenges and seize market opportunities. This dimension is critical in today's fast-paced business environment, where differentiation often hinges on the ability to innovate jointly. For example, a retail chain and its supplier might collaborate on developing eco-friendly packaging solutions to meet sustainability goals, combining expertise in materials and consumer preferences.

Joint innovation allows suppliers and key accounts to tackle complex problems that require diverse skill sets and perspectives. By pooling their resources and creativity, they can develop groundbreaking solutions. For instance, an automotive manufacturer might work with a key supplier to design lightweight components that improve fuel efficiency without compromising safety. Such collaborative innovation not only strengthens the relationship but also positions both parties as leaders in their respective markets.

Beyond product or service innovation, this dimension also encompasses process and business model innovation. A key account and supplier might co-develop more efficient supply chain processes or explore new revenue-sharing models. For example, a software company and a corporate client might jointly design a subscription-based pricing structure that aligns with the client's seasonal cash flow. By innovating together, both parties not only enhance their competitive advantage but also deepen their strategic alignment.

Designing the end-to-end co-creation process

Co-creation is an encompassing process that includes nuanced practices with one thing in common: the customer puts into the process a similar amount of effort (if not more) and resources than the supplier.

A study[9] revealed that co-creation often starts from co-diagnosis, the collection and organization of information for collaborative use. This can be articulated in the form of a customer forum, where the strategic account manager engages key customers in problem formulation. For instance, Interfood, a leading manufacturer of high-quality dairy ingredients for industrial applications, would involve Danone in high-level discussions to find ways to better address the nutritional concerns of their consumers. This would then lead, often using design thinking methods, to the *co-ideation* or generation of ideas, and a more granular definition of the nature of the problem to address.

Typically, a well-defined purpose leads to a phase of *co-design*; in other words, developing concepts and knowledge that help the customer succeed. For instance, another leading food manufacturer, Unilever Food Solutions – known by the slogan 'Created by Chefs for Chefs' – co-designs with customers a comprehensive set of menus that are nutritious and healthy, but also profitable.

Other approaches that help co-create customer value relate to *co-testing*; that is, prototyping and improving the offering, and *co-evaluation*, commenting and generating insights for further improvement of value propositions. For example, software company SAP co-creates knowledge and new solutions not only by involving customers, but also by deliberately bringing together several different partners from their ecosystems such as universities or governmental groups. This results in a co-creative process with a pronounced emphasis on connecting stakeholders with complementary capabilities.

How to foster value-based selling and co-create solutions

So far, the reasons for key account managers to foster value-based selling and co-creating solutions have been established, as well as an understanding of the key foundations and dimensions of this important capability.

In today's business environment, the exercise of this capability is increasingly mediated through digital platforms, AI and advanced analytics to enable more sophisticated collaborative mechanisms. Also, virtual collaboration tools expand possibilities for co-creation in global KAM.

Moreover, VBS and cocreating solutions progressively includes sustainability considerations. Collaborative risk assessment and resource integration must account for environmental and social impacts, and joint learning requires the addition of sustainable innovation capabilities.

From an ethical perspective, selling based on value and co-creation needs a greater emphasis on responsible innovation. Transparency now includes ethical technology use and co-creation processes must address potential societal and environmental consequences.

Additionally, since the business environment has become more uncertain and complex, value-based selling and co-creation in KAM must be extremely agile, responsive and adaptable. The ability to rapidly reconfigure collaborative approaches becomes a key competitive advantage.

Ultimately, the dimensions of value-based selling and value co-creation are not static checklist items but dynamic, interconnected principles that require continuous refinement. They represent a fundamental shift from transactional business relationships to collaborative, ecosystem-based value generation. The most successful KAM organizations will be those that can most effectively create flexible, ethical and innovative collaborative environments with their key accounts.

Articulating and measuring the value created

Most companies know the features of their offerings and develop a detailed understanding of their customer's challenges. However, fewer than 5 per cent make it truly meaningful for their customers according to the analysis of 55 sales pitches from 29 different companies in Europe by Business Acceleration, a Dutch consulting practice.

The key account manager needs to translate selling and co-creation practices into concrete evidence of value using examples such as:

- Top-line growth value indicators (sales/quarter, market penetration, budget growth, consumer satisfaction).

- Bottom line value indexes (reduced break rates, reduced employment costs, reduced energy costs).

- Business reputation and continuity measures to eliminate accidents and reduce rejections due to quality issues.

- Strategy value to achieve new market entry and diversify into a new product range.

Moreover, a convincing articulation of value and value propositions captures an improved future scenario for the strategic customer in compelling ways. It describes how unique combinations of products, services and a particular relationship ethos will help the customer get the job done.

Thus, developing the approaches to value-based selling and co-creation is a necessary but not sufficient skill for the SAM: it is important to measure the results of your efforts. Joona Keränen, an Associate Professor at RMIT who specializes in shared value creation, developed a framework for assessing customer value in B2B markets that includes five processes.[10] The first – value potential identification – comprises identifying the customer's explicit needs, understanding the customer's processes and understanding the financial implications for the customer's business. The second process includes a baseline assessment, determining customers' current performance, specifying mutual outcomes and conducting trial runs. Once value is created, the ensuing processes involve performance evaluation, specifying the value impact for customer's performance, followed by long-term value realization. This requires verifying and documenting the realized customer value.

Organizational enablers for value-based selling and co-creation

To effectively implement value co-creation, suppliers need to develop the following organizational capabilities and characteristics.

1. Customer-centric culture and co-creation mindset

The entire organization must be aligned around creating value with and for customers[11] and developing an organizational mindset that values and prioritizes collaborative value creation.[12]

A customer-centric culture transcends traditional customer service approaches, embedding customer value creation into the organizational DNA. This requires a fundamental reimagining of organizational purpose, where every employee understands their role in creating value beyond their immediate functional responsibilities. For example, Salesforce demonstrates this through its V2MOM (Vision, Values, Methods, Obstacles, Measures) framework, where customer success is explicitly integrated into every level of organizational strategy. Every employee, from software developers to customer support representatives, is evaluated not just on individual performance but on their contribution to customer value creation.

A co-creation mindset represents a philosophical shift from transactional thinking to collaborative value generation. It involves seeing customers as active partners in value creation rather than passive recipients of products or services. For example: LEGO's open innovation platform allows customers to propose and vote on new product ideas, fundamentally transforming the relationship from manufacturer-consumer to collaborative value creators.

2. Flexible organizational structure and cross-functional integration

The organization should be able to adapt processes and structures to accommodate customer-specific co-creation initiatives[13] and to mobilize diverse internal resources and expertise to support co-creation efforts.

Flexibility is about creating adaptive organizational architectures that can rapidly reconfigure resources, processes and teams to address specific customer co-creation needs. This goes beyond traditional hierarchical models to create more fluid, project-based and customer-responsive configurations. For instance, Spotify's 'squad' model illustrates this approach. Small, cross-functional teams are organized around specific customer value streams, with the ability to quickly form, dissolve and reconfigure based on emerging customer needs and technological opportunities.

On the other hand, cross-functional integration breaks down traditional organizational silos, creating holistic approaches to value creation that leverage diverse organizational expertise and perspectives. For example, Tesla's approach to product development involves continuous integration of engineering, design, manufacturing and customer experience teams. This allows for rapid innovation and customer-responsive product development across traditional functional boundaries.[14]

3. Advanced collaboration tools and knowledge management systems

The organization needs technological infrastructure to facilitate seamless communication and joint working[15] and robust processes for capturing, sharing and leveraging insights gained from co-creation activities.[16]

Collaboration tools are not just technological solutions but strategic enablers of value co-creation. They must provide seamless, secure and intelligent platforms that facilitate knowledge sharing, joint problem-solving and real-time collaboration. To illustrate, Microsoft Teams, integrated with advanced AI capabilities, offers more than communication – it provides intelligent collaboration features like real-time translation, contextual insights and seamless integration with project management and knowledge management systems.[17]

Advanced knowledge management systems are intelligent, dynamic platforms that capture, synthesize and leverage insights from co-creation activities, transforming individual interactions into organizational learning. For example,

FIGURE 7.4 Organizational characteristics associated with the enablers of value-based selling and co-creation

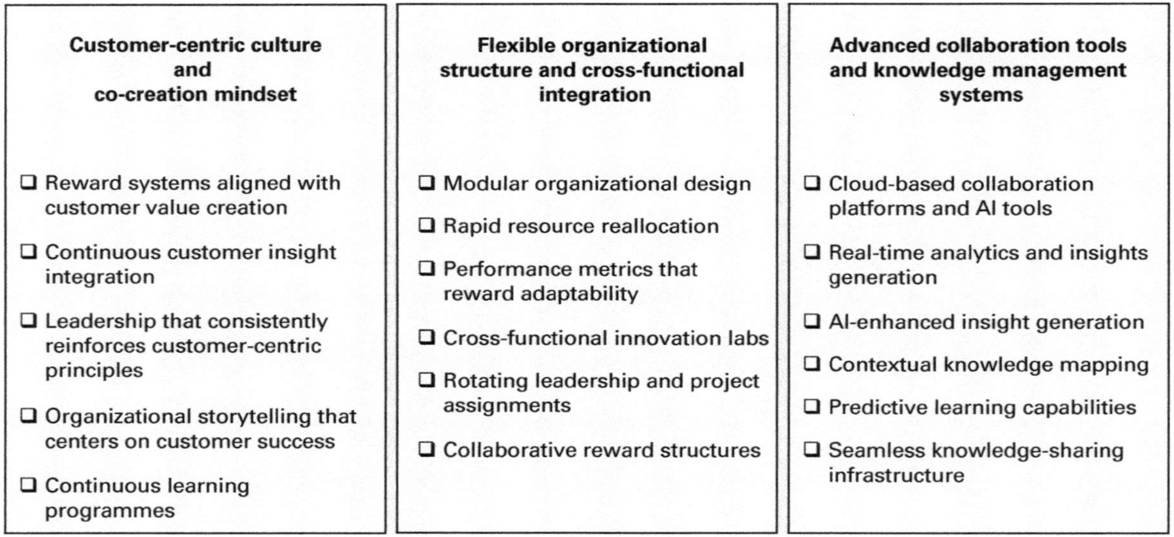

Customer-centric culture and co-creation mindset

- ❑ Reward systems aligned with customer value creation
- ❑ Continuous customer insight integration
- ❑ Leadership that consistently reinforces customer-centric principles
- ❑ Organizational storytelling that centers on customer success
- ❑ Continuous learning programmes

Flexible organizational structure and cross-functional integration

- ❑ Modular organizational design
- ❑ Rapid resource reallocation
- ❑ Performance metrics that reward adaptability
- ❑ Cross-functional innovation labs
- ❑ Rotating leadership and project assignments
- ❑ Collaborative reward structures

Advanced collaboration tools and knowledge management systems

- ❑ Cloud-based collaboration platforms and AI tools
- ❑ Real-time analytics and insights generation
- ❑ AI-enhanced insight generation
- ❑ Contextual knowledge mapping
- ❑ Predictive learning capabilities
- ❑ Seamless knowledge-sharing infrastructure

Procter & Gamble's Connect + Develop platform systematically captures, categorizes and makes actionable the insights generated through customer and partner collaborations, creating a continuous learning ecosystem.[18]

4. Organizational characteristics associated with these enablers

Figure 7.4 presents the main organizational characteristics that are expected to be associated with the discussed enablers for value-based selling and cocreation in KAM.

HOW TO INCORPORATE ELEMENTS OF SUSTAINABLE DEVELOPMENT IN VALUE PROPOSITIONS

In an era of unprecedented global challenges – climate change, social inequality, resource scarcity and technological disruption – businesses can no longer afford to view sustainability as a peripheral concern or a mere marketing strategy. The convergence of environmental degradation, social transformation and economic volatility has fundamentally reshaped the landscape of value creation. Today's most forward-thinking organizations recognize that sustainable development is not just an ethical imperative but a strategic necessity. B2B value propositions that fail to integrate comprehensive sustainability considerations risk becoming obsolete, as stakeholders – from investors and customers to employees and regulators – demand holistic approaches that demonstrate genuine commitment to addressing systemic global challenges.

The digital transformation and the rise of artificial intelligence have paradoxically both complicated and enabled more sophisticated sustainability strategies. On one hand, technological advancement has accelerated resource consumption and potential environmental harm; on the other, it provides unprecedented tools for measuring, understanding and mitigating negative impacts. In this complex ecosystem, B2B value propositions must transcend traditional metrics of financial performance and operational efficiency. They must now articulate value through a multidimensional lens that encompasses environmental stewardship, social responsibility, economic resilience and ethical innovation. By embedding sustainable development principles into their core value propositions, companies can transform potential challenges into opportunities for differentiation, creating solutions that not only solve immediate business problems but also contribute to broader societal and ecological regeneration.

Figure 7.5 proposes some sustainability elements of value that key account managers might consider including when developing and cocreating value with their strategic customers, with support from their own company.

FIGURE 7.5 Environmental sustainability elements of value

ENVIRONMENTAL SUSTAINABILITY

Element of value	What it entails	Example
Carbon footprint reduction	✓ Moving beyond cost savings to demonstrate environmental impact ✓ Quantifying emissions reductions ✓ Offering solutions that directly contribute to climate change mitigation	A logistics company that doesn't just optimize routes for efficiency, but explicitly calculates and commits to carbon emission reductions
Circular economy integration	✓ Designing products and services with lifecycle sustainability in mind ✓ Emphasizing recyclability, reusability and minimal waste ✓ Creating closed-loop systems that regenerate resources	Electronics manufacturers offering comprehensive recycling programmes and designing products for easy disassembly and material recovery
Renewable energy and clean technology	✓ Proposing solutions that leverage or enable clean energy transitions ✓ Demonstrating how technologies can support decarbonization ✓ Providing tools for energy efficiency and sustainable resource management	Solar panel installers who offer comprehensive carbon impact assessments alongside financial savings projections

Summary and application

In conclusion, fostering value-based selling and co-creating solutions constitute a critical capability for successful key account managers in the way they approach strategic customer relationships. The shifting economic environment and customer expectations, and the opportunities for differentiation and learning, enhance the importance of this capability in a key account manager.

Value-based selling, on the one hand, is both a solution to a problem and a strategic sales approach, and includes understanding the customer's business model, crafting the value proposition, and communicating value. Value co-creation, on the other hand, is a strategic decision based on mutual trust, shared goals and commitment, which includes four dimensions, depicted as the Four Is: interaction, integration, investigation and innovation.

There are several organizational enablers for value-based selling and co-creation, including a customer-centric culture and a co-creation mindset, a flexible organizational structure and cross-functional integration, and advanced collaboration tools and knowledge management systems. As businesses increasingly recognize the limitations of traditional value creation models, value-based selling and value co-creation are likely to become an essential strategy for key account management in complex B2B environments.

Table 7.1 provides 10 recommended actions that should help key account managers foster value-based selling and co-create solutions.

TABLE 7.1 Recommended actions for key account managers

Action	Description
1. Conduct customer business analysis	Perform deep analysis of the customer's business model, including operations, challenges and strategic goals. Use data analytics and industry insights to identify specific pain points and value creation opportunities.
2. Create value measurement frameworks	Develop clear metrics and KPIs to quantify the value delivered to customers, including financial impact, operational improvements and strategic benefits. Track and document these metrics systematically.
3. Establish cross-functional teams	Form dedicated teams that combine expertise from different departments (sales, technical, operations) to support value co-creation initiatives with key accounts. Ensure clear roles and communication channels.

(continued)

TABLE 7.1 (Continued)

	Action	Description
4.	Design co-creation workshops	Organize regular structured sessions with customers to jointly explore challenges, brainstorm solutions and develop innovative approaches. Include both strategic and operational stakeholders from both organizations.
5.	Implement value documentation process	Create systematic ways to capture and share success stories, learnings and best practices from value co-creation initiatives. Use these insights to improve future customer engagements.
6.	Build customer-specific value propositions	Develop tailored value propositions that align with each customer's specific business objectives, incorporating sustainability and innovation elements that matter to them.
7.	Create joint innovation roadmaps	Work with customers to develop shared innovation goals and timelines, identifying specific projects and initiatives for collaborative development over the medium to long term.
8.	Establish value governance structure	Set up regular value review meetings with customers to monitor progress, assess outcomes and adjust co-creation initiatives as needed. Include both operational and strategic reviews.
9.	Develop digital collaboration platform	Implement tools and technologies that facilitate real-time collaboration, knowledge sharing and joint project management with key accounts.
10.	Build sustainability integration plan	Create specific plans to incorporate environmental and social value elements into customer solutions, aligning with both organizations' sustainability goals and market demands.

Notes

1 J C Anderson, J A Narus and W Van Rossum. Customer value propositions in business markets, *Harvard Business Review*, 2007, 85 (3), 90–99

2 H Terho, A Haas, A Eggert and W Ulaga. 'It's almost like taking the sales out of selling'—Towards a conceptualization of value-based selling in business markets, *Industrial Marketing Management*, 2012, 41 (1), 174–85

3 J Keränen, D Totzek, A Salonen and M Kienzler. Advancing value-based selling research in B2B markets: A theoretical toolbox and research agenda, *Industrial Marketing Management*, 2023, 111, 55–68

4   A Hinterhuber and S M Liozu. Sales value quantification capabilities: A review of the literature and conceptual framework, *Journal of Business & Industrial Marketing*, 2018, 33 (7), 1046–59

5   H Terho, A Haas, A Eggert and W Ulaga. How sales strategy translates into performance: The role of salesperson customer orientation and value-based selling, *Industrial Marketing Management*, 2015, 45, 12–21

6   C K Prahalad and V Ramaswamy. Co-creation experiences: The next practice in value creation, *Journal of Interactive Marketing*, 2004, 18 (3), 5–14

7   S L Vargo and R F Lusch. Service-dominant logic: continuing the evolution, *Journal of the Academy of Marketing Science*, 2008, 36 (1), 1–10

8   E Jaakkola and T Hakanen. Value co-creation in solution networks, *Industrial Marketing Management*, 2013, 42 (1), 47–58

9   J Marcos-Cuevas, S Nätti, T Palo and J Baumann. Value co-creation practices and capabilities: Sustained purposeful engagement across B2B systems, *Industrial Marketing Management*, 2016, 56, 97–107

10 J Keränen and A Jalkala. Towards a framework of customer value assessment in B2B markets: An exploratory study, *Industrial Marketing Management*, 2013, 42 (8), 1307–17

11 L A Bettencourt, R F Lusch and S L Varg. A service lens on value creation: marketing's role in achieving strategic advantage, *California Management Review*, 2014, 57 (1), 44–66

12 V Ramaswamy and F Gouillart. Building the co-creative enterprise, *Harvard Business Review*, 2010, 88 (10), 100–09

13 K Storbacka, R J, Brodie, T Böhmann, PP P Maglio and S Nenonen. Actor engagement as a microfoundation for value co-creation, *Journal of Business Research*, 2016, 69 (8), 3008–17

14 N Furr and J Dyer. Lessons from Tesla's approach to innovation, *Harvard Business Review*, 2020, 18

15 V Ramaswamy and K Ozcan. What is co-creation? An interactional creation framework and its implications for value creation, *Journal of Business Research*, 2018, 84, 196–205

16 A F Payne, K Storbacka and P Frow. Managing the co-creation of value, *Journal of the Academy of Marketing Science*, 2008, 36 (1), 83–96

17 A de Lucas Ancillo, S G Gavrila, J Á Tébar-Sáez and A O Rocha (2024) Technologies and team management to increase productivity in a digital age. In *Artificial Intelligence and Business Transformation: Impact in HR Management, Innovation and Technology Challenges*, 177–87, Springer Nature Switzerland, Cham

18 L Huston and N Sakkab. Inside Procter & Gamble's new model for innovation, *Harvard Business Review*, 2006, 84 (3), 58–66

Dominique Côté

In my experience as a KAM professional, the role of a key account manager in general, but particularly in the pharmaceutical industry, is rich and nuanced. Primarily, it involves orchestrating the entire account team and shifting the mindset from an inside-out to an outside-in perspective. In my view, the key account manager's role is to move beyond being a mere marketing billboard to becoming a customer-centric partner who understands and addresses the needs of the entire customer ecosystem.

One of the critical aspects of KAM, in my opinion, is the orchestration of various roles within the pharmaceutical industry, such as market access, medical liaison and commercial teams. The key account manager acts as a connector, bringing together different functions to create a cohesive strategy aligned with the customer's objectives. This involves regular knowledge sharing and strategy development that considers the entire portfolio of opportunities and partnerships.

When it comes to measuring KAM performance, I believe there's still work to be done in the pharmaceutical industry. Traditionally, the focus has been on quantitative metrics like market share and prescription data. However, I strongly advocate for the inclusion of qualitative criteria, such as understanding customer objectives and bringing value beyond product offerings. In my experience, aligning measurement with customer-defined success metrics is crucial but often challenging to implement due to short-term revenue pressures.

Regarding the capabilities required for effective key account management, I find that a combination of hard and soft skills is essential. In my view, some of the most critical capabilities include strategizing, developing lasting relationships, promoting customer centricity and creating value. However, I believe that soft skills, particularly what I call a 'growth mindset', are becoming increasingly important in today's environment.

From my perspective, the ability to adapt, learn and operate in uncertain situations is crucial for key account managers. This growth mindset enables them to co-create solutions with customers, even when the path forward isn't clear. In the pharmaceutical industry, where there's often a tendency to rely on technical knowledge and predefined solutions, this ability to embrace ambiguity and co-create can lead to breakthrough results.

In terms of developing these capabilities, I strongly believe that it requires a combination of factors. First and foremost, having the right mindset is crucial. However, this needs to be supported by a clear process and skill set development. In my experience, effective KAM development involves not just training individuals but also creating an organizational environment that supports growth and experimentation.

Leadership support is, in my opinion, absolutely critical for the success of KAM initiatives. This includes not just verbal support but also empowering key account managers to try new approaches in a safe environment. I've observed that when leadership is not fully on board, KAM often becomes just another training initiative rather than a true business transformation.

When it comes to the future of KAM, particularly in light of increasing digitalization, I remain optimistic. While some may question the relevance of key account managers in an increasingly digital world, I believe their role will become even more crucial. In my view, as we embrace digital tools and AI, the need for human judgment, insight and relationship-building skills will only increase.

To develop highly effective key account managers, I recommend a holistic approach. This includes careful selection of individuals with the right mindset, providing them with a clear process and tools, and offering ongoing coaching and support. Moreover, I believe it's crucial to have a high-level centre of excellence within the organization that can drive strategic initiatives and provide continuous support to key account managers.

In conclusion, based on my experience in the field, I believe that key account management, especially in the pharmaceutical industry, is not just a sales initiative but a business transformation. It requires a shift in mindset at all levels of the organization, from individual key account managers to top leadership. While the role is challenging, it also offers great opportunities for those who can effectively navigate the complexities of modern healthcare systems and create genuine partnerships with key accounts.

The future of KAM, in my opinion, lies in embracing both the human and technological aspects of the role. As we move forward, key account managers who can leverage digital tools while also providing deep insights and building strong relationships will be invaluable to their organizations. By focusing on developing these multifaceted capabilities and creating supportive organizational structures, companies can position themselves to thrive in the evolving landscape of key account management.

As an accomplished executive with 30 years of experience in global life sciences organizations, Dominique has built an impressive career leading commercial teams before founding her boutique consultancy group. Her extensive experience includes key leadership roles at major pharmaceutical companies, including Novartis, Pfizer, Zoetis and UCB, where she spearheaded Global Go-to-Market transformations, KAM initiatives and Commercial Excellence programmes. As a chief commercial operation executive, she also led global marketing and innovation for pharmaceutical and biotech groups, managing teams across 36 countries and developing deep expertise in global markets and diverse business cultures.

Dominique leverages her expertise as a certified executive coach and consultant, focusing on go-to-market strategies and commercial transformations while serving on several prestigious boards, including NFL Biosciences and SAMA (Strategic Account Management Association). Her commitment to industry leadership extends to her involvement with organizations such as Women in Bio and the Healthcare Businesswomen's Association, where she contributes to international strategy. As a bilingual professional between Montreal and Brussels, she continues to influence the industry through international keynote speaking engagements and publications in respected journals like the Journal of Sales Transformation *and* Velocity, *sharing her unique perspective on commercial excellence and customer-centricity.*

www.linkedin.com/in/dominiquecote1 (archived at https://perma.cc/ EM7D-H8KE)

08

Negotiating in supplier-key customer relationships

Overview

Key account managers (KAMgrs) spend a significant amount of their customer-facing time seeking agreements, resolving product and service delivery issues, and negotiating deals. During negotiation skills development programmes with KAMgrs, we often get asked questions about tips and tactics to be used during the negotiation, in other words, 'at the table' or 'in front of the computer' if negotiating online. Interestingly, the most effective negotiation approaches are those that consider not just the activities conducted during but also before and after negotiation rounds. Thus, this chapter focuses on approaches to conduct end-to-end negotiation processes before, during and after commercial negotiation interactions with key customers. Overall, in this chapter, we address the question: *How can key account managers better design the end-to-end negotiation process with strategic customers?*

Negotiating with key customers is often characterized by a set of premises we would like to outline up front. First, if you're negotiating with a key account, maintaining a future working relationship with the customer is essential, as is the substantive content of the deal. This means that collaborative approaches to negotiating are more likely to produce the desired short and long-term outcomes. Our second assumption is that you will typically negotiate with customers for whom you are also an important supplier; therefore, a degree of interdependence and power balance exists. This suggests that the other party will have a strong incentive to negotiate, often using principled approaches and limiting the use of 'dirty tricks'. Third, we assume that the future value of the strategic customer business is greater than the value of the deal at hand.

Why is it important to develop negotiation capabilities?

Suppliers and key customers engage in negotiation processes constantly. Thus, negotiation competence is a cornerstone of successful key account managers. We argue that negotiation skills in key account management (KAM) transcend the traditional concept of price discussions and extend into the realm of strategic value creation (see Chapter 7) and relationship-building (see Chapters 5 and 6).

WHY DEVELOPING NEGOTIATION CAPABILITIES IS IMPORTANT

Strategic value creation:

- Enhances value proposition development
- Enables risk-sharing agreements
- Improves profit-sharing schemes
- Strengthens collaborative outcomes

Relationship development:

- Builds long-term partnerships
- Improves stakeholder engagement
- Enables conflict resolution
- Strengthens trust through transparency

Business performance:

- Improves deal effectiveness
- Enhances pricing outcomes
- Increases mutual benefits
- Optimizes resource allocation

Team leadership:

- Strengthens cross-functional coordination
- Improves negotiation team dynamics
- Enables role clarity
- Enhances collective performance

Process management:

- Enables systematic preparation
- Improves concession management
- Strengthens follow-through
- Enhances agreement implementation

Our research and extensive work with key account managers across industries reveals that negotiation capabilities directly influence not only immediate commercial outcomes but also the long-term sustainability of strategic customer relationships. When we examine the most successful KAMgrs, we consistently observe their ability to navigate complex multi-stakeholder negotiations while maintaining delicate balances between customer value creation and organizational profitability.

As we have seen already, today's KAMgrs must orchestrate relationships across multiple organizational levels, often involving diverse stakeholder groups with competing interests. This diversity of priorities results in the need to engage in 'negotiated orchestrations' to move forward supplier-key customer relationships. Recent studies[1] demonstrate how superior KAMgr performance is associated with the ability to negotiate and persuade in the context of managing supplier-customer projects, the use of internal experts, and creating and capturing value for both their organizations.

Negotiation in KAM underpins strategic alignment discussions, value proposition development, joint business planning and the establishment of long-term collaborative frameworks. These processes blend complex negotiation ability with technical expertise and sophisticated relationship management capabilities.

Another key dimension of negotiation capability is the need to operate within multi-cultural contexts, demanding a more nuanced and comprehensive approach to negotiation skill development.

Developing negotiation capabilities will reinforce KAMgrs' ability to enhance:

- Strategic value creation and communication
- Stakeholder management and influence
- Cross-functional team orchestration
- Complex decision-making processes
- Long-term relationship-building

Understanding and developing negotiation capabilities is not merely an optional enhancement to a KAMgr's skill set – it is a fundamental prerequisite for success in modern KAM. As we progress through this chapter, we will provide practical insights, evidence-based methods and guidelines for developing negotiation know-how.

A framework for commercial negotiation in KAM

Before delving into the description of negotiation tactics to define value-based negotiation, I'd like to define negotiation as the process of reaching a *mutually acceptable agreement* that *satisfies* each party's *interests*. This process comprises *bargaining* and exchanging *concessions*, balancing *power*, born *costs* and gained *value*, and enabling the continuation of the *relationship* in the future. The words in italics denote core concepts that apply to negotiating with strategic customers that may not be relevant in highly distributive deals with non-key customers. Here are 10 guidelines to enhance mutual value in deals with strategic accounts.

Before the negotiation

1. SETTING YOUR MINDSET FOR 'STRATEGIC' NEGOTIATION

We refer to 'strategic' negotiation precisely because you're negotiating with 'strategic' customers. Therefore, the focus and emphasis are on creating value over the long term. The way you negotiate and the types of deals you shape set the tone for the future relationship with your key customer.

To achieve success in negotiating with key customers, it is essential to adopt a strategic mindset that goes beyond basic bargaining tactics. This means approaching the negotiation as a collaborative process aimed at creating mutual value and strengthening the long-term relationship.[2]

> While many companies I've worked with have excellent key account management teams who excel at customer satisfaction and retention, they struggle to drive additional revenue from existing clients. The ideal key account manager needs to balance both customer service and sales skills, which is a rare combination.
>
> Tim Chapman

The first step in cultivating this strategic mindset is to prepare thoroughly. This involves understanding your own interests and priorities, as well as those of your customer.[3] Similar to an investigator at a crime scene, effective negotiators gather as much information as possible about the situation, the customer's needs and constraints, and the broader market context.[4] This investigative approach helps identify potential areas of common ground and opportunities for creating value, ensuring that you are not solely focused on areas of conflict.

Next, it is essential to regulate your emotions and maintain a calm and objective demeanour. The sources highlight the importance of managing fear and anger, particularly in challenging negotiations.[5] Techniques such as taking a break to regain composure or recalling a pleasant experience to calm down can be helpful. Remember, negotiation is about addressing the issues at hand, not engaging in personal attacks or letting emotions derail the process.[6]

Finally, adopt a flexible and adaptable approach, recognizing that negotiation is a dynamic process. Be willing to make concessions and consider alternative solutions. As the sources explain, skilled negotiators are more likely to plan in terms of a range, setting upper and lower limits, rather than fixating on a single objective.[7] By embracing this strategic mindset, you can transform negotiations from adversarial battles into collaborative opportunities to build lasting and mutually beneficial relationships with your key customers.

> Your approach to negotiation also sets a precedent for forthcoming deals. KAMgrs and complex project managers often tell me that the real negotiation is the one that follows the signature of the contract. The British Airports Authority negotiated a landmark contract for constructing the London Heathrow Terminal.[8] This project's on-time and almost-on-budget delivery was a major achievement, partly enabled by the approach taken to negotiations with tier-one suppliers, not just before the contract but after the deal(s) were agreed to.

2. EMBEDDING RISK-SHARING AND PROFIT-SHARING SCHEMES

Breakthrough innovations in industrial, life sciences, defence and other sectors require significant investments from the supplier and the strategic customer. Indeed, key account managers engage in complex contracts with key customers. We argue that KAMgrs need to develop the ability to negotiate deals that balance risk-sharing and profit-sharing schemes.

When Airbus designed the A350 aircraft, it engaged key suppliers such as GKN Aerospace to deliver expert support for metallic and composite wing structures across all A350 XWB programmes. This was supported by a long-term partnership known as a 'risk-sharing part ownership', creating mechanisms for the collaborative design and construction of these complex aircraft subsystems.

First, it's essential to understand the nature of the risks involved and how they might impact both parties. Thorough preparation and customer due diligence are vital for identifying potential risks, assessing their likelihood and quantifying their potential impact. This might involve analysing market trends, competitor activities, technological advancements and regulatory changes, as well as carefully evaluating the partners' operational capabilities.

Once the risks are clearly understood, the next step is to determine how they can be shared fairly. This involves a careful negotiation of contractual terms that allocate responsibility and liability in a way that mitigates risk for both parties. For example, KAMgrs can negotiate contracts that can include clauses that outline specific performance metrics, establish clear roles and responsibilities, define acceptable levels of risk exposure and outline procedures for dispute resolution.

Profit-sharing schemes can involve linking profit-sharing percentages to specific performance targets, such as sales growth, cost reductions or innovation milestones. Additionally, the profit-sharing mechanism should be transparent and easily understandable for both parties, fostering trust and open communication.

Negotiating these types of agreements requires a delicate balance between protecting your company's interests and fostering a strong, collaborative relationship with the customer. A key principle to keep in mind is the concept of reciprocity.[9] By demonstrating a willingness to share risks fairly and offer attractive profit-sharing incentives, you can encourage a similar spirit of cooperation from the customer. This can lead to a win-win outcome where both parties are motivated to contribute to the success of the partnership.

The uncertain nature of long-term programmes means that both risks and benefits need to be considered. When negotiating with strategic customers, KAMgrs need to embed into their negotiation approaches a carefully crafted formula for balancing cost, value and risk across their and their customer's organizations.

3. FOCUSING ON COMPATIBLE INTERESTS AND CONVERGING PRIORITIES

Effective negotiators give much more time and attention to discussing compatible issues than average negotiators.[10] They focus on common ground before addressing more difficult topics between the parties. Thus, they build momentum, enabling progress, particularly when the parties seem far apart in reaching an agreement. However, they also realize that value can emerge from differences in priorities.

> Large technology vendors like IBM work with their clients to design and deliver complex transformational projects. Key negotiation variables in these deals may include functionality, implementation time, scalability and, of course, price. A detailed analysis of these projects may reveal that a shorter implementation period can facilitate a faster time to market, allowing a company to capture market share and secure a prominent position in the market. This can be much more valuable than a discount on the price of a contract.

Rather than fixating solely on potential points of conflict, skilled negotiation KAMgrs prioritize exploring areas where the interests of both supplier and key customer align. This approach promotes a positive and constructive negotiation environment, enhancing the likelihood of reaching an agreement that satisfies both sides. Highlighting shared interests and compatible goals is crucial in building and maintaining strong relationships with key customers. By demonstrating a genuine understanding of the customer's needs and priorities and showcasing how these align with your own objectives, KAMgrs create a foundation of trust and shared purpose.

> If you're trying to create value, you've got to understand the client's processes, their business model, their market, their customers, their strengths and weaknesses. Otherwise, you've got no chance of creating value.
>
> Prof Malcolm McDonald

Using inclusive language in framing proposals and making suggestions invite collaboration. This can involve explicitly acknowledging points of agreement, using phrases like 'It's encouraging to see we share an interest in...' or 'What I like about your proposal is...' By emphasizing the 'we' rather than the 'I', you reinforce the notion that both parties are working together towards a shared goal.

4. PREPARING TO DISAGREE

Not all negotiation situations develop within agreeable environments. Divergence of perspectives is normal and KAMgrs need to learn how to express disagreement effectively. Neil Rackham's research on the behaviours of successful negotiators offer strategies on how to disagree constructively and minimize potential negative consequences:[11]

> Avoid behaviour labelling when disagreeing. Unlike others, skilled negotiators avoid explicitly stating that they disagree. Instead of saying 'I disagree with that because...', they prefer to present their reasoning first, leading indirectly to their point of disagreement. This subtle approach allows the other party to consider their perspective without feeling directly challenged, preserving their ego and reducing defensiveness.

> Focus on reasons, not disagreement. This strategy emphasizes shifting the focus from the act of disagreeing to the rationale behind it. By presenting well-reasoned arguments, skilled negotiators aim to persuade the other party through logic and evidence, rather than relying on blunt disagreement. This approach encourages a more objective and less emotionally charged discussion.

> Questioning as an alternative to direct disagreement. Questions can serve as effective alternatives to direct disagreement. Rather than outright rejecting a proposal, skilled negotiators might ask clarifying questions that highlight potential issues or concerns. This approach encourages the other party to re-evaluate their position and consider alternative perspectives without feeling directly confronted.

> Maintain a calm and objective demeanour. Regulating emotions and maintaining a neutral tone is crucial, especially when expressing disagreement. By avoiding emotional outbursts or personal attacks, you can keep the conversation focused on the issue at hand and prevent the negotiation from devolving into a heated argument. Remember, expressing disagreement doesn't have to be confrontational. It can be a constructive step towards finding a mutually acceptable solution.

> Consider the importance of timing. Timing is a crucial element in expressing disagreement effectively. Raising a contentious point early in the negotiation

could create an adversarial atmosphere and hinder progress. Conversely, delaying disagreement until the final stages might appear disingenuous or manipulative. A strategic approach involves carefully choosing the appropriate moment to voice concerns, ensuring your perspective is heard while maintaining a collaborative spirit.

By understanding and implementing these strategies, key account managers can navigate disagreements effectively, fostering productive dialogue and preserving the long-term relationships with their key customers. As discussed, in general, strategic negotiation involves prioritizing the identification and articulation of compatible interests and converging priorities before addressing areas of conflict.

During the negotiation

5. ADDRESSING THE PRICE NEGOTIATION

At this point in the chapter, we can imagine you thinking, 'This idea of negotiating based on value is nice, but the reality is that my customers, all they seem to care about is price!'

We acknowledge that the pressure to negotiate cost reductions often precludes or limits collaborative arrangements between suppliers and customers. This is the perceived reality in contexts such as consumer goods and large retailers, large construction projects, supply contracts of components for original equipment manufacturers, etc. The purchasing power of these customers and their demands for discounts means that, very often, win-win negotiation seems impossible to achieve. Here are some strategies that KAMgrs can use to negotiate prices effectively:

1 *Involve negotiation parties upstream and downstream.* Buyers are often tasked with focusing on price reductions and this becomes as key performance indicator for them. An approach you can consider to counter the excessive focus price is to involve additional parties in the negotiation: the suppliers of the supplier, what we call *upstream*, and the customer's customer, in other words, *downstream*.

In their book *3D Negotiation*, Lax and Sebenious refer to the example of Sweetheart Cup Company, a North American company that made paper cups, plastic cups and related products. One of their major customers, McDonald's, issued a request for a price reduction of 10 per cent, warning suppliers of lost business if this reduction was not offered. Instead of engaging in a lengthy bargaining process, the Sweetheart Cup Company engaged a major paper supplier, Georgia-Pacific, and several McDonald's key stakeholders. Equipped with insights into McDonald's consumers, the company sought ways to optimize overall costs for all parties involved and avoid having to provide the requested discount.

KAMgrs can highlight value chain interdependencies, demonstrating the interconnectedness of the value chain and emphasizing the importance of factors beyond price. This can involve showcasing how specific suppliers contribute to the overall quality and performance of the product or service, ultimately benefiting the end customer.

Another strategy is shifting focus from price to *total cost of ownership*. Key account managers engage their supplier organization to collaboratively present a comprehensive cost analysis that extends beyond the initial purchase price. This analysis can encompass factors like maintenance, operating costs and the potential for long-term savings through improved efficiency or reduced downtime, which can resonate with buyers concerned about the total cost of ownership. For example, a key account manager selling industrial machinery could bring in their specialized component manufacturer to explain advanced features and organize site visits where successful end-users demonstrate improved productivity and reduced operational costs. This multilateral approach shifts discussions from pure price negotiations to value creation across the supply chain. It helps buyers understand that aggressive price reductions could compromise quality or service levels that their own customers value, ultimately affecting their market position and customer satisfaction.

KAMgrs can showcase the value for the end customer. By involving the customer's customer, the key account manager can directly demonstrate the value proposition of the product or service to the end-user. Testimonials, case studies or even a joint presentation with the customer's customer can provide compelling evidence of the positive impact on the end-customer's business, emphasizing the value created beyond a narrow focus on price.

These approaches can help reframe the negotiation by shifting the buyer's attention from a purely transactional, price-driven perspective to a more holistic view of value creation throughout the entire value chain. This, in turn, can create opportunities for the key account manager to secure a more favourable outcome that reflects the true value of their offering.

2 *Value First, Then Price* is the title of a book[12] our colleagues Andreas Hinterhuber and Todd Snelgrove edited. This statement nicely captures the essence of this particular strategy. A supplier can build trust and rapport with a buyer by focusing on areas of agreement and shared interests first. This can be achieved by discussing issues related to the supplier's offering, such as technical specifications, quality assurance and service level agreements, before addressing the potentially more contentious issue of price. Once the buyer is convinced of the value proposition and has developed a degree of commitment, the supplier can then introduce the price discussion, potentially achieving a higher price than if the price had been discussed at the outset. This strategy can backfire, however, if the buyer perceives it as an attempt to manipulate them into agreeing to a higher price.

3 *Gain commitment to your solution.* Similar to the 'value first, price second' approach, this strategy focuses on gaining commitment from the buyer regarding the non-price related aspects of the offering before discussing price. In industries such as power plant engineering or industrial automation, where technical specifications and project scope are paramount, a supplier can leverage its expertise and differentiation to convince the buyer of the superiority of its solution before the price negotiation begins. By focusing on the value and benefits of their solution, a supplier can potentially increase the buyer's willingness to pay and achieve a higher price.

4 *Expand the offering.* You can use this tactic to introduce a new issue or service that was not previously discussed midway through the negotiation. For example, a supplier of measurement and control equipment might initially focus on selling hardware to a customer. Later in the negotiation, the supplier might subtly introduce the idea of providing regular software updates and maintenance services as part of the package. If the buyer doesn't perceive the importance of these additional services to the supplier, they might agree without much resistance, giving the supplier an advantage in the negotiation.

5 *Bundle different components of the offering.* A supplier can increase the perceived value of their offering and make it more difficult for the buyer to negotiate individual components by including and bundling a wider range of issues and services in the negotiation. The more complex and comprehensive the offering, the less transparent it becomes for the buyer, potentially leading to higher overall prices. A railway construction

company, for instance, could transition from being solely a product supplier to offering comprehensive systems solutions, thereby justifying higher prices due to the reduced risk and increased value provided to the customer.

6 *Present multiple simultaneous offerings (MESO)*. This a sophisticated negotiation strategy where a party presents several complete proposals at the same time, each with different combinations of terms but representing equivalent overall value to the party presenting it.[13] This approach provides flexibility and choice to the counterparty while maintaining the negotiator's interests. Offering multiple options simultaneously helps overcome negotiation deadlocks, reveals the other party's preferences through their reactions to different proposals and creates a more collaborative atmosphere by demonstrating a willingness to consider various solutions.

For example, a software company negotiating with a client might present three equivalent packages: Package A offers the software at a higher price with extensive training and support; Package B provides the software at a moderate price with standard support and additional user licenses; and Package C features a lower base price with usage-based pricing and minimal support. Each package represents similar value to the vendor but appeals to different client priorities regarding upfront costs, scalability and support needs.

7 *Issue amplification*. This tactic involves amplifying the importance of an issue or potential challenge to secure concessions from the buyer. For example, a supplier could emphasize the complexity of training requirements or the potential difficulties in project implementation, knowing they have the expertise to handle these challenges effectively. By strategically exaggerating these issues, the supplier can potentially secure a higher price or more favourable terms in exchange for their perceived ability to mitigate the buyer's concerns. It is important to note that this tactic should be used judiciously and ethically, as over-exaggeration or deception may damage the relationship and lead to mistrust.

6. INVOKING NEGOTIATED CONTINGENT AGREEMENTS

Value-based negotiation is built on the assumption that the promised value will be realized. Several circumstances could combine to prevent the potential value from being accomplished. In these circumstances, contingent agreements can be established; in other words, contractual arrangements or provisions that depend on the occurrence or non-occurrence of specific future events. These can be contingent liabilities, performance-based bonuses or insurance agreements. Another common form of contingent agreement is earnouts: the purchase price of a business is contingent on the future performance of the acquired company. For instance, if you were negotiating on behalf of an electricity company, you could agree with a supplier of wind turbines, such as Siemens Gamesa, on specific commercial terms and conditions based on the performance of the installed turbines.

7. OFFERING AND MANAGING CONCESSIONS

Regardless of whether you are negotiating a long-term contract with a major client or bargaining over a one-off deal, negotiation requires exchanging concessions. Flexibility is a cornerstone of effective negotiation. Nobody likes to negotiate with an inflexible counterpart.

Before the negotiation, carefully consider your priorities and identify potential concessions you are willing to make. These should be items or issues that are of lower priority to you but hold value for the other party. Consider offering to the other party concessions that are 'high value' to them and 'low cost' to you and to demand from them the opposite: concessions that are 'low cost' to them but 'high value' to you. Additionally, focus on concessions that have minimal intrinsic cost to you, maximizing the value you receive in return.[14]

> Throughout my career, I've encountered situations where key account managers, in their eagerness to please clients, compromised profitability by making unnecessary concessions. Understanding value creation, not just price, has been fundamental to my success.
>
> Stuart Roberts

Having a clear plan outlining the concessions you are willing to make and the conditions under which you will offer them can help you stay focused and avoid making impulsive decisions during the negotiation. Determine the sequence in which you will present your concessions, starting with those of lesser importance and gradually moving towards more significant ones. This approach allows you to gauge the other party's willingness to reciprocate and adjust your strategy accordingly.[15]

When offering concessions, label them as such,[16] emphasizing their inherent value to each party. Ensure that you offer contingent concessions, stating that you can make a concession only if the other party agrees to make a reciprocal one. The perception of value is typically enhanced when you offer incremental concessions, which are increasingly smaller at each negotiation round.[17]

Finally, avoid excessive justification: while explaining the rationale behind a concession can sometimes be helpful, avoid over-justifying your position, as this can weaken your negotiating stance. Focus on the value exchange and the mutual benefits of the concession rather than providing elaborate explanations that can invite further scrutiny or counterarguments.

8. ORCHESTRATING DIFFERENT ROLES IN TEAM-BASED NEGOTIATIONS

KAMgrs' negotiations with strategic accounts will almost always involve other people. Therefore, the effectiveness of the process and the level of satisfaction with the agreement will depend not just on the KAMgr's personal skills but also on the ability of the negotiation team to work in a coordinated fashion. Complex negotiations undertaken by teams often require a number of roles that can be allocated based on factors such as seniority and experience. These roles may include:

Chief negotiator: This role is typically held by the most senior member of the delegation, responsible for overseeing the overall negotiation process and ensuring alignment with the team's objectives.

Spokesperson: The spokesperson articulates the team's position, presents offers and counteroffers, and engages in direct communication with the other party.

Analyst: An analyst plays a crucial role in evaluating the value and cost of concessions, analysing the other party's proposals, and providing insights to inform the team's decision-making process.

Observer: An observer focuses on non-verbal cues and the social dynamics of the negotiation. They pay attention to the other party's body language, tone of voice and interactions, providing valuable insights that go beyond the spoken words. In negotiation, it is not just what you say but what you don't say that matters. Someone who can 'read the room' needs to be encouraged to observe the other party's behaviour and emotions and to decode what they mean in the context of the ongoing negotiation

Note-taker: A dedicated note-taker ensures that all key points, offers, counteroffers and agreements are accurately recorded. This documentation is crucial for maintaining a clear understanding of the negotiation's progress and preventing misunderstandings.

> The key account manager's role is to move beyond the traditional sales approach of being a mere marketing billboard to becoming a customer-centric partner who understands and addresses the needs of the entire customer ecosystem: A strategist and mini key account CEO.
>
> Dominique Côté

Meredith Belbin's team roles theory[18] offers valuable perspectives on how individuals work together. This established diagnostic allows for evaluating individuals' preferences when working with others, differentiating among social, action and thinking orientations. Individuals with a social orientation can become ideal negotiation orchestrators and observers. People characterized by strong thinking orientation are likely to be good negotiation analysts. Finally, action-oriented people are often best suited to claim value in challenging deals.

After the negotiation

9. AGREEING ON A POST-AGREEMENT AGREEMENT

Key account managers are often under pressure to get deals over the line, particularly close to year-end periods. In our experience, this makes some KAMgrs wonder, 'Could I have achieved a better deal... if I had more time?' Well, this is a very human reaction and thought. The question is whether, after having finalized and signed an agreement, you can lose your credibility if you propose a renegotiation. In order to address this situation, you can consider the post-settlement settlement.[19]

> Imagine you work for TechCo, a large technology company. You've just concluded a tough negotiation with a key customer. You've signed the contract, shaken hands and everyone's ready to go home. However, your key contact with the customer, Sarah Holmes, the procurement director, after reaching an agreement on pricing and basic service levels, suggests spending an extra hour exploring additional possibilities. You are initially hesitant, but Sarah explains

that the original deal would remain intact unless you found something better for both parties.

During your discussion, several untapped opportunities are outlined. Your company was planning to enter new markets where Sarah's company had strong connections. Meanwhile, Sarah's team realized they needed specialized training that your company could provide. By the end of their conversation, they had enhanced the original agreement: TechCo would provide premium training services in exchange for introductions to key players in the new markets.

This approach, known as 'post-settlement settlement' or 'post-agreement agreement', can transform a standard deal into a value-creating one. The key is to create a safe space to explore improvements while keeping the original deal as a safety net. The focal question becomes, 'Is there any way we could make our agreement better for both of us?'

Here are some tips on how to implement post-agreement agreements in business deals:

1 Secure the initial agreement first – this serves as a guard and reduces tension since both parties know they have at least one acceptable solution.

2 Explicitly agree to explore additional options – make it clear that any changes must benefit both parties, and either party can fall back on the original agreement.

3 Use brainstorming techniques to identify new value – encourage both parties to think creatively about additional terms, resources or opportunities that weren't considered initially.

4 Consider different dimensions – explore various aspects like timing, delivery methods, payment terms, additional services or future collaboration opportunities.

The factors that help post-agreement agreements include maintaining transparency about intentions to improve the deal, keeping the original agreement intact until both parties agree to modifications, and focusing on creating additional value rather than redistributing existing value.

Post-agreement agreements work particularly well in complex business deals where multiple variables are involved and when there's potential for ongoing relationships between the parties.

10. REINFORCING THE 'SIGNATURE' QUALITIES OF VALUE-BASED NEGOTIATORS

We have argued that value-based strategies are among the most effective approaches to sustaining negotiation effectiveness with strategic customers. Short-term financial and operational pressures may mean that both suppliers and customers find it difficult to exhibit value-based negotiation behaviours consistently. Thus, following a negotiation and in preparation for the next one, the following behaviours need to be reinforced:

- **Creativity**: Identifying shared interests, exploring joint ventures or finding mutually beneficial trade-offs.

- **Flexibility**: Demonstrating adaptability in their approach. Value-based negotiators are willing to adjust their strategies based on new information, changing circumstances or unexpected developments during the negotiation process.

- **Innovative thinking**: Approaching challenges with a problem-solving mindset, relentlessly exploring alternative solutions and being open to creative ideas that meet all parties' interests.

- **Transparency**: Openly declaring constraints and genuine interests.

Bain & Company's study on business value[20] shows how B2B customers care about the functional elements of your offering and the ease of doing business with your company. These are traditionally negotiated in service-level agreements, performance clauses, etc. However, value also manifests for individuals when their priorities, such as peace of mind, design and aesthetics, are addressed.

Furthermore, subtle sources of value emerge when your offering tackles the customer's hopes, deep motivations and future vision. These are rarely captured in formal agreements. However, they can become dealmakers. Therefore, the narrative of negotiation processes with strategic accounts needs to balance the concrete and specific with the holistic and aspirational. When KAMgrs help their customers become more aware and address value drivers across the dimensions outlined, the chances are that the thorniest issues, such as price, become easier to agree on.

As previously mentioned, certain behaviours enable the surfacing of hidden value drivers that can supersede the value of the negotiated items. The 10 guidelines described above, when implemented regularly so they become a habit, will help in designing and delivering negotiation processes to enhance mutual value in deals with strategic accounts.

Summary and application

Enhancing negotiation effectiveness

In the previous chapter, we addressed the capability of fostering value-based selling and co-creation. Value creation and value capture (i.e. negotiation) are often inextricably connected.

Managing value creation and value capture simultaneously is a central challenge in any negotiation in the context of KAM. Table 8.1 suggests some guidance to KAMgrs on achieving this delicate balance.

TABLE 8.1 Managing value creation and value capture simultaneously

Action	Description
1. Prepare thoroughly	Thorough preparation involves detailed research, analysis of the customer's needs and constraints, and identification of potential areas of common ground. By understanding where interests align, negotiators can proactively propose solutions that create value for both parties, leading to mutually beneficial agreements that strengthen the long-term relationship.
2. Leverage the power of questions	Asking questions is a vital tool for both value creation and value capture. Questions serve multiple purposes in negotiation, including but not restricted to:
	Information gathering: Questions help understand the other party's thinking, priorities and constraints, revealing potential areas for value creation.
	Control and pacing: Questions allow skilled negotiators to guide the conversation's flow and maintain a sense of control, which can be beneficial for value capture.
	Challenging assertions: Questions can effectively challenge the other party's assumptions or proposals without resorting to direct confrontation, enabling a more nuanced approach to value capture.
	Creating a breathing space: Questions provide negotiators with time to gather their thoughts and strategize, enhancing their ability to manage both value creation and capture.

(continued)

TABLE 8.1 (Continued)

Action	Description
3 Prioritize compatible interests	Framing proposals in a way that highlights shared interests and compatible goals, fosters a sense of partnership and establishes a strong foundation for mutually beneficial agreements. For example, phrases such as 'It is encouraging to see we share an interest in...' can help establish collegiality, leading to more cooperative negotiations.
	To ensure both parties achieve their desired outcomes, it's essential to understand each other's needs and constraints. Skilled negotiators leverage this information to identify potential areas for value creation. For instance, in a scenario where a construction company is negotiating a contract, understanding the constraints faced by the other party can lead to discovering opportunities for mutual gains. Thorough preparation, including analysing the customer's needs and constraints, is crucial in identifying compatible interests and formulating solutions that create value for both parties.
4 Cultivate tactical empathy	The concept of 'tactical empathy' is a powerful tool for navigating complex negotiations. Balancing emotional intelligence and assertive influence, tactical empathy involves understanding the other party's perspective and acknowledging their emotions, even when those emotions run high. This approach builds rapport and trust, facilitating a collaborative environment conducive to value creation. However, it's important to note that tactical empathy doesn't equate to weakness. It's a strategic tool for gaining insight into the other party's needs and motivations, ultimately enabling more effective value capture.
5 Employ conditional language (If... then)	Employing phrases like 'If... then' signal your willingness to make concessions while ensuring reciprocity. This tactic is vital in KAM for balancing value creation and capture. By framing concessions as contingent upon corresponding actions from the other party, KAMgrs can create value while simultaneously protecting their own interests. This conditional approach ensures that any value created is shared reasonably, preventing one party from disproportionately benefiting from the negotiation.

(continued)

TABLE 8.1 (Continued)

Action	Description
6 Master the art of silence	In key customer relationships, where negotiations are often strategic, the use of silence is a vital skill in certain moments such as after proposing a concession. Silence can be a powerful tool for subtly shifting the power dynamic, prompting the other party to fill the void with further concessions or revealing valuable information. This tactic may allow you to capture more value than initially anticipated. However, the effective use of silence requires patience and the ability to read non-verbal cues, ensuring that the silence is perceived as thoughtful consideration rather than disinterest or hostility.
7 Negotiate the agenda and the process	In complex business-to-business negotiations, understanding the nature and order of negotiation issues plays a significant role in both value creation and capture. We encourage you to negotiate the overall agenda and the negotiation process. Focus on the scope and ultimate goal of the negotiation rather than any particular sequence of issues. Setting the agenda can give a party the advantage of steering the negotiation's flow and potentially leading to increased profits. For example, sellers in competitive situations might employ the 'save the best for last' tactic, building trust and satisfaction before addressing more difficult issues, thereby remaining in the negotiation longer and potentially gaining commitment from the buyer.
8 Understand and adapt to different negotiation styles	Very often we hear 'you have to treat others in the way you like to be treated'. Actually, it is the opposite. You should treat others in the way they like to be treated. In commercial negotiations, parties often adopt a mix of distributive and integrative strategies. Your preferred style may lean towards a collaborative strategy to strengthen relationships and maximize long-term returns. Others with whom you negotiate might focus on substantial results and cost management, sometimes adopting competitive strategies. Therefore, it is crucial to assess the other party's strategy and adapt accordingly to manage both value creation and capture effectively.

(continued)

TABLE 8.1 (Continued)

Action	Description
9 Regulate your emotions	The best negotiators learn how to regulate emotions, particularly fear and anger, during negotiations. Self-awareness is paramount, particularly in large deals. As a KAMgr, you need to recognize your own emotional triggers and physical manifestations of anger (e.g. increased heart rate). Developing strategies to address anger before it escalates is crucial, so learn when to take a break or use relaxation techniques.
	Recognizing how fear manifests (e.g. shaky voice or discomfort maintaining eye contact) is also essential. You can combat fear by focusing on your strengths and engaging in thorough preparation, including rehearsing the negotiation process.
	In team-based negotiations, regulating emotions extends to the entire team. Clear communication and defined roles will help manage individual emotions and ensure a unified front.
10. Build strong relationships	Remember that optimal negotiation outcomes do not need to be in conflict with supporting the development of long-term, collaborative relationships with key customers.
	When you negotiate, ensure you request your agreements to be based on objective and reasonable criteria. Emphasize establishing trust and commitment to the agreed process. For example, during the initial phases of negotiation, focus on collaborative problem-solving to enhance value co-creation. As the process evolves, strive to maintain open communication and remain alert to capture value.

This chapter offers a number of insights to complement the processes of value creation with effective value capture techniques. By employing these strategies, key account managers will navigate complex negotiation processes, achieving the best balance across the commercial, operational and relational agendas with key customers. Finally, negotiation capabilities grow through practice and reflection. Make sure you receive feedback from colleagues (even sometimes the customer) to become an effective negotiator in supplier-key customer relationships.

FIGURE 8.1 Key drivers, tools, behaviours and success factors for negotiating in supplier- key customer relationships

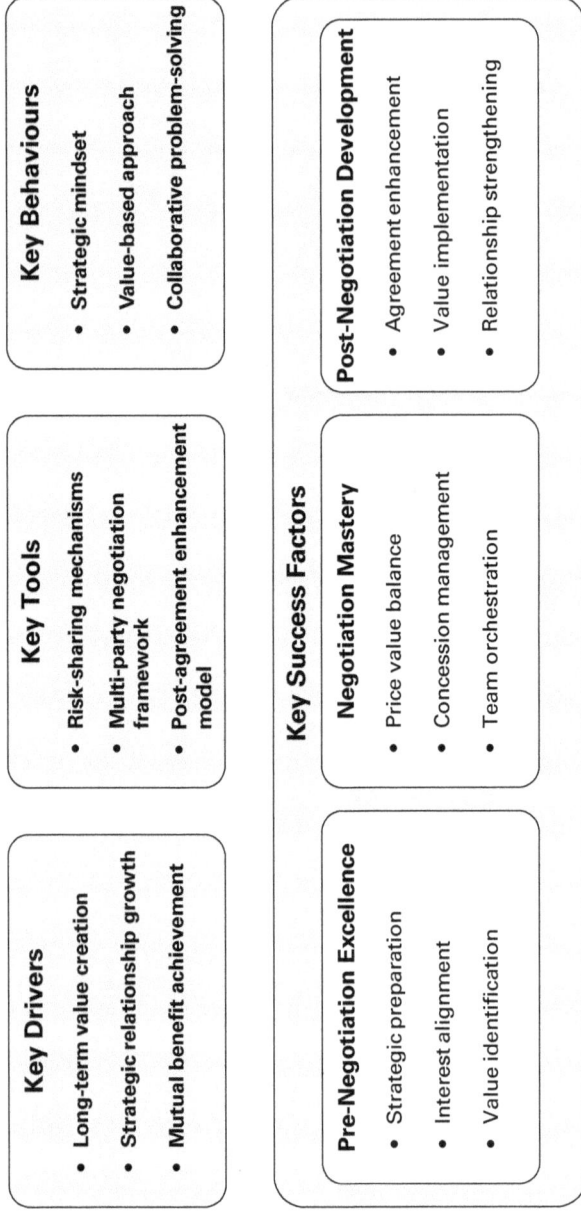

Key Drivers

- Long-term value creation
- Strategic relationship growth
- Mutual benefit achievement

Key Tools

- Risk-sharing mechanisms
- Multi-party negotiation framework
- Post-agreement enhancement model

Key Behaviours

- Strategic mindset
- Value-based approach
- Collaborative problem-solving

Key Success Factors

Pre-Negotiation Excellence

- Strategic preparation
- Interest alignment
- Value identification

Negotiation Mastery

- Price value balance
- Concession management
- Team orchestration

Post-Negotiation Development

- Agreement enhancement
- Value implementation
- Relationship strengthening

Notes

1   B B Hengstebeck, R Kassemeie and J Wieseke. What comprises a successful key account manager? Differences in the drivers of sales performance between key account managers and regular salespeople, *Industrial Marketing Management*, 2022, 106, 392–404, https://doi.org/10.1016/j.indmarman.2022.09.003 (archived at https://perma.cc/245G-CJEZ)

2   H Agndal, L J Åge and J Eklinder-Frick. Two decades of business negotiation research: An overview and suggestions for future studies, *Journal of Business and Industrial Marketing*, 2017, 32 (4), 487–504, https://doi.org/10.1108/JBIM-11-2015-0233 (archived at https://perma.cc/3QKL-7PHA)

3   W Watkins (2008) *Be a Smarter Negotiator*, IMD

4   D Malhotra and M Bazerman. Investigative Negotiation, *Harvard Business Review*, 2007 (September), 72–79

5   R S Adler, B Rosen and E M Silverstein. Emotions in negotiation: How to manage fear and anger, *Negotiation Journal*, 1998, 14 (2), 161–79

6   N Rackham (1999) The behavior of successful negotiators. In R J Lewicki, D M Saunders and J W Minton (eds.) *Negotiation: Readings, exercises, and cases*, 3rd edn, 341–53, McGraw-Hill Education

7   Ibid.

8   E Jaakkola and T Hakanen. Value co-creation in solution networks, *Industrial Marketing Management*, 2013, 42 (1), 47–58

9   J Marcos (2021) *The View from Across the Table: Effective behaviours in strategic negotiations*, Cranfield School of Management

10 J Keränen and A Jalkala. Towards a framework of customer value assessment in B2B markets: An exploratory study, *Industrial Marketing Management*, 2013, 42 (8), 1307–17

11 Rackham. The behavior of successful negotiators

12 A Hinterhuber and T C. Snelgrove, eds. (2021) *Value First, Then Price: Building value-based pricing strategies*, Taylor & Francis

13 D Malhotra and M Bazerman (2007) *Negotiation Genius: How to overcome obstacles and achieve brilliant results at the bargaining table and beyond*, Bantam, New York

14 L Sciencia do Prado and D P Martinelli. Analysis of negotiation strategies between buyers and sellers: An applied study on crop protection products distribution, *RAUSP Management Journal*, 2018, 53 (2), 225–40, https://doi.org/10.1016/j.rauspm.2018.01.001 (archived at https://perma.cc/WXN7-DV3Y)

15 R D D'Andrea. Executing profitable sales negotiations: Selling value, not price, *Industrial and Commercial Training*, 2005, 37 (1), 18–24

16 Ibid.

17 A de Lucas Ancillo, S G Gavrila, J Á Tébar-Sáez and A O Rocha (2024) Technologies and team management to increase productivity in a digital age. In *Artificial Intelligence and Business Transformation: Impact in HR management, innovation and technology challenges*, 177–87, Springer Nature

18 R M Belbin and V Brown (2022) *Team Roles at Work*, Routledge

19 Malhotra and Bazerman. *Negotiation Genius*

20 E Almquist, J Senior and N Bloch. The elements of value, *Harvard Business Review*, 2016, 94 (9), 47–53

Sue Holt

As an expert in KAM, I'd like to share some key insights from our discussion about the evolving nature of this critical business function and the role of the KAMgr. In my view, one of the most fundamental shifts in recent years has been the recognition of key account managers as true 'customer experts' within their organizations. This perspective has been particularly transformative in companies like Royal Mail and CCS, where it helped bridge the gap between traditional supply chain experts and customer-facing roles.

From my experience, the role of key account managers has become increasingly sophisticated and multifaceted. In traditional sales organizations, we often had various specialized experts – IT experts, accountancy experts, supply chain experts – but nobody was specifically designated as the customer expert. In my opinion, this new positioning has given key account managers a clearer identity and purpose within their organizations.

When it comes to the profile of modern key account managers, I've observed a significant evolution. Interestingly, we're seeing more people entering the role without traditional sales backgrounds. Instead, many successful key account managers come with broader management experience and diverse skill sets. This shift is reflected in the changing personality profiles we see in the role. Through Belbin team role assessments, we've noticed a move away from dominant 'Shaper' personalities toward more 'Coordinator' and 'Resource Investigator' types, suggesting a greater emphasis on collaborative and investigative skills rather than pure sales ability.

One particularly interesting aspect I've noticed is the increasing importance of managing internal relationships. Key account managers typically spend around 75 per cent of their time on internal coordination and negotiations, with only 25 per cent spent directly with customers. This might surprise many, as job advertisements often suggest the opposite ratio, but it reflects the complex nature of modern key account management.

In terms of performance measurement, organizations are adopting more sophisticated metrics. At the organizational level, companies are increasingly looking at:

- Growth and shareholder value

- Performance against business plans

- Overall growth of the key account portfolio

- Share of wallet and customer profitability

- Net promoter scores

In terms of performance measurement of individual key account managers, as well as the usual supply-side measures (profitability, relationship strength, share of wallet, etc), the main changes we have seen are around bringing the customer into the measurements, for example:

- Individual net promoter score (NPS): for each key account manager

- Meeting customer critical performance indicators (CPIs): critical measures from the customer's point of view

- Meeting customer key performance indicators (KPIs): key performance measures from the customer's point of view

Reflecting on the role of key account manager, the most successful excel in several critical capabilities. The first and most fundamental is strategizing and planning, which involves developing a deep understanding of the customer's business, their market position and their future directions. This strategic understanding has become even more crucial as it forms the foundation for building value propositions and maintaining long-term relationships.

Another critical capability, in my view, is the ability to manage information effectively. I've observed that many key account managers could improve in utilizing information from various sources within their organization. High-performing managers stand out by taking a holistic view and actively gathering insights from all customer touchpoints.

Regarding personal characteristics, I believe certain traits are particularly important for succeeding in this role. These include integrity and transparency, which can be challenging for those from traditional sales backgrounds who might have been trained in more aggressive sales closing techniques. Political astuteness is also crucial – the ability to read and navigate both customer and internal organizational dynamics while maintaining one's integrity.

One aspect that I believe is often overlooked is the importance of stamina and persistence. Key account managers need to be resilient, able to take knocks and keep moving forward. As I often say, we can't have 'rabbits in the headlights' when problems arise. This resilience needs to be coupled with the ability to influence without authority, which is becoming increasingly important in matrix organizations.

Looking toward the future, I believe the role of key account manager will become even more strategic. While artificial intelligence and automation will handle many transactional aspects, I'm convinced there will always be a place for human relationships in strategic business partnerships. The traditional B2B salesperson might be a dying breed, but key account managers are evolving into highly skilled strategic partners who can navigate complex business relationships and drive mutual value creation.

What I find particularly interesting is how the role is becoming increasingly important in the context of global business relationships. The challenges of managing international accounts add another layer of complexity that requires sophisticated management skills and cultural awareness.

In terms of development, I believe most key account management capabilities can be developed through proper training and support. However, there are certain inherent qualities that are harder to train, such as political astuteness, the ability to inspire confidence and emotional resilience. These characteristics often need to be present in candidates from the start.

Looking ahead to the next decade, I envision key account managers becoming even more strategic in their approach, with many holding MBA-level qualifications. While technology will undoubtedly play a larger role in data analysis and relationship mapping, the human element of building trust and managing complex relationships will remain crucial. In fact, I believe procurement teams will increasingly look for strategic suppliers who can truly partner with them to tackle market challenges together.

In my assessment, organizations need to recognize that this evolution requires a different approach to talent management. The key account managers of tomorrow will need to be of a high calibre, combining business acumen with relationship management skills and strategic thinking. While some traditional sales roles may be replaced by technology, the strategic key account management function is likely to become more, not less, important in driving business success.

To conclude, I believe we're seeing a fundamental shift in key account management from a pure sales function to a strategic business role that requires a unique combination of business acumen, relationship management skills and strategic thinking ability. This evolution presents both challenges and opportunities for organizations as they adapt to the changing business landscape.

Dr Sue Holt is an independent educator and consultant, a Visiting Fellow at Cranfield School of Management and a Visiting Professor at IESEG School of Management. Her main areas of interest are key and global account management and strategic sales. Sue is the Programme Director of Cranfield's flagship Key Account Management Best Practice (KAMBP) programme and has been the Programme Director for many customized company programmes across a wide range of industries and countries globally, as well as undertaking major consulting assignments on KAM. She has been the author of many academic and practitioner reports and articles and is a leading proponent of fighting for the formal professionalization and recognition of strategic sales and KAM as critical functions in the organizations of the future. Sue is also a co-author of the seminal book Implementing Key Account Management.

Sue has been involved in lecturing, research and consultancy in a number of key areas of marketing for over 20 years. Her main interests lie in the fields of global and key account management and strategic sales. Prior to working with Cranfield, Sue pursued a wide-ranging management career in both the public and private sectors, including working for the Prime Minister at 10 Downing Street and for the Speaker in the House of Commons. This was followed by a number of years in marketing management gaining practical expertise in marketing research, strategic and marketing planning and business-to-business marketing. As Sales and Marketing Director for a major printing company, she was instrumental in developing strategic marketing planning within the organization and introduced key account management as an approach to successfully managing major customers.

www.cranfield.ac.uk/som/people/dr-sue-holt-735315

PART THREE

Intra-organizational capabilities

09

Promoting customer centricity

*Empowering key account managers
to drive strategic customer value*

Overview

Customer centricity has become a fundamental paradigm shift in key account management, moving beyond traditional customer service to become a comprehensive organizational philosophy. The chapter emphasizes that true customer centricity requires placing the customer at the centre of all business decisions and operations, while ensuring this approach creates value for both the customer and the supplier organization.

The chapter identifies four key pillars of customer centricity: culture, structure, processes and metrics. These pillars are complemented by five critical premises: customer understanding, organizational alignment, decision-making focus, holistic approach and long-term goals. The interaction between these pillars and premises creates a framework for implementing customer centricity effectively.

The text emphasizes that customer centricity is not just about saying 'yes' to customers or providing good service. Instead, it requires a deep understanding of customer needs, systematic organizational alignment, customer-focused decision-making, a holistic approach to customer relationships and a long-term orientation. The chapter provides practical guidance through a matrix that connects the pillars with the premises, offering specific strategies and actions for key account managers.

For key account managers (KAMgrs), the chapter outlines concrete ways to promote customer centricity, including developing cross-functional teams, implementing customer feedback systems, creating value-based metrics and establishing long-term strategic planning processes. It emphasizes that success in customer centricity requires both strategic vision and tactical execution.

The chapter concludes by highlighting that in today's competitive business environment, customer centricity is no longer just a differentiator but a fundamental requirement for survival and growth. Key account managers play a crucial role in this transformation, serving as the bridge between customer needs and organizational capabilities, and ensuring that customer centricity becomes deeply embedded in the organization's DNA.

Why does promoting customer centricity matter?

To state that customers are vital to the success of any company is not exactly groundbreaking news. However, it would be defendable to say that many organizations don't realize that they have become too internally focused on their outcomes and the processes and practices that support them. To show customers that sellers care about them and their outcomes, a concept known as 'customer-centricity' has gathered pace in recent years. This paradigm shift that places the customer at the heart of all business decisions and operations is something every company is keen to promote. But what exactly is customer centricity, and why has it become such a crucial focus for modern enterprises? Why are KAMgrs responsible for leading every aspect of their company to achieve it?

As we navigate through an era marked by unprecedented technological advancements, shifting consumer behaviours and intense global competition, the importance of customer centricity has never been more pronounced. It's no longer enough for businesses to offer good products or services; they must create meaningful, lasting relationships with their customers to thrive in this new reality.

To understand the importance of customer centricity, we must first define what it entails. According to Gartner,[1] a leading research and advisory company who are as well placed to define it as anyone, the concept can be encapsulated as follows: *Customer centricity is the ability of people in an organization to understand customers' situations, perceptions and expectations.* Customer centricity demands that the customer is the focal point of all decisions about delivering products, services and experiences to create customer satisfaction, loyalty and advocacy.

Let's explore why customer centricity is so important in today's business environment.

Increasing power and value of customers

The digital age has empowered customers like never before. With vast information at their fingertips and numerous options, customers now hold significant market power. The internet and social media have given prospects and customers unprecedented information about products, services and companies. They can easily compare offerings, read customer reviews and share their experiences with a global audience. This transparency has shifted the balance of power from businesses to customers. Companies can no longer rely on information asymmetry or brand loyalty to retain customers; they must consistently deliver value and meet customer expectations to remain competitive. Thus, organizations that fail to recognize and adapt to this shift risk becoming obsolete.

Customer centricity focuses on building lasting relationships rather than just securing one-time transactions. This approach increases customer lifetime value, as satisfied customers are more likely to make repeat purchases, upgrade their services and recommend the business to others. The cost of acquiring a new customer is typically much higher than retaining an existing one. By focusing on customer centricity, businesses can increase customer retention rates, encourage repeat purchases and maximize the lifetime value of each customer. This leads to more stable revenue streams and reduces marketing and acquisition costs.

In an era where switching costs are often low, customer loyalty is more valuable than ever. Customer-centric organizations are better equipped to build strong emotional connections with their customers, fostering brand advocacy and other forms of loyalty that can withstand competitive pressures and market fluctuations, as well as significantly impact a company's reputation and growth. Loyalty goes beyond repeat purchases; it involves positive word-of-mouth and an emotional attachment to a brand. Customer-centric companies that consistently deliver positive experiences and genuinely understand customer needs can create this emotional connection. Loyal customers are less likely to switch to competitors and more likely to be forgiving when issues arise, giving the company opportunities to recover and strengthen the relationship.

Ultimately, customer centricity can significantly impact a company's bottom line. Research has consistently shown that customer-centric companies outperform their competitors regarding profitability and shareholder value. The financial benefits of customer centricity are multifaceted. Increased customer loyalty leads to higher retention rates and more stable revenue streams. Positive word-of-mouth reduces customer acquisition costs. Improved product development leads to higher success rates and better resource allocation. Enhanced operational efficiency reduces costs. All these factors contribute to improved financial performance over time. While the initial investment in becoming customer-centric can be significant, the long-term financial benefits often far outweigh the costs.

Business and development opportunities

While becoming customer-centric often requires initial investment, it can lead to greater operational efficiency in the long run. By aligning all business processes around customer needs, organizations can eliminate inefficiencies and focus resources on activities that truly add value for the customer. Customer centricity often leads to a more streamlined organization. By understanding what truly matters to customers, companies can eliminate processes or features that don't add value, reducing waste and improving efficiency. Moreover, by addressing customer needs effectively the first time, customer-centric organizations can reduce the resources spent on handling complaints or fixing issues, leading to overall operational cost savings. Importantly, to maximize its benefits to the supplier company, customer centricity needs to be clearly perceived by the customers themselves.[2]

As products and services become increasingly commoditized, customer experience has emerged as a key differentiator. A customer-centric approach allows businesses to stand out by providing superior, personalized experiences beyond the primary offering. In many industries, core products or services have become so similar that it's difficult for companies to differentiate based on features or price alone. Consider the smartphone market, where most devices offer similar basic functionalities. The overall customer experience – from purchase to after-sales support – becomes a crucial differentiator in such scenarios. Companies that excel in understanding and catering to customer needs can create unique value propositions that set them apart from competitors.

Additionally, by profoundly understanding customer needs and preferences, organizations can develop products and services that resonate with their target market. This not only increases the chances of success for new offerings but also reduces the risk of investing in products that don't meet customer needs. Customer-centric organizations are better positioned to identify unmet needs in the market and develop innovative solutions. Companies can create products and services that solve real problems and deliver genuine value by maintaining close relationships with customers and actively seeking their input. This approach can lead to higher success rates for new product launches, reduced development costs and faster time-to-market.

From an organizational development perspective, a customer-centric culture often leads to higher employee engagement. When employees understand how their work directly impacts customer satisfaction, they find more meaning in their roles and are more motivated to perform at their best. In short, they see what they do as being worthwhile and making a difference, and they may get the opportunity to engage with happy customers who value them. Customer centricity provides a clear purpose for employees across the organization. Understanding how their work contributes to customer satisfaction can increase job satisfaction and motivation. Moreover, in customer-centric organizations, employees are often empowered to make decisions that benefit the customer, leading to a sense of ownership and pride in their work. This increased engagement can lead to higher productivity, lower turnover rates and better overall performance.

Finally, customer-centric organizations are inherently more attuned to changes in customer preferences and market conditions. This awareness allows them to adapt quickly to evolving landscapes, ensuring long-term sustainability. In today's fast-paced business environment, adapting quickly is crucial for survival. Customer-centric organizations, with their finger on the pulse of customer needs and market trends, are better positioned to anticipate and respond to changes. This adaptability can be a significant competitive advantage, allowing companies to pivot their strategies or offerings before competitors realize the need for change.

The following box provides a summary of the main points that justify promoting customer centricity.

WHY PROMOTING CUSTOMER CENTRICITY IS IMPORTANT

Increased power and value of customers:

- Empowered customers with more sources of influence
- Opportunity to increase customer lifetime value
- Build customer loyalty and connect emotionally
- Improve profitability through stable revenue

Enabling innovation, organizational learning and sustainability:

- Operational efficiency
- Differentiation through customer experience
- Enhanced product development
- Cultural and adaptive advantages
- Long-term sustainability

Customer centricity

In today's business world, there is a consensus on the importance of centring the business strategy around the customer. It is not about doing what the customer wants, but rather starting with the customer's needs and then determining the company's value offerings. Customer centricity follows an outside-in approach rather than an inside-out one. Let's illustrate this idea with an example.

Figure 9.1 shows two drawings to illustrate two different suppliers: Supplier A and Supplier B. Both companies are in the wood business, but there is a relevant difference in terms of the scope and orientation of each other's business. The picture representing Supplier A shows wood pieces that could be utilized in furniture or house construction. The drawing for Supplier B, on the other hand, presents a furniture-based solution for two people to have breakfast, a coffee or perhaps lunch in a reduced space.

FIGURE 9.1 Two different suppliers in the wood business

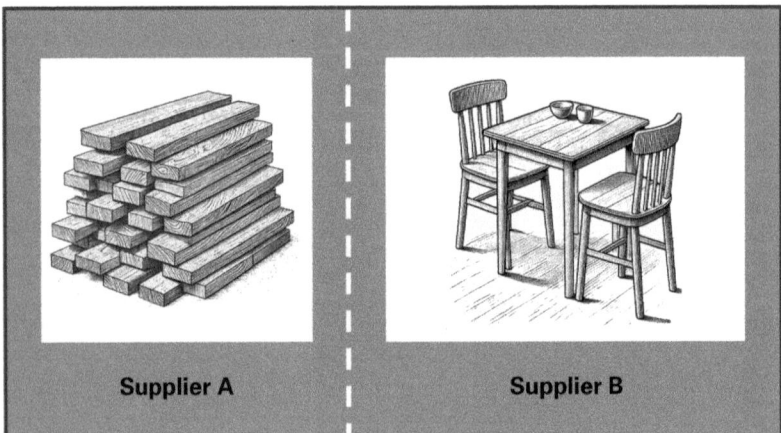

Supplier A | Supplier B

One could argue that Supplier A follows a product-centric business approach whilst Supplier B adheres to a customer-centric approach. A key aspect in this distinction is that the customer-oriented company, Supplier B, could even decide to use other materials different from wood in the future, according to the evolution of customer needs. Supplier A, instead, would probably struggle more to reinvent their business if for any reason wood – as a raw material – becomes less valuable for the market or experiences any problem.

What customer centricity is not

Before exploring in depth what it is let's define what customer centricity is not. This is important, because otherwise it is easy and even tempting for supplier companies and key account managers to behave in ways that *look* customer centric, but that could prevent the supplier company from capturing significant value from KAM relationships.

It's not just good customer service: While excellent customer service is a component of customer centricity, the latter is a much broader, organization-wide philosophy. Customer service typically deals with interactions after a customer has engaged with a company. Customer centricity, on the other hand, informs every aspect of the business, from product conception to long-term relationship management. It's about proactively designing the entire customer experience, not just reacting to customer needs.

It's not about always saying 'yes': Being customer-centric doesn't mean acquiescing to every customer demand. It's about understanding customer needs and finding the best way to meet them within the context of the business's capabilities and goals. Sometimes, this might mean saying no to a customer request if it doesn't align with the company's values or long-term strategy. The key is to communicate transparently and offer alternatives or explanations that show the customer that their needs are being considered, even if they can't be met in the exact way requested.

It's not a one-time initiative: Customer centricity is not a project that can be implemented and then forgotten. It's an ongoing commitment that requires continuous effort and refinement. Customer needs and expectations evolve over time, and so must an organization's approach to meeting them. This requires regular assessment, feedback loops and a willingness to adapt and innovate continuously. It's not a campaign produced by marketing in the hope of attracting new clients.

It's not just about collecting data: While data is crucial for understanding customers, customer centricity goes beyond mere data collection to include empathy, interpretation and insights-based action. It's about turning data into actionable insights and then using them to create meaningful customer experience improvements. This often requires a blend of quantitative analysis and qualitative understanding, combining complex data with softer skills such as empathy and intuition.

It's not a department or a role: Customer centricity isn't the responsibility of a single department or individual within an organization. While teams or roles may be specifically focused on customer experience, true customer centricity is a company-wide mindset and approach. It should inform decisions and actions at every level of the organization, from the CEO to the newest hire.

It's not about short-term gains: Customer centricity is a long-term strategy. While it can certainly lead to short-term improvements in customer satisfaction and sales, its real power lies in building lasting relationships that drive sustainable growth over time. This may sometimes mean making decisions that prioritize long-term customer value over short-term profits.

What customer centricity really is

In key account management, customer centricity has emerged as a fundamental paradigm shift that places the customer at the heart of all business decisions and operations.

According to Gartner:[3] *Customer centricity is the ability of people in an organization to understand customers' situations, perceptions, and expectations.* Customer centricity demands that the customer is the focal point of all decisions about delivering products, services and experiences to create customer satisfaction, loyalty and advocacy. This definition highlights the importance of focusing the business strategy on the customer, establishing customer metrics to assess performance, and to embrace customer understanding as a key for success. Another definition that is worthwhile considering is this one:

> A business approach that places the value perception of the customer at the center of attention and takes it as the starting point for all organizational activities. Strategy development starts consistently with the customer and flows back to the organization (as opposed to inside-out thinking; that is, from the

organization to the customer). The aim is to create an optimal and distinctive fit between the value perception of the customer and the products/services offered. In this way, superior value is created for the customer, and superior value is captured by the organization.[4]

This definition complements the one by Gartner as it also emphasizes the relevance of creating a unique fit between the customer's needs and the supplier's offering, to both creating and capturing greater value.

Customer centricity is at the intersection of three critical activities:

Customer understanding. Developing a deep knowledge of customer needs, behaviours and expectations. It informs decision-making and ensures that all actions are aligned with customer priorities and acts as the foundation for guiding efforts in experience design and continuous improvement.

Experience design. Creating tailored and meaningful customer experiences, emphasizing measures of success such as customer satisfaction and loyalty and ensuring that interactions with the company consistently deliver value and align with customer expectations.

Continuous improvement. Promoting an ongoing process of refining products, services and processes based on customer feedback, encouraging leading innovation and empowering teams to adapt to changing customer needs. It drives efficiency and alignment with customer goals over time.

At the intersection of these activities lies **customer centricity**, where:

- 'Lead' ensures leadership focuses on driving customer-first strategies.
- 'Measure' involves tracking key performance indicators to refine experiences.
- 'Empower' highlights the need to enable teams and systems to act in the best interest of the customer.

Figure 9.2 illustrates customer centricity as the intersection of customer understanding, experience design, and continuous improvement.

The four pillars of customer centricity

Together with understanding the nature of customer centricity, executives from supplier companies need to be able to assess whether their company is sufficiently customer centric. This requires being able to show concrete evidence of commitment to it.

FIGURE 9.2 Critical activities that intersect on customer centricity

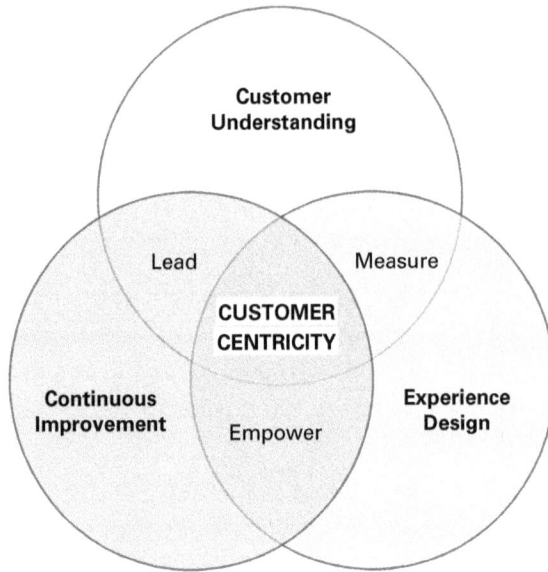

In a seminal work,[5] the authors refer to four critical pillars, which they even call organizational barriers in the path to customer centricity. We adopt and adapt their approach, to propose culture, structure, processes and metrics as the key pillars that companies need to evaluate to check the extent of their customer centricity.

FOUR PILLARS TO DEMONSTRATE CUSTOMER CENTRICITY

1. Culture

The foundation of a customer-centric organization lies in its culture, which emphasizes putting the customer at the heart of every decision. In B2B settings, this means fostering values that prioritize understanding and addressing customer needs over simply promoting products. Likewise, it is expected that in a customer-centric company all employees will know how their work connects with customers and create value. Finally, a customer-centric culture should provide evidence of significant involvement from top management in customer management.

Business leaders can promote a customer-centric culture by instilling empathy as a critical value, educating every employee about the organization's customers, and facilitating direct interaction with customers, among other actions.[6] For example, companies such as Microsoft have reshaped their cultures to focus on customer success by embedding customer feedback into their product development cycles. A critical aspect is nurturing norms where employees are advocates for the customer, ensuring cross-departmental collaboration to meet client needs. Transitioning to such a culture often requires senior leadership to champion these values, as demonstrated by firms such as GE, where executives spend time with customers to better understand their challenges.

2. Structure

A customer-centric structure in B2B organizations integrates all functional areas to deliver consistent value. Unlike product-centric silos, customer-centric structures often include roles like Key Account Managers who act as single points of contact for strategic clients, and Customer Success Managers to focus on the value obtained from all customers. Additionally, a customer-centric structure should have significant customer representation in the board of directors and top management; this could be by formally having a Chief Customer Officer, or by making sure there is profound commitment and expertise with customers in the upper echelons of the organization.

For instance, Wells Fargo employs a matrix organization with relationship managers focusing on client needs and product specialists providing technical support. This dual approach ensures alignment between product offerings and customer requirements. Realigning organizational structures to focus on customer needs rather than products is a significant challenge but can lead to improved accountability and client satisfaction.

3. Processes

Customer-centric processes are designed to build and sustain long-term relationships rather than solely facilitating transactions. This includes customer planning and value co-creation in its several forms, like co-investigating a market opportunity and then co-designing a solution. In B2B settings, these processes involve developing strategies that cater to individual customer needs through tools like customer relationship management (CRM) systems. Furthermore, artificial intelligence (AI) technology can enhance customer centricity by facilitating customer feedback and, thus, learn more deeply about their needs.[7]

To illustrate, Salesforce uses its CRM software to track customer interactions and predict future needs, creating opportunities for personalized solutions. Multichannel integration and robust data management processes are essential, allowing firms to provide seamless customer experiences across touchpoints. However, achieving this requires cross-functional coordination and often significant investments in IT infrastructure.

4. Metrics

Many business leaders claim to be customer-centric, but measure performance through company-focused indicators.[8] Metrics in a customer-centric B2B organization shift focus from traditional indicators like market share to customer-oriented measures such as customer profitability and customer lifetime value (CLV) to assess financial performance, and customer engagement, satisfaction and loyalty to evaluate relational performance. Likewise, customer experience metrics become fundamental to map customer journeys and to analyse its impact on other customer metrics.

For example, IBM measures customer advocacy to assess the effectiveness of its service and product delivery. Aligning employee incentives with these metrics ensures that all levels of the organization remain committed to customer-centric goals. Moreover, using metrics like share of wallet helps B2B firms identify growth opportunities within existing accounts, driving both customer retention and revenue growth.

Figure 9.3 proposes a self-assessment on customer centricity, with some questions that managers from supplier companies may ask themselves.

The five premises for customer centricity

To make the definition of customer centricity *live* throughout the organization and the four mentioned pillars, supplier companies need to follow five very important *premises*, which are:

FIGURE 9.3 Self-assessment on customer centricity

Culture	Structure	Processes	Metrics
Does decision-making start with the customer?	Does the sales force organize in customer segments and key accounts?	Do we elaborate and execute business plans at the customer level?	Do we measure customer profitability and lifetime value?
Do all employees in our company contribute to customer management and success?	Are the different functional units aligned to provide value to customers?	Do we have advanced CRM systems, supported by digitalization and AI?	Do we measure customer engagement, satisfaction and loyalty?
Does top management allocate significant time to customers?	Do we have a Chief Customer Officer in the Board of Directors?	Do we engage in joint solution development and value creation with customers?	Do we measure and manage customers' experience and journey?

1. CUSTOMER UNDERSTANDING

At the heart of customer centricity lies a commitment to developing a deep and multifaceted understanding of customers. This understanding goes far beyond basic demographic data or transactional history. It requires a nuanced appreciation of the emotional, psychological and contextual factors that influence the customer's decisions, challenges and aspirations. In the context of KAM, such insights are essential for building strong, trust-based relationships and delivering value that is truly aligned with the customer's priorities.

Previous research[9] emphasizes that customer centricity involves the alignment of the firm's operations around the needs of valuable customers. This alignment requires deep empathy and the ability to see the world from the customer's perspective. For key account managers, this means not just understanding the immediate needs of their accounts but also anticipating future challenges and opportunities that may affect their clients' businesses. It involves actively listening to customers, observing their behaviours and constantly seeking to deepen one's understanding of their industry, competitive landscape and internal dynamics.

Customer-centric decision-making is not just about addressing current challenges – it also involves looking ahead to anticipate future needs and opportunities. To maintain relevance and deliver sustained value, key account managers must view customer understanding as a dynamic, ongoing process, proactively identifying potential risks and help their accounts navigate them while positioning their organization as a valuable partner in the customer's success. For instance: monitoring emerging trends in the customer's industry and suggesting solutions that can help them stay ahead of the curve; identifying inefficiencies in the customer's processes and recommending improvements to enhance productivity or reduce costs; and proposing innovative ideas that align with the customer's strategic goals, even before the customer explicitly requests them.

By prioritizing customer understanding, organizations can make decisions that align with the true needs and expectations of their key accounts. This approach fosters trust, strengthens relationships and positions the organization as an indispensable partner in the customer's success. In the long run, a profound understanding of customers not only enhances the customer experience but also drives loyalty, retention and sustainable growth in KAM.

ON CUSTOMER CENTRICITY FOR KEY ACCOUNT UNDERSTANDING

The primary responsibility of our key account managers is to facilitate value creation. They do this by developing a deep understanding of the customer's current and future needs and then drawing upon various parts of Fujitsu to create opportunities or respond to customer requests.

Andrea Clatworthy

2. ORGANIZATIONAL ALIGNMENT

Customer centricity is not confined to a single department such as customer service or key account management; it is a comprehensive organizational philosophy. True customer centricity requires that the entire organization – at every level and across every function – be relentlessly focused on creating value for the customer.[10] This commitment must be embedded into the DNA of the organization, ensuring that all decisions, whether strategic or operational, are grounded in a deep understanding of customer needs and expectations.

To achieve this level of alignment, the mindset of putting the customer first must permeate all roles and departments. From C-suite executives to frontline employees, from product development to finance, every part of the organization must be aligned to deliver value to the customer. For example, the product development unit may design solutions based on customer insights and feedback to address their specific pain points, while the finance department should develop pricing models and payment structures that balance customer value creation with profitability. This often necessitates a significant cultural shift within the organization, and key account managers play a crucial role in leading this transformation. It requires breaking down silos, fostering cross-functional collaboration and ensuring that every employee understands how their role contributes to customer value. This might involve changes in organizational structure, incentive systems and communication processes to ensure that the customer's voice is heard and considered in all decision-making processes.

Achieving organization-wide alignment around customer centricity often necessitates fundamental changes to structure, processes and culture. These changes may include: building a culture where customer value is prioritized above short-term gains or internal convenience; establishing processes and forums that encourage departments to work together, share information and align their efforts around customer outcomes; revising performance metrics and reward systems to encourage behaviours that contribute to customer-centric objectives; and ensuring the customer's voice is consistently heard across the organization by leveraging tools such as Voice of the Customer (VoC) programmes, regular customer feedback sessions and transparent reporting of customer-related insights.

ON ALIGNING WITH CUSTOMER-DEFINED SUCCESS METRICS

I strongly advocate for the inclusion of qualitative criteria, such as understanding customer objectives and bringing value beyond product offerings... aligning measurement with customer-defined success metrics is crucial.

Dominique Côté

3. DECISION-MAKING FOCUS

Customer centricity isn't about always saying yes to customers or being overly accommodating at the expense of business viability. Instead, it is about placing the customer at the centre of all decision-making processes, ensuring that decisions across the organization – from product development to service delivery – are aligned with the needs, expectations and value of the business's most important customers.

Customer-centric organizations align their products and services with the wants and needs of their most valuable customers, and therefore, customer impact should be a primary consideration in every decision, from strategic planning to daily operations.[11] Key account managers must consistently ask questions such as: 'How will this decision affect our key accounts?' 'Does this align with our customers' needs and expectations?' and 'Will this create long-term value for our most important customers?'

A decision-making focus requires a thorough understanding of customer needs and preferences, as well as the ability to balance these with the organization's strategic objectives, capabilities and resource constraints. For example, while it is critical to address specific customer demands, these efforts must also align with broader organizational goals such as profitability, innovation and competitive differentiation. This balance might involve making tough choices, such as discontinuing products or services that no longer meet the needs of priority customers or that do not contribute to long-term value, investing in new technologies, capabilities, or processes to enhance value delivery for key accounts, or streamlining internal workflows to improve responsiveness and customer experience without compromising operational efficiency.

ON THE SCOPE OF CUSTOMER CENTRICITY IN KAM

It's not about pushing products; it's about truly understanding the customer's business and working together to create solutions that drive their success.

Mark Bailey

4. HOLISTIC APPROACH

Customer centricity applies to all aspects of what a business provides, and it encompasses the entire experience surrounding a customer's interactions with the organization. This holistic approach ensures that every touchpoint contributes to building value and fostering trust, creating a seamless and positive experience for key accounts. It requires key account managers to consider not just their direct dealings with the customer but the broader ecosystem of interactions that shape the customer's perception and satisfaction.

Customer experience is a multidimensional concept focusing on cognitive, emotional, behavioural, sensorial and social responses to a firm's offerings along the customer journey.[12] For KAMgrs, this means considering every touchpoint, including the user interface of digital products, the ambience of physical meeting spaces, the tone and content of marketing communications, the efficiency and effectiveness of after-sales support, and the alignment of the supplier's internal processes with the customer's workflows.

This holistic approach requires key account managers to think beyond their immediate interactions with the customer and consider the full spectrum of customer touchpoints, to include pre-sale interactions, product or service delivery, post-sale support and ongoing relationship management. They must consider how all aspects of their organization's offerings and operations impact the customer experience. This might involve collaborating with various internal departments to ensure consistency and quality across all customer touchpoints or working with customers to map out their entire journey and identify opportunities for improvement.

A holistic approach to customer centricity also requires aligning the organization's internal operations with the customer's workflows. This alignment ensures that the organization not only meets but enhances the customer's efficiency and effectiveness. For example: streamlining delivery schedules to match the customer's production timelines; providing data and insights in formats that integrate seamlessly with the customer's systems; and ensuring that communication channels are accessible and responsive to customer preferences.

5. LONG-TERM GOALS

The essence of customer centricity goes beyond achieving momentary satisfaction; it aspires to foster deep-rooted loyalty and proactive advocacy. This long-term orientation ensures that KAMgrs not only deliver value but also cultivate relationships that generate sustainable growth for both the customer and the organization. Research shows that customer engagement is a major determinant of business-to-business sales success, and therefore, should be promoted.[13]

Customer engagement value integrates several critical dimensions:[14]

- **Customer lifetime value:** The total earnings a customer generates throughout their relationship with the company.

- **Customer referral value:** The potential revenue generated through referrals and introductions to new accounts.

- **Customer influence value:** The positive impact of customer advocacy on the brand's reputation and market presence, often amplified in today's digital and interconnected world.

These dimensions underline the fact that loyal and engaged customers do more than purchase – they actively contribute to the organization's success by promoting its offerings, providing feedback and enhancing its brand image.

For key account managers, this means focusing on turning customers into long-term supporters and promoters of the business. In today's interconnected world, satisfied customers who become loyal advocates can drive word-of-mouth marketing, provide valuable feedback for product and service improvement, contribute to a positive brand image in ways that traditional marketing efforts often struggle to achieve and serve as references for potential new key accounts.

This long-term perspective requires key account managers to look beyond short-term sales targets and focus on building enduring relationships. It might involve investing in customer success initiatives, creating customer advisory boards or developing loyalty programmes tailored to key accounts. The goal is to make such significant value for customers that they become repeat buyers and active advocates for the organization.

How can key account managers promote customer centricity?

For key account managers, embracing customer centricity means going beyond traditional account management practices. It requires them to become true client partners, deeply embedded in their business challenges and opportunities. By doing so, they can drive significant value not only for their customers but also for their own organizations.

As markets become increasingly competitive and customer expectations continue to rise, customer centricity will likely become not just a competitive advantage but a necessity for survival and growth in key account management. The key account managers and organizations that can truly embed customer centricity into their operations will be well-positioned to thrive in this challenging but exciting landscape.

Key account managers play a pivotal role in promoting customer centricity within their organizations and in fostering strategic, mutually beneficial relationships with clients. Having established that customer centricity is crucial in modern key account management, how does a KAMgr implement this approach?

A practical way to identify how KAMgrs can promote customer centricity is by building a matrix that connects each pillar (culture, structure, processes and metrics) with each premise (customer understanding, organizational alignment, decision-making focus, holistic approach and long-term goals). For each resulting cell, key account managers could develop a strategy and specific actions to promote customer centricity. Figure 9.4 shows an overview of this matrix.

To illustrate how this methodology works, we propose strategies and concrete actions that key account managers could develop to promote customer centricity across the premises and the pillars. The reader should not take this as comprehensive, but as examples of strategies and actions.

1. Customer understanding

Central to customer centricity is a dedication to gaining a comprehensive and layered understanding of customers.[15] This extends well beyond simple

FIGURE 9.4 Premises and pillars matrix for customer centricity in KAM

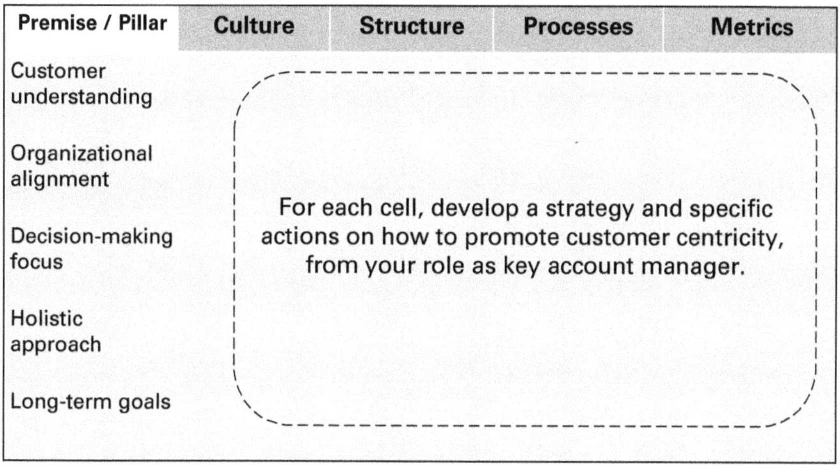

Premise / Pillar	Culture	Structure	Processes	Metrics
Customer understanding				
Organizational alignment				
Decision-making focus	For each cell, develop a strategy and specific actions on how to promote customer centricity, from your role as key account manager.			
Holistic approach				
Long-term goals				

demographic information or transactional records, encompassing a deeper awareness of the emotional, psychological and situational factors that shape customer decisions, challenges and goals. In KAM, these insights are crucial for fostering trust-based relationships and providing value that genuinely reflects the customer's priorities.

Table 9.1 provides recommendations on how key account managers can promote customer centricity through customer understanding, by defining a purpose, a strategy and concrete actions related to the pillars of culture, structure, processes and metrics.

2. Organizational alignment

Customer centricity extends beyond specific departments like customer service or key account management; it is a holistic organizational mindset. Achieving true customer centricity requires every level and function of the organization to prioritize delivering value to the customer. This focus must be deeply ingrained in the organization's culture, driving all strategic and operational decisions to reflect a thorough understanding of customer needs and expectations.

Table 9.2 suggests purposes, strategies and specific actions for KAMgrs, so they can promote customer centricity by means of organizational alignment, affecting the culture, the structure, the processes and the metrics.

TABLE 9.1 Promoting customer centricity through customer understanding

	CULTURE	STRUCTURE	PROCESSES	METRICS
Purpose	Embed customer-centric values across the organization	Facilitate cross-functional collaboration	Integrate customer understanding into workflows	Measure and reward customer outcomes
Strategy	Promote customer needs and outcomes, fostering empathy and highlighting the customer's perspective.	Establish teams/roles that explicitly integrate customer insights into decision-making and product/service delivery.	Redesign key processes to incorporate customer feedback and ensure that customer voice informs decisions.	Develop customer-focused metrics and align incentives with customer success.
Actions	Organize customer-centric workshops or 'customer day' events to interact directly with customers and understand their challenges. Share stories about how the company's products or services impact customers, emphasizing both successes and areas for improvement. Recognize and reward employees or teams who demonstrate customer-centric behaviour.	Form task forces that bring together sales, product development, marketing and customer support to address customer issues. Create a 'customer advocate' role within teams to ensure the customer perspective is considered in all decisions. Secure executive sponsorship for customer initiatives to elevate their importance.	Implement structured post-interaction surveys and feed the insights into product/service development cycles. Conduct customer journey mapping sessions with cross-functional teams to identify pain points and opportunities for improvement. Test new processes directly with key customers to validate their effectiveness before broader implementation.	Integrate customer satisfaction and loyalty as core performance indicators across departments. Measure and track customer retention, upsell/cross-sell success and customer lifetime value as key metrics. Tie bonuses or team incentives to improvements in customer metrics, such as reducing churn or increasing customer satisfaction scores.

TABLE 9.2 Promoting customer centricity through organizational alignment

	CULTURE	STRUCTURE	PROCESSES	METRICS
Purpose	Build a shared vision around the customer	Establish accountability and collaboration across functions	Standardize customer-centric workflows	Drive alignment through unified customer-centric KPIs
Strategy	Align teams and leadership on customer outcomes by fostering a unified mindset across all departments.	Create structures that facilitate cross-functional accountability and communication around customer goals.	Align processes to prioritize customer needs and ensure seamless handoffs between functions.	Develop shared metrics that encourage collaboration across departments and seek customer success.
Actions	Develop a customer-centric mission statement and communicate it internally in team meetings, and leadership speeches. Organize 'shadowing' days where employees spend time with customers to experience their challenges firsthand. Partner with executives to model and reinforce customer-first values in their decision-making and communications.	Establish cross-functional KAM teams, ensuring a shared responsibility for the customer's success. Develop shared objectives and key results (OKRs) for customer outcomes, such as satisfaction or loyalty. Create a governance committee with representatives from key departments to review customer initiatives and resolve conflicts.	Implement a structured process for transitioning customers among departments to avoid information silos. Conduct customer health review meetings with stakeholders from all relevant departments to identify and address issues proactively. Ensure all customer-facing teams use the same tools and frameworks for gathering and acting on customer feedback.	Create dashboards with different customer metrics and make them accessible to all teams for transparency and collaboration. Tie compensation for all teams to shared customer metrics (e.g. retention rate, satisfaction scores). Conduct collaborative reviews of performance on customer metrics to inform improvements in implementing KAM.

3. Decision-making focus

Effective decision-making demands a deep comprehension of customer needs and preferences, coupled with the skill to align these insights with the organization's strategic goals, available capabilities and resource limitations.

Table 9.3 recommends how key account managers can promote customer centricity through the premise of decision-making focus. For each of the four pillars of customer centricity (culture, structure, processes and metrics), we organize suggestions on purpose, strategy and concrete actions.

4. Holistic approach

For key account managers, a holistic approach demands attention to every aspect of the customer journey, including cognitive, emotional and social dimensions. By recognizing that each touchpoint – from pre-sale engagements and product delivery to post-sale support – shapes the customer's perception, key account managers can ensure a seamless and consistent experience. This requires proactive collaboration across departments, such as marketing, logistics and customer support, to align internal processes with customer needs. Such alignment not only builds trust but also positions the organization as a true partner in the customer's success.

Table 9.4 provides ideas of how a key account manager can promote customer centricity through culture, structure, processes and metrics under a holistic approach.

5. Long-term goals

Key account managers are central to translating long-term goals into actionable strategies that deepen customer engagement and ensure sustained value creation. This may involve implementing initiatives like customer success programmes, advisory boards or loyalty schemes designed specifically for key accounts. These efforts demonstrate a commitment to the customer's success, fostering a sense of partnership and collaboration. By shifting the focus from short-term sales targets to enduring relationships, key account managers not only drive repeat business but also cultivate customer advocates who enhance brand credibility and attract new opportunities. This long-term approach positions the organization as a trusted partner, ensuring mutual growth and resilience in competitive markets.

TABLE 9.3 Promoting customer centricity through decision-making focus

	CULTURE	STRUCTURE	PROCESSES	METRICS
Purpose	Foster a customer-first decision-making mindset	Enable transparency and accountability in decision-making	Embed customer considerations in decision frameworks	Align success measurement with customer value
Strategy	Ensure that decisions at all organizational levels are guided by customer impact and key accounts' perspectives.	Establish decision-making structures that require cross-functional alignment around customer needs.	Integrate customer-centric criteria and key accounts' feedback into decision-making and evaluations.	Use metrics on customer experience, satisfaction, loyalty and success to guide future decision-making.
Actions	Develop and socialize a detailed customer journey map to help teams understand who they are making decisions for.	Establish customer advisory boards with key accounts for them to provide inputs on major decisions.	Include customer impact as a weighted criterion in the decision matrix, alongside costs, risks and timelines.	Track customer satisfaction before and after implementing significant decisions to assess their impact.
	Designate a 'customer champion' in leadership meetings to represent the customer's voice in key decisions.	Form cross-functional committees to evaluate strategic customer decisions and anticipate the impact of such decisions.	Require teams to integrate insights from customer data (e.g. surveys, usage analytics) as evidence in proposals or decisions.	Assess how well decisions meet predefined customer-centric objectives, such as growth or loyalty.
	Reinforce cultural norms with questions such as 'How does this benefit the customer?' before decisions are made.	Create clear processes for resolving decisions that negatively impact customers, ensuring accountability and swift resolution.	Conduct 'customer impact assessments' before implementing changes, such as new pricing models or product features.	Track and report the percentage of decisions influenced by direct customer input to monitor alignment with customer needs.

TABLE 9.4 Promoting customer centricity through holistic approach

	CULTURE	STRUCTURE	PROCESSES	METRICS
Purpose	Instil a comprehensive view of customer value	Enable cross-functional integration	Focus on the entire customer journey	Measure end-to-end customer outcomes
Strategy	Cultivate a culture where every employee understands their role in delivering value to customers.	Design structures that promote seamless collaboration and shared responsibility for the key account lifecycle.	Redesign processes to address customer needs comprehensively.	Use metrics that capture the overall health of the customer relationship, spanning all stages of their journey.
Actions	Host regular sessions where key account managers present updates on customer journeys, showcasing challenges and successes. Share real-life customer stories that emphasize the interconnected efforts of multiple teams in delivering value. Incorporate training on customer-centricity during onboarding, emphasizing how all roles contribute to the customer experience.	Create 'customer squads' that bring together sales, marketing, support and operations to co-manage key accounts. Develop shared accountability for customer performance across departments, ensuring no single team works in isolation. Assign executive sponsors to strategic accounts to advocate for customer needs and ensure alignment across functions.	Conduct cross-department workshops to map the customer journey, identify pain points and co-create solutions. Implement a clear process for managing the customer lifecycle, with stages, ownership and handoff protocols. Set up a process for periodic check-ins with customers to anticipate needs and address issues before they escalate.	Develop a composite score that includes metrics such as satisfaction, retention likelihood, usage and engagement. Establish shared KPIs such as customer lifetime value (CLV), engagement and loyalty, ensuring all teams are aligned. Generate regular reports that evaluate how different departments contribute to overall customer outcomes and success.

Table 9.5 illustrates how key account managers can promote customer centricity's premise of long-term goals within the organizational elements of culture, structure, processes and metrics.

Summary and application

Key account managers play a pivotal role in driving customer centricity across their organizations, serving as the bridge between customer needs and organizational capabilities. This is a tall order, since in practice companies struggle to be customer-centric and face traps, like being too ambitious, failing to execute or missing the right alignment with customers.[16] Through the systematic application of the premises and pillars matrix, KAMgrs can implement concrete strategies and actions that transform abstract customer-centric principles into tangible business practices. This structured approach ensures that customer centricity isn't just a theoretical concept but becomes deeply embedded in the organization's culture, structure, processes and metrics.

The success of customer centricity initiatives largely depends on the key account managers' ability to orchestrate change across multiple dimensions simultaneously. By focusing on customer understanding, organizational alignment, decision-making focus, a holistic approach and long-term goals, KAMgrs can create a comprehensive framework that touches every aspect of the customer relationship. This multifaceted approach ensures that customer centricity becomes a sustainable competitive advantage rather than a temporary initiative.

The implementation of customer centricity requires both strategic vision and tactical execution.[17] Key account managers must balance the need for immediate results with long-term relationship building, ensuring that every action taken strengthens the bond between the organization and its key accounts. This involves not only managing external relationships with customers but also fostering internal collaboration and alignment across different departments and functions.

In today's rapidly evolving business landscape, customer centricity has become more than just a differentiator – it's a fundamental requirement for survival and growth. As organizations continue to face increasing competition and changing customer expectations, the role of KAMgrs in promoting and maintaining customer centricity will become even more crucial. By embracing these principles and consistently working to embed them

TABLE 9.5 Promoting customer centricity through long-term goals

	CULTURE	STRUCTURE	PROCESSES	METRICS
Purpose	Embed long-term customer value in organizational mindset	Align teams around long-term customer success	Plan for and support long-term relationship growth	Focus on metrics that reflect long-term success
Strategy	Shift the focus from short-term wins to fostering enduring customer relationships.	Build organizational structures that support sustained collaboration and strategic KAM planning.	Create processes that prioritize sustained customer growth and improvements over time.	Implement metrics that measure long-term customer outcomes, such as satisfaction, retention and growth.
Actions	Share case studies on how long-term customer partnerships have driven mutual success over time.	Assign cross-functional teams to manage long-term strategies for strategic customers.	Co-develop with key accounts multi-year plans with clear milestones and joint goals.	Use customer lifetime value (CLV) to track the long-term financial impact of customer relationships.
	Encourage executives to publicly champion the importance of long-term customer goals in meetings and communications.	Ensure continuity in KAM by implementing robust succession plans for key account roles.	Schedule periodic strategic reviews with customers on long-term objectives and refine plans.	Measure contract renewal and cross-sell rates as indicators of sustained customer satisfaction and trust.
	Implement training sessions focused on the benefits of long-term thinking and its positive consequences for KAM.	Establish formal programmes that focus on co-developing long-term strategies with key customers, such as joint product roadmaps or multi-year growth plans.	Gather customer input on long-term innovation or improvement initiatives, ensuring they are involved in shaping future solutions.	Track how much value a key account contributes to the company's long-term strategy, factoring in innovation or co-creation opportunities.

throughout their organizations, key account managers can help create resilient, customer-focused enterprises that are well-positioned to thrive in an increasingly complex and demanding business environment.

Table 9.6 provides recommended actions for key account managers to foster customer centricity.

TABLE 9.6 Recommended actions for key account managers

Action	Description
Establish customer journey mapping sessions	Lead regular cross-functional workshops to map the complete customer journey, identifying pain points and opportunities for improvement. Involve key stakeholders from both organizations to ensure comprehensive understanding.
Create customer health dashboards	Develop and maintain comprehensive dashboards that track key customer metrics (satisfaction, retention, lifetime value) and share these regularly with internal stakeholders to drive customer-focused decisions.
Implement strategic account reviews	Conduct bi-annual strategic reviews with customers that go beyond performance metrics to include long-term planning, innovation opportunities and value creation initiatives.
Launch customer advisory programmes	Establish formal customer advisory boards where key accounts can provide input on product development, service improvements and strategic direction.
Develop cross-functional account teams	Form dedicated teams that bring together representatives from sales, product development, operations and support to provide holistic account management.
Institute customer impact assessments	Create and implement a structured process to evaluate how major business decisions will affect key accounts before implementation.
Build customer success stories	Document and share detailed case studies of successful customer initiatives, focusing on value creation and problem-solving approaches to promote internal learning.
Establish executive sponsorship programmes	Create formal programmes matching senior executives with key accounts, including clear guidelines for engagement and regular touchpoints.
Implement voice of the customer programmes	Set up systematic processes to gather, analyse and act on customer feedback across all touchpoints, ensuring insights drive organizational improvements.
Create customer-centric KPIs	Develop and track metrics that measure true customer value creation (beyond sales figures) and integrate these into regular business reviews and team objectives.

Notes

1 M P McDonald. How to know when you're really customer-centric, Gartner, 3 May 2022, www.gartner.com/en/articles/how-to-know-whether-you-re-really-customer-centric (archived at https://perma.cc/3SNR-UXKA)

2 J Habel, R Kassemeier, S Alavi, P Haaf, C Schmitz and J Wieseke. When do customers perceive customer centricity? The role of a firm's and salespeople's customer orientation, *Journal of Personal Selling & Sales Management*, 2020, 40 (1), 25–42

3 McDonald. How to know when you're really customer-centric

4 D Shah, R T Rust, A Parasuraman, R Staelin and G S Day. The path to customer centricity, *Journal of Service Research*, 2006, 9 (2), 113–24

5 Ibid.

6 Ibid.

7 D L Yohn. Ways to build a customer-centric culture, *Harvard Business Review*, 2018, October, 2

8 G Cornfield. The most important metrics you're not tracking (yet), *Harvard Business Review*, 2020, 16 (6), 74–85

9 P C Verhoef, K N Lemon, A Parasuraman, A Roggeveen, M Tsiros and L A Schlesinger. Customer experience creation: Determinants, dynamics and management strategies, *Journal of Retailing*, 2009, 85 (1), 31–41

10 C V D Hemel and M F Rademakers. Building customer-centric organizations: Shaping factors and barriers, *Journal of Creating Value*, 2016, 2 (2), 211–30

11 P Fader (2020) *Customer Centricity: Focus on the right customers for strategic advantage*, University of Pennsylvania Press

12 K N Lemon and P C Verhoef. Understanding customer experience throughout the customer journey, *Journal of Marketing*, 2016, 80 (6), 69–96

13 R Guesalaga, J L Ruiz-Alba and P J López-Tenorio. Drivers of business-to-business sales success and the role of digitalization after COVID-19 disruptions, *Journal of Business & Industrial Marketing*, 2024, 39 (4), 708–20

14 V Kumar and A Pansari. Competitive advantage through engagement, *Journal of Marketing Research*, 2016, 53 (4), 497–514

15 C Senn and M Gandhi. 3 traps on the way to becoming a customer-centric company, *Harvard Business Review*, 1 October 2024, https://hbr.org/2024/10/3-traps-on-the-way-to-becoming-a-customer-centric-company (archived at https://perma.cc/LQ3E-U94P)

16 P Fader and S E Toms (2018) *The Customer Centricity Playbook: Implement a winning strategy driven by customer lifetime value*, University of Pennsylvania Press

17 Customer Contact Week Digital. Turning customer centricity into a business differentiator, 24 November 2023, https://europe.customercontactweekdigital.com/customer-experience/articles/turning-customer-centricity-into-a-business-differentiator (archived at https://perma.cc/97VE-XXW6)

Beth Rogers

As an expert in KAM with extensive experience at companies like IBM and Logicalis, I'd like to share key insights from our discussion about the evolving role of key account managers and their essential capabilities.

In my view, one of the most fundamental aspects of key account management today is the strong focus on customer retention, particularly given the current economic climate. However, the role goes far beyond just maintaining relationships. Key account managers are expected to be entrepreneurs within their organizations, driving innovation that can transform both their customers' businesses and their own organizations. While they might only manage one significant innovative project per year, these initiatives can have substantial impact when successful.

From my experience, successful key account managers typically spend around 75 per cent of their time on internal negotiations and coordination, with only 25 per cent spent directly with customers. This might surprise many, as job advertisements often suggest the opposite ratio. The reality is that key account managers spend considerable time negotiating internally for resources and building support for customer initiatives. Even in more streamlined organizations like HP, the internal-to-external ratio was typically around 60-40.

When it comes to what makes an account truly 'key', I've observed that while revenue volume is still important, two factors stand out as crucial indicators: the customer's willingness to undertake innovative projects and the strength of the relationship. Interestingly, research by Gartner (in 2022) indicates that the single most important indicator of a successful key account programme is its focus on growth within the account. In my opinion, while the traditional 80-20 rule is often cited, a more realistic target is for key accounts to represent about 60 per cent of revenue – any more than this might indicate an unhealthy concentration of risk.

For truly strategic accounts, I strongly believe there should be one dedicated key account manager per account. While some companies might label someone managing multiple accounts as a key account manager, these are more accurately described as mid-tier account managers. The scale of true key account management can be substantial – I've seen cases where global accounts have teams of up to 200 people with specific responsibilities for that account.

Regarding qualifications and background, I believe that most key account managers today should have at least five years of experience and typically possess a first degree. While traditionally many came from sales backgrounds, I've seen successful key account managers emerge from technical and professional service backgrounds, particularly in sectors such as manufacturing and pharmaceuticals. The role typically attracts professionals in their late 30s to early 40s, and while still predominantly male, the gender balance is gradually shifting.

In terms of essential capabilities, based on my experience, I would prioritize four key areas:

1 Engaging, communicating and building trust with key customers (50 per cent importance)

2 Building teams and enhancing cross-functional collaboration (20 per cent)

3 Negotiating and designing supplier-customer partnerships (20 per cent)

4 Achieving top management involvement and support (10 per cent)

In my assessment, these capabilities can be developed through various means, but mentoring stands out as particularly effective. Professional development should be ongoing and comprehensive, potentially including formal education like MBA programmes or executive education. The MBA environment, with its emphasis on teamwork and case studies, provides valuable practice for the collaborative nature of key account management.

Technology plays an increasingly important role, particularly in relationship mapping and management. Modern CRM systems with relationship mapping capabilities can help track and analyse the strength and frequency of customer connections across different organizational levels. This systematic approach to relationship management, which I call 'multi-threading', has become crucial for success. These tools can help identify gaps in customer relationships and guide strategic relationship development.

One of the most challenging aspects I've observed is managing team performance and rewards. I advocate for a balanced approach where individual bonuses are tied to team success. For instance, in one effective system I encountered, team members received individual bonuses only if everyone achieved their objectives, followed by team bonuses and additional managerial bonuses for leaders. This approach helps prevent the 'free rider' problem and encourages genuine collaboration.

The role of HR and line management in developing key account managers is also crucial. While HR should drive strategic talent management and skill development, line managers need to provide day-to-day coaching and support. I've noticed that many companies struggle with this balance, particularly when performance issues arise.

A particularly interesting case study from my experience involved relationship mapping in the IT sector. In one instance, a supplier lost their position during a supplier rationalization because they had strong technical relationships but poor connections with senior management. This underscores the importance of maintaining relationships at all levels within customer organizations.

Looking to the future, I believe key account management must continue to evolve. The pandemic has shown how quickly business practices can change, forcing many to adapt to online communications despite initial resistance. In my view, successful key account management programmes must stay proactive in developing new capabilities and tools to avoid falling behind competitors.

From my perspective, perhaps the most crucial takeaway is that development in key account management is lifelong. You don't simply create a key account manager and leave them be – there are always new skills to learn and new challenges to overcome. Success requires both experiential learning and knowledge-based development, supported by proper organizational structures and resources. The key is maintaining a growth mindset and staying adaptable in an ever-changing business environment.

Dr Beth Rogers has established herself as a prominent academic and thought leader in sales management and KAM, with a particularly strong focus at Portsmouth Business School, where she served as Head of the Marketing and Sales Subject Group. During her academic career, she conducted significant research in key account management, contract sales organizations, and the integration of systems and salespeople in business relationships. Her expertise in KAM is evidenced by her co-authorship of three books on the subject with Malcolm McDonald and her own book Rethinking Sales Management, *which received praise from the Strategic Account Management Association's (SAMA) President for its strategic approach to account management.*

Beth's experience combines academic and practical industry perspectives, having worked as a Business Development Manager at Logicalis and as a consultant at the Cranfield Marketing Planning Centre. She has maintained a long-standing relationship with Cranfield School of Management, where she has served as a Visiting Fellow for 25 years. Her influence in the sales profession is further demonstrated through her roles as a Fellow of the Institute of Sales Professionals, an Honorary Fellow of the Sales Performance Association and her chairmanship of the UK Sales Board, where she helped develop National Occupational Standards for Sales. This blend of academic research and practical experience has made her a respected voice in key account management, as evidenced by her contributions to The Times *on sales performance topics.*

www.linkedin.com/in/bethrogerssales

10

Building teams and enhancing cross-functional collaboration

Overview

Key account managers (KAMgrs) are the orchestrators of multifaceted relationships across supplier and customer organizations. These relationships are typically multilevel and multifunctional in nature, and thus require the coordination and alignment of teams to create value and to deliver complex solutions to strategic accounts.

The success of key account management programmes often extends far beyond the capabilities of individual account managers. The intricate needs of strategic customers demand a coordinated effort that spans multiple functions of the company, expertise areas and organizational levels. Thus, building and stimulating high-performing customer teams and fostering meaningful cross-functional collaboration is a capability needed in key account managers to sustain business relationships with key customers.

This chapter explores key dimensions in building and developing teams to deliver value to your most important customers. We'll examine how to identify and bring together the right mix of talent, establish clear roles and responsibilities, and create an environment where diverse skills and perspectives converge to drive innovation and customer success.

We address cross-functional collaboration, distilling practical strategies for breaking down silos and aligning different departments toward common customer-centric goals. In this chapter, we also tackle common challenges that arise when individuals work together in teams. We blend research insights of effective teams with the context of supplier-seller relationships to offer practical insights to answer the question of how KAMgrs can enhance their effectiveness by working in teams and promoting cross-functional collaboration.

WHY BUILDING TEAMS AND ENHANCING CROSS-FUNCTIONAL COLLABORATION IS IMPORTANT

Complexity management:

- Addresses multifaceted customer requirements
- Enables consistent service delivery worldwide
- Handles intricate technical solutions
- Coordinates across multiple geographies

Knowledge integration:

- Enhances customer knowledge acquisition
- Facilitates knowledge dissemination
- Enables better solution development
- Combines diverse expertise areas

Relationship continuity:

- Maintains institutional knowledge
- Ensures smooth handovers
- Sustains long-term partnerships
- Preserves customer-specific expertise

Resource optimization:

- Enables efficient resource sharing
- Maximizes complementary skills
- Improves project delivery
- Strengthens organizational capabilities

Value creation:

- Delivers integrated solutions
- Drives innovation through diversity
- Enhances problem-solving capacity
- Creates competitive advantage

Cross-functional alignment:

- Breaks down organizational silos
- Coordinates multiple departments
- Aligns diverse stakeholder goals
- Streamlines decision-making processes

Why do teams matter in KAM?

Traditionally, strategic account management has put emphasis on the performance of individual KAMgrs. We argue that it is the ability to assemble multifunctional teams that increasingly multifaceted customer relationships require. Teams are needed in key account relationships for at least four reasons: to cope with the complexity of the inter-organizational relationships, to establish collaboration across functions, to provide continuity to supplier-customer partnerships when a single individual leaves an organization and to foster innovation, promoting new ways of thinking. None of these customer outcomes could be realized by high-performing individuals but by high-performing teams.

> We treated key account management as a team sport, focusing on overall targets rather than individual performance. This approach allowed us to be flexible, shifting resources between accounts as needed.
>
> John Downer

Complexity

It is largely accepted that customer relationships in business markets have become more nuanced and complex, and that buying organizations are expecting more from their suppliers, amongst others, in terms of performance, compliance, and adherence to ethical and sustainable practices. No single individual can develop the requisite variety to excel across all these functional domains. Thus, teams need to be created to address the complexity of customer requirements.

A study of large industrial firms[1] in Europe, compared the differences between supplier firms having a team and those not having a team for managing the key customers. The result of this research revealed higher key account performance in the group adopting team-based KAM than the non-team group of companies. Moreover, this work showed that key customer teams can enhance customer knowledge acquisition and better enable the dissemination and utilization of knowledge.

The complexity in key customer relations stems from the need for consistency in product performance, service delivery and operations while simultaneously delivering additional value in strategic partnerships.

In global account management, complexity is exacerbated by the geographical dispersion of customer operations, and the need to coordinate activities across multiple geographies.

Individual KAMgrs rarely possess the comprehensive knowledge or influence needed to manage such intricate relationships effectively. Research demonstrates that KAM teams provide a base of collective expertise that enables better customer knowledge processing and facilitates consistent service delivery worldwide.

The relationship between logistics suppliers and aerospace manufacturers serves as an example of complex supplier-customer relationships that KAM teams can facilitate. For instance, DHL has been involved in the logistics of delivering large aircraft components and engine parts to assembly plants. The relationship between companies like DHL and Airbus would typically involve supply chain optimization, parts transportation and maintenance support, requiring a high level of coordination for seamless manufacturing and airline services. Marja-Liisa Turtiainen was appointed Vice President of Engineering & Manufacturing, Aviation & Aerospace at DHL Customer Solutions and Innovation to look after DHL's relationship with Airbus. She initiated a major redesign of DHL's relationship with the aircraft manufacturer, engaging a team that comprised information systems, inventory management, global supply chain and commercial expertise. Her expert ability to craft a team across the two organizations earned her the 'Best in Class Partner' award for DHL's excellence in being the aircraft manufacturer's logistics partner.[2] When accepting the award, Marja-Liisa said, 'It's an honour to be recognized as best performer. Only market-leading *teamwork* makes it possible to deliver these performance levels.'

Award-winning, high performance in complex relationships can only be delivered by a strong account team that brings together commercial, technical and relational capabilities in a customer-centric fashion.

Underpinning the award was DHL's approach to optimizing logistics flows, increasing end-to-end supply chain visibility, reducing logistics spend and, overall, achieving higher levels of operational excellence, transparency, communication and innovation.

Collaboration

KAM teams influence collaboration both directly and indirectly. Collaborative relationships benefit supplier-customer partnerships at least in two ways: first, an increased ability to share resources, expertise and know-how, and second, reinforced relationships necessary to delivery major projects.[3]

> Key account managers rarely have direct authority over all the resources they need. They must be skilled at influencing and coordinating across different departments and levels of the organization. This requires excellent communication skills, a deep understanding of the company's operations and the ability to align diverse stakeholders around common goals.
>
> Mark Bailey

Resource sharing is an area of increasing interest in business-to-business relationships,[4] and there is a growing shift toward collaborative resource sharing. This trend, a key feature of the sharing economy, has experienced major developments in digital platforms that enable organizations to access and share intangible resources efficiently. Collaboration for resource sharing creates an interconnected network of markets where various forms of value exchange flourish. While much attention has focused on consumer-facing platforms (like Uber and Airbnb), the true potential of sharing extends far beyond these well-known examples, and it is projected to reach $1.5 trillion by 2024.[5] These unprecedented opportunities for business-to-business relationships are contingent upon collaborative approaches to generate value in multiple forms – economic, environmental and social. Businesses that embrace collaborative approaches gain significant competitive advantages while contributing to more sustainable and efficient economic systems. At the heart of establishing and developing inter-organizational relationships lies key account managers' ability to initiate and develop strategic interactions amongst resource sharing partners.

Another area of collaboration where key account managers can make a difference is supplier-customer relationships in major projects. For instance, companies like Jacobs design and deliver engineering and solutions to rail infrastructure owners such as Network Rail in the UK or public transport entities like the Metropolitan Transportation Authority (MTA) in New York.[6] These advanced solutions allow clients to plan, develop, finance, design, construct, maintain and operate smarter transportation infrastructure. Key account managers, working alongside project managers, orchestrate a complex web of deliverables and interconnected dependencies, bringing together contractual, commercial and project management disciplines. The ability to produce increasingly demanding outcomes in complex projects requires a variety of perspectives and areas of expertise. These outcomes need to be supported by cohesive teams.

> A crucial piece of advice for key account managers is to recognize when to involve other team members. Rather than attempting to handle everything personally, it's important to bring in the right expertise at appropriate times to showcase the company's capabilities and add credibility to your propositions.
>
> Nicolaas Smit

Continuity

Very often, breakthrough developments in supplier-customer relationships are the result of protracted timeframes. For instance, the award that Marja-Liisa Turtiainen received from Airbus was the result of seven years' work! During this time, she created an approach that enabled her to deliver 'one-team, one-process, one-company'.

However, you very rarely find a KAMgr in the same role for more than five years. Teams are required to provide continuity in the acquisition, dissemination and utilization of customer-specific knowledge that leads to sustained value creation.

KAM teams represent semi-formal structures that coordinate complex sales processes across products, functional units and geographical regions, while also serving as a consultative partner to the customer.

The study referred to in the section on 'Complexity' reveals that suppliers with established KAM teams demonstrate higher levels of customer knowledge acquisition, particularly in strategic areas such as technological developments, planned moves and financial positions. This comprehensive understanding allows suppliers to better anticipate customer needs and create solutions that competitors find difficult to imitate. Furthermore, team-based KAM has shown superior performance outcomes compared to non-team approaches, suggesting that the organizational investment in establishing and maintaining these teams is justified by their ability to manage the nuanced demands of modern business relationships.

Best practice companies in KAM like Siemens emphasize long-term relationships and the need to become a trusted partner.[7] They recognize the value of relational assets and the fact that customer relationships can span up to 30 years and beyond. It would be unrealistic to expect that a key account manager would be looking after a customer for three decades. That is why maintaining the institutional know-how and expertise accumulated over such period needs a handover process supported by teams. Only KAM teams can sustain the lifecycle of value creation throughout such protracted periods of time.

The nature of teams in KAM

Jon R. Katzenbach[8] describes a high-performing team as a 'small number of people with complementary skills who are equally committed and hold themselves mutually accountable for a common purpose, goals, and working approach'. Key account managers are at the heart of creating such teams in key customer relationships.

First, effective teams are typically comprised by a small number of people. You may be wondering, 'What number is a small number?' We advise to refer to the classic rule of the magical number seven, plus/minus two that cognitive psychologist George Miller created. He argued that the number of elements an average human can hold in short-term memory is 7 ± 2. Ideally, a KAM team would comprise this number of members in order to ensure an appropriate span of control as well as coordination.

Second, the number 7 ± 2 is enough to integrate into the KAM team professionals with the required complementary skills such as commercial, operational/technical, financial and digital technologies backgrounds. KAM teams integrate requisite variety with non-trivial customer insights into common relationship goals with well-defined performance measures. As we referred to in Chapter 1, the KAMgr synthesizes key dimensions of the customer's strategy and connects these to the suppliers' approach to create value for the customer, and even beyond, for the customer's consumer. Tom Muccio, former President of Global Customer Teams at Procter & Gamble,[9] brought together multi-disciplinary teams to redefine the relationship of P&G with its key customer, Walmart.

Third, in order to build effective strategic customer teams, KAMs devote a significant amount of energy and time to bring about commitment and a sense of accountability in their account teams. Very often, KAMs do not have formal authority over the individuals that are part of the SA team. Thus, they must engage informal influencing techniques; they need to create impact without authority. Allan Cohen and David Bradford[10] advocate for the use of alliances, reciprocity and exchange to help individuals meet their objectives within organizations (see the section on cross-functional collaboration later in this chapter). Barry Callebaut, the world's leading manufacturer of high-quality chocolate and cocoa products, assemble key account teams who, using consumer insights, new ingredients and streamlined supply chain operations, commit themselves to helping key customers like Mr Cheney, the specialist American-style cookies manufacturer based in São Paulo, succeed in seasonal campaigns and new product launches.[11]

Key account teams are designed and carefully assembled to provide complete solutions to key customers. The skills required transcend any single individual's area of knowledge, thus requiring the engagement of teams. For example, Onyx Insight, an award-winning global renewable technology business, brings together sensing, analytics and engineering expertise to enhance the performance of wind turbines. The KAM for a key customer, such as General Electric, involves a small number of individuals with complementary skills and expertise to create an innovative solution for a key customer.

Creating high-performing KAM teams

Is it enough to understand the nature of teams in organizations to deliver high performing customer relations? Not really. KAMgrs must understand both the dynamic processes that underpin effective teams and some of the silent killers of team performance.

> For truly strategic accounts, I strongly believe there should be one dedicated key account manager per account... The scale of true key account management can be substantial – I've seen cases where global accounts have teams of up to 200 people with specific responsibilities for that account.
>
> Dr Beth Rogers

Underpinning processes of effective teams

Unilever is a strategic supplier to the French-headquartered retailer Carrefour. Product managers, supply chain executives, IT specialists and finance experts, amongst others, come together, coordinated by an account director. As a team, each member contributes to the design and execution of campaigns to help this retailer grow sales of Unilever's consumer products in food, home and personal care categories. But how can an account director effectively orchestrate these disparate resources and areas of expertise?

Gregory Huszczo[12] work *Tools for Team Excellence* suggests that the creation of high-performing key account management teams requires more than just assembling skilled individuals. As Huszczo emphasizes, excellence emerges from the deliberate cultivation of seven critical elements: clear goals, talent, roles, procedures, relationships, leadership and organizational support.

In the context of KAM, these elements take on particular significance as teams must navigate complex customer relationships while coordinating internal resources across functional boundaries. Success in KAM teams depends not only on individual expertise but also on the team's collective ability to deliver integrated solutions to strategic customers. KAM teams can develop the necessary synergies to move beyond traditional seller-buyer relationships and create genuine strategic partnerships that drive value for both organizations. Understanding these dynamics is crucial, as KAM teams can become the cornerstone of key B2B relationships by developing the following processes and KAM teams' characteristics.

> I estimate that they spend about one-third of their time with the customer and two-thirds internally, which aligns with my experience of the necessary balance for effective account management.
>
> Andrea Clatworthy

1. Clear sense of direction and specific targets. KAMs will often face multiple demands. Having a clear roadmap for developing their relationships with their key accounts is essential. Account teams in suppliers like Unilever craft their account strategy in a way that supports their key customers' ambitions. For instance, on 8 November 2022, Carrefour presented its 2026 strategic plan, stating as a key priority the requirement for the group's top 100 suppliers to adopt a 1.5°C trajectory by 2026. This provides clear guidance to work together toward the achievement of a specific environmental target.

HOW COULD A KAM TEAM AT UNILEVER HELP CARREFOUR
IN THEIR ENVIRONMENTAL INITIATIVES?

As Unilever's KAM team for Carrefour, you would recognize that helping your
strategic retail partner achieve their ambitious environmental target requires
more than traditional one-to-one relationships and supplier-retailer
collaboration. Your team could leverage Unilever's established environmental
leadership and combine it with Carrefour's market presence to create
meaningful impact. By sharing your expertise in science-based targets and your
successful emissions reduction initiatives, you can help accelerate Carrefour's
journey while strengthening this key customer relationship.

Your strategy could centre on creating multiple layers of value exchange. At
the operational level, you could offer detailed carbon footprint data for all
Unilever products. You could champion a set of training workshops for
Carrefour category and marketing teams on environmental impact assessment,
and access to your supply chain optimization tools and carbon measurement
frameworks. You could also propose the development of exclusive sustainable
product lines and co-created packaging reduction initiatives that can
demonstrate tangible progress toward the 1.5°C trajectory goal. These practical
initiatives could be supported by regular knowledge sharing, including market
intelligence on consumer sustainability preferences and benchmarking data
from other markets.

To ensure meaningful progress, you could develop a phased approach that
begins with a joint baseline assessment and identification of quick wins in
packaging and logistics. This could evolve into medium-term initiatives such as
implementing joint carbon tracking systems and pilot programmes for circular
economy initiatives. Throughout this journey, you would enhance both
partners' commitment to transparent emissions reporting and shared KPIs that
demonstrate your contribution to Carrefour's environmental goals. By
combining your environmental expertise with Carrefour's retail leadership, you
could create a model for sustainable supplier-retailer partnerships that delivers
both environmental impact and business value.

These and other similar actions and initiatives would inevitably involve
teams guided by a clear sense of direction and mutually agreed specific targets.

2. **Diverse talent and skills.** High-performing teams, as mentioned earlier, are
characterized by the integration of diverse skills. Meredith Belbin conducted
some pioneering work to understand the composition of high-performing

teams[13] that led him to develop what we know as Belbin's Team Roles theory. This framework identifies nine roles individuals typically assume within teams, grouped into Action-Oriented, People-Oriented and Thinking-Oriented categories. Each role highlights strengths and possible weaknesses, contributing to team dynamics. A high-performing team balances these roles, leveraging their diversity to address complex challenges effectively. Recognizing and valuing different roles maximizes strengths enabling teams to achieve their goals efficiently.

Belbin's Team Roles theory aligns closely with the dynamics of key account teams given the need for diverse roles to deliver exceptional value to strategic clients. Key account teams require a mix of strategic thinking, interpersonal skills and execution capabilities to manage complex client relationships effectively. For example, *Coordinators* can align team efforts with client objectives, while *Resource Investigators* bring external opportunities and insights to the table. *Shapers* focus on delivering against agreed KPI. *Plants* create innovative solutions, ensuring the team remains proactive in addressing client needs. *Teamworkers* are best placed for ensuring collaboration and *Monitor-Evaluators* balanced decision-making.

By leveraging Belbin's framework, KAM teams can build a balanced structure where each member's strengths contribute to managing critical accounts holistically, sustaining long-term partnerships.

THE ORIGINS OF BELBIN'S TEAM ROLES THEORY

The genesis of Team Roles theory can be traced back to 1969 when Dr Belbin started to study the behaviour of teams at Henley Business School. Successful managers with board potential took part in a business simulation during a ten-week course. The business simulation contained all the principal variables that typify the problems of decision-making in a business environment. The experiment was designed along scientific lines with careful measurement at each stage.

Having an interest in group as well as individual behaviour, but with no particular theories about teams, Dr Belbin enlisted the aid of three other scholars: Bill Hartston, mathematician and international chess master; Jeanne Fisher, an anthropologist who had studied Kenyan tribes; and Roger Mottram, an occupational psychologist. Together they began what was to be a nine-year task. Three business games a year with eight teams in each game, and then in meeting after meeting, observing, categorizing and recording all the different kinds of contribution from team members.

Those participating were invited to take psychometric tests plus a test of high-level reasoning ability called the Critical Thinking Appraisal (CTA). Teams of various designs were composed based on these individual test scores. Every half-minute the contribution of the person speaking was recorded and classified into one of seven categories by trained observers. At the end of the exercise, which ran off and on throughout a week, the results of each team (operating as a company) were presented financially, which allowed more effective and less effective teams to be compared.

At first it was thought that high-intellect teams would succeed where lower intellect teams would not. However, the outcome of this research was that certain teams, predicted to be excellent based on intellect, failed to fulfil their potential. In fact, it became apparent by looking at the various combinations that it was not intellect, but balance that enabled a team to succeed. Successful teams were characterized by the compatibility of the roles that their members played, while unsuccessful teams were subject to role conflict. Using information from psychometric tests and the CTA, predictions could be made on the roles that individuals played and ultimately on whether the company would be more likely to figure among the winners or losers.

One interesting point to observe from the experiment was that individuals reacted very differently within the same broad situation. It is a common experience that individual differences can cause a group to fall apart. People just don't fit in. On the other hand, variation in personal characteristics can become a source of strength if they are recognized and taken into account. So, understanding the nature of these differences can become an essential first step in the management of people, providing one can recognize what is useful for a given situation and what is not.

The most successful teams tended to be those with a mix of different people, i.e. those with a range of different behaviours. In fact, eight separate clusters of behaviour turned out to be distinctive and useful. These were called 'Team Roles', and a ninth based on specialist knowledge was to emerge later. These Team Roles have been used in organizations and teams across the world ever since.

Action-oriented roles:

- Shaper: Challenges norms and drives the team forward.
- Implementer: Turns ideas into practical actions.
- Completer-Finisher: Ensures work is completed thoroughly and on time.

Social-oriented roles:

- Coordinator: Focuses on team organization and delegating tasks.
- Teamworker: Promotes harmony and supports collaboration.
- Resource Investigator: Explores external opportunities and brings new ideas.

3. Clear roles and responsibilities. In order to facilitate the performance of KAM teams, individuals must have clarity in terms of the scope of the work they are expected to deliver. When clarity of expectations is balanced and blended with the needed flexibility to cater to the changes occurring in the customer environment, account teams perform at their best.

Role clarity typically has a positive effect on the sellers' ability to execute sales strategies.[14] Clear responsibilities are paramount in opportunity identification, selection and management. In complex sales, where these phases are separated across different individuals, understanding of when one process starts and when the next ends help seamless strategy execution and better customer outcomes.

Furthermore, Guenzi and Storbacka's work in implementing KAM shows[15] that role clarity reduces ambiguity and conflicts, allowing team members to focus effectively on their specific contributions while understanding how their work integrates with others. Successful KAM implementation requires mapping and redesigning critical processes using tools like the RASIC (Responsible, Accountable, Supporting, Informing and Contributing) matrix to clearly indicate each team member's role in different phases of implementing KAM. This structured approach to role definition supports both internal cross-functional coordination and external customer-facing activities. When roles and responsibilities are well-defined, teams can better orchestrate resources and deliver integrated solutions that create value for both the organization and its key accounts.

4. Efficient procedures. Large organizations can become bureaucratic and the needed agility and responsiveness to deliver against customer requirements suggest reviewing the procedures that teams adopt to ensure they are externally focused, not just internally oriented. Effective processes and procedures are needed to ensure that the 'promised' value proposition sales professionals make to customers is actually delivered. Thus, such processes may point to effectively linking sales functions and other functions.

FIGURE 10.1 Processes and supporting elements that underpin effective teams

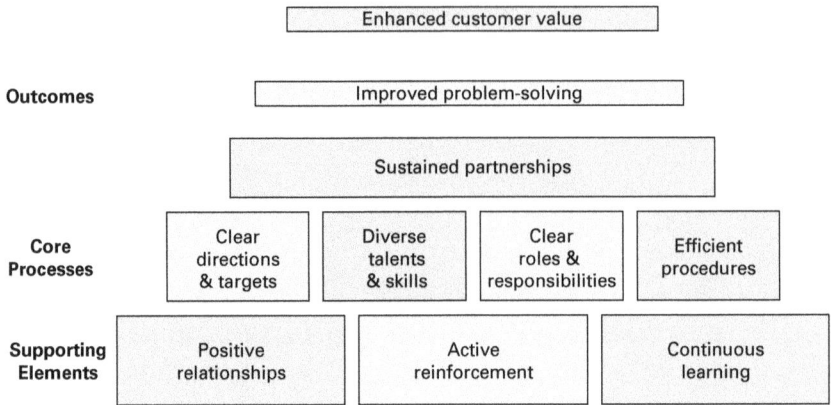

Successful KAM implementation requires systematically analysing and redesigning critical processes, particularly to streamline decision-making and reduce bureaucracy in customer-facing activities. Suppliers map and redesign key processes to improve response times and bring flexibility to matters such as pricing and discount policies.[16] Efficient procedures need to balance standardization for consistency with flexibility for customization – allowing KAM teams to respond quickly to customer needs while maintaining control. This can be achieved through well-designed information systems, clear approval pathways and streamlined administrative processes that empower KAM teams to make decisions at the appropriate level. Organizations should focus on eliminating unnecessary complexity in procedures while ensuring adequate controls remain in place to manage risk and maintain quality in key account relationships.

Huszczo's work in high performing teams also suggest the need for positive interpersonal relationships. Although conflict is ubiquitous and the ability to handle conflict is a key skill in KAMs, constructive personal relationships are often associated with higher levels of performance. Also, active reinforcement systems that promote continuous learning, collegiality and alignment are part of the ingredients of the recipe for high performance in teams. Many key-account and internal-team relationships are sustained through solid social and personal bonds between the buyer and supplier staff.

Addressing common pitfalls in designing teams

The complexity of managing strategic customer relationships often masks a fundamental truth: the success of key account management ultimately depends on how well teams function together. While organizations invest heavily in processes, systems and customer strategies, they frequently overlook the human dynamics that can make or break a KAM programme.

We have looked at the characteristics of high performing KAM teams. A good way to address common shortcomings in teams is by first understanding what these are. Lencioni's *The Five Dysfunctions of a Team*[16] outlines a framework with the pitfalls that undermine team effectiveness. He presents these dysfunctions as a pyramid, with each level building on the one below, illustrating how one weakness can cascade into broader challenges.

At the foundation lies the **absence of trust**. Without trust, team members avoid vulnerability, hesitating to admit mistakes or ask for help. This creates a defensive environment that stifles collaboration and lays the groundwork for the next dysfunction: **Fear of conflict**. Without trust, teams shy away from honest, open discussions, replacing meaningful debates with guarded comments or artificial harmony. As a result, they fail to address real issues.

This leads to a **lack of commitment,** as team members cannot fully buy into decisions when they haven't engaged in healthy conflict to clarify and debate ideas. Ambiguity thrives, and false agreement becomes the norm. A lack of commitment then gives rise to the **avoidance of accountability**, where individuals hesitate to hold peers accountable for low standards, allowing mediocrity to creep in. Finally, the pyramid peaks with **inattention to results,** as personal goals and egos overshadow collective team objectives, leading to failure.

Lencioni suggests remedies for each dysfunction: building trust through vulnerability, encouraging constructive conflict, ensuring clarity and alignment, embracing accountability and maintaining a results-focused mindset. Together, these steps create a cohesive, high-performing team. Let us investigate these in more detail in the context of KAM teams.

Building trust: The foundation of customer-centric teams

At the base of every high-performing key account team lies intra-group trust. Yet, this fundamental element is often compromised by the very structure of KAM teams. Cross-functional team members, often coming from different departments with competing priorities, may hesitate to show or admit limitations. For instance, a KAMgr may be reluctant to acknowledge her limited understanding of technical specifications, while a product manager might hide his discomfort with customer negotiations. This lack of trust manifests in subtle ways – withholding information, avoiding difficult conversations about customer challenges, or presenting an artificially optimistic view of account progress.

Building trust in KAM teams requires deliberate effort. Successful teams often schedule regular off-site meetings where members share their professional journeys, challenges and aspirations. When a member of the KAM team can openly discuss struggles with value quantification, or when someone admits uncertainty about how to engage the key customer senior management team or other customer-related matters, the team starts building the psychological safety essential for peak performance.

Encouraging constructive conflict: The engine of innovation

The fear of conflict particularly plagues key account teams because they often operate in high-stakes environments where major customer relationships hang in the balance. Team members might avoid challenging a colleague's approach to account planning or resist questioning a proposed solution's viability, fearing they might damage internal relationships or appear uncooperative. However, this artificial harmony prevents teams from developing truly innovative solutions for their key accounts.

Successful KAM teams learn to embrace productive disagreement. They understand that robust debate about account strategies, solution design or resource allocation leads to better outcomes. Regular account review sessions become forums for honest discussion rather than mere progress reports. Team members feel empowered to question assumptions and challenge conventional approaches, knowing that constructive conflict strengthens rather than weakens team cohesion.

Ensuring clarity and alignment behind account strategies

The lack of commitment often manifests in key account teams through passive resistance to agreed strategies. Team members might nominally agree to a customer engagement plan during meetings but fail to prioritize their commitments once they return to their functional roles. This is particularly challenging in matrix organizations where team members report to both functional and account managers.

Effective KAM teams address this by ensuring all members have a voice in strategy development. They create clear decision-making frameworks and document specific commitments. Regular team sessions focus on reviewing not just progress but also the level of buy-in and understanding of the agreed approach. Leadership ensures that functional goals align with account objectives, reducing the tension between departmental and account priorities.

Embracing accountability: Delivering on customer promises

The avoidance of accountability is particularly damaging in key account management, where complex customer solutions require coordinated execution across multiple functions. Team members might hesitate to call out delays or quality issues, especially when they involve colleagues from other departments. This reluctance can lead to missed deadlines, quality problems and, ultimately, disappointed customers.

High-performing KAM teams establish clear performance standards and make accountability a shared responsibility. They create transparent tracking systems for commitments and make it safe for team members to raise concerns early. Regular account reviews include frank discussions about team performance, with all members feeling responsible for the overall success of the account relationship.

Maintaining a results-oriented mindset: Focusing on customer success

The ultimate dysfunction – inattention to results – manifests when team members prioritize their functional or personal objectives over customer success. A product manager might push for selling new features that don't address customer needs, or a service team might optimize for internal efficiency rather than customer value.

Successful key account teams maintain an unwavering focus on customer outcomes. They establish clear metrics that reflect customer success rather than just internal targets. Team incentives align with account objectives, and regular customer feedback sessions help maintain focus on what truly matters.

Addressing these dysfunctions requires a systematic approach. Organizations must recognize that forming effective key account teams involves more than just selecting capable individuals or establishing clear processes. It requires creating an environment where trust flourishes, healthy conflict is encouraged, commitment is clear, accountability is embraced and customer results remain the primary focus.

Leadership plays a crucial role in this transformation. Key account directors must model the desired behaviours, facilitate open communication and create the psychological safety needed for teams to overcome these common dysfunctions. Regular team assessment and coaching help identify and address issues before they impact customer relationships.

The investment in building cohesive key account teams pays dividends through stronger customer relationships, innovative solutions and sustained competitive advantage. By understanding and actively addressing these common team dysfunctions, organizations can unlock the full potential of their key account management programs.

Towards cross-functional collaboration in KAM

Cross-collaboration is vital in KAM because, as we have argued, serving strategic clients requires contributions from multiple departments across an organization. Key accounts typically have complex needs that span several

FIGURE 10.2 Common pitfalls encountered in designing teams

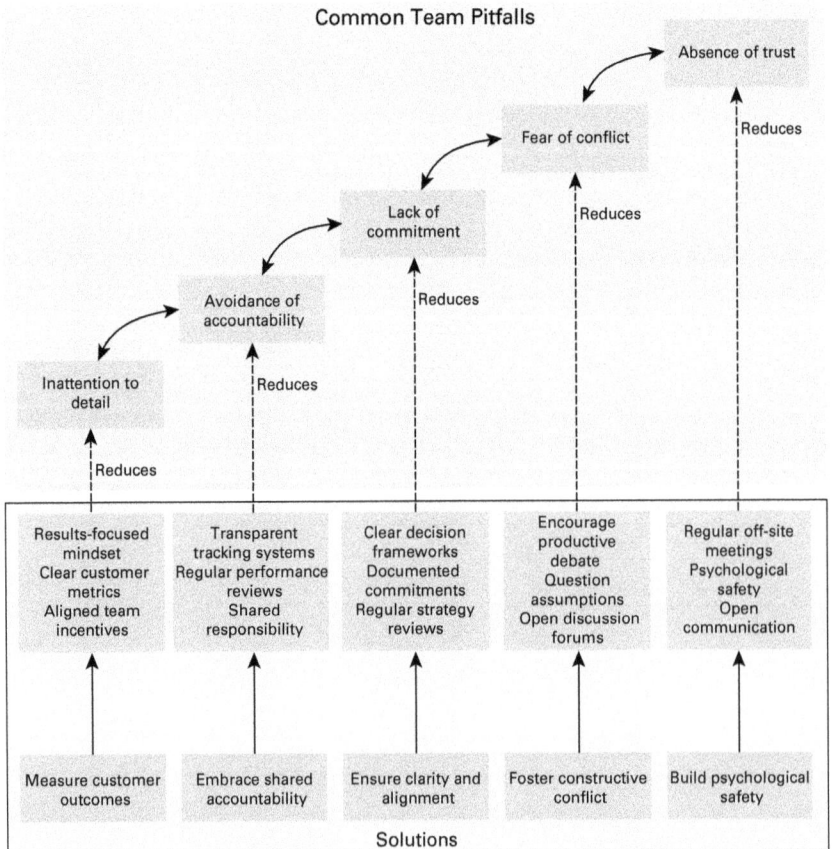

areas, like sales, marketing, operations, product development, customer support, etc. These areas go beyond customer-facing jobs. Collaboration ensures these functions work together to deliver tailored solutions, strengthen relationships, and drive mutual success.

Fostering cross-functional collaboration calls for KAMgrs to act like orchestra conductors, coordinating different sections to deliver a harmonious performance for the customer. For instance, Dan Ahern, group account manager at ABB, was pivotal in fostering collaboration both within ABB and between ABB and one of their key accounts, Caterpillar. Recognizing the need for a unified approach, Dan positioned himself as the representative for all of ABB's activities with Caterpillar, emphasizing the importance of acting as 'one ABB'. He understood that the existing issues with the Turbocharger business unit threatened ABB's overall relationship with Caterpillar. To address this, Dan took decisive action, facilitating communication between ABB and Caterpillar, particularly at the executive level. He arranged meetings and workshops to align goals and strategies. Further demonstrating his commitment to collaboration, he actively sought involvement in the steering committee for Caterpillar, aiming to work closely with all stakeholders to repair the strained relationship and improve cooperation. By championing a collaborative approach, Dan aimed to shift ABB's position from a mere supplier to a true partner for Caterpillar.

In the case of ABB, the role of fostering collaboration was far from easy. The path to collaborative harmony is not without its obstacles that often manifest in:

- Silo mentality and lack of trust: Departments working in isolation, clinging to their own knowledge and resources, can stifle collaboration. Overcoming this requires a culture shift that emphasizes trust and openness, encouraging a willingness to share information and work together.

- Inadequate communication: Poor communication can lead to misunderstandings and missed opportunities. Regularly sharing information, using clear language and establishing robust feedback mechanisms are vital for effective communication.

- Misaligned goals and incentives: When departments are working at cross-purposes, with differing goals and incentives, collaboration can break down. It is critical to ensure that individual incentives align with the overall success of the KAM initiative and the shared goals of the supplier and the customer.

- Lack of resources or support: Collaboration requires dedicated time, effort and resources. Without adequate support from management, in the form of time allocation, budget and access to necessary tools, collaborative efforts will falter.

- Resistance to change: Moving towards a collaborative model can be challenging for individuals accustomed to traditional ways of working. Effective change management, clear communication about the benefits of collaboration and addressing concerns openly can help overcome resistance.

- Cultural differences: In global organizations, cultural differences can present communication challenges and require sensitivity to diverse communication styles, values and expectations.

- Technological barriers: Outdated technology or a lack of integration between systems can hinder collaboration. Investing in modern, integrated technology solutions can significantly improve communication and streamline collaborative processes.

Addressing these barriers requires a multifaceted approach that focuses on building trust, improving communication, aligning goals, providing support and embracing a culture of change. When done successfully, cross-collaboration transforms KAM, moving it from a transactional, supplier-centric approach to a true partnership where the supplier and the customer work together to achieve remarkable results.

Thus, KAMgrs can embed several factors to enable cross-functional and inter-organizational collaboration:

- Proactivity: KAMs who demonstrate proactiveness are more likely to actively seek out collaborative opportunities and build strong relationships. They are naturally inclined to anticipate challenges and take the initiative to solve them, making them invaluable drivers of collaboration.

- Strong leadership support: A company culture that champions collaboration starts at the top. Leaders must clearly communicate a vision for collaboration, empower KAMs to collaborate and allocate resources to support collaborative initiatives. The creation of dedicated leadership positions, like a Chief Technology Officer (CTO) or Head of KAM, reinforces the importance of cross-functional teamwork.

- Effective communication channels: Open and transparent communication is the lifeblood of collaboration. This can be achieved through regular meetings, shared platforms like a CRM system and other easily accessible tools for communication and collaboration. For example, using a shared CRM system keeps all account information in one central location, fostering synchronized communication and eliminating information silos.

- Shared goals and metrics: Aligning goals and metrics across departments, and including the customer in this process, creates a shared sense of purpose. When everyone is working towards the same objectives and can clearly see how their efforts contribute to success, collaboration becomes a natural and effective way of working.

- Development of collaborative skills: Collaboration requires specific skills, and it is important to provide training and development opportunities for employees. These programmes should focus on crucial areas like communication, negotiation, conflict resolution and team building.

- Supportive tools and resources: Practical tools and resources can make a significant difference in facilitating and streamlining collaboration. For example, a competency map can provide KAMs with detailed information about the supplier's capabilities, enabling them to propose tailored solutions to customers.

TABLE 10.1 Key actions to contribute to and lead high performance teams

Action		Description
1.	Establish an optimal team composition	Configure teams of 7+2 members with complementary skills across commercial, technical, financial and digital technology domains to ensure comprehensive customer value delivery.
2.	Implement role clarity frameworks	Deploy tools like the RASIC matrix to clearly delineate responsibilities, accountability and support functions within the key account team structure.
3	Foster psychological safety	Create an environment where team members can openly acknowledge limitations and share challenges without fear of repercussion, establishing the foundational trust described in Lencioni's framework.
4	Institutionalize knowledge retention	Develop systematic processes for capturing and transferring customer-specific knowledge to ensure continuity of relationship value beyond individual tenure.

(continued)

TABLE 10.1 (Continued)

	Action	Description
5	Enable constructive conflict	Establish structured forums for robust debate about account strategies and solution design, encouraging productive disagreement that drives innovation.
6	Align cross-functional incentives	Create shared performance metrics and reward systems that promote collaboration across departmental boundaries and support customer-centric outcomes.
7	Streamline decision processes	Design efficient procedures that balance standardization for consistency with flexibility for customization, enabling rapid response to customer needs.
8	Cultivate team role diversity	Apply Belbin's Team Role theory to ensure balanced representation across action-oriented, people-oriented and thinking-oriented roles.
9	Establish accountability mechanisms	Implement transparent tracking systems for commitments and regular performance reviews that maintain focus on customer success metrics.
10.	Develop collaborative capabilities	Invest in training programmes focused on essential skills, including communication, negotiation, conflict resolution and cross-functional leadership.

Summary and application

Having come to the end of the chapter on building teams and fostering collaboration, Table 10.1 summarizes some key actions you can consider both to contribute to, and to lead, high-performing teams.

Figure 10.3 shows key drivers, tools, behaviours and success factors when building teams and enhancing cross-functional collaboration.

FIGURE 10.3 Key drivers, tools, behaviours and success factors

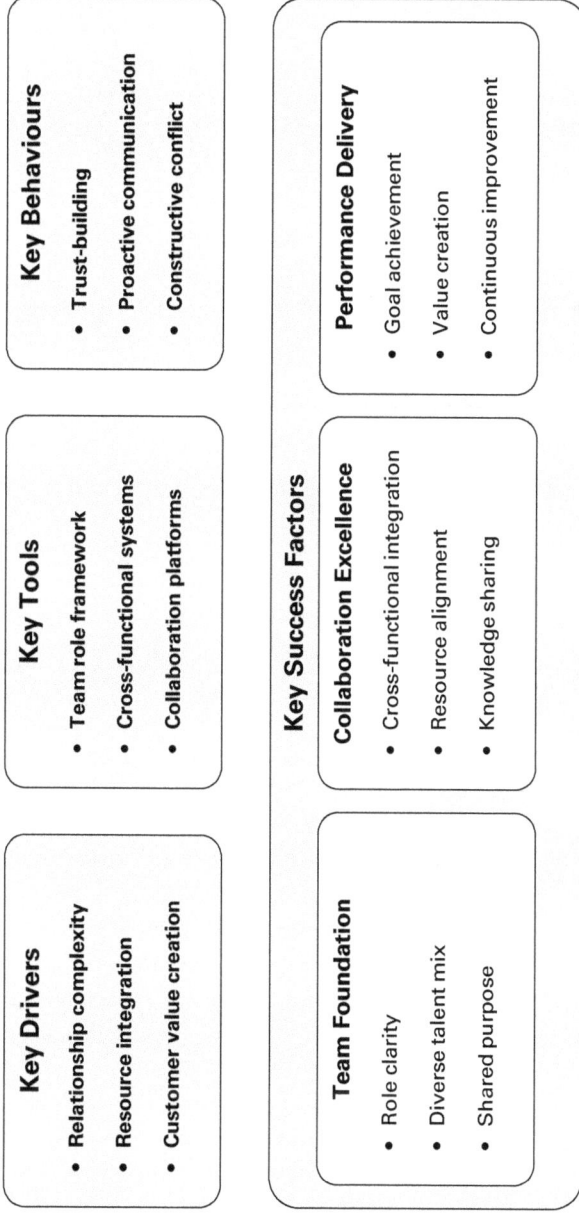

Key Drivers
- Relationship complexity
- Resource integration
- Customer value creation

Key Tools
- Team role framework
- Cross-functional systems
- Collaboration platforms

Key Behaviours
- Trust-building
- Proactive communication
- Constructive conflict

Key Success Factors

Team Foundation
- Role clarity
- Diverse talent mix
- Shared purpose

Collaboration Excellence
- Cross-functional integration
- Resource alignment
- Knowledge sharing

Performance Delivery
- Goal achievement
- Value creation
- Continuous improvement

Notes

1   J Salojärvi and S Saarenketo. The effect of teams on customer knowledge processing, esprit de corps and account performance in international key account management, *European Journal of Marketing*, 2013, 47(5/6), 987–1005

2   DHL. Press Release Bonn, Airbus honors DHL with Best Performer Award, 13 October 2016, https://dhl-freight-connections.com/en/business/starthilfe-fuer-grosse-voegel/#:~:text=%E2%80%9CDHL%20is%20proud%20of%20 its,is%20right%20for%20this%20customer (archived at https://perma. cc/25M5-GLQU)

3   D B Arnett, B A Macy and J B Wilcox. The role of core selling teams in supplier-buyer relationships, *Journal of Personal Selling & Sales Management*, 2005, 25 (1), 27–42

4   K von dem Berge (2024) Resource sharing in B2B contexts: Enhancing utilisation among allies and competitors, unpublished PhD thesis, Cranfield University, School of Management

5   BCC Research (2020) Shared Economy: WeWork, Uber, Airbnb and Lyft, www.bccresearch.com/market-research/finance/shared-economy-wework-uber-airbandb-lyft-market.html?srsltid=AfmBOorkOs8UbzjvPXV_ VLGcJHW8SAu_Hr1fer46J43YcHtlsMD2fscG (archived at https://perma. cc/4KN3-K6X7)

6   Jacobs (n.d.) Grand Central Madison project, www.jacobs.com/projects/ grand-central-madison (archived at https://perma.cc/UD9T-RGUD)

7   SAMA – Strategic Account Management Association. Case Study: Impact of sustainability, YouTube, 17 January 2011, www.youtube.com/watch?v=oF61-omUQAYQ (archived at https://perma.cc/K4UL-VG9K)

8   K Katzenbach and K Douglas (2015) *The Wisdom of Teams: Creating the High-performance organization*, Harvard Business Review Press

9   8th & Walton. One on One: Tom Muccio, President of Global Customer Teams (ret.), Procter & Gamble, YouTube, 24 July 2013, www.youtube.com/ watch?v=siTVSiXEQws (archived at https://perma.cc/9R9H-ZXNU)

10 A R Cohen and D L Bradford. Influence without authority: The use of alliances, reciprocity, and exchange to accomplish work, *Organizational Dynamics*, 1989, 17 (3), 5–17

11 Foodbiz. Mr. Cheney faz parceria especial com a Callebaut para a Páscoa, 25 March 2021, https://foodbizbrasil.com/negocios/mr-cheney-faz-parceria-especial-com-a-callebaut-para-a-pascoa/ (archived at https://perma.cc/MKE7-UWK5)

12 G Huszczo (2010) *Tools for Team Excellence: Getting your team into high gear and keeping it there*, Davies-Black Publishing

13 R M Belbin and V Brown (2022) *Team Roles at Work*, Routledge

14 P D Kerr and J Marcos-Cuevas. Reclaiming the contingent nature of the determinants of salesperson performance: An extended meta-analysis, *Journal of Personal Selling & Sales Management*, 2023, 44 (4), 414–31

15 P Guenzi and K Storbacka. The organizational implications of implementing key account management: A case-based examination, *Industrial Marketing Management*, 2015, 45, 84–97

16 P M Lencioni (2010) *The Five Dysfunctions of a Team: A leadership fable,* John Wiley & Sons

Tim Chapman

As a seasoned professional with extensive experience in key account management, I've held roles ranging from managing large manufacturing clients at ICL Fujitsu to overseeing global accounts at Vodafone. My career has given me a unique perspective on the evolution of key account management and the skills required to excel in this field.

In my view, the role of a key account manager today is multifaceted and challenging. It requires a delicate balance between retention and growth. While customer retention has always been important, I've noticed that in recent years, clients are switching suppliers more frequently. This makes the defensive aspect of the role – maintaining and nurturing existing relationships – even more critical.

However, growth remains a key objective. Many companies I've worked with have excellent key account management teams who excel at customer satisfaction and retention, but struggle to drive additional revenue from existing clients. The ideal key account manager needs to balance both customer service and sales skills, which is a rare combination.

Looking ahead, I believe the role will continue to evolve. While many core processes remain similar to what they were 20–30 years ago, the environment and available technology have changed dramatically. Key account managers need to adapt to these changes, leveraging new tools and technologies to be more effective in their roles.

In terms of performance measurement, I've seen various approaches throughout my career. Early on, it was very much driven by financial targets. As markets matured, other factors like customer satisfaction began to play a larger role. In some industries, there's been a shift away from commission-based compensation to salary-based structures, often driven by regulatory concerns or past mis-selling issues.

Based on my experience, particularly from designing commission schemes at Vodafone Global Enterprise, I believe the ideal performance measurement scheme for key account managers should be achievable and realistic. A good balance might be 80 per cent based on financial targets and 20 per cent on customer satisfaction metrics. It's crucial that these metrics align with the company's overall objectives and drive the desired behaviours.

When it comes to the capabilities that underpin high performance in key account management, I would highlight three as particularly important:

1 Strategic thinking with a balance between long-term vision and short-term tactical execution

2 The ability to lead and influence without formal authority

3 Relationship building, but from a network perspective rather than just individual relationships

Developing these capabilities often requires a combination of innate qualities and learned skills. For strategic thinking, I've found it helpful to encourage key account managers to develop a clear, long-term vision for their accounts. This provides a 'North Star' to guide all activities, both long term and short term.

The ability to lead and influence without authority is crucial, particularly given that about 60 per cent of the job involves managing internal resources. This requires strong interpersonal skills, emotional intelligence and the ability to manage stakeholders effectively.

For relationship-building, I've found that bringing in people from diverse backgrounds – not just traditional sales – can be beneficial. These individuals often bring different perspectives and may have stronger listening and empathy skills, which are crucial for building trust and psychological safety with clients.

Adaptability is another key skill for key account managers. The business world is constantly changing, and key account managers need to keep pace. This might involve embracing new technologies, understanding new industries or adapting to different communication styles with younger generations of decision-makers.

In terms of developing these skills, I believe in a combination of formal training, on-the-job learning and personal development. As a leader, I've always tried to create diverse teams, bringing in people from different backgrounds to foster mutual learning and adaptability.

Finally, I can't stress enough the importance of building and maintaining a broad professional network. This network should extend beyond just your key accounts, as it can provide valuable insights, opportunities and support throughout your career.

In conclusion, key account management is a challenging but rewarding field that requires a unique blend of skills. The most successful key account managers are those who can balance strategic thinking with tactical execution, build and leverage broad networks, and continually adapt to changing business environments. As the business world continues to evolve, so too must the skills and approaches of key account managers.

Tim Chapman has built an impressive career spanning key leadership roles in enterprise sales and consulting. Starting at Vodafone Global Enterprise, he progressed from Global Account Manager to VP of New Business Sales, Americas, over a nearly eight-year tenure. As Global Account Manager, he managed strategic relationships with major corporations such as SKY, News Corporation and BP, notably securing a 16-country global agreement with BP. His progression continued through roles as a Sales Effectiveness Executive, where he implemented sales excellence programmes for 750 managers globally, and as a Regional Sales Manager, leading a team of nine account managers overseeing 150 US-based multinational customers.

In more recent years, Tim has expanded his influence in sales leadership, serving as Vice President of Sales at Elliptic and Managing Partner at Sales EQ, a position he's held since 2015. At Vodafone, his experience with key accounts was particularly noteworthy, especially during his final role as VP of New Business Sales, Americas, where he led a team of 20 account managers responsible for 300 US-based multinational customers and delivered double-digit growth from an €80 million revenue base. His current work at Sales EQ focuses on international sales consultancy and training, where he leverages his extensive enterprise sales experience to help clients enhance their sales capabilities and achieve measurable returns on investment.

www.linkedin.com/in/tichapman

11

Securing top management involvement and support

Overview

Top management involvement is fundamental to the success of key account management programmes. Given that key accounts represent an organization's most valuable customers, executive support becomes essential for strategic success and long-term profitability.

The chapter explores three distinct drivers of top management involvement in KAM. Strategic drivers focus on building long-term partnerships and gaining market intelligence. Operational drivers centre on developing KAM competence and resolving operational barriers. Individual drivers stem from personal interests and professional advancement opportunities.

Executive sponsors can adopt multiple roles when supporting KAM initiatives. As strategic visionaries, they set direction and align KAM with corporate strategy. Through resource allocation, they ensure adequate support for KAM programmes. In their organizational alignment role, they foster cross-functional collaboration. Some executives excel as relationship builders, engaging directly with key accounts at a senior level. Others focus on decision-making, performance monitoring or championing a customer-centric culture. In times of crisis, sponsors can intervene to resolve critical situations.

> Leadership support is absolutely critical for the success of KAM initiatives. This includes not just verbal support, but also empowering key account managers to try new approaches in a safe environment.
>
> Dr Beth Rogers

The chapter provides practical guidance for key account managers (KAMgrs) to leverage executive sponsorship effectively. This includes a structured approach to identifying suitable sponsors, aligning initiatives with business strategy, establishing clear expectations and engaging sponsors strategically in customer interactions. Success depends on creating mutual benefits that add value to both the KAM programme and the sponsor's objectives.

WHY TOP MANAGEMENT INVOLVEMENT MATTERS IN KEY ACCOUNT MANAGEMENT

Strategic direction and alignment:

- Corporate strategy integration
- Long-term partnership development
- Market intelligence gathering
- Strategic decision-making frameworks

Resource management:

- Appropriate resource allocation
- Investment prioritization
- Budget authorization
- Human capital deployment

Organizational effectiveness:

- Cross-functional coordination
- Departmental barrier reduction
- Process optimization
- Internal alignment enhancement

Customer relationship enhancement:

- Strategic commitment signalling
- Senior-level relationship building
- Crisis management support
- Partnership value amplification

Cultural transformation:

- Customer-centric culture promotion
- Organizational value alignment
- Change management facilitation
- Innovation encouragement

Performance oversight:

- KAM effectiveness monitoring
- Accountability establishment
- Results measurement
- Success recognition

Knowledge management:

- Best practice sharing
- Organizational learning promotion
- Capability development
- Experience transfer

Risk management:

- Strategic risk assessment
- Operational issue resolution
- Compliance oversight
- Relationship continuity assurance

Effective sponsor engagement requires regular but focused communication, strategic involvement in customer interactions and clear protocols for crisis management. While some organizations have formal sponsorship programmes, this chapter emphasizes that key account managers can secure and leverage senior executive support through thoughtful planning and structured approaches, regardless of the formal structures in place.

Why is it important for top management to be involved in KAM?

Top management involvement (TMI) is a critical element for the success of KAM programmes. As we have outlined earlier in the book, key accounts represent the company's most valuable customers, essential to the firm's long-term success and profitability. Given their strategic significance, top management must be directly involved in shaping and supporting the overall KAM strategy and approach.[1] The effective implementation of KAM involves dedicating and allocating significant resources to strategic customers. Therefore, top management involvement is necessary to ensure appropriate resources are assigned to key customers in alignment with the overall corporate strategy and priorities. Also, the involvement of top managers who have the authority to make important strategic decisions regarding key accounts allows for quicker, higher-level decision-making. Besides, since KAM requires coordination and collaboration across different functional areas of the organization, top management plays a crucial role in aligning goals, promoting cooperation and breaking down silos between departments to support key account initiatives.[2]

Very often, from the customer perspective, senior executives' involvement in customer contact and relationship-building, particularly through social interactions, is taken as a proxy for the real importance of the relationship. Therefore, top management involvement can help strengthen ties with key accounts and signal the strategic importance of the relationship with customers.[3]

> Having our CEO involved also makes a big difference for our clients because it gives them a sense of importance and establishes a direct connection.
>
> Dominique Côté

If the management of key customers is to become a capability to sustain customer value over the long term, a customer-centric culture needs to be created and nurtured. Top management support and participation help create a culture that prioritizes key accounts throughout the organization.

A key question is, how important is it for a KAM programme to have the support and sponsorship of top executives? One could argue that since the customer-facing activities are driven by the key account manager, the senior executives can be seen more like figureheads. Evidence shows that when top management is involved, the importance of KAM is elevated within and across organizations, creating greater accountability for KAM and enhancing its performance and results.[4] In Table 11.1 we summarize the studies that link TMI with performance outcomes in KAM.

TABLE 11.1 The relationship between TMI and KAM effectiveness

Study	Key insights
Homburg, Workman and Jensen[1] conducted a major study with 375 organizations and defined four clusters that shape KAM: (1) activities, (2) actors, (3) resources and (4) approach formalization.	Their observations reveal that TMI in KAM is positively related to KAM effectiveness. Senior executives set an example and demonstrate commitment to KAM.
In their conceptual review, Piercy and Lane[2] argue that a challenge for leaders is to understand better the potential weaknesses in KAM strategy to balance these against the benefits.	Top management are crucial, particularly in ensuring they do not underestimate the changes in the environment to effect the necessary changes in KAM and thereby cannot enhance KAM effectiveness.
Zupancic[3] examines the elements of key account management programmes, to understand the success factors and to create an integrated framework.	Top management support, manifested both in strategy statements as well as concrete actions, contributes to establishing a professional KAM programme and define appropriate structures, processes and people.
Guesalaga[4] conducted 27 interviews with senior executives and a survey of 261 key account managers to examine how the dimensions of TMI relate to KAM outcomes.	Top management plays a pivotal role in KAM implementation through executive sponsorship programmes. The study found that top managers' social interaction with customers is more relevant than business-related interaction, which can even be detrimental when focused on tactical issues. High level of interventions from the top-level might confuse customers and signal a lack of confidence in the key account manager.

(continued)

TABLE 11.1 (Continued)

Study	Key insights
Salojärvi et al.[5] conducted a survey to understand the relationships between various intra-organizational factors and customer knowledge utilization in the context of key account management.	TMI is positively related to obtaining good relational outcomes through promoting customer knowledge utilization.
Al Hussan[6] and colleagues conducted a qualitative study to explore the role of senior managers in managing intra- and inter-organizational relationships with key customers and the factors that influence such involvement in the Arab Middle East region.	TMI is critical in developing business relationships and creating value for the firms. Arab senior managers' participation is imperative, and a hands-on approach is advised when dealing with the Arab key customer. The study reveals the need to focus more on the relational aspect of key account management.

1   C Homburg, J P Workman and O Jensen. A configurational perspective on key account management, *Journal of Marketing*, 2002, 66 (2), 38–60, https://doi.org/10.1509/jmkg.66.2.38.18471 (archived at https://perma.cc/X7PR-VEXT)

2   N Piercy and N Lane. The underlying vulnerabilities in key account management strategies, *European Management Journal*, 2006, 24 (2–3), 151–62, https://doi.org/10.1016/j.emj.2006.03.005 (archived at https://perma.cc/KSK8-WJJU)

3   D Zupancic. Towards an integrated framework of key account management. *Journal of Business & Industrial Marketing*, 2008, 23 (5), 323–331, https://doi.org/10.1108/08858620810881593 (archived at https://perma.cc/D6YZ-LNWJ)

4   R Guesalaga. Top management involvement with key accounts: The concept, its dimensions, and strategic outcomes, *Industrial Marketing Management*, 2014, 43 (7), 1146–56

5   H Salojärvi, L-M Sainio and A Tarkiainen. Organizational factors enhancing customer knowledge utilization in the management of key account relationships, *Industrial Marketing Management*, 2010, 39 (8), 1395–402

6   F B Al Hussan, F B Al-Husan and L Alhesan. The role of senior executives in managing key customers in Arab context, *Journal of Business & Industrial Marketing*, 2017, 32 (6), 825–35

Hence, for a KAMgr, the ability to engage and secure the support of senior executives in his/her organization is part of the capabilities to enhance personal effectiveness and the outcomes sought by KAM programmes.

In order to help you better understand the nuances of the involvement of key executives in KAM, we now look at the drivers and motives behind the involvement. We then outline different roles senior managers can adopt before providing a few guidelines to help you leverage the power of their involvement.

The drivers for top management involvement

We have established the importance of the involvement of top executives in shaping KAM programmes, but what are their drivers? What are the factors that explain the involvement of these, often busy, individuals in creating customer centricity?

According to research conducted by Liang Sun at Cranfield School of Management in the UK,[5] three clusters of factors explain top management involvement in KAM: strategic drivers, in other words, wide-ranging and long-term oriented drivers; operational drivers, that is specific elements to enhance KAM programmes; and finally individual drivers or factors related to personal preferences and motives.

Strategic drivers

Building long-term partnerships and developing trust with customers is a primary driver, and the one that underpins top executives' intent when involved in KAM initiative. They aim to promote a relational approach to support strategic customer development over the long run. Top executives also get involved to help establish a rational decision-making framework based on customer needs and knowledge. In other words, to make KAM investments more systematic and aligned to corporate strategy. When asked about the reasons that motivate their involvement, executives explain that they often find value in gaining market intelligence from the customer perspective, engaging in dialogues and conversations with them. A key source of insight, in addition to the companies' information systems and the account manager know-how, is the description of the priorities of their key suppliers that customers often reveal to senior representatives.

Executives find that their involvement with key accounts is part of their efforts to identify trends and anticipate market shifts that can generate both opportunities and risks. Anticipating these opportunities and risks allows suppliers to reconfigure resource allocation to maintain KAM effectiveness.

Operational drivers

The first of these drivers is the interest in developing competence and high performance in key account managers. Executives realize that building a high-performing KAM function requires coaching and mentoring interventions.

TABLE 11.2 Drivers of top executive involvement in KAM

Strategic	*Commercial effectiveness* • Achieving success with key accounts • Enhancing resource allocation by establishing robust decision-making frameworks based on customer needs • Creating more value for customers *Cross-boundary relational developments* • Building long-term partnerships and a high level of trust • Facilitating internal alignment to enable closing the deal *Market sensing & alignment* • Identifying market changes earlier for new opportunities • Gaining deeper insights into customers perspectives • Identifying market dynamics and potential risks • Gaining inputs for strategy formulation • Seizing new market opportunities that come from environmental change *Governance and accountability* • Meeting investor expectations and deliver on promises to increase business with high-value clients • Providing consistency and stability within the organization • Demonstrating administrative commitment to strategic customer • Ensuring role stability during organizational restructuring or mergers
Operational	*Organizational processes* • Directly intervening to resolve issues • Facilitating coordination across departments *Organizational and professional development* • Ensuring incoming and current account managers are qualified • Helping account managers develop problem-solving capabilities • Boosting the motivation of KAM teams
Individual	• Personal interest in sales based on previous sales background • Professional advancement • Substantiating commitment to employees • Obtaining information and ideas from strategic customers • Fostering social relationships with senior executives of strategic customers to expand industrial networking • Boosting the motivation of KAM teams • Executive compensation-related interests

Top managers become involved in KAM to resolve operational barriers that often emerge in the relationship with key customers. For instance, legal or financial due diligence can delay agreements and contracts. Therefore, top managers help show commitment to establishing seamless administrative operations and service levels.

In major inter-organizational relationships which typically characterize key customer-key suppliers' relationships, top managers become instrumental in helping articulate KAM processes and procedures transparently. They can also 'defend' the status of particular customers within the top management team and board of directors. Given that customer information is rarely entirely objective and complete, TMI can mitigate bias in managers' debriefing and obtain direct customer feedback on KAM implementation matters.

Individual drivers

TMI in KAM would not be completely explained if we didn't add intrinsic personal motives that often become a powerful driver for engaging in supporting KAM programmes. Personal interest in sales and customer management operations based on previous sales backgrounds drive TMI. These executives seek to foster social relationships with their counterparts in strategic customer organizations to expand networks and complement formal inter-organizational governance systems with informal interactions. These strategies create social capital that can prove very helpful in contexts of rapid change such as during organizational restructuring or mergers in either the supplier or the customer organizations.

The roles of the executive sponsor

Categorization of roles in top management

Executives utilize a set of underlying managerial resources, namely, managerial cognition, managerial social capital and managerial human capital, to leverage their administrative authority and to make decisions[6] such as whether to continue to cooperate with a key customer, or whether to adjust investments and direct these to other accounts. The link between managerial capability and firm strategy is well documented, but not in the context of KAM, where there is increased interest but still relatively scarce evidence on the role top management plays in KAM.[7]

There is agreement that executive sponsors play an important role in developing KAM and that they need to be appropriately matched with the right account to deepen the relationships and drive revenue growth. Dominique Côté,[8] who has designed executive sponsorship programmes for more than three decades, suggests that the first aspect to consider is securing the sponsor's time commitment. She even argues that, as a minimum, this should be 10 to 12 hours per year, though this can vary from business to business. In addition, her advice is for regular (monthly) touchpoints with the key account manager to debrief and coach them and to be up to date on the dealings with the account and upcoming meetings. The second aspect to consider is that the KAMgr needs to have her/his say in selecting the executive sponsor and be comfortable with the appointed sponsor. Thirdly, once the top executive is selected, a structured dialogue needs to be organized to discuss and agree on the approach and the role the executive sponsors will adopt.

Typically, executive sponsors can adopt various roles to support KAM initiatives. Each role entails specific responsibilities and can have both advantages and disadvantages. Let us explore the roles that executive sponsors typically assume in KAM contexts.

STRATEGIC VISIONARY

As a strategic visionary, the executive sponsor sets the overall direction and vision for the KAM programme, aligning it with the company's broader strategic objectives and defining the growth priorities and range of investments in the account.

Top executives can provide valuable strategic insights based on their understanding of market trends, competitive dynamics and customer behaviour.

This role often entails defining long-term KAM goals and objectives and participating in their delivery. It also requires actively connecting the KAM strategy with the corporate strategy to create coherence between the two. The strategic visionary communicates the importance of KAM throughout the organization, helping create a culture of customer centricity.

This role brings a number of benefits to KAM programmes: it ensures KAM is aligned with overall business strategy, it provides clear direction for KAM initiatives and elevates the importance of KAM within the organization.

On the other hand, the strategic visionary may be too detached from day-to-day KAM operations which could lead to unrealistic expectations if not grounded in operational realities.

RESOURCE ALLOCATOR

In this role, the executive sponsor ensures that adequate resources are allocated to support KAM initiatives. Fundamentally, this approach translates into approving budgets for KAM programmes and facilitating the allocation of human resources to key account teams. Executives may adopt this role informally, for instance, when finance executives engage in prioritizing investments in KAM-related technologies and tools.

KAM programmes are resource-intensive endeavours; therefore, this role ensures KAM has the necessary resources to succeed and is a powerful way to demonstrate tangible commitment to KAM. However, this approach may lead to resource conflicts with other organizational priorities and could result in over-investment if not carefully managed.

ORGANIZATIONAL ALIGNER

This executive sponsor acts as a bridge between different departments and functions, fostering cross-functional collaboration to support key accounts. These executives work to break down silos between departments, facilitating cross-functional teamwork and aligning KAM goals across different business units.

This level of alignment improves coordination and efficiency in serving key accounts and reduces internal conflicts and barriers. As a result, supplier organizations enhance their ability to deliver integrated solutions to strategic accounts.

Proper organizational alignment is often time-consuming and challenging in large, complex organizations. Organizational structures and the need to navigate across business units make this approach difficult, and prone to face resistance from entrenched departmental interests.

> Typically, our CALs spent about 30 per cent of their time directly engaging with clients. The rest was dedicated to internal preparation, coordination, and influencing.
>
> John Downer

RELATIONSHIP BUILDER

This approach of executive sponsorship emphasizes engaging with key accounts at a senior level, building and strengthening relationships with key decision-makers and influencing personnel in the customer organization.

Typically, relationship builders participate in high-level meetings, such as annual reviews. The nature of these interactions is primarily social. This role is similar to the 'social visitor' that Noel Capon and Christoph Senn identified.[9] This approach demonstrates a commitment to the customer relationship at the highest level, often helping strengthen strategic partnerships with key accounts. This involvement can provide valuable insights into customer needs and priorities. However, it can be time-intensive for busy executives and can inadvertently undermine the role of key account managers if not carefully balanced. The relationship building needs to be genuine and authentic, as customers can become disenfranchised if the sponsors only develop relationships at a superficial level.

DECISION-MAKER

In some organizations, the senior executive not only supports growth with key accounts but also makes decisions regarding the customer, particularly those with significant strategic or financial implications. They, therefore, approve major proposals or investments in the customers, decide on the selection of key or, indeed, the de-selection of key customers, and are often involved in helping to resolve conflicts or issues with key accounts.

Having a decision-maker sponsor enables quick, high-level decision-making, and provides a clear demonstration of the importance of key accounts to the organization. However, it can create bottlenecks if too many decisions require executive approval. A major concern is that this role could potentially disempower key account managers.

THE PERFORMANCE MONITOR

Most supplier-key account relationships generate high volumes of financial and commercial information, performance data, measures of service level agreements, etc., all of which need to be consolidated, structured and managed. This role describes the type of executive sponsor who oversees KAM performance to ensure accountability and drive results through.

Very often they set and/or review performance metrics for KAM programmes, trying to balance inputs and outcomes. Regularly reviewing KAM-related activities helps establish a better link between the performing of activities and the results obtained; thus, being able to hold key account teams accountable for the outcomes expected of them.

Reviewing KAM initiatives using a combination of leading and lagging indicators helps identify opportunities for continuous improvement in KAM programmes and better establish the link between customer activities and their ROI.

In large organizations, it is often challenging to create coherence between the corporate objectives and priorities and the day-to-day account processes. In other words bridging the gap between strategy articulation and strategy execution is not a trivial endeavour. The performance monitor sponsorship approach facilitates alignment between strategy definition and implementation. However, this approach needs to be balanced, to avoid creating unnecessary pressure that may lead to short-term thinking, or stifle innovation if it is too focused on immediate results.

CULTURAL CHAMPION

No matter how well-thought-out your business strategy is, it won't succeed if it's not supported by the right organizational culture. For a strategy to work, it needs to be supported by the company's values, beliefs and behaviours – in other words, its culture. The cultural champion is a sponsorship style that promotes customer centricity, thus, the culture that prioritizes key accounts throughout the organization.

If you have a cultural champion in your organization, you should expect this executive to actively communicate the importance of key accounts to all employees. In board meetings and staff briefings, these sponsors will openly recognize and reward KAM's successes. They will model and appreciate customer-centric behaviours. Fostering this culture creates a virtuous circle, which legitimizes collaboration across functions and business units. Typically, a strong customer-oriented culture reinforces role clarity and enhances employee engagement, first with KAM initiatives and, second, with the wider organization.

Changing the culture of an organization may be hard, slow and challenging to implement. Thus, cultural champions will need patience and perseverance with the intended transformations toward a customer-centric business. They will need to bring on board both the community of key account managers and also other employees not directly involved in KAM. At the end of the day, your KAM business should be everybody's business.

KNOWLEDGE FACILITATOR AND COACH

As discussed in the case of the performance monitor, key account relationships generate a wealth of information, insights and knowledge. This executive sponsor promotes knowledge sharing and learning related to KAM practices and processes. Knowledge facilitators enable the sharing of best practices across key account teams. They are eager to support investments in KAM training and development to achieve higher levels of effectiveness and growth with key customers. These executives focus on reviewing key account plans with a view to understanding the underlying mechanisms that generate customer value and loyalty. These insights are then shared and disseminated throughout the organization.

This type of executive sponsorship enhances organizational learning and reinforces KAM capabilities. It also improves consistency in KAM practices across the organization, creating a stronger knowledge base of effective practices to be leveraged for broader business benefits.

On occasions, this particular approach could lead to information overload if knowledge assets are not properly managed, and sometimes may require significant time and resources to roll out effectively.

CRISIS MANAGER

No major supplier-customer relationship is ever free from tensions or problems. Issues will emerge particularly when the collaboration occurs in the context of frontier technologies, complex projects and multiple stakeholders. This executive sponsor helps the KAMgr by intervening in critical situations or crises involving key accounts.

The crisis manager will engage when a problem or an issue has been escalated or when a problem could cause major operational, financial, relational or reputational risk. When tough decisions are needed in crisis situations, these sponsors will provide reassurance and senior management backing. Often, this sponsorship is associated with engaging in negotiations or settlement processes.

A key advantage of this approach is the clear demonstration of commitment to key account relationships. Senior executives provide a safety net for key account managers in difficult situations that help quickly resolve critical issues restoring key account's confidence and trustworthiness.

Dominique Côté, an expert in strategic account management and member of the board of SAMA, describes the role of an executive sponsor as one that:

- Serves as the voice of the customer internally and as a champion for the strategic account manager

- Helps eliminate internal barriers and advocates for resources to be allocated towards opportunities within the top accounts

- Stays informed on the dealings with the account through an established and systematic account process

- Contributes to, and has accountability for, the key account plan
- Challenges account strategy and tactics before they are deployed with the customer
- Coaches key account managers on business matters
- Participates in internal leadership and customer account meetings to anticipate issues and address them before they become a problem

However, this approach can create dependency on executive interventions, and could potentially undermine key account managers' authority and legitimacy if overused.

In conclusion, executive sponsors can adopt multiple roles in supporting KAM initiatives, each with its own set of responsibilities, advantages and potential drawbacks. The most effective executive sponsors are likely to balance these roles, adapting their approach based on the specific needs of the KAM programme, the organization as a whole and the nature of the business relationship with the key account. By thoughtfully adopting these various roles, executive sponsors can significantly enhance your success as key account manager and, overall, the success of your organization's KAM programme.

The support of key account management programmes: A dynamic contingency approach

The roles depicted in the previous section are by no means static and unchangeable. Quite the contrary. Research[10] suggests that top managers evolve and adapt their approach in supporting KAM programmes transitioning from one role to another. This adaptation fundamentally depends on the perceived nature of the contingencies in the marketplace and the external environment. The recent years have shaken markets with events such as a global pandemic, geo-political tensions, financial instability such as hyperinflation, disrupted supply chains, etc. How would TMI in KAM adapt to these contingencies?

Higher vs lower time commitment

Top executives, often time-poor professionals, must be protective of their time when deciding how much of it to invest in supporting KAM. In his TMI research, Liang Sun[11] revealed that the higher the perceived volatility in the

FIGURE 11.1 Roles of executive sponsors

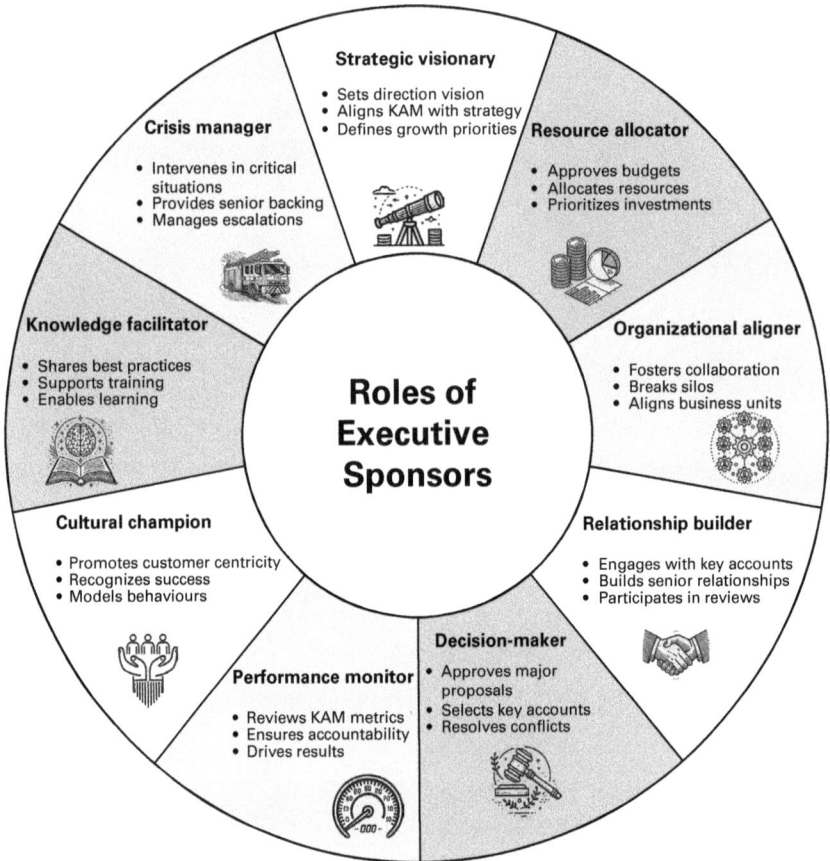

market, the higher the likelihood of increasing their time commitment as a mechanism to respond/cope with market and environmental contingencies. No senior executives mentioned reducing their time commitment. One can argue that KAM programmes help mitigate uncertainty when they facilitate addressing internal as well as customer-related challenges. In fast-evolving environments, decisive backing from senior executives is crucial for deploying rapid responses to unforeseen market contingencies.

Centralized control vs delegated decision-making authority

When unexpected events occur, the key account managers interviewed felt that their companies, rather than increasing their authority and ability to respond, constrained their ability to make major strategic decisions. Case-study evidence into TMI suggests that account managers are often not seen as key decision-makers in contingency situations. Even though they have direct access to critical information on emergent issues and close contact with the market and customers, most executives prefer to revert to centralized decision-making authority in uncertain situations. While senior executives were comfortable with account managers making decisions during routine operations, they viewed themselves as more reliable decision-makers in contingency contexts. Only a few companies believed that with their detailed understanding of customers and markets, account managers would make decisions that align well with the company's strategic interests.

Internal vs external orientation

Executives typically often rely on personal experience for decision-making. However, in contingent situations where uncertainty is amplified, experienced executives seek additional data-driven validation. This data may come from external quantitative market analyses and customer feedback, but also from internal discussions and deliberations.

In the face of unexpected events, increasing customer interaction is a common response. Participating in customer meetings or visits, executives may gain valuable customer and market insights. However, the external perspective needs to be balanced with re-engaging internally. If, in the face of unconventional events, executives focus too much externally, account managers may feel sidelined, perceiving a diminished role and decreased motivation. These interactions can also set a precedent, inviting key customers to contact top executives directly when faced with future contingencies.

Table 11.3 illustrates a dynamic contingent approach.

TABLE 11.3 A dynamic contingent approach

Key Dimensions	
Displayed commitment	Time commitment
	Resource commitment
	Accountability commitment
Approach to exercising control and making decisions	Decision-making authority
	Decision-making bias
	Ad hoc directive adjustment
Establishing the locus of interaction	Internal leadership interaction
	Customer interaction

How to leverage the support of a senior sponsor

In this chapter, so far, we have tried to help key account managers by building the case for appointing executive sponsors who can support the KAMgr role and KAM programmes in their organizations. We have explored the different forms or styles their sponsorship can take. The question you may have now is, how to leverage the support of a senior sponsor?

> Through my experience, I've found that stakeholder management requires penetration at multiple organizational levels. A key account manager must establish authentic relationships across various functions – from finance to procurement, operations to HR.
>
> Stuart Roberts

Some organizations have formalized senior executive sponsorship programmes, but other businesses do not. Whether your organization has an established programme or not, as a key account manager, you can effectively engage the support of senior executives to help enhance your growth agenda with your key accounts. The following are strategies and actions you can take to gain and maximize the sponsorship of top executives.

Identify the right sponsor

The first step is to identify the most appropriate senior executive to sponsor your key account(s). You will want to look for someone who has a strategic view of the business and understands the importance of key accounts, which may be in an outward-looking function or in an internal one. The right sponsor shows genuine interest in customer relationships, has the authority to make decisions and allocate resources and is respected within the organization so she/he can influence other departments.

So, think about potential sponsors considering their roles, influence and track record with customer-focused initiatives. Prepare a shortlist of candidates you can discuss with your Sales/Commercial director. Before approaching a potential sponsor, prepare a strong case for their involvement. Your chosen sponsor is likely to be persuaded if you are able to demonstrate the strategic importance of the key account, the current and potential value of the account for the company and specific ways in which executive sponsorship can drive growth. Remember, the 'ideal' sponsors are likely to be very busy people and, thus, will often request a set of clear objectives and expected outcomes of their involvement.

Align with your business strategy and establish clear expectations

To help move things forward, frame the key account initiatives you want support for in the context of broader corporate goals. Clearly articulate how your key account plans support the company's strategic objectives. Use the language of your executive leadership in your communications. For example, if the company's focus is on innovation, highlight how your key account strategy drives customer-driven innovation. This will enhance the relevance of your request in the eyes of your sponsor.

Then, once you've secured the commitment of a sponsor, set clear expectations for their involvement. Discuss the nature of their involvement and how you see your sponsor's specific roles (e.g. strategic visionary, resource allocator, etc.)

Some of the principles that apply to establishing external relationships also apply to the development of your relationship with your executive sponsor. In addition to formal meetings, seek opportunities to understand their broader goals and challenges within the business and, if appropriate, offer support for their other initiatives.

Engage sponsors in customer interactions and updates strategically

One of the most visible contributions of senior sponsors is in your interactions with the people in your key customers. Inter-organizational relationships need to be carefully planned and designed, and clarity is needed in how and when to engage your sponsor in customer interactions.

Identify high-impact opportunities for executive involvement, such as annual business reviews with C-level customer executives. Or consider other opportunities linked to the launching of major new initiatives or partnerships or resolving significant issues or conflicts.

Brief your sponsor thoroughly before these interactions, providing context, objectives and talking points so they are aligned with you and your commercial and relational strategy with the account.

Key account performance reviews may be unique opportunities to gain their input on your account strategy and secure their continued support.

These account performance reviews can be scheduled on an annual or bi-annual basis and offer an opportunity to conduct a comprehensive overview of the account performance against set KPIs, progress on strategic objectives, current profit margins and future growth plans and its supporting initiatives.

In addition to the interactions with the customer, your sponsor will want to be kept informed but not overwhelmed with details. Thus, you will need to develop a regular reporting cadence (e.g. monthly or quarterly) using a concise format, such as an updated key account plan executive summary. That summary can contain short narrative descriptions and dashboards that can encompass:

- Key performance indicators, both quantitative indicators (e.g. revenue, completion of service level agreements) and qualitative metrics (e.g. customer satisfaction and activity measures)
- Major wins, if relevant
- Strategic opportunities
- Current challenges
- Required decisions
- Resources needed and support

In addition to regular meetings, your sponsor can be very valuable if you need to manage critical issues with your key account. If a crisis or major event happens, it is helpful to define a crisis management protocol that outlines when and how to involve your executive sponsor. If a significant issue emerges, brief your executive sponsor providing a clear, concise summary of the situation, an explanation of potential impacts on the account and a recommended course of action.

> One of us authors had a boss that used to say:
>
> If you come to me with a problem and you want my support, you also need to propose three solutions.

Utilize their influence and expertise

Your sponsor can open doors and break down silos within the business. Coordination and alignment in most organizations function as a result of both formal and informal relationships and interactions. Senior executives can utilize their position to trigger formal decisions within companies. Thus, having identified the specific areas where cross-functional collaboration is needed, you can ask your sponsor to help resolve conflicts between departments that impact your key account. They can also become instrumental in allowing you to build an informal network with other departments to access the resources you need to create and deliver value to your key customers.

Your sponsor can become a conduit for sharing key account insights across the organization, enabling cross-functional collaboration and cooperation. You can stimulate knowledge sharing by providing your sponsor with insights and learnings from your key account that could benefit other parts of the business.

When critical decisions that affect more than one department need to be made, you can use your sponsor's authority to expedite these decisions. Develop a clear escalation/issue-handling process in such a way that the nature of the issue and its impact on the account are clear, the options with pros and cons are articulated and, given that you are closer to the customer, your recommendation and the timeline for making the decision.

If you need to secure resources beyond what you would normally have available, request your sponsor's help to obtain the means you need to serve your key account effectively. Show how these resources will drive account growth and ROI. Use your sponsor's influence to champion your requests in budget discussions and resource allocation meetings.

Finally, you need to be prepared for potential changes in your executive sponsorship. Your sponsor is likely to change positions and role, and, thus, you need to develop a succession plan that includes a potential alternative sponsor within the organization, a knowledge transfer process to brief a new sponsor and a plan for maintaining continuity in the key account relationship.

By implementing the strategies and actions outlined in this section, you will effectively leverage executive sponsorship to drive success in your KAM efforts. A key to the success of senior executive sponsorship is that the scheme is mutually beneficial – valuable for your key account initiatives, and reinforcing your sponsor's personal and organizational objectives.

Summary and application

Having come to the end of the chapter on executive sponsorship, we now summarize some key actions you can consider to identify a suitable executive sponsor, engage the sponsor and develop a fruitful relationship with them.

> In my experience, if you're creating shareholder value for the company and you can prove it, then the board will support you. If you can't prove it, you don't know what you're doing.
>
> Prof Malcolm McDonald

Table 11.4 shows 10 key actions to enhance your ability to secure top management involvement and support.

Figure 11.2 Shows key drivers, tools, behaviours and success factors when strategizing and planning for your key customers.

TABLE 11.4 Ten key actions to enhance your ability to secure top management involvement and support

Action	Description
1. Create sponsor profile	Build a profile of the ideal sponsor based on criteria such as strategic vision, customer orientation, decision-making authority and cross-functional influence. Use this to evaluate potential candidates.
2. Prepare business case	Develop a compelling case that outlines why sponsorship is needed, including account value, growth potential and specific ways the sponsor can contribute. Make it data-driven and aligned with corporate objectives.
3. Consult with sales leadership	Discuss potential sponsor candidates with your Sales/Commercial Director to validate your choices and gain support for approaching them.
4. Define clear expectations	Create a clear outline of expected involvement (e.g. 10–12 hours per year), specific roles they might play (e.g. strategic visionary, resource allocator) and desired outcomes.
5. Design engagement framework	Develop a structured approach for sponsor involvement, including regular update meetings, crisis protocols and customer interaction guidelines.
6. Create executive brief	Prepare a concise overview of the account's current status, strategic importance, challenges and opportunities to facilitate initial sponsor engagement.
7. Establish regular updates	Implement a consistent but streamlined reporting rhythm (monthly/quarterly) focusing on KPIs, strategic opportunities and required decisions. Keep communications focused and action-oriented.
8. Plan strategic interactions	Carefully select and prepare for key moments of sponsor involvement, such as annual reviews or major customer meetings. Provide thorough briefings with clear objectives.
9. Support sponsor's objectives	Understand your sponsor's broader business goals and challenges, offering relevant customer insights and support for their other initiatives when appropriate.
10. Drive mutual value	Ensure sponsorship delivers value both ways – demonstrate how their involvement benefits the account while also supporting their personal and organizational objectives.

FIGURE 11.2 Key drivers, tools, behaviours and success factors when securing top management involvement and support

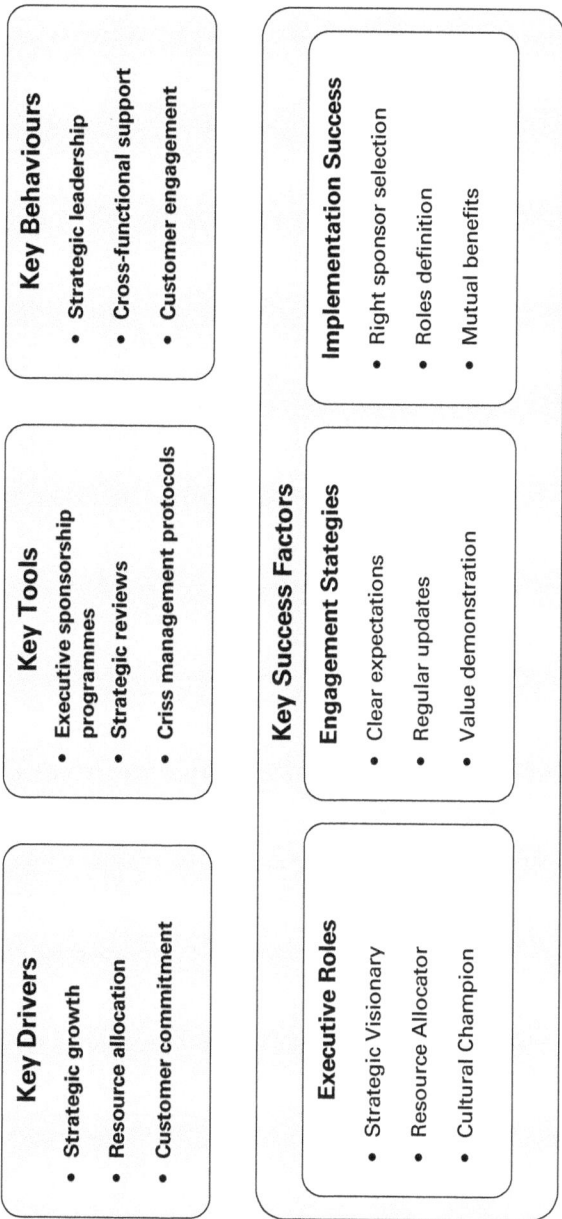

Key Drivers

- **Strategic growth**
- **Resource allocation**
- **Customer commitment**

Key Tools

- **Executive sponsorship programmes**
- **Strategic reviews**
- **Criss management protocols**

Key Behaviours

- **Strategic leadership**
- **Cross-functional support**
- **Customer engagement**

Key Success Factors

Executive Roles

- Strategic Visionary
- Resource Allocator
- Cultural Champion

Engagement Statgies

- Clear expectations
- Regular updates
- Value demonstration

Implementation Success

- Right sponsor selection
- Roles definition
- Mutual benefits

Notes

1 R Guesalaga. Top management involvement with key accounts: The concept, its dimensions, and strategic outcomes, *Industrial Marketing Management*, 2014, 43 (7), 1146–56; D Zupancic. Towards an integrated framework of key account management, *Journal of Business & Industrial Marketing*, 2008, 23 (5), 323–31

2 Guesalaga. Top management involvement with key accounts; G Pereira, N Tzempelikos, L R Trento, C R Trento, M Borchardt and C V Viegas, Top managers' role in key account management, *Journal of Business & Industrial Marketing*, 2019, 34 (5), 977–93

3 Ibid.

4 N Tzempelikos and S Gounaris. Linking key account management practices to performance outcomes, *Industrial Marketing Management*, 2015, 45, 22–34, www.sciencedirect.com/science/article/abs/pii/S001985011500053X (archived at https://perma.cc/L34P-6U24)

5 L Sun. Top management involvement in enhancing the effectiveness of key account management: A contingency model, unpublished doctoral research

6 R Adne and C E Helfat. Corporate effects and dynamic managerial capabilities, *Strategic Management Journal*, 2003, 24 (10), 1011–25

7 P Kumar, A Sharma and J Salo. A bibliometric analysis of extended key account management literature, *Industrial Marketing Management*, 2019, 82, 276–92

8 D Côté (2021) *From Executive Sponsorship to Executive Engagement: Having the right sponsor can accelerate impact in your strategic account management journey*, Velocity

9 N Capon and C Senn. When CEOs make sales calls. How top-management involvement in B2B relationships can drive-or kill-deals, *Harvard Business Review*, 2021, 99 (2), 41

10 Sun. Top management involvement in enhancing the effectiveness of key account management

11 Ibid

Andrea Clatworthy

As the Head of Marketing Transformation for Fujitsu Europe and a recognized expert in account-based marketing (ABM), I've been in the IT and consulting industry for over 20 years. I joined Fujitsu in 2011 and have been pioneering ABM within the company since 2013. This experience has given me a unique perspective on key account management in our industry.

At Fujitsu, we refer to our key account managers as Client Executives (CEs). Their role is comprehensive, covering everything that happens within their assigned customer accounts. For our largest accounts, each CE is responsible for a single customer, while smaller accounts might share a CE. Some CEs operate in specific regions, while others manage global accounts.

The primary responsibility of our CEs is to facilitate value creation. They do this by developing a deep understanding of the customer's current and future needs and then drawing upon various parts of Fujitsu to create opportunities or respond to customer requests. This involves both reactive and proactive approaches.

In terms of daily interactions, our CEs engage with a wide range of stakeholders, both within Fujitsu and at the customer. They're typically the instigators of ideas, putting together virtual teams from our side and sometimes from the customer's side to make things happen. I estimate that they spend about one-third of their time with the customer and two-thirds internally, which aligns with my experience of the necessary balance for effective account management.

We define key accounts based on current size, future business potential and strategic importance. We use a segmentation approach, with key accounts typically at the top of our segmentation pyramid. We also have a category called 'Next Flagship' for accounts we see as potential future stars.

One of the unique aspects of our approach is the high level of empowerment we give our CEs. They have a lot of authority to make decisions and drive initiatives forward. We also integrate customer success managers into our account teams, who typically report to the CE but are also part of a broader customer success community.

When it comes to measuring performance, we look at a range of factors. These include net promoter score (NPS), revenue, pipeline, profit and delivery against service level agreements (SLAs). We also consider adherence to the account plan. We use both objective and subjective measures in our assessments, recognizing the importance of factors like trust and relationship quality, even if they're harder to quantify.

From my perspective, the four most crucial capabilities for a key account manager are:

1 Engaging, communicating and building trust with key customers
2 Leading and influencing both with and without authority
3 Building teams and enhancing cross-functional collaboration
4 Fostering value-based selling and co-creating solutions

I place the highest importance on engaging, communicating and building trust with key customers. I'm convinced that people buy from people, regardless of RFPs or other formal processes. The best key account managers know all the important people in their customer organizations, often on a personal level.

The ability to lead and influence both with and without authority is also critical. Our CEs need to be able to fire up people, get them engaged and bring them into cross-functional teams. They need to be able to put forward business justifications for investments and rely on their influencing skills when they don't have direct authority.

Building teams and enhancing cross-functional collaboration is essential because our CEs can't do everything themselves. They need to be great orchestrators, bringing together the right people and resources to meet customer needs.

Fostering value-based selling and co-creating solutions is about truly understanding the customer's business and working together to create solutions that drive their success.

In terms of developing these capabilities, I believe some are innate, while others can be developed. For example, emotional intelligence is a crucial soft skill that great key account managers possess. Some technical skills, like financial analysis, can be delegated to team members if the CE isn't strong in that area.

A specific example that illustrates the importance of these capabilities involved one of our CEs working with a major UK-based retailer. After a reorganization at the customer, our CE recognized the need to build relationships at different levels. Noticing a community engagement initiative on a notice board during a visit, he proposed that Fujitsu get involved in a tree-planting event. This simple act of engagement led to a day spent working alongside the customer's team, building relationships in an informal setting. It's a perfect example of how being alert to opportunities and taking initiative can strengthen customer relationships.

In conclusion, effective key account management is about much more than just sales. It requires a combination of strategic thinking, relationship-building, leadership and the ability to orchestrate resources across the organization. At Fujitsu, we strive to empower our CEs to excel in these areas, recognizing that their success is crucial to our overall business performance. As we continue to evolve our approach, we're always looking for ways to strengthen our key account management capabilities and deliver even greater value to our customers.

Andrea Clatworthy has established herself as a pioneering leader in account-based marketing (ABM) and marketing transformation at Fujitsu over a 14-year tenure. Her career trajectory at Fujitsu shows significant progression, starting in sector-specific roles before moving into increasingly strategic positions. As Head of Client Marketing from 2012 to 2016, she led sector-, bid- and account-based marketing initiatives across the UK & Ireland business. She managed a diverse team while overseeing ABM for the EMEIA strategic growth programme.

Her expertise in ABM became particularly evident as she progressed to global head of ABM and later to her current role as director and head of Europe's marketing transformation. As Head of ABM (2016–2020), she led an award-winning ABM strategy across EMEIA, defining ABM as a strategic approach to coordinate marketing and sales efforts for specific accounts. She notably scaled the ABM programme globally from 2020 to 2023, working with colleagues worldwide to ensure consistency and excellence in practice. In her current position since January 2023, she has led the transformation of Fujitsu's European Marketing function, which represents the company's largest region outside of Japan, demonstrating her ability to drive large-scale organizational change and strategic initiatives.

www.linkedin.com/in/andrea-clatworthy (archived at https://perma.cc/MQ2X-YP97)

12

Leading and influencing with and without authority

Overview

As a key account manager (KAMgr), you are the person who will face the reactions from your key customers about the delivery (or lack thereof) of your company's offerings. Managing key account relationships in most cases requires KAMgrs to mobilize their organizations to deliver the promised value to the customer. As we saw in the previous chapter, having an effective executive sponsor will help, but whilst this is necessary, it is rarely sufficient to ensure full customer satisfaction. You will need to persuade your organization to secure the necessary support from other teams in marketing, sales and other departments to deliver to the customer the solution that meets the identified requirements. The ability of the KAMgr to influence internally leads to increased customer commitment and has positive effects on the performance of the relationship. In short, a good KAMgr needs to be able to influence to get things done for their key customers.

> The ability to lead and influence without authority is crucial, particularly given that about 60 per cent of the job involves managing internal resources. This requires strong interpersonal skills, emotional intelligence and the ability to manage stakeholders effectively.
>
> Tim Chapman

Leading and influencing in key account management are two capabilities that are both required and vital in equal measure in a KAM role. In terms of leadership, as a KAMgr you may or may not have direct line reports within the business. However, you will rely on other people with whom there is no formal reporting line, only a 'dotted line' one. That means that as the KAMgr you must lead indirectly and through influence. In addition, you will need to get things done in the customer's organization, particularly driving strategic initiatives, achieving mutually beneficial outcomes and managing complex stakeholder maps.

Thus, KAMgrs often face the unique challenge of leading and influencing without formal authority. This chapter will offer you practical frameworks for understanding the dynamics of power and influence, and for developing effective strategies to lead and persuade both within and across organizations, regardless of your position in the organizational hierarchy.

The following box summarizes why this is important.

WHY LEADING WITH OR WITHOUT AUTHORITY IS IMPORTANT

Strategic decision-making:

- Supports evidence-based proposals
- Validates investment decisions
- Quantifies value creation opportunities
- Enables risk assessment modelling

Stakeholder influence:

- Strengthens negotiation positions
- Demonstrates ROI to key decision-makers
- Builds credibility with financial stakeholders
- Supports internal resource allocation requests

Performance tracking:

- Measures implementation success rates
- Monitors relationship health metrics
- Tracks value delivery commitments
- Evaluates strategic initiative outcomes

Value demonstration:

- Validates cost reduction achievements
- Quantifies efficiency improvements

- Documents shared success stories
- Measures impact across stakeholder groups

Resource optimization:

- Identifies resource allocation priorities
- Justifies investment in key accounts
- Evaluates team performance metrics
- Assesses project viability

Relationship development:

- Builds trust through transparency
- Supports data-driven conversations
- Enables fact-based problem-solving
- Strengthens strategic partnerships

Understanding power when leading and influencing

To effectively lead and influence in KAM, it is crucial to understand your sources of power as they underpin leading and influencing strategies. The intersection of leadership and influence in KAM represents a critical domain where traditional leadership approaches meet specialized influence tactics. While leadership encompasses the broader scope of inspiring and guiding others toward shared goals, influence represents the tactical ability to shape decisions and behaviours in specific situations.[1] This distinction becomes particularly relevant in the complex B2B relationships that KAMgrs navigate. As we have argued, KAMgrs rarely have hierarchical power, so what are the other sources that they can rely on to enhance their authority?

Sources of power in KAM

Expert power: This stems from the KAMgr's deep knowledge and expertise. A strong understanding of the customer's business, industry trends and the supplier's capabilities enables the KAMgr to provide valuable insights and advice, positioning them as a trusted advisor (see Chapter 6). Research[2] identifies expert power as a sustainable form of influence in KAM and channel relationships. KAMgrs who consistently demonstrate expertise are 2.3 times more likely to achieve their strategic objectives compared to those who rely primarily on other power bases.[3] This expertise is manifested in deep industry knowledge, technical proficiency and strategic business acumen, enabling KAMgrs to engage credibly with C-level executives and provide valuable insights based on the customer's business model.

Referent power: This power is rooted in the quality of relationships. KAMgrs who consistently demonstrate integrity, trustworthiness and a genuine commitment to the customer's success earn respect and build strong rapport, enhancing their ability to influence decisions. In longitudinal studies[4] referent power has been shown to develop through consistent value delivery, ethical behaviour and trust building. As this research indicates, strong referent power could increase contract renewal by 47 per cent and share of wallet by 31 per cent. Building referent power requires establishing a track record of consistent value delivery while maintaining unwavering ethical standards in all business interactions.

Information power: Access to and control over valuable information grants KAMgrs a strategic advantage. Gathering insights from various sources and strategically sharing relevant information can shape perceptions and influence the decision-making process. Work by Davies & Ryals in 2014[5] highlights the critical role of information power in modern KAM, emphasizing systematic approaches to gathering and leveraging market intelligence, competitive analysis and customer insights. Their study found that KAMgrs who effectively leverage information power achieve 28 per cent higher average deal values than their peers. This involves developing both formal and informal channels for gathering and validating customer insights while maintaining robust systems for tracking and communicating performance metrics.

Network power: KAMgrs operate within a web of relationships. Cultivating a diverse network of contacts within the supplier and customer organizations allows them to access resources, gather information and mobilize support for key initiatives. This is evidenced through belonging to professional bodies and using social media to highlight the breadth and quality of networks, supported by valid thought leadership articles. A KAMgr with a visible large network will be more attractive than those who do not.

> I'm convinced that people buy from people, regardless of RFPs or other formal processes. The best key account managers know all the important people in their customer organizations, often on a personal level.
>
> Andrea Clatworthy

Ethical considerations

It is crucial to emphasize that **all power and influence tactics should be used ethically and responsibly.** Power does not equal bullying or unprofessional behaviours, it means power in the sense of ability, energy and respect from others. It is therefore essential that authenticity and ethical behaviours are considered. Manipulating others, misrepresenting information or using undue pressure to achieve personal gain is detrimental to long-term success in KAM.

Research by Wilson & Millman in 2003[6] demonstrates that successful KAMgrs transcend traditional sales roles by becoming strategic leaders who orchestrate value creation across organizational boundaries. This leadership manifests through vision articulation, where KAMgrs serve as strategic bridges between their organization and customer enterprises, translating high-level objectives into tangible value propositions. Furthermore, they demonstrate leadership through cross-functional team coordination, managing virtual teams across organizational boundaries and ensuring cohesive execution of complex initiatives.

REAL-WORLD EXAMPLE
Influencing without authority

Dan Ahern, as the newly appointed Group Account Manager for Caterpillar at ABB, faced a significant challenge in influencing a resistant business unit (BU). Despite his formal role, the BU had established a long-standing relationship with Caterpillar and was reluctant to cede control.

- **Challenge**: The BU perceived Dan's involvement as interference and attempted to exclude him from key decisions and interactions with Caterpillar.

- **Strategy**:
  - Dan asserted his authority as the Group Account Manager, emphasizing that Caterpillar was a shared customer and that a unified approach was essential for success.
  - He highlighted the potential risks to ABB's overall business with Caterpillar if the BU continued to operate in isolation.
  - He directly challenged the BU leader, requesting an open discussion to resolve the issue and establish a collaborative path forward.

- **Outcome**:

  o While the initial response was met with resistance, Dan's assertive yet collaborative approach eventually led to a dialogue and a more unified strategy for managing the Caterpillar account.

  o This case demonstrates the importance of asserting authority when necessary while also seeking to build consensus and find mutually beneficial solutions.

SOURCE ABB and Caterpillar[7]

Understanding influencing strategies

In the complex landscape of KAM, the ability to influence effectively is not just a skill – it's a critical success factor. Key account managers must navigate multiple stakeholders, competing priorities and diverse organizational cultures while maintaining productive long-term relationships.

Figure 12.1 shows the variety of the stakeholders that need to be considered.

Influence in KAM differs significantly from traditional sales approaches. While sales often focuses on short-term transactions, KAM requires a sophisticated understanding of influence that supports sustainable, mutually beneficial relationships. Effective influence in KAM:

- Builds and maintains trust over extended periods
- Aligns with both organizational and individual stakeholder objectives
- Adapts to changing business environments and stakeholder needs
- Considers the complex network of relationships within client organizations

Coercive tactics

Coercive influence represents the most challenging category of tactics in KAM, requiring careful consideration and strategic deployment. Coercive tactics rely on pressure, authority or consequences to achieve desired outcomes. While these approaches can yield immediate results, they carry significant risks to long-term relationship health. Applications of coercive tactics are:

- Contract enforcement during critical compliance issues
- Risk mitigation in time-sensitive situations
- Protection of intellectual property or confidential information
- Addressing serious breaches of agreement or trust

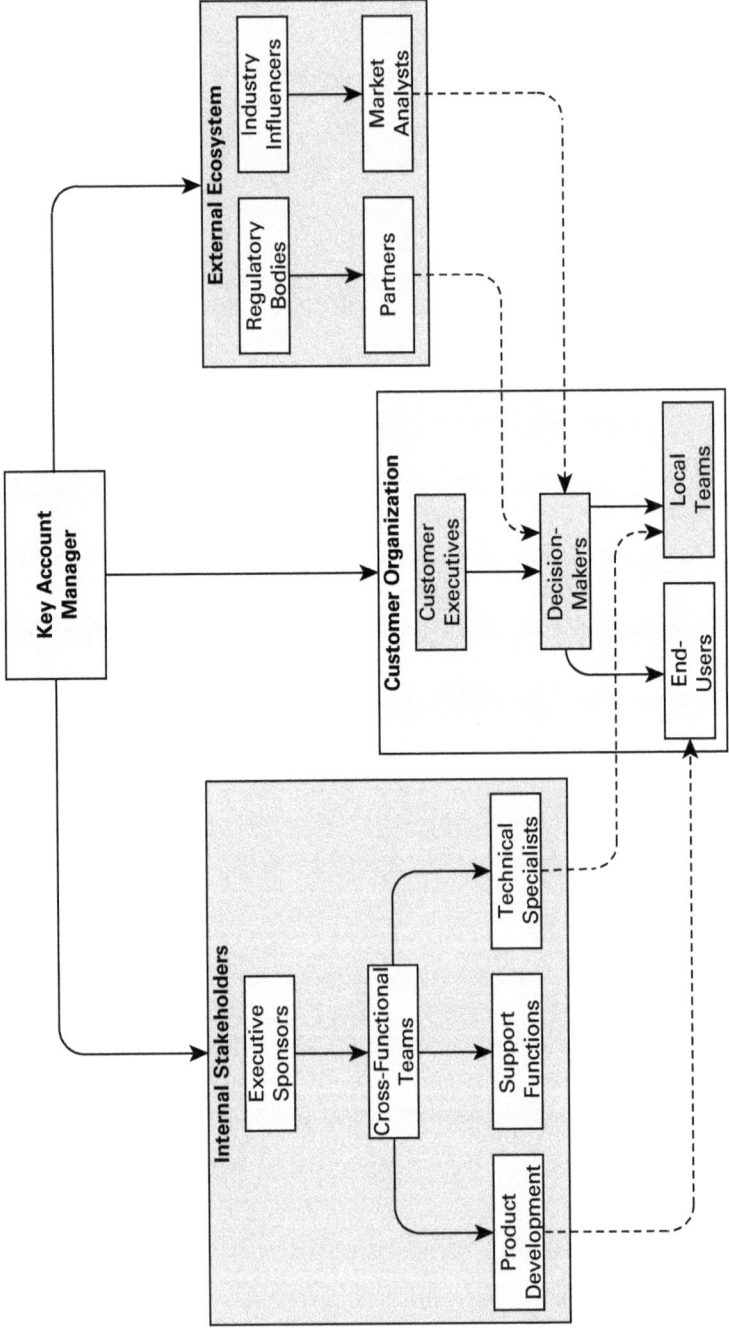

FIGURE 12.1 Stakeholders and their relationships

It is inevitable that at some point in complex relationships between supplier and customer in a KAM context coercive influence is required, but if executed professionally and respectfully it will not damage the relationship. Conversely, if applied authentically and ethically it may serve to strengthen relationships. However, it is wise to reserve this option for situations where other approaches have failed, and you have ensured organizational alignment before deployment. Document all interactions and decisions and prepare contingency plans for potential relationship damage. It may be wise to test your approach out with an internal customer coach to gain an understanding of the customer's likely reactions. And, as noted above, always maintain a professional tone and ethical approach throughout.

To mitigate risk consider the following points:

- Balance firmness with respect
- Provide clear paths to resolution
- Keep senior management informed
- Document all communications and decisions
- Plan relationship recovery strategies

Rational tactics

Rational influence forms the backbone of professional KAM relationships, leveraging logic, data and mutual benefit to drive decisions. The components of rational influence are:

- Data-driven argumentation
- Economic value demonstration
- Process optimization proposals
- Risk-benefit analysis
- Market intelligence sharing
- Competitive positioning
- Technical expertise

PRACTICAL IMPLEMENTATION OF RATIONAL INFLUENCE IN KEY ACCOUNT MANAGEMENT

Throughout this section, we'll follow Sarah Chen, a fictional KAM at TechServe Solutions, a global IT services provider. She's working to expand services with her key account, GlobalBank (again fictional), specifically proposing a cloud migration and security enhancement project worth $2.5 million annually. The stakeholder landscape includes the CTO (final decision maker), IT Directors (technical evaluators), CFO (financial oversight) and various department heads (end users).

The following is her detailed implementation framework, set out in nine steps.

Step 1 – Gathering comprehensive data

- **Internal data collection sources**
  - Historical account performance metrics
  - Service delivery statistics
  - Past project success rates
  - Current contract utilization rates

Example: Sarah analyses three years of TechServe's service delivery data for GlobalBank, identifying a 99.99 per cent uptime for current services and a 42 per cent cost reduction in managed services areas.

Step 2 – Stakeholder priority analysis

- **Stakeholder mapping**
  - Primary decision-makers' objectives
  - Secondary influencers' concerns
  - Department-specific needs
  - Personal and professional motivations

Example: Sarah creates a stakeholder matrix revealing the CTO's priority is cybersecurity enhancement, while the CFO focuses on cost-optimization. Department heads are primarily concerned with minimal disruption to operations. She then can create a message for each of the stakeholders to show their solution meets their priorities and measurement.

Step 3 – Visual preparation

- **Data visualization strategy**
  - Executive summaries
  - Technical architecture diagrams

- o Financial models
- o Timeline roadmaps
- o Risk assessment matrices

Example: Sarah develops a multi-layer dashboard showing:

- o *Current vs proposed security posture*
- o *Implementation timeline with minimal disruption periods*
- o *Cost comparison charts with three-year ROI projections*
- o *Resource utilization graphs*

These build confidence in Sarah and the KAM, and increase her position in the eyes of the client as the trusted advisor. This is very important in the later stages of closing as it helps reduce risk in the eyes of clients and increase the likelihood of closure.

Step 4 – Scenario development

- **Multiple scenario planning**
  - o Best case implementation
  - o Conservative approach
  - o Hybrid solutions
  - o Phased rollout options

Example: Sarah prepares three scenarios:

1 *Full immediate implementation ($2.5 million annually)*
2 *Phased approach over 18 months ($2.7 million annually)*
3 *Hybrid solution maintaining some legacy systems ($2.3 million annually with limited benefits)*

Step 5 – Question anticipation

- **Preparation matrix**
  - o Technical concerns
  - o Financial implications
  - o Operational impacts
  - o Risk factors
  - o Resource requirements

Example: Sarah creates a comprehensive FAQ document addressing 50+ potential questions, categorized by stakeholder type and concern area.

Step 6 – Presentation phase   Using a logical structure the proposition are professionally articulated and with the help of the wider supplier team, using executives and technical experts.

- **Presentation framework**
  - Current situation analysis
  - Challenge identification
  - Solution overview
  - Implementation approach
  - Expected outcomes
  - Risk mitigation strategies

Example: Sarah structures her presentation in modular segments, allowing for deep dives based on stakeholder interest:

1 *Executive summary (5 minutes)*
2 *Technical overview (15 minutes)*
3 *Financial analysis (10 minutes)*
4 *Implementation plan (15 minutes)*
5 *Risk management (10 minutes)*

Step 7 – Case study integration

- **Relevant experience showcase**
  - Similar client successes
  - Industry-specific examples
  - Problem-solution scenarios
  - Lessons learned

Example: Sarah includes three case studies:

1 *A similar migration for a regional bank*
2 *A security enhancement project for a financial services firm*
3 *A phased implementation for a global insurance company*

Step 8 – Metrics presentation

- **Key performance indicators**
  - Current state metrics
  - Target state metrics
  - Industry benchmarks
  - Performance guarantees

Example: Sarah presents clear metrics including:
  - *99.999 per cent uptime guarantee*
  - *45 per cent reduction in security incidents*
  - *30 per cent improvement in processing speed*
  - *25 per cent cost reduction over three years*

Step 9 – Strategic alignment

- **Business outcome linking**
  - Corporate strategy alignment
  - Departmental goal support
  - Innovation roadmap fit
  - Competitive advantage creation

Example: Sarah directly links her proposal to GlobalBank's published strategic objectives:

1 *Digital transformation acceleration*
2 *Customer experience enhancement*
3 *Operational efficiency improvement*
4 *Risk reduction initiatives*

Following through

COMPREHENSIVE DECISION DOCUMENTATION

The foundation of effective follow-through lies in meticulous documentation of all decisions and agreements. Key account managers must maintain detailed records that capture not only the final decisions but also the underlying rationale and context. This documentation should encompass meeting minutes, explicit terms of agreement and clearly defined responsibilities for all parties involved.

In our case study, Sarah demonstrates this principle by creating comprehensive documentation packages tailored to different organizational needs. Her approach includes detailed briefing documents for the executive steering committee that focus on strategic outcomes and high-level milestones. For the project implementation team, she develops technical specifications and detailed workflow documents. The contract management team receives comprehensive terms and conditions documentation, while the service delivery team gets detailed operational guidelines and service level agreements.

IMPLEMENTATION TRACKING

Effective implementation tracking requires a sophisticated approach to monitoring progress across multiple dimensions. Rather than treating tracking as a simple checklist exercise, successful KAMgrs develop integrated monitoring systems that provide real-time insights into project health and potential issues. This system should seamlessly combine milestone tracking, resource utilization monitoring, budget management and timeline compliance into a cohesive overview of project status.

Sarah exemplifies this approach through her implementation of a comprehensive weekly dashboard. Her system provides stakeholders with immediate visibility into project phase completion, offering insights into resource allocation effectiveness and detailed budget variance analysis. The dashboard particularly shines in its ability to track risk mitigation progress, allowing for proactive management of potential issues before they impact project outcomes.

OUTCOME MEASUREMENT AND SUCCESS METRICS

The measurement of outcomes extends beyond simple performance metrics to encompass a holistic view of project success. This approach requires the integration of multiple data points to create a comprehensive picture of project impact across various organizational dimensions. Key account managers must develop measurement frameworks that capture both quantitative and qualitative aspects of success.

Sarah's monthly reporting structure exemplifies this comprehensive approach to outcome measurement. Her reports integrate system performance metrics with tangible cost savings achievements, providing a clear picture of project ROI. She also tracks user adoption rates alongside security incident reduction statistics, offering insights into both technical and operational improvements. Process efficiency gains are measured through a combination of quantitative metrics and qualitative feedback from end users.

STRATEGIC COMMUNICATION AND SUCCESS SHARING

The communication of success requires a strategic approach that goes beyond simple status updates to tell a compelling story of value creation and achievement. This narrative should resonate with different stakeholder groups while maintaining consistency in core messages and key metrics. Key account managers must develop multi-channel communication strategies that ensure appropriate information flow to all stakeholder levels.

Sarah's multi-channel communication plan demonstrates this strategic approach. Her monthly executive briefings focus on strategic value and ROI, while quarterly business review presentations provide detailed analysis of progress and achievements. Weekly project status updates keep operational teams aligned, and daily operational dashboards ensure immediate visibility into system performance and issues.

CONTINUOUS IMPROVEMENT THROUGH FEEDBACK

The feedback collection process should be viewed as a continuous improvement engine rather than a simple gathering of opinions. This requires the implementation of structured feedback systems that capture insights across multiple organizational levels and translate them into actionable improvements. Key account managers must create feedback loops that drive ongoing optimization of both project outcomes and relationship management approaches.

In Sarah's case, she implements a comprehensive feedback system that combines formal and informal channels. Monthly stakeholder satisfaction surveys provide quantitative data on project performance and relationship health. Quarterly service review meetings offer forums for detailed discussion of challenges and opportunities. Continuous improvement workshops engage stakeholders in collaborative problem-solving, while dedicated end user feedback channels ensure ground-level insights are captured and addressed.

Emotional tactics

Emotional influence should be considered as *building lasting partnerships through connection*. The foundation of emotional influence in business relationships lies in the deliberate cultivation of deep interpersonal connections and the alignment of shared values. This approach transcends traditional business transactions, creating partnerships that withstand challenges and evolve over time. At its core, emotional influence begins with intentional relationship building that encompasses multiple dimensions of human connection. This process starts with developing genuine personal connections and establishing trust through consistent, authentic interactions. Successful practitioners focus on understanding and aligning with their partners' cultural perspectives while working together to create a compelling shared vision that resonates with all stakeholders.

Emotional intelligence serves as the cornerstone of effective emotional influence, requiring practitioners to develop and apply sophisticated interpersonal skills. This involves gaining a deep understanding of stakeholder motivations and adapting communication styles to match individual preferences and situations. Skilled professionals excel at navigating complex team dynamics and providing valuable support during periods of organizational change. Their ability to resolve conflicts effectively while maintaining positive relationships demonstrates the practical application of emotional intelligence in building lasting partnerships.[8]

> Strategic thinking with a balance between long-term vision and short-term tactical execution... I've found it helpful to encourage key account managers to develop a clear, long-term vision for their accounts. This provides a 'North Star' to guide all activities.
>
> Tim Chapman

The implementation of emotional influence strategies requires a systematic and patient approach. Successful practitioners invest significant time and resources in relationship development, recognizing that strong connections cannot be rushed or manufactured. They excel at identifying stakeholder values and finding meaningful ways to align organizational goals with these personal and professional principles. This process involves creating compelling narratives that highlight shared successes and demonstrate mutual benefit, reinforcing the value of the partnership.

Building effective coalitions represents another crucial aspect of emotional influence. This involves identifying and developing relationships with key champions who can advocate for shared initiatives and help navigate organizational complexity. These champion relationships often become instrumental in achieving strategic objectives and maintaining momentum during challenging periods. Through careful cultivation of these relationships, practitioners create a network of supporters who can help advance mutual interests and overcome potential obstacles.

The success of emotional influence tactics ultimately depends on the authenticity and consistency with which they are applied. Practitioners must maintain genuine interest in their partners' success while demonstrating unwavering commitment to shared goals and values. This approach creates a foundation of trust and mutual respect that enables both parties to navigate challenges effectively and achieve sustained success together. When executed skilfully, emotional influence transforms traditional business relationships into dynamic partnerships characterized by shared vision, aligned values and mutual growth.

REAL-WORLD EXAMPLE
Building expertise for influence

This case study, synthesized from various sources, highlights the importance of developing expert power to enhance influence in KAM.

- **Challenge**: A newly appointed KAM lacked deep knowledge of the customer's industry and the supplier's full range of offerings, limiting their ability to provide valuable insights and build credibility.

- **Strategy**:

  o The KAM proactively engaged in a structured learning process, studying industry reports, attending relevant conferences and shadowing experienced colleagues to gain a deeper understanding of the customer's business context and the supplier's capabilities.

  o They actively sought feedback from customers and internal stakeholders to identify knowledge gaps and tailor their learning efforts accordingly.

- **Outcome**:

  o Over time, the KAM's growing expertise earned them the respect of both customers and internal colleagues.

  o Their ability to provide valuable insights and propose solutions aligned with the customer's strategic goals significantly enhanced their influence within the account.

SOURCE Which resources and capabilities underpin strategic key account management?[9]

An integrated approach to influencing

The foundation of effective influence as a KAMgr begins with a comprehensive situational analysis. Understanding the nuanced landscape of each account requires careful consideration of multiple factors that shape the influence strategy. Key account managers must first evaluate the maturity of their client relationships, as this determines the depth and type of influence approaches available. This assessment extends to understanding individual stakeholder preferences and the broader organizational culture that governs decision-making processes. Time constraints and potential risk factors also play crucial roles in shaping the strategic approach to influence.

The art of influence in key account management lies in the thoughtful integration of various tactical approaches. Successful KAMgrs recognize that influence is not a one-dimensional tool but rather a sophisticated blend of different methods. The most effective approach typically begins with rational tactics that establish a solid foundation based on logic and clear business value. These rational elements are then enhanced by emotional tactics that strengthen relationships and create deeper connections with stakeholders. While coercive tactics should be used sparingly, they remain a valuable tool for critical situations where traditional approaches may prove insufficient.

Measuring and adjusting influence strategies is essential for long-term success. Key account managers must continuously monitor their effectiveness through various indicators, including direct stakeholder feedback and concrete decision outcomes. The health of client relationships serves as a crucial metric, alongside implementation success rates and overall account growth patterns. This ongoing assessment enables KAMgrs to refine their approach and maintain optimal effectiveness.

In today's global business environment, cross-cultural considerations play an increasingly important role in influence strategies. Effective key account managers develop a deep understanding of cultural preferences in influence and adapt their tactics accordingly. This includes modifying communication styles, respecting local hierarchical structures and aligning with cultural expectations around business relationships. Success in cross-cultural influence requires flexibility and cultural intelligence to navigate diverse business environments effectively.

The digital transformation of business has created new dimensions in the influence landscape. Modern key account managers must master digital communication platforms while maintaining the personal connection that remains crucial for relationship building. This includes effectively utilizing data visualization tools to enhance communication and creating virtual collaboration spaces that facilitate engagement. Building and maintaining digital relationship networks has become as equally important as traditional face-to-face relationships, requiring KAMgrs to develop new skills in virtual influence and engagement.

Success in influence as a key account manager requires an integrated approach that combines traditional relationship-building skills with modern digital capabilities, all while remaining sensitive to cultural nuances and organizational dynamics. This comprehensive approach enables KAMgrs to build stronger, more resilient client relationships that drive mutual success and long-term value creation.

While understanding the dynamics of influence is crucial, KAMgrs must also **cultivate personal qualities and skills** that enhance their ability to lead and influence effectively. These attributes form the foundation for building trust, credibility and strong relationships, which are essential for influencing without authority.

Emotional intelligence (EQ)

Emotional intelligence is a cornerstone of effective leadership and influence. KAMgrs with high EQ are skilled in:

- **Self-awareness:** They understand their own strengths, weaknesses, emotions and how these impact their interactions with others. This self-awareness enables them to regulate their emotions and maintain composure in challenging situations.
- **Empathy:** They can understand and appreciate the perspectives, emotions and motivations of others, even those from different backgrounds and cultures. Empathy allows KAMgrs to build rapport, foster trust and navigate conflict more effectively.
- **Relationship management:** They excel at building and maintaining strong, mutually beneficial relationships. KAMgrs with strong relationship management skills are adept at communication, collaboration and conflict resolution, creating a positive and productive working environment.

Communication skills

Effective communication is paramount for influence. KAMgrs must be able to:

- **Listen actively:** They must go beyond simply hearing words and strive to understand the underlying meaning and intent behind what others are communicating. Active listening builds rapport, demonstrates respect and helps KAMgrs identify unstated needs and concerns.

- **Articulate ideas clearly**: They must express their thoughts, ideas and proposals in a clear, concise and persuasive manner. Using simple language, avoiding jargon and structuring arguments logically enhances understanding and increases the likelihood of buy-in.

- **Tailor communication style**: They must adapt their communication style to different audiences and situations. Understanding the preferences and communication norms of stakeholders, whether they are internal colleagues or customer representatives, allows KAMgrs to convey their message effectively and build stronger connections.

Strategic thinking

KAMgrs who can think strategically are better positioned to lead and influence. Strategic thinking in KAM involves:

- **Understanding the customer's business goals**: KAMgrs must delve deep into the customer's business, understanding their strategic priorities, challenges and opportunities. This insight enables them to develop solutions that align with the customer's overall goals and demonstrate the value of the partnership.

- **Identifying potential challenges and opportunities**: By analysing industry trends, competitive landscapes and the customer's internal dynamics, KAMgrs can anticipate future needs and proactively propose solutions that address potential challenges or leverage emerging opportunities.

- **Developing solutions that align with strategic priorities**: KAMgrs should focus on developing solutions that directly contribute to the customer's strategic goals, rather than simply selling products or services. This strategic approach positions the KAM as a valuable partner and enhances their influence within the customer organization.

Internal selling

Internal selling is the process of building support for key accounts within the supplier organization. It involves:

- **Cultivating relationships**: KAMgrs must develop strong relationships with colleagues from different departments, fostering a sense of shared ownership and commitment to key account success.

- **Securing resources:** KAMgrs often need to advocate for the allocation of resources, such as budget, personnel or technology, to support key account initiatives. They must be able to articulate the value of these investments and persuade decision-makers to prioritize key account needs.

- **Advocating for key account needs:** KAMgrs must act as champions for their key accounts, ensuring that their voices are heard and that their needs are understood and met by the supplier organization.

Harnessing principles of influence

Robert Cialdini's principles of influence are six universal psychological principles that explain how people can be persuaded.[10] Below is a brief explanation of each principle:

1. RECIPROCITY

People feel obligated to return favours or kindnesses. When someone gives something to us, we tend to feel a need to give back. For example, in a negotiation, a KAMgr may concede something to the customer, which will make more likely that the customer will reciprocate with a concession as well

2. COMMITMENT AND CONSISTENCY

Once people commit to something, they are more likely to follow through to maintain consistency with their self-image or previous actions. To illustrate, if a KAMgr expects to expand information exchange with a key account, by encouraging small initial commitments from the customer, such as exchanging tactical information on a regular basis, he/she could obtain larger commitments over time, like sharing more strategic insights about their companies.

3. SOCIAL PROOF

People look to others to determine how to act, especially in uncertain situations. Seeing others engage in a behaviour makes it seem more acceptable or desirable. Typically, testimonials, reviews and 'bestseller' labels leverage social proof to persuade potential customers. In KAM, providing evidence of the successful adoption of a supplier's solution by other customers can induce another key account to consider it as well.

4. AUTHORITY

People tend to obey or trust experts or authoritative figures. Therefore, featuring endorsements from credible experts, certifications or professional appearances can increase the persuasiveness of a message. In KAM, the seniority of key account managers and other sources of authority can boost the influence he/she may have on the customer.

5. LIKING

People are more easily influenced by those they like, such as friends, attractive individuals or those with whom they share similarities. Building rapport with customers is important in KAM and also finding commonalities between the KAMgr and the main points of contact in the customer.

6. SCARCITY

Items or opportunities become more desirable when they are perceived as rare or limited. A key account manager could use this principle when there is scarcity of products and services, of course rooted in the truth.

Leading and influencing in specific KAM situations

KAMgrs encounter a variety of situations where their leadership and influence skills are tested. This section explores specific strategies for leading and influencing in common KAM scenarios.

Internal stakeholder management

Managing internal stakeholders is critical for KAMgrs to secure resources and support for their key accounts. Even without direct authority over colleagues from other departments, KAMgrs can effectively influence decision-making by:

- **Building strong relationships:** Cultivating positive relationships with key decision-makers and influencers within the supplier organization is essential. KAMgrs who invest time in understanding the perspectives, goals and priorities of their colleagues are better positioned to build rapport and secure their support.

- **Aligning key account objectives with business strategy:** Clearly demonstrating how key account initiatives align with the overall business strategy of the supplier organization is crucial for gaining buy-in from senior management. KAMgrs must highlight the potential benefits, such as increased revenue, market share or customer loyalty, that investing in key accounts can bring.

- **Demonstrating the value of investing in key accounts:** Using data and compelling business cases, KAMgrs can showcase the ROI of key account initiatives. Quantifying the value generated by KAM activities, such as increased sales, cost savings or improved customer satisfaction, strengthens their arguments for resource allocation.

Navigating cross-functional teams

KAMgrs often lead or participate in cross-functional teams that include members from different departments within the supplier organization and sometimes even representatives from the key account. To effectively lead and influence in this setting, KAMgrs can:

- **Facilitate open communication and information sharing:** Creating an environment where team members feel comfortable sharing their expertise, insights and concerns fosters collaboration and innovation.

- **Encourage active listening and respect for different perspectives:** Recognizing that team members bring diverse backgrounds and viewpoints to the table is crucial for harnessing the team's collective intelligence. Encouraging respectful dialogue and active listening helps to build understanding and identify solutions that address everyone's needs.

- **Clearly define goals and objectives:** Establishing clear goals, objectives and success metrics for the team ensures that everyone is working towards the same outcomes and that progress can be tracked effectively.

- **Celebrate successes and recognize individual contributions:** Acknowledging the achievements of the team and recognizing the valuable contributions of individual members fosters a sense of camaraderie and encourages ongoing commitment.

Influencing key account decision-makers

KAMgrs must also be adept at influencing decision-makers within the key account's organization. While building strong relationships is fundamental, understanding the customer's organizational dynamics and tailoring influence strategies accordingly is also crucial:

- **Understanding the customer's organizational structure:** Mapping the key decision-makers, influencers and stakeholders within the customer organization helps KAMgrs identify who they need to engage with and how decisions are made.

- **Identifying key decision-makers and influencers:** Recognizing the individuals who hold the power to approve or block decisions and those who can influence their thinking is essential for targeting influence efforts effectively.

- **Tailoring communication strategies to individual needs and preferences:** Adapting the communication style, message content and influence tactics to resonate with the individual personalities, motivations and communication preferences of key decision-makers increases the likelihood of success.

Managing conflict

Conflicts are inevitable in complex business relationships. However, KAMgrs who can effectively manage conflict can transform these challenges into opportunities to strengthen partnerships. Key strategies for conflict management include:

- **Active listening and seeking to understand different perspectives:** When conflicts arise, it is crucial to resist the urge to become defensive and instead focus on understanding the root cause of the disagreement. Actively listening to the concerns and perspectives of all parties involved lays the foundation for finding mutually agreeable solutions.

- **Identifying common ground and shared interests:** Focusing on areas of agreement and shared goals helps to shift the conversation from an adversarial stance to a more collaborative problem-solving approach.

- **Negotiating mutually acceptable solutions:** Approaching conflict resolution with a win-win mindset is essential. KAMgrs should be skilled in negotiation techniques, seeking to find creative solutions that address the needs of all parties involved.

- **Maintaining professionalism and respect throughout the process:** Even in heated disagreements, it is vital for KAMgrs to remain calm, respectful and focused on finding a constructive resolution. Losing control of emotions or resorting to personal attacks will only escalate the conflict and damage the relationship.

REAL-WORLD EXAMPLE
Leveraging network power for success

This case, drawn from research on knowledge integration in KAM, illustrates how KAMgrs can leverage network power to drive successful outcomes.

- **Challenge**: A KAM team, responsible for co-creating an integrated solution for a key account, faced challenges in accessing specialized expertise from different supplier companies within the network.
- **Strategy**:
    o The KAM team proactively cultivated relationships with key individuals across the supplier network, establishing clear communication channels and fostering a collaborative culture.
    o They mapped the expertise and resources available within the network and developed a process for efficiently accessing and sharing knowledge.
- **Outcome**:
    o By effectively leveraging their network connections, the KAM team was able to assemble the necessary expertise and resources to deliver a successful integrated solution for the key account.
    o This case demonstrates the power of building and utilizing a strong network to overcome challenges and achieve collaborative success in KAM.

SOURCE Co-creating integrated solutions within business networks: The KAM team as knowledge integrator[11]

Summary and application

Leading and influencing key accounts, particularly without formal authority, is a complex but crucial skill for high-performing KAMgrs. By understanding the dynamics of influence, developing key personal qualities and applying effective strategies tailored to different situations, KAMgrs can build strong relationships, navigate organizational complexities and drive mutually beneficial outcomes for both the supplier and the key account.

TABLE 12.1 Ten practical actions that can help improve performance when leading and influencing as a key account manager

	Action	Description
1.	Develop expert power	Build deep knowledge of customer's business, industry trends and supplier capabilities. Studies show KAMs who demonstrate expertise are 2.3 times more likely to achieve strategic objectives. Focus on developing industry knowledge, technical proficiency and strategic business acumen.
2.	Build referent power	Consistently demonstrate integrity, trustworthiness and genuine commitment to customer success. Establish track record of value delivery while maintaining ethical standards.
3.	Enhance information power	Systematically gather and strategically share valuable market intelligence, competitive analysis and customer insights.
4.	Cultivate network power	Develop diverse network of contacts within both supplier and customer organizations. Focus on building professional relationships through industry bodies and thought leadership. Use networks to access resources, gather information and mobilize support.
5.	Master rational influence	Implement data-driven argumentation using economic value demonstration, process optimization proposals and risk-benefit analysis. Create comprehensive business cases with clear metrics and ROI calculations.
6.	Practice emotional intelligence	Develop high EQ through self-awareness, empathy and relationship-management skills. Focus on understanding stakeholder motivations and adapting communication styles accordingly while maintaining professional boundaries.
7.	Lead cross-functional teams	Create environment for open communication, encourage active listening, define clear goals/metrics and recognize individual contributions. Focus on facilitating collaboration across organizational boundaries.
8.	Navigate internal stakeholders	Build strong relationships with key decision-makers, align initiatives with business strategy and demonstrate clear value of investing in key accounts through data and business cases.
9.	Manage conflict effectively	Use active listening to understand perspectives, identify common ground, negotiate win-win solutions and maintain professionalism throughout. Transform challenges into opportunities to strengthen partnerships.
10.	Implement strategic communication	Develop multi-channel approach with executive briefings focused on strategic value, detailed QBRs for progress analysis and regular operational updates. Ensure appropriate information flow to all stakeholder levels.

FIGURE 12.2 Key drivers, tools, behaviours and success factors when leading and influencing in a KAM environment

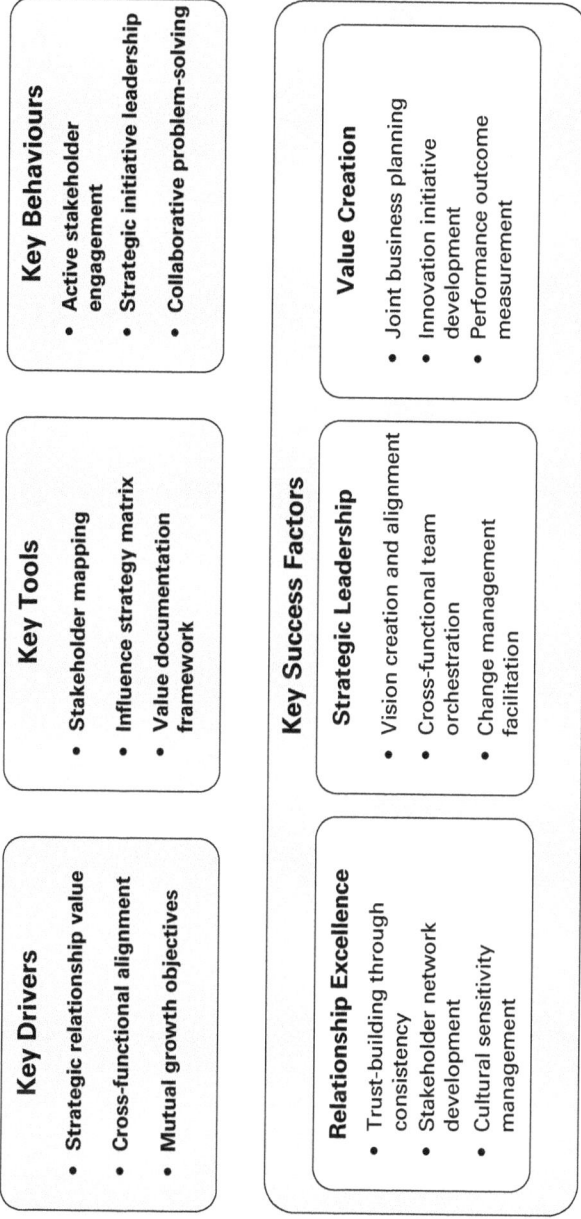

Key Drivers

- Strategic relationship value
- Cross-functional alignment
- Mutual growth objectives

Key Tools

- Stakeholder mapping
- Influence strategy matrix
- Value documentation framework

Key Behaviours

- Active stakeholder engagement
- Strategic initiative leadership
- Collaborative problem-solving

Key Success Factors

Relationship Excellence

- Trust-building through consistency
- Stakeholder network development
- Cultural sensitivity management

Strategic Leadership

- Vision creation and alignment
- Cross-functional team orchestration
- Change management facilitation

Value Creation

- Joint business planning
- Innovation initiative development
- Performance outcome measurement

As a KAMgr, you may want to consider that:

- Influence is not about wielding power but about building consensus, inspiring action and achieving shared goals.
- Developing expert power, building a strong network and mastering communication skills are essential for influencing effectively.
- Understanding the customer's business, aligning initiatives with strategic goals and demonstrating the value of KAM activities are critical for securing internal support and influencing key account decision-makers.
- Adapting leadership and influence strategies to different situations and individuals is key to success.
- Ethical conduct and a commitment to mutually beneficial outcomes are paramount for building trust and sustaining successful long-term partnerships.

Mastering influence in key account management requires a sophisticated understanding of available tactics and their appropriate application. Table 12.1 shows practical actions that can help improve performance when leading and influencing as a key account manager.

Figure 12.2 shows the key drivers, tools, behaviours and success factors when leading and influencing in a KAM environment.

Notes

1   N Tzempelikos and S Gounaris (2021) Key account management orientation and company performance: Does relationship quality matter? *American Marketing Association*, 2011, 269–77

2   S Sahadev. Exploring the role of expert power in channel management: An empirical study, *Industrial Marketing Management*, 2005, 34 (5), 487–94

3   M McDonald and B Rogers (2017) *Malcolm McDonald on Key Account Management*, Kogan Page

4   P Guenzi and K Storbacka. The organizational implications of implementing key account management: A case-based examination, *Industrial Marketing Management*, 2015, 45, 84–97

5   I A Davies and L J Ryals. The effectiveness of key account management practices, *Industrial Marketing Management*, 2014, 43 (7), 1182–94

6   K Wilson and T Millman. The global account manager as political entrepreneur, *Industrial Marketing Management*, 2003, 32 (2), 151–58

7 W Nie, T E Vollmann and I Francis. ABB and Caterpillar (A): Key Account Management, Case study, *Harvard Business Review*, 27 July 2007

8 R B Cialdini (2001) *Influence: Science and practice*, 5th edn, Allyn & Bacon

9 R Guesalaga, M Gabrielsson, B Rogers, L Ryals, and J M Cuevas. Which resources and capabilities underpin strategic key account management? *Industrial Marketing Management*, 2018, 75, 160–72

10 Cialdini. *Influence: Science and practice*; R B Cialdini (2016) *Pre-Suasion: A revolutionary way to influence and persuade*, Simon & Schuster

11 T Hakanen. Co-creating integrated solutions within business networks: The KAM team as knowledge integrator, *Industrial Marketing Management*, 2014, 43 (7), 1195–203

INDEX

Looking for another book?

Explore our award-winning
books from global business
experts in Marketing and Sales

Scan the code to browse

www.koganpage.com/marketing

More from Kogan Page

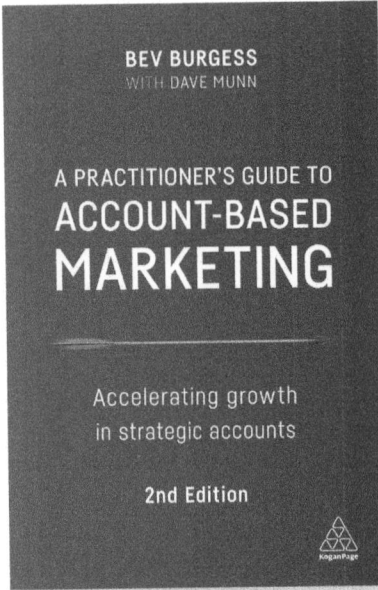

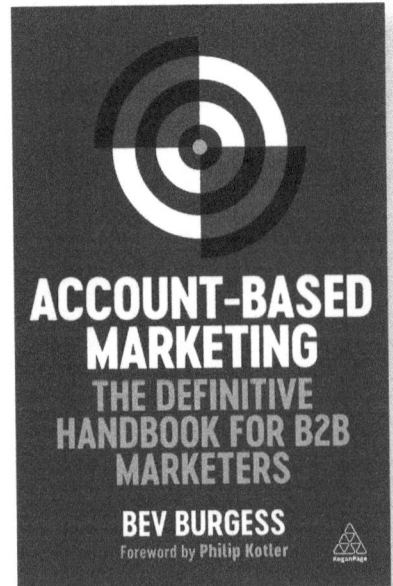

www.koganpage.com

From 4 December 2025 the EU Responsible Person (GPSR) is:
eucomply oÜ, Pärnu mnt. 139b – 14, 11317 Tallinn, Estonia
www.eucompliancepartner.com